Rentier Capitalism and Its Discontents

"This excellent but heart-breaking book describes the tragedy wrought by post-Soviet neoliberal remaking of Kazakhstan and Kyrgyzstan. Following the advice of U.S. officials, the World Bank and IMF to endow local kleptocracies with privatized public assets, these countries found themselves pressured to act more on behalf of foreign financial institutions and corporations than for their own populations. Their new 'rule of law' has turned out to be the rule of investment-dispute courts over-ruling public attempts to charge foreign investors for the ecological and social damages they cause. Domestically, the 'free market' law of 'property rights' supports creditor privileges leaving an expropriated population in its wake as smallholders are driven into debt, forfeit their homes and are marginalized."

— Professor Michael Hudson, *University of Missouri*

"This is a bravely-told analysis of parasitic rentier capitalism in an over-looked part of the global economy. It was unleashed by the folly of the west's shock therapy doctrine imposed on the region in the 1990s. Today's venal oligarchy are the offspring of neoliberal dogma."

— Professor Guy Standing, *SOAS, University of London*

"Combining rich empirics with sharp theoretical insights, Sanghera and Satybaldieva reveal how the neoliberalism has facilitated the expansion of wealth of the rentier class at the expense of the poor in Kazakhstan and Kyrgyzstan. This trenchant analysis is a must read for anyone interested in the nature and trajectories of contemporary capitalism and its unfolding in Central Asia."

— Professor Susanne Soederberg, *Queen's University*

"In this truly exceptional book, Balihar Sanghera and Elmira Satybaldieva have subjected the forms taken by capitalist social relations in post-Soviet Central Asia - especially, the extraction of rent and unearned income - to rigorous analysis. They bring to life the theoretical categories of 'moral economy', and illustrate the countermovements confronting capital, through interviews with people whose relationships with each other are being transformed: lenders and borrowers, city officials and informal settlement dwellers, trade unionists and community activists. This is a brilliant and insightful contrast to the weight of research that views Central Asia through the lens of the geopolitics of elsewhere."

— Professor Simon Pirani, *University of Durham*

Balihar Sanghera · Elmira Satybaldieva

Rentier Capitalism and Its Discontents

Power, Morality and Resistance in Central Asia

palgrave
macmillan

Balihar Sanghera
University of Kent
Canterbury, UK

Elmira Satybaldieva
University of Kent
Canterbury, UK

ISBN 978-3-030-76302-2 ISBN 978-3-030-76303-9 (eBook)
https://doi.org/10.1007/978-3-030-76303-9

This Palgrave Macmillan imprint is published by the registered company Springer Nature Switzerland AG
The registered company address is: Gewerbestrasse 11, 6330 Cham, Switzerland

To all those struggling against the rentier class

Foreword: Central Asia's Neoliberal Tragedy

In the mid-1980s, Soviet officials saw a need to open up their economy in the hope of achieving Western-style innovation and productivity. That was the decade in which Margaret Thatcher and Ronald Reagan were sponsoring the neoliberal pro-financial policies that have polarised the U.S., British and other economies and loaded them down with *rentier* overhead.

The Soviet Union followed a privatisation policy far more extreme than anything the social-democratic West would have tolerated. It agreed in December 1990 to adopt the neoliberal blueprint presented in Houston by the International Monetary Fund (IMF), the World Bank, the Organisation for Economic Cooperation and Development (OECD) and the European Bank for Reconstruction and Development (EBRD) to transfer hitherto public property into private hands.[1] The promise was that the privatisers would find their interest to lie in producing abundant new housing, consumer goods and prosperity.

The Soviet leaders believed that the neoliberal advice they received was about how to follow the path by which the advanced industrialised nations had developed and made their prosperity seem so attractive. But the advice actually turned out to be how to open up their economies and enable

[1] *The Economy of the USSR. A study undertaken to a request by the Houston Summit: Summary and Recommendations* (Washington, DC: The World Bank, December 19, 1990).

U.S. and other foreign investors to make money off the former Soviet republics, by creating client oligarchies of the sort that U.S. diplomacy had installed in Latin American and other puppet states. The Cold War's isolation of the former Soviet Union gave way to turning its republics into prey for financial and natural-resource exploitation by U.S. and other Western banks and corporations.

The result was kleptocracy, euphemised as a free market. Banking, real estate, natural resources and public utilities were privatised in the hands of appropriators who managed their acquisitions in their own self-interest, which they found to dovetail with that of foreign investors and banks. As a Russian joke of the 1990s expressed the ensuing crisis: 'Everything the Party old us about communism was false; but everything they told us about capitalism was true!'

Vladimir Putin described the destruction of the former Soviet Union as the great tragedy of the late twentieth century. What made it a classical Greek tragedy was how inevitable yet also how unanticipated its destiny was when the Soviet republics accepted shock therapy and abolished the government's role as investor, credit creator and regulator in 1991. Privatisation did not end dysfunctional planning. It merely privatised social dysfunction, soon proving to be as economically and demographically destructive as an outright military attack would have been.

Every economy is managed by some class or another. In the absence of public authority, planning passes to whomever is in control of banks, land and related sources of wealth, and above all the allocation of credit. Today, three decades after the post-Soviet carve up began, the concentration of banking has devastated, indebted and impoverished the population, leading to shorter lifespans and rising emigration.

This excellent but heart-breaking book describes the tragedy wrought by post-Soviet neoliberal remaking of Kazakhstan and Kyrgyzstan. Sanghera and Satybaldieva describe how U.S., World Bank and IMF officials, posing as helpful advisors claiming to help these republics adopt the model by which the Western economies had grown prosperous, pressured these countries to act on behalf of foreign financial institutions and corporations more than for their own populations. These 'aid-giving' (or more accurately, debt-creating) institutions acted on behalf of Western banks and investors to promote the carve up and financialisation of post-Soviet land, real estate, oil and mineral wealth.

Soviet planning had provided housing as a right, along with access to education and basic health care. There was no market for housing and no mortgage debt. Government financing of housing by its own credit creation kept housing charges low. There was overcrowding, but at least families were not driven into debt to obtain housing, education or medical treatment. That is a major reason why so many Russians and other post-Soviet populations now feel a certain nostalgia for Soviet times, bad as they seemed in 1991.

The subsequent malaise was unnecessary. The post-Soviet economies could easily have been made vibrant and affluent. In the immediate aftermath of the Soviet Union, existing occupants and users of real estate were given titles, obtaining property free of debt. But if state controls on rent and speculation had remained in place and social housing construction had been adequately financed, people would not have had to amass huge debts to own homes, buildings and land. This would have minimised the economy's cost of living, helping the post-Soviet states develop a low-cost agriculture and industry.

The Soviet planners paid little attention to how the course of rent and interest payments were polarising the Western economies. Not having levied charges for land rent or interest led them to miss their economy's great advantage compared to Western finance capitalism: freedom from land rent, monopoly rent, interest and usurious financial practices. It has been these *rentier* revenues that have ended up polarising and impoverishing the post-Soviet economies.

The post-Soviet republics could have used their own central banking systems to finance restructuring, keeping credit creation as a public utility as it was in the Soviet times. That would have freed these economies from reliance on foreign banks to extend dollar credit to be spent locally. Without wages being paid or other income received after their currency collapse wiped out domestic savings, there was an immediate need for debt financing to survive. Public banking would have freed economies from the need to borrow dollars or other foreign currency, especially to obtain housing.

National treasuries could have given value to this money by taxing the economic rents created in real estate, agriculture and industry. That was the ideal of classical economists, after all. Taxing the land's rental value would have prevented it from becoming an object of speculation. Instead, rental income was paid to the commercial bankers who emerged, financed by Western banks instead of a new national central bank. The post-Soviet tax systems burdened labour and industry, while property owners were largely untaxed, steering their economies along *rentier* lines.

The 'rule of law' sponsored by Western backers enabled managers and political insiders to register public land, oil and mineral resources, public utilities and factories in their own names, and 'cash out' in hard currency by selling many (and often most) shares in their new companies to Westerners. Most of the proceeds were kept abroad, leaving local economies in need of foreign credit to function.

To make this asset grabbing irreversible, the neoliberal rule of law and 'security of contract' were legal straitjackets giving creditors the right to foreclose on the property of debtors - without rights for debtors and renters, who were evicted if they could not meet their mortgage payments or pay higher rents as housing was gentrified. As Sanghera and Satybaldieva summarise, 'By instituting neoliberal financial policies, the Central Asian states rewrote the social contract, and created a new class dependency between financial elites and borrowers. Debtfare states were established that facilitated, justified and normalised unequal class relationships to ensure debt-led capital accumulation. They minimised the oversight of the financial sector, and eliminated strong protections against predatory lending. The political elites legitimised the neoliberal framing of debt as empowering.' The effect was not to empower the population but to marginalise it while driving smallholders into debt and depriving them of their homes.

What was lost was the concept of housing and other basic needs as a human right. 'In the Soviet Union there was a definite set of property rights that people could rely on, and the state would respect and implement,' the authors describe. 'The bundle of rights included rights to land and housing, and rights to occupancy and use for tenants and their families. Rent, interest and speculative gains were "non-labour" income, and were not allowed.'

After 1991, however, housing throughout the former Soviet republics had to be obtained by taking on debt. They thus traded away domestic state-sponsored financial, fiscal and real estate self-reliance to follow a dream of obtaining widespread U.S.-style prosperity, not realising how polarising the policy of debt-financing would be. In the absence of domestic savings (which had been wiped out by hyperinflation), commercial banks obtained loanable funds by borrowing abroad. Domestic private-sector debt thus found its counterpart in rising debts to foreign banks.

Describing how ambitious individuals obtained title to prime housing, shopping centres and marketplaces before entering political office, the authors provide a list of local mayors who enriched themselves further by selling off public land and municipal assets. Corporate housing became a vehicle for appropriators to evict former employees and long-time tenants, gentrifying real estate much as in the U.S. Rust Belt where factories were being closed down. The new owners were free to maximise whatever they could squeeze out, with no attempt made to provide the social protections taken for granted in the West for debtors or renters.

Obtaining housing after 1991, required going into debt. Unlike the 5% range of mortgage rates in the West, much of the population borrowed money at effective interest rates between 25 and 50%. It was like trying to buy a home by resorting to American-style payday loans. There was little way to pay them off. Moreover, women and the non-affluent rural influx into the cities had to rely on microcredit, bearing up to 80% annual interest.

Sanghera and Satybaldieva single out the World Bank's International Finance Corporation and the United States Agency for International Development (USAID) for their efforts to legitimise such usury while sanctimoniously claiming that it 'empowered' women as debtors. The reality, they point out, was that the International Finance Corporation and other international donors mandated these microfinance institutions (MFIs) to become fully commercialised to achieve high returns on equity. The average interest rate was 44%. The result, as Satybaldieva has pointed out elsewhere, has been a disaster:

> Many women, who were previously employed as factory and agricultural workers, and as teachers and healthcare specialists, were forced into petty trading through Western sponsored microcredit schemes. . . .
>
> Second, many women borrowed money to pay for services, such as health care and education, which were previously available for free. Key social services saw significant cuts in state spending, which not only reduced public sector pay but privatised and commodified basic necessities, enabling affluent groups to access better quality services while low-income groups were deprived of them. . . . A 2021 survey of online microcredit borrowers in Kazakhstan showed that 29% of respondents took out loans to pay for emergency expenses, 21% to make ends meet, and 16% to pay off debt

on bank loans. The rest used the loans to pay for medical treatment, utilities, educational fees. Only a small minority of loans was linked to buying consumer goods.[2]

To enforce collection, local microcredit lenders mobilised local district officials and elders to shame women for missing their repayments, even descending on families at funerals to insist that they bear collective responsibility for the debts of the deceased. The amounts involved are enormous, the authors report. 'Between 1995 and 2012 microcredit enabled a transfer of up to $125 billion from poor communities in the Global South to financial centres in the Global North.'

Women became the most radical opponents of Western-style neoliberal reforms. In Bishkek, Kyrgyzstan's capital and largest city: 'On 26 May 2016, about 700 people, mostly rural women, protested in front of the U.S. Embassy demanding debt amnesty from banks and MFIs that had been created and supported by the USAID and the World Bank's International Finance Corporation. Holding placards that read "Occupy FINCA", "Debt kills", "Save our homes from banks" and "Humans above profit", the protesters did something very significant that day.' They attributed responsibility and blame for their situation to Western financial institutions rather than on their personal failings. Similar anti-debt protests and attributions occurred in neighbouring Kazakhstan.

What made the debt burden a national problem was that homebuyers and businesses typically agreed to denominate their debts in dollars in order to lower the exorbitant interest rates charged for loans in local currency. As economies were dollarised, their local exchange rates depreciated as a result of the balance-of-payments deficits resulting from trade dependency and general economic imbalance. The cost of servicing foreign-currency debts rose in proportion to the depreciating exchange rate.

Poverty drove labour to emigrate. Ironically, this helped stabilise the balance of payments for many Central Asian countries. Remittances from Kyrgyzstan's exodus of migrant workers account for about 30% of its GDP. Similarly, Tajikistan's migrant workers in Russia sent their families back home income amounting to over 30% of its GDP.

[2] Elmira Satybaldieva, 'The Debt Oppression in Central Asia,' *Naked Capitalism*, June 7, 2021.

Post-Soviet Central Asia lacks the basic reforms almost universal for thousands of years. Already around 2350 BC, the Sumerian ruler Urukagina proclaimed a reform that stopped creditors from entering the homes of debtors and simply grabbing their possessions and animals. From Mesopotamia and Egypt down to Roman times the rights of debtors were protected by requiring written records to document all creditor claims and limiting interest rates. But Western advisors made no attempt to create such rule of law in Central Asia. What their legal system achieved is closer to barbarism, as Sanghera and Satybaldieva conclude:

> In seeking to liberate the population from the Soviet form of welfare dependency, the neoliberal architects produced new parasitic and exploitative forms of market dependency, in which the powerful propertied class appropriated and exploited surplus value that others generated. The asset-rich and transnational corporations became richer by taking from the asset-poor and the working class through interest, rent, capital gains and low wages. The massive transfer of wealth left most of the population in a state of indebtedness, poverty, misery and distress.

On the international level, the neoliberal rule of law is what corporate lawyers have written to enable Investor-State Dispute Settlement (ISDS) courts to block government attempts to fine or charge foreign investors for the ecological and social damages they cause. Global oil and mining monopolies confront governments in a united front, having mobilised the World Bank, IMF and World Trade Organisation to pressure host countries to abide by pro-corporate rules that limit the rights of their governments, and blocking democratic electoral oversight or pressure. In the face of these courts and the often naïve (or corrupt) contracts signed with government, no countervailing attempt was made to create state regulatory agencies, courts or international law to give post-Soviet economies the protections common in the United States and Europe.

What Western investors wanted most from Central Asia was its natural-resource wealth. The authors describe how U.S., World Bank and NGO advisors imposed contracts favouring the interests of Western oil and mining companies. Chevron set its eyes on the vast oil reserves in Kazakhstan's Tengiz oil field. What Kazakhstan wanted was Western expertise as contractor and minority investor. But Chevron wanted control - and to leave the host-country government with as little revenue as possible from the sale of its oil.

The result was one of the world's most predatory oil contracts - nothing like what Kazakhstan thought it was to get, but a bonanza for Chevron. The contract promised that the government would receive 80% of production, reflecting the normal 80%/20% production-sharing agreements for European and Middle Eastern countries. However, the authors describe, Kazakhstan ended up with only 2% of the project's revenue. Corporate lawyers drew up a contract obliging Kazakhstan's government not to receive any profits at all until it had borne the immense costs of developing the oil field itself (borrowing from the IMF) and met a long-term production target - by which time nearly a quarter of the Tengiz oil reserves would be emptied out and sold.

Chevron's operation proved to be as disastrous an ecological horror story as it had caused in Ecuador. It was fined $303 million for violating environmental protection laws, but pressured President Nazarbayev to repeal the fine to show the world how 'investor-friendly' Kazakhstan was! When popular opposition arose to demand a fair contract, the response by international investors and Western government officials and their front men at the IMF, World Bank and USAID was to claim that renegotiation would violate the rule of law and sanctity of contracts.

Kyrgyzstan suffered in a similar way from foreign gold-mining polluters. These 'externalities' were borne by the host countries, with no cost to the foreign investors for their illegal, irresponsible and predatory behaviour. If the West truly had sought to help the post-Soviet states become prosperous, its diplomats would have helped negotiate fair natural-resource investment agreements, environmental protection, worker safety and other public regulation. Instead, Sanghera and Satybaldieva conclude, 'The neoliberal investment rules regime binds governments to agreements signed with transnational corporations . . . If agreements are violated, investors feel justified to take host states to international arbitration for damages. . . . The rule of law . . . claimed that . . . the state cannot infringe individual rights and freedoms, and the domain of private property must be protected from majoritarian politics.' Neoliberalism thus did not get rid of state planning. It established corporate dominance over the state, forcing host-country governments to give 'the interests of transnational capital [priority] over those of their own population, and cooperate with foreign corporations to limit democratic voices and weaken resistance.'

Some conquered countries recover, as Germany and Japan after 1945. But conquest of the former Soviet states took the form of corrupting their economic structure by installing a kleptocracy. The destiny of Central Asia and other post-Soviet states remains shaped by the way in which their land, mineral resources and public enterprises have been privatised at the hands of a client kleptocracy in alliance with foreign capital. Like the land grants created by the Norman Conquest and those of Spain in the New World, the post-Soviet asset grab has created a new oligarchy empowered to collect land and natural-resource rents for themselves, and for U.S. and other foreign shareholders and creditors. The widening maldistribution of property and debt dependency is likely to block their development for many decades.

The accusation that Tacitus put into the mouth of Rome's adversary, the Celtic leader Calgacus two thousand years ago - 'They made a desert and called it peace' - might be levied against the Western neoliberals who impose financialised austerity, dependency and debt peonage, and call the takeover of government by *rentiers* a natural and inherent rule of law. The challenge for Central Asia is how to reform in the face of the vested interests that have been put in place over the past thirty years. Reform is resisted not only by the new *rentier* interests and their foreign sponsors, but also by the narrow 'middle-class', which does not find its interest to lie in joining with the majority to revive public spending and tax land rent and other economic rents.

Resilience cannot be restored without public spending, but the *rentier* business plan is to minimise taxes by shrinking the government, especially by privatising its public utilities and other functions to create opportunities for charging monopoly rents, and to oppose taxation of economic rent. Today's mainstream economic philosophy and academic curriculum throughout the West backs this neoliberal programme by denying that there is any such thing as unearned *rentier* income or wealth.

Yet only a rent tax can recapture what insiders have appropriated. At issue above all is whether credit, the banking and tax system will be managed as a public utility or for private gain. A national treasury or central bank must be empowered to create money so as not to rely on foreign banks. The guideline must be that no economy should borrow in a foreign currency that it does not earn, e.g., by exporting to earn the foreign currency needed to pay debts. There is no need to rely on foreign banks to lend dollars to be converted into domestic currency. In such cases the central bank has to create the domestic currency anyway. Foreign credit is needed only to pay for trade and payments deficits, not for domestic investment or consumption.

These tax and financial reforms failed as classical economics was rejected after World War I. The world today needs to recover its basic approach in order to free itself from the pro-*rentier* detour that it has taken, not only in the post-Soviet republics most conspicuously but now also plaguing Europe and the U.S. post-industrial economy itself.

To avoid the foreign dependency inherent in the neoliberalism sponsored by U.S. diplomacy, the World Bank and IMF requires an alternative body of economic theory, above all the distinction between earned and unearned income and the concept of economic rent as the excess of market pricing over intrinsic cost value. That was the thrust of classical political economy in the nineteenth century - to free markets from the *rentier* class. Value and price theory were the analytic tools to isolate economic rent as unearned income. These concepts provide the basis for managing a mixed public/private economy, public investment and credit creation, and for protecting domestic labour, industry and agriculture. In elaborating a theory to guide policy, the disastrous neoliberal promotion of *rentier* interests throughout the post-Soviet states provides an object lesson for what to avoid.

New York, USA
June 2021

Michael Hudson

Acknowledgements

There is a strange paradox. We are currently living through a severe crisis that poses multiple challenges for social reproduction and emancipatory politics. There are obscene levels of social inequalities, indebtedness, labour precarity, ecological disasters, political populism and state oppression. And yet there is limited critical and empirical attention on the social forces shaping the multidimensional crisis. This book uses a Southern standpoint to shed light on how rentier capitalism has contributed to this crisis.

Our journey for this book started in 2004 at the American University-Central Asia, when we began our first project to critically assess market reforms in Kyrgyzstan. The experiences and voices of different social groups were a productive entry point in understanding the neoliberal transformation that followed the collapse of the Soviet Union. Over the course of next 17 years, we researched social inequalities and politics in Kazakhstan and Kyrgyzstan. We gained a deeper understanding of people's interests and concerns, and untangled their complex social and economic relationships. This book is an outcome of a lengthy investigation on lenders, property developers, foreign investors, development agencies, judges, lawyers, state officials, borrowers, informal settlers, petty traders, grassroot activists, local elites and oppositional leaders.

Our research was possible because of the generosity and openness of ordinary people, who struggled with and against the oppression of rentier capitalism. Without their testimonies and support, we would never have been inspired to write this book. We are therefore thankful first and foremost to our interviewees and participants who gave us so much of their time, and shared their personal stories of daily struggles.

Many thanks to our research assistants, who shared our enthusiasm for the project, engaged in lengthy discussions, and encouraged our work. They are: Chyngyz, Adil Rodionov, Sabira Serikzhanova, Rasul Avaz uulu, Burul Usmanalieva, Timur Temirov, Saltanat Midin kyzy, Benazir Kanybek kyzy, Nurlan Choibekov, Kunduz Sultanmuratova, Aigul Muratova kyzy and Gulmira Churokova.

We would like to thank the British Academy, the University of Kent and the Open Society Foundations for their financial support. Our thanks also to the Kennan Institute at the Woodrow Wilson Center, the Davis Center for Russian and Eurasian Studies at Harvard University, and the Sociology Department at Boston University for providing us with research grants and space for critical reflection and analysis.

We want to acknowledge the many friends and colleagues who advanced our thinking at various stages of our work: Mehrigiul Ablezova, David Abramson, Laura Adams, Kuat Akizhanov, Margaret Archer, Gulzat Botoeva, Sally Cummings, Bhavna Dave, Julia Eder, Jeanne Feaux de la Croix, Julian Go, Joe Hanlon, Chris Hann, John Heathershaw, Michael Hudson, Eliza Isabaeva, Bob Jessop, Azamat Junisbai, Prajakti Kalra, Deniz Kandiyoti, Marlene Laruelle, Morgan Liu, Lorena Lombardozzi, Philipp Lottholz, Nick Megoran, Vince Miller, David Montgomery, Emil Nasritdinov, Cat Owens, Gul Ozcan, Sebastien Peyrouse, Chris Pickvance, Simon Pirani, William Pomeranz, Larry Ray, Madeleine Reeves, Matthew Rojansky, Vanessa Ruget, Richard Sakwa, Siddharth (Montu) Saxena, Andrew Sayer, Stuart Shields, Chris Shilling, Ngai-Ling Sum, David Swartz, Jorg Wiegratz, Iain Wilkinson, Yuliya Yurchenko and Xin Zhang.

We are grateful to the audience of the following universities, where this research was presented at various stages of development: American University-Central Asia, Cambridge, East China Normal, Eurasian National, Exeter, George Washington, Giessen, Harvard, KAZGUU, Kent, KIMEP, King's College, Laval, Open, Oxford, St Andrews, Warwick, Washington State and Zurich.

We would like to note our acknowledgement to Wyndham Pain, our editor at Palgrave Macmillan for his patience and encouragement.

Our special thanks to our families for their love and support.

The usual disclaimers apply, as we alone are responsible for any shortcomings of this book.

Quote from Your Book

"In seeking to liberate the population from the Soviet form of welfare dependency, the neoliberal architects produced new parasitic and exploitative forms of market dependency, in which the powerful propertied class appropriated and exploited surplus value that others generated. The asset-rich and transnational corporations became richer by taking from the asset-poor and the working class through interest, rent, capital gains and low wages. The massive transfer of wealth left most of the population in a state of indebtedness, poverty, misery and distress."

Contents

List of Tables

CHAPTER 1

Introduction

This book offers a moral economic critique of post-Soviet capitalism. In freeing markets from government regulation, neoliberalism enabled powerful economic actors to extract income by virtue of property rights that entitled them to a stream of income from mere ownership and control of existing scarce assets, including money credit, real estate and natural resources (Sayer, 2015). Neoliberalism created and expanded the role of rent and unearned income in post-Soviet economies. Income extraction through interest, rent, dividends and capital gains was justified and normalised as part of the 'free market' system. Rent-seeking practices went beyond natural resource extraction and illicit public and private takings.

The neoliberal process of marketisation did not merely enrich the propertied class, it produced dispossession, inequalities and harms. In Kazakhstan and Kyrgyzstan, most of the population moved between acquiescing to unjust and dominant economic relations and yearning for alternative arrangements based on fairness, dignity and flourishing. They evaluated the effects of 'free markets' on their lives, and many of them demanded state regulation, social protection and political change. Grassroots and social movement activists sought to better interpret their situation, and build alliances with others to mount effective resistance against the state and capital in what was an unequal struggle.

B. Sanghera and E. Satybaldieva, *Rentier Capitalism and Its Discontents*,
https://doi.org/10.1007/978-3-030-76303-9_1

This book also engages with the Polanyian double movement paradigm to analyse the economic and political processes in the region. After the collapse of the Soviet Union, Kazakhstan and Kyrgyzstan implemented extensive market reforms, the so-called neoliberal shock therapy. At the behest of international financial institutions and development agencies, major economic sectors, including oil and gas, minerals, finance, real estate, retail and construction, were privatised, liberalised and deregulated. The neoliberal system transformation commodified money, land and labour, creating largely unfettered markets for these fictitious commodities.

The commodification of money, land and labour generated unequal social relationships, in which the rich and powerful appropriated and exploited the surplus value that others had produced. Exclusion and unequal inclusion arose from commodification to become sources of countermovements (Burawoy, 2015). Kazakhstan and Kyrgyzstan faced mounting problems of indebtedness, usurious interest rates, land evictions, homelessness, low pay, job insecurity and environmental destruction. This spawned local and national resistance. While some social movements called for social protection against the harmful effects of commodification, others wanted strong constraints on the markets of fictitious commodities and/or decommodification.

Clearly, rent-seeking practices were a product of neoliberalising and countervailing powers, and were contingent, neither automatic nor inevitable. Income extraction was dependent on extra-economic institutions, which had powers to legitimise, facilitate and regulate rent-seeking. In Kazakhstan and Kyrgyzstan, the judiciary, regulatory bodies and other state institutions were important sites of struggles in which different social forces competed over rights, rules, norms and discourses regarding property rights and unearned income. While income-extractive arrangements arose out of powerful vested interests, unearned income still had to be morally justified, or rather rationalised. Moral claims and counter-claims were made regarding who should do, get and control what (Sayer, 2018).

International financial institutions, development agencies and Western capital-exporting countries were the neoliberal architects of the income-extractive regime (Soederberg, 2014). They bound Kazakhstan and Kyrgyzstan to the 'free market' system through fiscal, legal and judicial mechanisms, including investment treaties and constitutional rules. Their justifications for the regime were weak, but following the collapse of state socialism and no alternative economic imaginaries imminent, many people accepted the new economic order. While some normalised the operations of the 'free market' as just how things were, others politicised them. In many cases external actors were primarily blamed for social suffering, leading to collective action to address injustices.

The political regimes were not neutral to social forces, but privileged some actors, strategies and actions over others (Jessop, 2002). Dependent on natural resource exports, transnational capital and international donors, Kazakhstan and Kyrgyzstan were structurally orientated towards global capital and 'free market' interests. The political regimes tried to secure popular consent, justifying the foreign acquisition of natural resources, financial liberalisation and untamed markets as sources of economic development, empowerment, creativity and freedom. But faced with growing public discontent over social inequalities, suffering and corruption, the regimes eventually used coercive powers to violently quell political opposition and suppress grassroots movements.

In evaluating actually existing economic relations and their associated justifications and consequences, this book reveals how unearned income practices were based on power and unequal relations, had weak moral defences, and resulted in harmful effects. In addition to expanding unproductive and exploitative forms of capital, widening economic inequalities and exacerbating social suffering, rent-seeking had other damaging impacts. The neoliberal regime constrained democratic forces through state and regulatory capture by the rich (Gill, 2008). In Kazakhstan and Kyrgyzstan, plutocracy, the rule of the rich, emerged as wealth was converted into political positions, and vice versa. The excessive extraction of natural resources led to environmental destruction. Predatory drilling and mining were responsible for air and river pollution, melting mountain glaciers and ill-health in local communities.

30 Years on—Time for a Critical Assessment

After three decades of neoliberal changes, post-communist countries underwent an economic system transformation (Myant & Drahokoupil, 2011). Kazakhstan and Kyrgyzstan were among several post-communist countries that went beyond the implementation of standard Washington Consensus reforms (Appel & Orenstein, 2018). They adopted a range of radical neoliberal policies, including a flat tax, low corporate tax, extreme monetarism and the deregulation of financial markets. The Central Asian states were in a 'competitive signalling' process to prove to international investors and donors that they were open to global capital.

This book provides a critical assessment of neoliberal system transformation that has largely been missing in Central Asian scholarship. Writers on Central Asia have often been silent on the nature of post-Soviet capitalism and class relations (see also Ost, 2015). The western media have tended to portray the region 'as a shadowy region of crime, disreputability, authoritarian leadership, political corruption and incipient decay' (Stone, 2012: 175). Central Asian social science has given much attention on issues of natural resources, migration, informal and illicit economies, patron-based politics and illiberal regimes. Such writings risk essentialising, pathologising and exoticising the region (see Koch, 2019). Lottholtz et al. (2020: 421) note that '"authoritarian" and "illiberal" framings are part of an Orientalist and Western-centric worldview that distracts attention from the discontents and violence inherent in capitalist modernity.'

Polanyi (1944) argues that land, money and labour were never intended to be bought and sold, because their unregulated commodification would destroy their true character. Neoliberal scholars have blurred the distinction between productive and unproductive forms of income to mystify unearned income. Rent-seeking is only problematised when political actors used their powers to extract income from economic producers (Buchanan, 2008). Similarly, the post-socialist literature have viewed rent-seeking as illegal or illicit activities among political elites, involving nepotism, patronage, corruption and fraud (Cooley & Heathershaw, 2017; Engvall, 2014; McGlinchey, 2011; Mihalyi & Szelenyi, 2017, 2019; Peyrouse, 2012). But neoliberal and post-socialist scholars have failed to address licit forms of extraction in the private sector, where rent-seeking is more prevalent, unjust and harmful (Maclean, 2017).

The neoliberal commodification of money, land, natural resources and labour transformed the Central Asian economies. The new economic system was characterised by the dominance of value taking over value making, and exchange-value over use-value. The forms of income extraction were diverse, widespread and routinised. While several economic sectors, such as banking, real estate, natural resources, retail and telecommunications, thrived, manufacturing and agriculture languished (Pomfret, 2019). Gains from rent-seeking and speculative activities created disincentives for industrial and agricultural production, despite the latter accounting for a large proportion of employment. Rents and rentiers have dominated the new economic system to such an extent that it can be called ‘rentier capitalism’ (Christophers, 2020). Rentiers refer to individuals who extract income (rent) based on existing assets.

The marketisation of fictitious commodities involved a violent process of value taking, dispossession, exclusion and exploitation (Harvey, 2005). It generated multiple sources of social inequalities and suffering in Central Asia. Rich and powerful elites obtained unearned income through usurious interest rates, excessive land and property rent, high revenues from subsoil assets and indefensible monopoly rent. The majority of the population made exorbitant payments for basic goods and services, resulting in impoverishment, misery and distress.

Drawing on Polanyian ideas on the double movement, this book argues that the neoliberal wave of commodification was countered by grassroots movements (Burawoy, 2015; Goodwin, 2018; Hann, 2016). The Central Asian literature on protests has tended to neglect class tensions as a source of resistance. Moreover, very few studies have provided a thorough analysis of such movements. Kazakhstan’s countermovements were largely defensive that aimed to reshape but not transform market practices. For instance, the anti-debt movement primarily campaigned to reschedule debt payments, stop malpractices, and have some debt relief. The informal settlement movement was limited to demanding land legalisation. By contrast, Kyrgyzstan’s countermovements were more offensive. They aimed to problematise interest rates, nationalise mining industries, and redistribute land to poor and migrant groups.

The two movements of commodification and decommodification occurred simultaneously, and their associated class forces struggled to access and control state institutions and resources. Although the countermovements gained some concessions, they failed to challenge the neoliberal property regime and the marketisation of fictitious commodities. The Central Asian states facilitated and prioritised income extraction over industrial production, and investor interests over social needs. The strategic alliance of the wealthy propertied class and political elites produced plutocratic regimes. Moreover, the coercive tools of the state were employed to contain and repress democratic opposition and resistance. Grassroots movements were often too fragmented and too easily co-opted to offer effective resistance.

The financial and propertied class (aka Masters of the Universe and neo-feudal overlords) will continue to wreak chaos and suffering in

Central Asia unless the neoliberal economic imaginary is critiqued, and feasible alternatives are offered. This book is a small step towards that goal.

A Southern Perspective

This book discusses how the global class relations of the ownership and control of scarce assets were significant in creating unequal wealth and power. The Central Asian rentier class had more in common with their counterparts in the West than their fellow citizens. Likewise, Central Asian grassroots activists, who opposed the neoliberal commodification of things, related to similar struggles elsewhere in the world. While the book examines the unequal exchange between the Global North and the Global South, it particularly focuses on domination and opposition in Kazakhstan and Kyrgyzstan.

A Southern standpoint was employed to capture the complex sets of activities, experiences, concerns and evaluations in Central Asia (see also Go, 2016). Dilemmas, contradictions, harms and suffering were understood and evaluated from class-inflected perspectives, in particular those of domestic rentiers and grassroots activists. This avoided producing disparaging accounts from a Northern standpoint that tended to explain outcomes in terms of essentialised identities and cultures, or prioritised first-world interests (e.g. security and energy) over low-income countries' concerns.

While knowledge is always socially situated, it does not mean that social science must be confined to epistemic relativism, or a plethora of narrow particularisms (Go, 2016). In this book, the Southern standpoint involved abstracting significant attributes and relationships from multidimensional concrete social phenomena. This mode of theorising aimed not only to explain and evaluate rentier capitalism and countermovements in Central Asia, but illuminate possibly similar processes and struggles elsewhere in the Global South and the West.

Mainstream social science tends to operate on a series of dualisms, such as universalism/particularism, explanation/understanding, theory/data, truth/opinion, objective/subjective, reason/emotion, mind/body, fact/value, modern/tradition, and so on (see Sayer, 1992, 2000 for discussion on critical realism and social science). In each of these dualisms, the first term is often treated as superior, though this can also be reversed in some post-positivist paradigms. The Southern standpoint avoided these disabling dualisms, and recognised the space between the terms. It drew attention to the intelligence of emotions, thick ethical descriptions, evaluations, embodiment, ontological realism, stratified ontology, causal mechanisms and theory-laden observations.

The Southern standpoint adopted a retroductive research strategy, rather than inductive and deductive research strategies, which examine phenomena from the bottom-up and the top down respectively. Retroduction seeks to explain observed regularities and events in specific contexts by postulating material and discursive causal mechanisms and conditions (Sayer, 1992). Theoretical pluralism, or multiple theoretical lens, was necessary to analyse complex concrete events. Specific theories, mechanisms and concepts were always tentative, and fieldwork was required to test their practical adequacy. The standpoint was also committed to judgemental rationality, which asserts that there are criteria for judging which explanations about reality are better or worse.

Furthermore, the standpoint used intensive research design, which primarily focuses on what makes things happen in particular cases, as opposed to extensive research, which is concerned with discovering some common properties and general patterns of a population (Sayer, 2000). The intensive approach started with specific individuals, and then traced their main causal relationships and examined their qualitative and quantitative nature. In critically investigating local rentier activities, the approach scaled upward and outward, illuminating part-whole, local-national and South-North relationships. It identified substantial connections and causal groups across different scalar levels. Causal relationships were pursed not on the basis of disciplinary loyalties or imperialism, but of substantial arguments.

Research Designs and Methods

This book draws on four case studies on credit money, land, real estate and natural resources in Kazakhstan and Kyrgyzstan. These topics were chosen for investigation because of their regional significance as sources of unearned income. Researching them offered critical insights into how these egregious forms of income extraction were created, justified, promoted and resisted in the post-Soviet space. The four case studies explored how different social groups construed, de-/legitimised and evaluated scarce assets. The total number of participants was 241, comprising wealthy asset owners, lower middle and working class renters/users, senior state officials, judges, professional intermediaries, international financial institutions and leaders of grassroots movements and civil society organisations.

The Case Study On Credit/Debt

The first case study on finance was in two parts. The first part examined the issue of credit/debt through the perspectives of lenders and state officials. This involved thirty semi-structured interviews conducted in Nur-Sultan, Almaty and Bishkek in 2016–2017. The sample consisted of twelve banks, two microcredit companies, one pawnshop, nine international financial institutions, four government ministries and agencies, and two trade associations. The authors and four research assistants used purposive sampling to recruit participants (Bryman, 2012). The interviews were conducted in Russian or English, and each interview lasted on average 45 minutes. The interview questions examined how the financial elites and state and non-state actors evaluated lending practices, what moral discourses and norms predominated their understandings, and what economic pressures shaped their judgements.

The second part involved borrowers' experiences and understanding of indebtedness in Kyrgyzstan. Initially a focus group with thirteen national and regional leaders, who belonged to an anti-debt movement, was conducted. The group discussion consisted of five national leaders and seven regional leaders, and was held in Bishkek in 2016. Ten of the focus group participants were ethnic Kyrgyz women in their 50s and 60s, and two were ethnic Kyrgyz men. The focus group discussion was conducted in Russian and Kyrgyz, and lasted over two and a quarter hours. It consisted of three segments. The first segment asked the participants to recount how the anti-debt movement began and developed, and what were their motivations and goals. The second segment asked them to discuss what strategies they had undertaken over the years. The third segment asked them to describe their interactions with state and financial institutions and elites, and how the latter responded to the movement's demands.

In addition, this part of the study involved thirty-three semi-structured interviews with borrowers, of whom twenty-three were women, and ten were men. The interviews took place in Bishkek and Osh in 2016. Most of the interviewees were recruited through the leaders of the anti-debt movement, and others came through recommendations. Most interviewees came from lower middle and working class backgrounds.

The interviews, conducted in Russian or Kyrgyz, lasted on average an hour, consisting of two segments. In the first segment, the interviewees described their personal and economic difficulties in relation to debt. The second segment asked them to discuss how they sought to resolve their economic difficulties.

Desk-based research was used to obtain information on how borrowers in Kazakhstan understood and responded to indebtedness. Local newspapers, online media, special reports and activists' blogs were key sources of data to investigate borrowers' experiences and actions.

The Case Study on Real Estate

The second case study on real estate consisted of two parts. The first part investigated how property developers and state officials construed and developed urban real estate in Kyrgyzstan. The authors and two research assistants recruited eleven participants, of which six were directors and senior managers of property and construction companies, four were senior officials of government ministries and agencies, and one city council official. The interviews were held in Bishkek and Osh in 2016, and were conducted in Russian or English, lasting on average 45 minutes. The interview questions examined how property developers and state actors understood and shaped urban real estate and housing construction.

The second part involved tenants' rental experiences in Kyrgyzstan. The semi-structured interviews focused on market traders as tenants in large private marketplaces in Bishkek and Osh, and were held in 2016. The sample consisted of ten market traders, of whom seven were female, and three were male, and one market traders' association. The interviews were conducted in Russian or Kyrgyz, each lasting 30 minutes. The traders were asked to discuss the effects of rent on their business, and their interactions with marketplace owners.

Information on urban real estate and housing experience in Kazakhstan was collected using desk-based research. The main sources of data were local online media reports and documents by government agencies and international organisations. Some information was also drawn from the previous research project on informal settlements, where interviews were conducted with Kazakhstan's state officials and non-governmental organisation (NGO) activists.

The Case Study on Land

The third case study on land was in two parts. The first part examined the issue of land through informal settlers' experiences and perspectives. Seventy-five semi-structured interviews were conducted with informal settlers in Nur-Sultan, Almaty, Bishkek and Osh in 2011. The interviewees were lower middle and working class participants, most of whom were un-/semi-skilled migrant workers, unemployed and retired. A few were low-level public sector managers and petty market traders. The authors and four research assistants used opportunity and snowball sampling to recruit participants. The interviewees were encouraged to discuss how they survived and coped with the lack of property tenure and city registration, what interactions they had with the city administration, the courts, and NGOs, and what moral and legal obligations they thought the state had towards them. The interviews were conducted in Kyrgyz, Kazakh or Russian, and each interview was about 30 minutes long.

The second part involved the perspectives from state officials, judges, lawyers, NGOs and international donor organisations. Initially twenty-one semi-structured interviews were carried out in Nur-Sultan, Almaty, Bishkek and Osh in 2011. The sample consisted of senior state officials, NGO activists, independent lawyers, and staff from international donor organisations. The authors and four research assistants used purposive sampling to recruit them. The interviews offered legal and administrative perspectives on informal settlements. NGO activists explained the nature of legal action against the state. The interviews were conducted in Russian, and each interview lasted about an hour.

In the following year, twenty-nine semi-structured were conducted with judges and lawyers in Nur-Sultan, Almaty, Bishkek and Osh. The sample consisted of sixteen Supreme Court, city and retired senior judges, twelve high-profile and local lawyers, and one ombudsman. The authors and four research assistants used purposive and snowball sampling to recruit participants. The interviews were conducted in Russian, and each interview was on average 45 min. The interview questions examined how judges and lawyers evaluated land, property rights and informal settlements. The interviewees were encouraged to discuss what kind of justice underpinned their evaluations, and what were the rights and obligations of non-legal professionals, including local authorities, property owners and illegal settlers.

The Case Study on Natural Resources

The fourth case study on mining was based on several sources. Some information was drawn from one of the authors' month-long fieldwork in a mountainous village in southern Kyrgyzstan in 2008. Local mining problems and disputes were examined. Seventeen semi-structured interviews were also conducted. The sample consisted of local state officials, community leaders and residents. The interviews were in Kyrgyz, and sought to investigate how mining was interpreted and evaluated by different actors. Moreover, an interview was conducted with a senior state official about the Kumtor gold mine. The interview explored key issues around foreign ownership of mines, contractual rights and obligations.

Desk-based research offered considerable information on natural resources in Kazakhstan and Kyrgyzstan. Online reports from the media, government bodies and independent organisations provided details on disputes, settlements and grievances. They also gave information on labour dissatisfaction, strike action and environmental pollution in the sector.

All the interviews in the four case studies were digitally recorded, and then were transcribed and translated into English. All participants were assured of confidentiality, and their names have been pseudonymised. The authors read the transcripts several times to understand what themes were emerging (Silverman, 2011). While some initial codes were derived from the authors' research agenda for each study, others emerged from the interview data. In this way, the authors avoided their preconceptions distorting their interpretation of the data (Fletcher, 2017). The codes were changed, eliminated and supplemented as the data warranted. Some codes were recoded into theoretical-informed categories that allowed for greater conceptual clarity.

Outline of the Book

This book is divided into four parts. In Part I, Chapter 2 examines the significance and diversity of income extraction in Kazakhstan and Kyrgyzstan. This is then linked to the countries' high concentration of wealth, economic inequalities and emerging political and social harms. Chapter 3 discusses several theoretical ideas that underpin the book and the four case studies. The moral economy perspective and the Polanyian double movement are presented alongside ideas on the state, the judiciary and new constitutionalism.

Part II offers an empirical discussion on the moral, legal and political dimensions of the neoliberal movement and its regime of rent extraction in the region. It explores the marketisation of money, urban real estate and natural resources. Chapter 4 interrogates the financial elites' moral claims to charge interest on loans. Chapter 5 investigates the commodification of real estate properties, and its link to political power and corruption. Chapter 6 examines how legal and judicial mechanisms secure foreign investors' rights to own and extract income in the natural resource sector.

Part III provides an empirical discussion on the moral, class and gendered dimensions of the region's countermovements. It explores how grassroots movements pursued their goals to decommodify fictitious commodities. Chapter 7 investigates the development of informal settlement movements, and their tense and ambivalent interactions with political regimes. Chapter 8 explores the emergence and evolution of anti-debt movements, and their contrasting goals and strategies in Kazakhstan and Kyrgyzstan. Chapter 9 discusses how environmental and labour movements arose in the natural resource sector, and their struggles against transnational corporations and political regimes.

In Part IV, Chapter 10 critically discusses the book's key themes: neoliberalism, rentierism, the state, class and countermovements. It also provides a critical moral evaluation of rentierism in the region. Chapter 11 explores what can be done to tackle income extraction, and ensure human flourishing.

References

Appel, H., & Orenstein, M. (2018). *From triumph to crisis: Neoliberal economic reforms in postcommunist countries*. Cambridge University Press.

Bryman, A. (2012). *Social research methods* (4th ed.). Oxford University Press.

Buchanan, J. (2008). Same players, different game: How better rules make better politics. *Constitutional Political Economy, 19*(3), 171–179.

Burawoy, M. (2015). Facing an unequal world. *Current Sociology, 63*(1), 5–34.

Christophers, B. (2020). *Rentier capitalism: Who owns the economy, and who pays for it?* Verso.

Cooley, A., & Heathershaw, J. (2017). *Dictators without borders: Power and money in Central Asia*. Yale University Press.

Engvall, J. (2014). Why are public offices sold in Kyrgyzstan? *Post-Soviet Affairs, 30*(1), 67–85.

Fletcher, A. (2017). Applying critical realism in qualitative research: Methodology meets method. *International Journal of Social Research Methodology, 20*(2), 181–194.

Gill, S. (2008). *Power and resistance in the new world order* (2nd ed.). Palgrave.

Go, J. (2016). *Postcolonial thought and social theory*. Oxford University Press.

Goodwin, G. (2018). Rethinking the double movement: Expanding the frontiers of Polanyian analysis in the Global South. *Development and Change, 49*(5), 1268–1290.

Hann, C. (2016). Cucumbers and courgettes: Rural workfare and the new double movement in Hungary. *Intersections. East Europe Journal Society and Politics, 2*(2), 38–56.

Harvey, D. (2005). *A brief history of neoliberalism*. Oxford University Press.

Jessop, B. (2002). *The future of the capitalist state*. Polity.

Koch, N. (2019). Post-triumphalist geopolitics: Liberal selves, authoritarian others. *ACME: An International Journal for Critical Geographies, 18*(4), 909–924.

Lottholtz, P., Heathershaw, J., Ismailbekova, A., Moldalieva, J., McGlinchey, E., & Owen, C. (2020). Governance and order-making in Central Asia: From illiberalism to post-liberalism? *Central Asian Survey, 39*(3), 420–437. https://doi.org/10.1080/02634937.2020.1803794.

Maclean, N. (2017). *Democracy in chains: The deep history of the Radical Right's Stealth Plan for America*. Viking Press.

McGlinchey, E. (2011). *Chaos, violence, dynasty: politics and Islam in Central Asia*. University of Pittsburgh Press.

Mihalyi, P., & Szelenyi, I. (2017). The role of rents in the transition from socialist redistributive economies to market capitalism. *Comparative Sociology, 16*(1), 13–38.

Mihalyi, P., & Szelenyi, I. (2019). *Rent-seekers, profits, wages and inequality: The top 20%*. Palgrave Macmillan.

Myant, M., & Drahokoupil, J. (2011). *Transition economies: Political economy in Russia, Eastern Europe, and Central Asia*. Wiley.

Ost, D. (2015). Class after communism: Introduction to the special issue. *East European Politics and Societies and Cultures, 9*(3), 543–556.

Peyrouse, S. (2012). The Kazakh neopatrimonial regime: Balancing uncertainties among the 'family', oligarchs and technocrats. *Demokratizatsiya, 20*(4), 345–370.

Polanyi, K. (1944). *The great transformation: Economic and political origins of our time*. Rinehart.

Pomfret, R. (2019). *The Central Asia economies in the twenty-first century: Paving a New Silk Road*. Cambridge University Press.

Sayer, A. (1992). *Method in social science: A realist approach* (2nd ed.). Routledge.

Sayer, A. (2000). *Realism and social science*. Sage.

Sayer, A. (2015). *Why we can't afford the rich*. Policy Press.

Sayer, A. (2018). Welfare and moral economy. *Ethics and Social Welfare, 12*(1), 20–33.

Silverman, D. (2011). *Interpreting qualitative data: A guide to the principles of qualitative research*. Sage.

Soederberg, S. (2014). *Debtfare states and the poverty industry*. Routledge.

Stone, L. (2012). Central Asian studies. *Journal of Third World Studies, 29*(1), 175–202.

PART I

Theorising Rent Extraction

CHAPTER 2

The Rise of the Rentier Class and Widening Social Inequalities

This chapter discusses two key aspects of neoliberalism: rentierism and economic inequalities. The first part of the chapter provides some details of the different forms of rent in Central Asia, and the assets of the richest individuals in Kazakhstan and Kyrgyzstan that facilitated rent extraction. Business elites often merged with political elites to create plutocracy. The second part examines the nature of income and wealth inequalities in the region. It also explores the hardship and misery associated with the commodification of basic goods and services.

The Rentierisation of Central Asian Economies

Forms of Rent and Rentierism in Central Asian Economies

Rent and rentierism come in different forms, and their diversity is crucial to understand the nature of the post-Soviet Central Asian economies. There are several core forms (Christophers, 2019; Sayer, 2015; Tawney, 1921). First, financial rents can consist of interest income, dividends and capital gains derived from financial assets. Financial rentiers can create and allocate credit money, and can acquire financial assets (e.g. bonds and shares) in primary and secondary markets. International financial actors, including the European Bank of Reconstruction and Development, promoted and facilitated the growth of banking and micro-lending

B. Sanghera and E. Satybaldieva, *Rentier Capitalism and Its Discontents*,
https://doi.org/10.1007/978-3-030-76303-9_2

in the post-Soviet space (Charman, 2007; Guseva, 2005; Ruziev & Dow, 2013).

Second, land rents can comprise ground and housing rent and capital gains based on the ownership and control of land and real estate (esp. residential apartments and office buildings). Landowners' ability to extract income depends on the scarcity and attractiveness of landed property. The deregulation and privatisation of housing and land were significant in creating land rents in post-Soviet economies (Marcuse, 1996). Private property rights were re-bundled to remove regulatory controls on rent and multiple holdings.

Third, natural resource rents involve extracting income based on naturally occurring resources, including energy products (oil, gas and coal) and other minerals (metal ores, stones, sands and salts). The owner of natural resources can be either the state or a private body. It can sign a leasing agreement with a non-owner, often a foreign actor, who is given the exclusive right to develop and extract the resource, and thereby generate rent, for a fixed time period. The state itself can also act as a rentier, and Kazakhstan, Turkmenistan and Azerbaijan are often called rentier states, because they receive substantial rents from natural resources (Franke et al., 2009).

Fourth, natural monopoly rents occur when natural monopolies can charge excessive prices for their commodities because they are free from competition. Natural monopolies can use their market power to obtain economic rent. In post-Soviet countries, the privatisation of public utilities, such as gas, electricity, water and fixed line telephony, was often followed by price hikes (Appel & Orenstein, 2018). Wooden (2014) observes how an increase in electricity tariffs sparked protests in Kyrgyzstan, resulting in the 2010 political uprising.

Fifth, spectrum rents are based on income from audio and television broadcasting and the provision of mobile telephony and internet services. The radio spectrum refers to a range of frequencies of electromagnetic energy that can be used for various types of communication (Christophers, 2019). It is often likened to land. As the owner of the radio spectrum, the state licenses exclusive rights to a third-party to use certain frequencies for particular purposes over specified geographical areas. This enables licensees to generate revenues, which constitute rents derived from exclusive commercial control of a scarce asset.

The construction and maintenance of mobile phone networks may be the second-largest area of foreign direct investment in Central Asia after oil and gas (Pomfret, 2019). The huge potential to extract economic rent means that foreign investors are willing to spend money, and often bribe state officials, to obtain licenses.

Sixth, intellectual property rents include income from patents, trademarks and copyright. Patents feature significantly in the pharmaceutical and biotechnology sectors, trademarks are widespread in the consumer product industry; and copyright is prevalent in the entertainment and publishing sectors (Christophers, 2019). Rents can either arise from the owner exploiting the intellectual property, or the owner licensing the rights to a third-party. But the protection and enforcement of intellectual property rights tend to be weak in post-Soviet economies, resulting in an illicit and lucrative trade in counterfeit and pirated goods.

Seventh, contract rents occur when organisations outsource activities by awarding contracts to other companies for the services to be provided. These contracts become prized assets for companies delivering the services, because they guarantee income for a fixed period of time. For example, a US Department of Defense agency awarded lucrative contracts to local companies to supply jet fuel to its air base in Kyrgyzstan (Toktomushev, 2015). This afforded the political regime and business elites with opportunities for rent-seeking and siphoning off funds to tax havens.

Eighth, platform rents are revenues generated for owners of digital platforms, such as Google and Booking.com There are two types of revenues: advertising on platforms, and fees and commissions levied on transactions initiated through the platform. The platform's scarcity is neither inherent (e.g. land), nor state prescribed (e.g. radio spectrum), rather it is a feature of the business to monopolise the specific sector, so that there is only one Google and one Amazon. While digital platforms are growing in Central Asia, they are not developed as in the Global North. Western and Russian companies, such as WhatsApp and Mail.ru, dominate the platform economy.

Christophers (2019) argues that despite the different forms of rents, rentiers' strategy is the same: acquire and extract value from scarce assets. Many post-Soviet oligarchs captured valuable assets and resources to become rentiers, largely as a result of privatisation, patronage and corruption (Mihalyi & Szelenyi, 2017). In his sample of Russian oligarchs, Braguinsky (2009) distinguishes between 'insiders' and 'outsiders'. The former were managers of Soviet enterprises prior to 1991, members of the nomenklatura, and relatives or close colleagues of people in the first two groups. The latter had no ties to the previous system. Insider oligarchs initially dominated large-scale industrial sectors, such as natural resources and engineering. Nearly half of them made their wealth based on controlling Russia's oil, gas and minerals, and extracting natural resource rents. In contrast, outsider oligarchs made their initial fortunes in service sectors, such as banking, consumer goods and the media. Almost half of them derived their wealth based on controlling finance and banking, establishing their own banks and investment companies, and appropriating financial rents.

While the nature of rentierism is similar across the world, there are some specificities in Central Asia and the wider post-Soviet space. First, rentierism was largely absent during the Soviet Union (Marcuse, 1996). International financial institutions' neoliberal reforms helped to create, legitimise and promote rentierism in post-Soviet economies, as Chapters 4–6 will show. Second, many early rentiers had occupied privileged political and economic positions during the Soviet Union (Braguinsky, 2009). They used their knowledge and power to quickly, and in some cases indiscreetly, acquire valuable resources and assets.

Third, many later acquisitions were characterised by nepotism, patronage, fraudulent privatisation, corruption, violence and criminality (McGlinchey, 2011). In some cases, political and business elites engaged in corporate raiding, seizing lucrative businesses with the aid of corrupt law-enforcement officials and judges. In Kyrgyzstan, political elites also used intimidation and violence to transfer the ownership and control of valuable assets.

Fourth, Central Asia is rich in natural resources, and the sector is a significant source of rent (Franke et al., 2009). Though barely acknowledged in the literature on Central Asia, finance and real estate have emerged as key sectors for income extraction, as will be shown in the next sub-section.

The Significance of Rent in Kazakhstan and Kyrgyzstan

Christophers (2019) observes that while the significance of rent in the economy cannot be accurately measured, it is possible to assess it in a sufficiently meaningful way to draw out some conclusions about the relative importance of rent and rentiers. Using a range of open sources, this sub-section examines the nature and extent of rent among the richest individuals in Kazakhstan and Kyrgyzstan.

Table 2.1 shows the top twenty richest business people in 2018 in

Table 2.1 Top 20 richest business people in Kazakhstan

Name	*Personal wealth ($m)*	*Main economic sectors*
Vladimir Kim	4500	Minerals, banking, finance, telecommunications and intellectual property
Bulat Utemuratov	3400	Banking, finance, minerals, telecommunications, real estate and fast-food franchisees
Timur Kulibayev	3100	Energy, banking, finance, real estate and shopping malls
Dinara Kulibayeva	3100	Real estate, shopping malls, energy, minerals, banking and education
Alijan Ibragimov	2300	Minerals, banking, finance and real estate
Rashit Sarsenov	780	Banking, finance, insurance and energy
Kenes Rakishev	610	Banking, finance, minerals, energy and insurance
Galimzhan Yessenov	545	Banking, finance, minerals and insurance
Bakhytbek Baiseitov	540	Banking, finance and energy
Nurlan Smagulov	525	Car dealership, car assembly plants, shopping malls and real estate
Aydin Rakhimbaev	485	Construction, real estate and telecommunications
Alexander Belovich	480	Construction and real estate
Kairat Boranbayev	445	Real estate, shopping malls, fast-food franchisees, fitness clubs, petrochemical and construction
Daniyar Abulgazin	430	Energy and shopping malls
Vyacheslav Kim	415	Banking, finance, retailing and information technology
Yerkin Tatishev	412	Real estate, construction, energy, minerals and agri-business
Alexander Klebanov	390	Finance and telecommunications
The Seitzhanovich Family	360	Energy, construction and hotels
Aigul Nuriyeva	350	Telecommunications
Serik Tulbassov	340	Construction, real estate and shopping malls

Source Adapted from Forbes Kazakhstan, 13 May 2019, available at https://forbes.kz//leader/50_bogateyshih_biznesmenov_kazahstana_-_2019_1557664676/

Kazakhstan according to Forbes' ranking. It details their estimated wealth, and which sectors of the economy their companies operated in. Data was formed from public sources and financial information provided by each person. The evaluation of the total value of their assets was conservative; i.e. not less than the estimated figure. The list does not include citizens of other countries who have substantial wealth in Kazakhstan.

Unearned income occurred in two ways: shares in companies entitled owners to dividends, profit and capital gains; and companies extracted specific forms of rent depending on the economic sector. All but one on the rich list had two or more forms of rent. They owned multiple companies, and many participated in several sectors.

The financialisation of the economy and the scarcity of land have been important for the rentier class (Hudson, 2014; Sayer, 2015). Of the 20 richest individuals, ten extracted income through banking activities, in particular creating and lending credit money, as will be discussed in Chapter 4. The same number siphoned off income through managing a broad range of financial assets and services. Ten business people had property companies that extracted rent through the ownership and control of residential and commercial real estate. There were six property developers, who facilitated and participated in rentier activities.

Given the abundance of natural resources in Kazakhstan, energy and minerals have been significant sources of rent for wealthy individuals (Franke et al., 2009). Eight business people wholly or partly owned companies that had leasing rights to extract and/or distribute oil and gas. Owning petrol stations allowed some individuals to have a degree of control of the local market, and make quasi-monopoly rent. Seven on the list were involved in the mining sector.

The shift to a market economy has seen retail trade and consumption boom in post-Soviet countries. Shopping malls, retail centres and marketplaces are a significant source of economic rent for owners. They are often located in prime sites, giving owners spatial monopoly power, and retail units are usually leased to companies and traders (Spector, 2017). Six individuals on the rich list owned several high-end shopping malls. Moreover, three business people had a degree of local monopoly power in specific retail markets—cars and fast-food.

Some forms of rent have become more important because of technological change and innovation. Five wealthy individuals owned telecommunication companies, which had exclusive rights to provide broadband internet access services and mobile networks. Their commercial control of the radio spectrum enabled them to extract rent.

Table 2.2 shows the top twenty richest people in Kyrgyzstan. The list was adapted from a 2013 ranking of the top 100 richest people in the country. The table details their estimated wealth, and which sectors of the economy their companies operated in. Data was formed from a range of open sources, including newspapers and media platforms (e.g. Vecherniy Bishkek, Kloop.kg, Sputnik.kg, Gezitter.org, Stan Radar and Beli Parus). The list only includes Kyrgyzstani citizens.

There are four caveats to the table. First, there is no up-to-date rich list for Kyrgyzstan similar to Forbes 2018 ranking in Kazakhstan. While the list should be treated with some caution, it does provide some insights into who are some of the wealthy individuals in the country. Second, most people on the list have held public office, and they have tried to hide their true financial situation. It is widely believed that fraud, corruption, plunder and other illegal and illicit activities have helped them to acquire valuable assets and income (Cooley & Heathershaw, 2017; Engvall, 2014; McGlinchey, 2011). There have been many criminal investigations, and in some cases, the state has confiscated their assets.

Third, some names from the 2013 ranking have been omitted, because there was insufficient information on their wealth. Fourth, most individuals on the list have declared themselves to be honest, hard-working and not rich. Their assets are often held either by close family members, or holding companies, which are usually secretive about their true owners (Cooley & Sharman, 2015). Through careful investigation of open sources, it has been possible to identify what assets the rich and their close relatives have. The table offers some valuable insights into the broad range of rents in the country. All but two on the rich list had multiple forms of rent.

For the rentier class in Kyrgyzstan, as in Kazakhstan, land and money were two major instruments to acquire wealth without doing creative work, as Tawney (1921) noted of the British rentier class. Owning real estate was the most popular way to obtain unearned income. Sixteen wealthy individuals had a substantial number of residential apartments and other properties, which were either rented or re-sold. There were ten property developers, who engaged in extractive and speculative investment in the real estate sector, as will be discussed in Chapter 5. Six

Table 2.2 Top 20 richest people in Kyrgyzstan

Name	*Personal wealth ($m)*	*Main economic sectors*
Omurbek Babanov	1500	Banking, energy, minerals, construction, real estate, shopping malls and pharmaceutical trade
Askar Salymbekov	1200–500	Retail and wholesale marketplaces, shopping malls, real estate, retail trade, construction and insurance
Almazbek Atambaev	600	Private equity, finance and real estate
Nariman Tuleyev	400–500	Banking, real estate, shopping malls, retail, construction, telecommunications and tourism
Chynybay Tursunbekov	280–300	Banking, real estate, food processing, construction, retail and distillery
Akylbek Zhaparov	200–250	Real estate, agriculture, farming, hotels, restaurant and shopping malls
Tursuntai Salimov	200–250	Retail marketplaces, restaurants, real estate, ski resort and retail
Dinara Isaeva	200–250	Banking, construction, real estate, shopping malls, retail marketplaces, minerals, tourism and airline
Isa Omurkulov	200–220	Shopping malls, real estate, catering and retail
Osmonbek Artykbaev	200–220	Construction, retail pharmacy chain and medical supplies
Temir Sariev	200–210	Construction, real estate, agri-business, agriculture, commodity trade, finance and industry
Akmatbek Keldibekov	180–200	Real estate, boarding houses, retail marketplaces, telecommunications, transport services and agriculture
Askarbek Shadiev*	180–200	Construction, real estate and wholesale trade
The Egemberdiev Family	180–200	Production and distribution of soft drinks and restaurants

(continued)

Table 2.2 (continued)

Name	*Personal wealth ($m)*	*Main economic sectors*
Kubanychbek Zhumaliev	150–170	Shopping malls, marketplaces, real estate, telecommunications, minerals, energy, horticulture and computer factory
Asirbekov Temirbek	100–120	Construction, real estate and financial management
Alexander Niyazov	100–120	Energy
Kamchybek Zholdoshbaev	100–110	Shopping malls, energy, microfinance and pharmaceutical trade
Sharipa Sadybakasova	90–100	Banking, real estate and wholesale trade
Melis Myrzakmatov*	90–100	Retail marketplaces, shopping malls, restaurants, telecommunications, construction and real estate

*Assets confiscated by the state

Source Adapted from Aimak.kg, 21 December 2013, available at http://aimak.kg/ru/novosti/politika_i_obshestvo/427-100-samyh-bogatyh-lyudey-kyrgyzstana.html

individuals siphoned off interest and other charges based on the ownership and control of credit money. Four persons on the rich list extracted income through other financial services, including insurance.

Shopping malls and marketplaces were important rent-generating assets for eleven wealthy individuals. Askar Salymbekov owned Dordoi Bazaar, one of the largest retail and wholesale marketplaces in Central Asia (Spector, 2017). Of the eleven individuals, several either wholly or partly owned retail marketplaces, and some were large shareholders of prestigious shopping malls. Three persons on the list had a degree of monopoly power in the pharmaceutical market through their ownership of retail chains and exclusive licences, enabling them to extract economic rent. The Egemberdiev Family extracted income through their famous brand of 'Shoro' and their control of distribution channels in the soft drinks market.

The dominance of foreign capital in the natural resource and telecommunication sectors in Kazakhstan and Kyrgyzstan (Pomfret, 2019) means that the scale of natural resource and spectrum rents is greater than shown in Tables 2.1 and 2.2, which only detail the wealth of local elites.

Energy and minerals were seemingly less significant for the rentier class in Kyrgyzstan than in Kazakhstan. Energy was a source of rent for four individuals on the rich list. Two of them owned a number of petrol stations, which gave them some spatial monopoly power, especially in Bishkek.

Three wealthy individuals used minerals to extract rent. One of them had leasing rights to a gold mine. Given that about a half of foreign direct investment in the country has been directed towards the mining sector, it was surprising that that it did not appear more prominently in the table. But gold mining companies have used complex financial schemes (such as shareholding companies) to hide final beneficiaries (Doolot & Heathershaw, 2015).

Four wealthy individuals owned companies with exclusive rights to broadcast radio and television, and provide mobile broadband. One of the largest mobile operators, Megacom, was owned by former President Bakiev's son, Maxim. It was later confiscated and nationalised by the state after Bakiev's overthrow in the 2010 uprising.

Contract rents were significant for two wealthy individuals. Omurbek Babanov had exclusive rights to supply jet fuel to Manas Airport and the US airbase (Toktomushev, 2015). Osmonbek Artykbaev had a contract to deliver medical drugs and equipment to state hospitals and clinics throughout the country. These contracts guaranteed income for a period of time, and protected Babanov and Artykbaev from competition, thereby allowing them to receive economic rent.

Plutocracy has come to dominate the post-Soviet political landscape. The rentier class has largely captured the state, and political elites have often been allied to rentier interests (Braguinsky, 2009; Mihalyi & Szelenyi, 2017). Tables 2.1 and 2.2 reveal how economic and political structures have become intertwined, partly as a result of nepotism, patronage, fraud and corruption (McGlinchey, 2011). In Kyrgyzstan, several rentiers occupied powerful political positions. Omurbek Babanov and Almazbek Atambaev were former Prime Ministers. Atambaev was also an ex-President. Nariman Tuleyev, Isa Omurkulov, Askar Salymbekov, Melis Myrzakmatov and Dinara Isaeva's husband were former city mayors. Some rentiers were cabinet ministers, and several were speakers and members of the Parliament.

In Kazakhstan, some rentiers were related or close to ex-President Nursultan Nazarbayev. Dinara Kulibayeva is his second eldest daughter, and her husband is Timur Kulibayev. Vladimir Kim is part of Nazarbayev's inner political circle, and Bulat Utemuratov was for a long time the head of the presidential administration, i.e. the 'number two' of the state apparatus (Peyrouse, 2012). Several rentiers have benefitted from Nazarbayev's patronage: resources and assets were distributed to them on the basis of their loyalty to the president.

In promoting neoliberalism and rentierism, Western governments and international financial institutions have helped to create and sustain the post-Soviet political landscape (see Cooley & Heathershaw, 2017 on the illicit role of international financial networks in Central Asia). One of the unintended consequences of neoliberalism has been that plutocracy, and not democracy, has tended to prevail in this region, contrary to international expectations and hopes (Hudson, 2014; Standing, 2016).

While there are broad similarities in rentierism and plutocracy between Kazakhstan and Kyrgyzstan, there are some differences. First, the significance of natural resource rents has varied over time, partly in response to exogenous factors, such as global recession and political instability. In Kazakhstan, the total natural resource rents as a percentage of Gross Domestic Product (GDP) was 16% in 2017 (World Bank, 2020a). At the peak of oil and gas prices in 2008, it reached 33%. But since then, it has declined as world prices started to fall.

In Kyrgyzstan, the total natural resource rents as a percentage of GDP was 8% in 2017 (World Bank, 2020a). Its highest value was 12% in 2011, partly reflecting rising gold prices at the start of the 2007–2008 crisis. Its value began to drop due to operational disruptions at major gold mines as a result of economic and political uncertainties following the 2010 political uprising in the country. Migrant remittances have been more important than natural resource rents for economic development. In 2018 Kyrgyzstan's personal remittances as a percentage of GDP was 33%, whereas Kazakhstan's figure was 0.35% (World Bank, 2020b).

Second, the development of household credit and debt has been different in the two countries. In resource-poor Kyrgyzstan, international financial institutions and development agencies created and promoted microcredit programmes, aiming to alleviate poverty through women's empowerment, microenterprises and rural development. But interests on micro-loans were much higher than on bank loans, and many borrowers experienced a high level of indebtedness and repossession. Protests against predatory lending and financial malpractices successfully led to the government capping interest rates, as will be discussed in Chapter 8. Major microfinance institutions later became commercial banks.

Resource-rich Kazakhstan attracted a large share of foreign direct investment. Cheap access to global credit expanded US dollar-denominated loans in the country. Easy credit fuelled a housing bubble until the 2007–2008 financial crisis, which left many mortgage-holders struggling to make repayments (Yessenova, 2010). Several construction companies and banks collapsed, and mortgage-holders called on the government to safeguard their homes. The government injected funds to stabilise the national currency against the US dollar, nationalised troubled banks, and provided some assistance to the construction sector.

Third, Kyrgyzstan and Kazakhstan have had different post-1991 political developments. Kyrgyzstan experienced the 2005 Tulip Revolution and the 2010 political uprising that removed incumbent governments by force and violence. In both cases civil society played a critical role in ousting corrupt political regimes, which had accumulated significant personal wealth (Cooley & Heathershaw, 2017; McGlinchey, 2011; Reeves, 2010). In light of these events, Kyrgyzstan's elites have tended to hide or understate their wealth and assets for fear that their holdings would be perceived as corrupt or undeserved. The tendency towards rentierism and plutocracy in the country has been countered by moral criticism and social activism.

Kazakhstan has had a relatively stable political environment. But there were several violent riots and clashes, including the 2005 Shanyrak protest over informal settlements and housing rights; and the 2011 Zhanaozen protest over union representation and workers' rights. In both cases, the protests were suppressed by state violence, and activists were arrested and imprisoned. Junisbai (2010) argues that Kazakhstan's relative economic prosperity has shaped attitudes about economic justice. In his study, many social groups believed that economic opportunities and outcomes were largely fair and just, thereby reducing support for egalitarianism and redistributive economic policies. In this context, Kazakhstan's elites have been less discreet about accumulating wealth or power, having little fear of moral and social scrutiny.

Economic Inequalities

Beyond Statistics on Low-Income

In Kazakhstan, official statistics claimed that absolute poverty rate fell from 47% in 2001 to 8% in 2009 (Roelen & Gassmann, 2014). Extreme poverty based on the minimum food-consumption level dropped from 16% to 1% over the same period. In 2012, the share the poor population was only 3.8%. In 2018, Kyrgyzstan's poverty rate had decreased throughout the 2009–2018 period to 22.4%.

While official statistics on poverty can be important to hold governments to account, they have severe limitations (Lister, 2015). Governments can manipulate concepts and measurements to hide the depth of economic malaise. Despite government claims to the contrary, according to international methodology, more than half of the population in Kazakhstan lived in poverty (Aliev, 2015). Moreover, statistics miss the relational aspects of poverty. Impoverishment and enrichment are essentially linked in rent relations, which involve a transfer of income from the asset-poor to the asset-rich. To understand the nature and dynamics of economic inequalities requires moving beyond the statistics on poverty to include an analysis of the rich.

Class inequalities cannot be solely assessed on the basis of employment and wage, but need to take account of asset holdings and capital gains (Adkins et al., 2019). Rentierism in Kazakhstan and Kyrgyzstan produced a high concentration of income and assets in the hands of elites. Class inequalities also necessitate an analysis of a wide variety of rent relations, including debt relation, which engulfed most of the population in Central Asia. Numerous studies reveal how class inequalities negatively affect many aspects of life from mental health, education and life expectancy to political participation, violence and crime (Abdoubaetova, 2020; Danilovich, 2010; El-Hodiri et al., 2015; Green, 2016; Hasanova, 2018; Kopeyeva, 2020; Kussainov, 2018; Mikhalev & Heinrich, 1999; Satybaldieva, 2015; Sharipova, 2015; Steimann, 2011; Ursulenko, 2010).

The figures for income and wealth distribution offered a stark picture of Central Asia's class stratification. It was characterised by a minority of wealthy rentiers at the top, and a large section of rural and urban poor at the bottom. The middle class, which included professionals and small business owners, remained small. In Kazakhstan, income obtained by the wealthiest 10% was 29 times greater than that earned by the poorest 10% (Sharipova, 2015). Only 3.5% of adult population had income above 10,000 USD per annum (Kaztag, 2020). Moreover, 162 individuals (or 0.001% of the population) owned 50% of the total wealth of the population (KPMG, 2019). The top 50 richest businesspersons owned 42% of the total wealth of the adult population.

In Kyrgyzstan, the Gini income coefficient fluctuated around 40%, which was the highest in the Eurasian Economic Union (Hasanova, 2018). 75% of Kyrgyzstan's poor population lived in rural areas. Their income was small, consisting of remittances, state pensions and other welfare support. Moreover, in Steimann's (2011) survey of rural areas, although rich households constituted no more than 3% of the population, they owned large tracts of land and livestock. Most rural households had little to no livestock and farmland.

Misery of Poverty

Official statistics on low-income are inadequate to understand the nature of hardship and deprivation of poor and working class groups. They also ignore how poverty is understood and experienced in everyday lives. In particular, social suffering and misery are removed in official accounts of inequality. But recent studies paint a vivid picture of the multidimensional nature of poverty in Central Asia.

Kazakhstan's spatial inequalities were stark. In 2014, the gross regional product per person in the country's capital Nur-Sultan was 12,701 USD (El-Hodiri et al., 2015). In the densely populated region of South Kazakhstan, it was 2985 USD. In Almaty region almost 90% of the households were in the low-income category. A survey on deprivation showed that 36.7% of respondents in South Kazakhstan, 28.1% in Mangistau and 23.9% in Atyrau were unable to afford food, clothing or essential consumer products (Sakal, 2015).

While Mangistau region produced about 70% of the country's oil output, its population did not benefit from oil revenues. Nur-Sultan was the main beneficiary, as the political regime sought to develop the capital into a global city for the rich and powerful with luxury apartments, shopping malls and financial institutions. Local communities in oil producing regions largely experienced a poor provision of social services, air and water pollution and land degradation (Ursulenko, 2010).

In Kazakhstan, 47% of the population lived in rural areas, and most of them experienced hardship, especially in relation to basic utilities. Only 24.2% of the rural population had access to water sources, and 8.9% were connected to a sewage system (Rolnik, 2011). 68% of rural households experienced energy poverty, and 77% lacked access to electricity (Kerimray et al., 2017). Due to high electricity costs, 40% of rural households relied on coal and firewood for heating and cooking in one of the coldest countries in the world. Kazakhstan had one of the highest coal consumption per capita in the world (Kerimray et al., 2017).

In Kyrgyzstan, 64% of the population lived in rural areas, and the vast majority of them lacked adequate water and energy supplies. Of the 1805 rural villages in the country, 595 villages did not have access to a centralised drinking water system, and 390 were not connected to any water supply network (Nunnally, 2017). Many rural households were unable to meet their basic energy needs (Liu & Pistorious, 2012). The country's energy crisis resulted in unstable electricity supply in the regions, and power outages were common outside of the capital Bishkek.

Lack of social protection and inadequate access to basic goods exacerbated the lived experience of poverty. Central Asia's social programmes were ineffective in protecting poor households, because the coverage was very limited and the benefits were too small (Grassmann, 2011). In 2008, the Kyrgyzstani government, guided by the international donor community, passed legislation to raise the income threshold for social assistance, thereby further impoverishing working class families. While the Soviet model of redistributive social support aimed to reduce inequalities, its neoliberal replacement of targeted assistance schemes led to the commodification of basic goods and deepening inequalities.

In Kazakhstan and Kyrgyzstan, the marketisation of healthcare systems reduced poor women's access to reproductive healthcare. A comparative study on access to reproductive health services in Kazakhstan and Belarus showed that low-income women in Kazakhstan could not afford reproductive care and hospital stays, whereas low income was not a significant barrier to medical services in Belarus (Danilovich, 2010). Due to inaccessibility and high costs, most women in Kyrgyzstan did not receive adequate reproductive healthcare (*The Guardian*, 2019). The country had the highest maternal mortality rate in the post-Soviet space, with 90% of those deaths found to be preventable.

Pre-school education was poorly funded by the state as well as increasingly commodified, so that for many working class families kindergartens were either inaccessible or unaffordable. In Kazakhstan's rural areas, only 41% of children aged five were enrolled in kindergartens (Roelen & Gassmann, 2014). While state-supported childcare attendance increased from 11% in 1995 to 39% in 2011, this was largely achieved through part-time attendance (Habibov, 2014). In Kyrgyzstan, on average only 23% of young children attended kindergartens. In rural areas, attendance was 16%. Only 17% of children from the poorest households had access to childcare.

The post-Soviet secondary education system has favoured children from richer households. In Kazakhstan, the establishment of a network of selective schools called the Nazarbayev Intellectual Schools (NISs) has benefitted affluent families and their children. Initially, these schools aimed to provide free high-quality education access to children from poor families (Kussainov, 2018). But strict entrance criteria meant that the schools had to recruit children from rich households, who could also pay tuition fees from 5800 to 10,600 USD a year. In 2017, the NISs accounted for almost 7% of the Ministry of Education and Science's budget, but had only 0.47% of the total number of pupils. In effect, taxpayers were subsidising the education of privileged children, many of whom continued their education abroad.

In Kyrgyzstan, secondary education has become commodified and a lucrative business. The number of private schools has grown in Bishkek. In 2017, there were 114 private schools, which were described as preparing students 'for export' (Abdoubaetova, 2020). Both countries testified to the trend of 'elitisation' in secondary education (Kussainov, 2018).

The class-based schooling did not merely contribute to the reproduction of social inequality in Central Asia, it failed to educate many children. In Kazakhstan, the 2015 PISA results showed that half of 15-year-old pupils in Atyrau, South Kazakhstan and Mangystau regions were 'functionally illiterate' in science, meaning that the pupils could not complete tasks of the first level of difficulty (Kopeyeva, 2020). In 2006 and 2009, Kyrgyzstan was bottom in the PISA rankings, after which the country refused to participate in the tests. The country's 2009 results showed that more than 80% of 15-year-old pupils had reading skills below the baseline level of proficiency.

During the 30 years of neoliberalisation, poor and working class groups have experienced multiple harms from inadequate income and employment to lack of affordable housing, childcare, healthcare and education. As state welfare institutions became delegitimised and defunded, Central Asia's political regimes legitimised and promoted the credit market as a way to meet basic needs. The Soviet welfare state became post-Soviet debtfare states. In Kazakhstan, 46% of households used loans to pay for basic goods and services that had become commodified (Shedenova & Beimisheva, 2013). But in the process, many working class and poor families fell into heavy debts, exacerbating their hardship and misery. In response to such class injustice and social suffering, countermovements emerged, attempting to decommodify basic goods and services and restore human dignity and well-being.

References

Abdoubaetova, A. (2020). Secondary schools and inequality: Navigating the fragmented landscape of educational choices in Bishkek. In M. Laruelle (Ed.), *New voices from Central Asia: Societal transformations* (pp. 85–106). The George Washington University.

Adkins, L., Cooper, M., & Konings, M. (2019). Class in the 21st century: Asset inflation and the new logic of inequality. *Environment and Planning A: Economy and Space*. https://doi.org/10.1177/0308518X19873673.

Aliev, T. (2015). Kazakhstan: Resource curse or Dutch disease? *Problems of Economic Transition, 57*(10), 1–28.

Appel, H., & Orenstein, M. (2018). *From triumph to crisis: Neoliberal economic reforms in postcommunist countries*. Cambridge University Press.

Braguinsky, S. (2009). Postcommunist oligarchs in Russia: Quantitative analysis. *Journal of Law and Economics, 52*(2), 307–350.

Charman, K. (2007). Kazakhstan: A state-led liberalized market economy? In D. Lane & M. Myant (Eds.), *Varieties of capitalism in post-Communist countries* (pp. 165–182). Palgrave Macmillan.

Christophers, B. (2019). The rentierization of the United Kingdom economy. *Environment and Planning A: Economy and Space*. https://doi.org/10.1177/0308518X19873007.

Cooley, A., & Heathershaw, J. (2017). *Dictators without borders: Power and money in Central Asia*. Yale University Press.

Cooley, A., & Sharman, J. C. (2015). Blurring the line between licit and illicit: Transnational corruption networks in Central Asia and beyond. *Central Asian Survey, 34*(1), 11–28.

Danilovich, N. (2010). Growing inequalities and reproductive health in transitional countries: Kazakhstan and Belarus. *Journal of Public Health Policy, 31*(1), 30–50.

Doolot, A., & Heathershaw, J. (2015). State as resource, mediator and performer: Understanding the local and global politics of gold mining in Kyrgyzstan. *Central Asian Survey, 34*(1), 93–109.

El-Hodiri, M., Kudasheva, T., & Kunitsa, S. (2015). Methods of measurement of socio-geographical inequality in Kazakhstan, a consequence to the distribution of oil development? *Journal of Economic Sociology, 3*(1), 7–23.

Engvall, J. (2014). Why are public offices sold in Kyrgyzstan? *Post-Soviet Affairs, 30*(1), 67–85.

Franke, A., Gawrich, A., & Alakbarov, G. (2009). Kazakhstan and Azerbaijan as post-Soviet rentier states: Resource incomes and autocracy as a double 'curse' in post-Soviet regimes. *Europe-Asia Studies, 61*(1), 109–140.

Grassmann, F. (2011). *Protecting vulnerable families in Central Asia: Poverty, vulnerability and the impact of the economic crisis* (Innocenti Working Papers No. 2011-05). https://www.unicef-irc.org/publications/639-protecting-vulnerable-families-in-central-asia-poverty-vulnerability-and-the-impact.html.

Green, J. E. (2016). Liberalism and the problem of plutocracy. *Constellations, 23*(1), 84–95.

Guseva, A. (2005). Building new markets: A comparison of the Russian and American credit card markets. *Socio-Economic Review, 3*(3), 437–466.

Habibov, N. (2014, May). Does reform in Kazakhstan improve access to childcare? Evidence from nationally-representative surveys. *Children and Youth Services Review, 40*, 13–19.

Hasanova, S. (2018). Income inequality in Kyrgyzstan: The redistributive effect of social benefits. In M. Laruelle (Ed.), *New voices from Central Asia: Political, economic, and societal challenges and opportunities* (pp. 105–117). The George Washington University.

Hudson, M. (2014). *The bubble and beyond* (New). ISLET.

Junisbai, A. (2010). Understanding economic justice attitudes in two countries: Kazakhstan and Kyrgyzstan. *Social Forces, 88*(4), 1677–1702.

Kaztag. (2020). *Nereal'nymi nazval deputat protsenty po kreditam v Kazakhstane*. https://kaztag.kz/ru/news/nerealnymi-nazval-deputat-protsenty-po-kreditam-v-kazakhstane.

Kerimray, A., De Miglio, R., Rojas-Solórzano, L., & Ó Gallachóir, B. (2017). Household energy consumption and energy poverty in Kazakhstan. *IAEE Energy Forum, 26*, 31–34.

Kopeyeva, A. (2020). Factors behind regional inequality in education in Kazakhstan. In M. Laruelle (Ed.), *New voices from Central Asia: societal transformations* (pp. 53–85). The George Washington University.

KPMG. (2019). *Private equity market in Kazakhstan*. https://assets.kpmg/content/dam/kpmg/kz/pdf/2019/09/KPMG-Private-Equity-Market-in-Kazakhstan-ENG-2019.pdf. Accessed Sept 2020.

Kussainov, D. (2018). Inequality in secondary education and Kazakhstan's risk of becoming a fragmented society. In M. Laruelle (Ed.), *New voices from Central Asia: Political, economic, and societal challenges and opportunities* (pp. 117–124). The George Washington University.

Lister, R. (2015). 'To count for nothing': Poverty beyond the statistics. *Journal of the British Academy, 3*, 139–165.

Liu, M., & Pistorious, T. (2012). Coping with the energy crisis: Impact assessment and potentials of non-traditional renewable energy in rural Kyrgyzstan. *Energy Policy, 44*(C), 130–139. https://doi.org/10.1016/j.enpol.2012.01.025.

Marcuse, P. (1996). Privatization and its discontents: Property rights in land and housing in the transition in Eastern Europe. In G. Andrusz, M. Harloe, & I. Szelenyi (Eds.), *Cities after socialism: Urban and regional change and conflict in post-socialist societies* (pp. 119–191). Blackwell.

McGlinchey, E. (2011). *Chaos, violence, dynasty: politics and Islam in Central Asia*. University of Pittsburgh Press.

Mihalyi, P., & Szelenyi, I. (2017). The role of rents in the transition from socialist redistributive economies to market capitalism. *Comparative Sociology, 16*(1), 13–38.

Mikhalev,V., & Heinrich, G. (1999). *Kyrgyzstan: A case study of social stratification* (World Institute for Development Economic Research Working Paper 164). http://www.wider.unu.edu/publications/working-papers/previous/en_GB/wp164/_files/82530858910950029/default/wp164.pdf. Accessed Sept 2020.

Nunnally, S. (2017). *Eight facts about water quality in Kyrgyzstan*. The Borgen Project. https://borgenproject.org/eight-facts-about-water-quality-in-kyrgyzstan/.

Peyrouse, S. (2012). The Kazakh neopatrimonial regime: Balancing uncertainties among the 'family', oligarchs and technocrats. *Demokratizatsiya, 20*(4), 345–370.

Pomfret, R. (2019). *The Central Asia economies in the twenty-first century: Paving a New Silk Road*. Cambridge University Press.

Reeves, M. (2010). The latest revolution. *London Review of Books, 32*, 9.

Roelen, K., & Gassmann, F. (2014). Beyond averages: Child well-being in Kazakhstan. *Journal of Children and Poverty, 20*(2), 91–110. https://doi.org/10.1080/10796126.2014.979139.

Rolnik, R. (2011). *Report of the Special Rapporteur on adequate housing as a component of the right to an adequate standard of living, and on the right to non-discrimination in this context.* UN Human Rights Council. https://www.ohchr.org/EN/HRBodies/HRC/RegularSessions/Session25/Documents/A_HRC_25_54_Add.2_ENG.DOC. Accessed July 2020.

Ruziev, K., & Dow, S. (2013). *A review of banking sector reforms in transition economies* (Working Paper 03/13). Centre for Global Finance, University of the West of England.

Sakal, H. B. (2015). Natural resource policies and standard of living in Kazakhstan. *Central Asian Survey, 34*(2), 237–254. https://doi.org/10.1080/02634937.2014.987970.

Satybaldieva, E. (2015). Why class matters in Kyrgyzstan: Everyday experiences, moral sentiments, and the politics of the poor. In M. Laruelle & J. Engvall (Eds.), *Kyrgyzstan beyond 'Democracy Island' and 'Failing State': Social and political changes in a post-Soviet society* (pp. 99–123). Lexington Books.

Sayer, A. (2015). *Why we can't afford the rich*. Policy Press.

Sharipova, D. (2015). Who gets what, when and how? Housing and informal institutions in the Soviet Union and post-Soviet Kazakhstan. *Central Asian Affairs, 2*(2), 140–167.

Shedenova, N., & Beimisheva, A. (2013). Social and economic status of urban and rural households in Kazakhstan. *Procedia—Social and Behavioral Sciences, 82*, 585–591. https://doi.org/10.1016/j.sbspro.2013.06.314.

Spector, R. (2017). *Order at the bazaar: Power and trade in Central Asia*. Cornell University Press.

Standing, G. (2016). *The corruption of capitalism: Why Rentiers thrive and work does not pay*. Biteback Publishing.

Steimann, B. (2011). *Making a living in uncertainty: Agro-pastoral livelihoods and institutional transformations in post-socialist rural Kyrgyzstan*. University of Zurich.

Tawney, R. H. (1921). *The acquisitive society*. G. Bell and Sons.

The Guardian. (2019, October 17). Life in limbo: Inside Bishkek's illegal 'new buildings'. https://www.theguardian.com/cities/2017/oct/17/life-limbo-inside-bishkek-illegal-new-builds-kyrgyzstan.

Toktomushev, K. (2015). Regime security, base politics and rent-seeking: The local and global political economies of the American air base in Kyrgyzstan, 2001–2010. *Central Asian Survey, 34*(1), 57–77.

Ursulenko, K. (2010). Regional development in Kazakhstan. *Kurzanalysen und Informationen*, No 47, 1–10. https://www.dokumente.ios-regensburg.de/publikationen/info/info-47.pdf.

Wooden, A. (2014). Kyrgyzstan's dark ages: Framing and the 2010 hydroelectric revolution. *Central Asian Survey, 33*(4), 463–481.

World Bank. (2020a). *Total natural resources rent (% of GDP)—Kazakhstan and Kyrgyz Republic*. https://data.worldbank.org/indicator/NY.GDP.TOTL.RT.ZS?locations=KZ-KG.

World Bank. (2020b). *Personal remittances, received (% of GDP)—Kyrgyz Republic and Kazakhstan*. https://data.worldbank.org/indicator/BX.TRF.PWKR.DT.GD.ZS?locations=KG-KZ.

Yessenova, S. (2010). Borrowed places: Eviction wars and property rights formalization in Kazakhstan. In *Economic action in theory and practice: Anthropological investigations, research in economic anthropology* (30, pp. 11–45).

CHAPTER 3

Moral Economy, the State and Social Movements

This chapter offers a theoretical discussion that underpins the book. It consists of five sections, each of which focuses on a particular set of abstract ideas. The first section explicates the moral economy as both an object and a perspective. It also discusses how morality and power are intertwined. A vital distinction is made between earned and unearned income. Several key insights from the Polanyian double movement are elucidated in the second section. The commodification of money, land and labour, its dissatisfaction and harms, and the complex interactions between the state and countermovements are explored.

The third section examinesthe state as a site of contestation of social forces. It also highlights the role the state plays in capitalist societies, in particular privileging capital over other interests. The nature of neoliberal constitutionalism and its focus on the rule of law are critically discussed in the fourth section. While neoliberal scholars criticise rent-seeking by political actors, they fail to challenge private rent-seeking practices. The fifth section explains how neoliberalism and regulatory capture can contribute towards criminogenic environments in economic sectors. It also explores how corruption and fraud can become normalised and routinised.

B. Sanghera and E. Satybaldieva, *Rentier Capitalism and Its Discontents*, https://doi.org/10.1007/978-3-030-76303-9_3

Moral Economy

'Moral economy' can refer to either an object of study, or an approach to thinking about economies (Sayer, 2000). In the first mode, all economies are 'moral' economies, because moral sentiments, norms, rules, rights and discourses underpin economic relations and practices (Booth, 1994; Keat, 2000). Moral emotions, virtues and qualities, however partial or imperfect, are the pre-conditions of economic practices. Though economic power and pressures can reinforce, compromise and override normative features. Social inequalities can affect people's fellow-feelings, moral sentiments and judgements of others' motives and actions (Smith, 1976 [1759]). Competitive markets can accentuate traders' self-interest as well as their sensitivity to customers' wants and desires.

Rights, customs, values and beliefs are important in shaping and naturalising moral economies. For instance, paying one's debts is portrayed as a moral and legal right that locks borrowers into financial servitude to banks (Hudson, 2015). Borrowers are expected to have a personal ethic of responsibility, and to honour their promise to banks to pay their debts despite experiencing personal hardship. Banks call on borrowers to be morally responsible, using shame, guilt and honour to deter default. By contrast, 'irresponsible' debtors are seen to lack moral discipline and integrity.

In the second mode, the moral economy examines and evaluates the moral justifications of economic relations and institutions, in particular property relations. It also explores and assesses the moral influences on economic activities, and their implications on social and economic development. The moral economy approach evaluates the fairness, legitimacy and justifications of actually existing economic arrangements (Sayer, 2007). In recognising how economic activities affect human flourishing, social analysis cannot avoid normative implications.

The neoliberal discourse frames market relations as formally equal and voluntary, and economic actors as free choosers. The discourse focuses on individual liberty and choice, and reduces economic relations to transactions between free-standing individuals pursuing their self-interest. Poor and disadvantaged individuals are abstracted from their social positions, in which they often act under duress, facing weak options. The discourse serves to abstract them from their unequal social relationship, and justify exploitative practices in terms of individual rights and responsibilities.

Normative features do not merely regularise and normalise economic activities, they justify and rationalise who should do, get or control what

(Sayer, 2018). Property rights and relations are particularly significant, because they legitimise and depoliticise income extraction based on the ownership and control of existing scarce assets.

The economy is a complex set of relationships between people and nature. People are dependent on others and nature for economic provisioning, but dependency can be a source of domination, exploitation and harm. While moral justifications and influences can shape the basic features of economic relations, it cannot be imagined that the latter are outcomes of democratic moral deliberations. Often power plays a significant role in forming economic arrangements, with justifications serving as ex-post rationalisations or as legitimations of vested interests (Sayer, 2015b). This makes it all the more important to critically assess justifications.

Bourdieu (2000) notes that acceptance and submission are less a product of conscious consent or force of ideas than a tacit and practical belief that becomes self-evident and common sense in the context of lack of alternatives. Once economic practices have become established, normative questions about their features tend to be forgotten, and the politics of accommodation and entrenchment prevails (Sayer, 2015b). In this way, economic practices become regularised and normalised. For instance, property owners' right to income despite contributing nothing to production often goes unchallenged. Rights to own, speculate and dispose at a profit are naturalised and depoliticised as how 'free markets' work.

But in times of crises and discontent, people's faith in established institutions and norms can break, and find visible expressions through protests and social movements. During such crises, powerful groups are involved in a continuous effort to secure the necessary acceptance of dominant institutions, and create a perception of legitimacy (Fairclough & Fairclough, 2012). They provide reasons to adhere to established practices, ensure unequal social relationships are described in legitimising ways, fend off questions of validity of economic institutions, and delegitimise opposition and alternatives to the economic order. Their rationales primarily serve as rationalisations of their position and power (Fairclough & Fairclough, 2012).

People's relation to the world is one of concern. They continually have to monitor and evaluate how the things they care about are faring, and what to do next (Sayer, 2011). But their ability to evaluate economic practices can be limited by economic pressure to survive in a competitive environment. Short-term financial concerns can be prioritised over long-term social ones. Economic relations and practices have innumerable unintended consequences, which are likely to affect people's well-being. These consequences can be categorised as positive, negative or perverse. Outcomes are open to ethical evaluations and regulation because of their ethical implications.

While intended and unintended consequences are vital in evaluating and justifying economic institutions, people can also appeal to other criteria, such as need, desert and justice. In addition, environmental criteria can be considered to evaluate economic relations (Sayer, 2015b). It is important to take care of the environment because material wealth and human flourishing ultimately depend on it. Moral economy examines whether people's relations to the environment are sustainable or not. It particularly explores how liberal property relations can degrade the environment. The privatisation of natural resources can cause excessive extraction with damaging consequences for local ecosystems. Owners' voracious desire to amass wealth is unsustainable, threatening the future of humanity.

Some Moral Economic Distinctions

Classical political economy makes an important moral economic distinction between earned and unearned income (Tawney, 1921). Earned income is what waged and salaried employees and self-employed people get for contributing to the provision of goods and services that others use (Sayer, 2016). Unearned income is not conditional on contributing to the production of new goods and services, but is extracted on the basis of unequal ownership and control of existing scarce assets, including money and land. For instance, banks can receive unearned income by virtue of having property rights that they are entitled to create and control money, which others lack but need and want. Pettifor (2017) argues that interest is rent on money that allows banks to make vast capital gains by siphoning rent (interest) from debt.

Relatedly, another distinction is between property and improperty (Hobson, 1937). Property is held and justified for its use-value, and for aiding and protecting creative work. In the case of improperty, owners possess scarce assets to extract payments from others. They obtain income not based on work (i.e. earned income), but because they are entitled to use existing scarce assets to extract payments from others (Sayer, 2015a). This form of income is asset-based and unearned, reflecting owners' power over assets and their lack of contribution to the production of new goods or services. Their mere ownership produces nothing, but is a source of unearned income. Rent, interest, capital gains, dividends and royalties are unearned, supporting functionless rentiers and creating deadweight costs.

In post-socialist economies, a significant share of property is held not for use or enjoyment, but for acquisition or power (Mihalyi & Szelenyi, 2017). The propertied class have an interest in passive ownership for acquisition, and are not restricted on how much improperty they can hold. The law affirms their rights to own, dispose and speculate (Marcuse, 1996). Whereas in earlier ages, the protection of property was legitimised to aid and protect creative work, it now protects rentiers from work (Tawney, 1921). Improperty is not merely an alternative to work, it is functionless and harmful.

In addition to individual rentiers, there are rentier organisations, which employ people to extract income (Sayer, 2015a). These organisations predominately operate in the financial, insurance and property sectors. They collect unearned income, and seek new sources. As well as pure rentiership, it is possible for individuals and organisations to have both earned and unearned incomes, so being part-rentiers.

The Double Movement

The Polanyian concept of the double movement has inspired a rich and diverse body of scholarship on social and economic change (Block, 2008; Burawoy, 2015; Hann, 2016). The neoliberal expansion of global capital and the marketisation of goods and services in transition and developing countries produced devastating socio-economic, political and environmental outcomes (Sandbrook, 2011; Satgar & Williams, 2019; Silva, 2012). In response, countermovements sought to protect societies from unfettered markets through state regulation of markets and global capital. Contemporary social struggles cannot be understood through merely national or local frames, because the processes of market liberalisation and diverse mobilisations (or countermovements) are conditioned by the global context (Block, 2008).

The Polanyian double movement offers four insights into contemporary social tensions and conflicts. First, the Polanyian normative critique of marketisation is based upon Aristotle's concept of unnatural exchange (Clark, 2014). The market society transforms money, land and labour into commodities, where 'interest is the price for the use of money and forms the income of those who are in the position to provide it; rent is the price for the use of land and forms the income of those who supply it; wages are the price for the use of labour power and form the income of those who sell it' (Polanyi, 1944: 112).

Money, land and labour are known as fictitious commodities, because they are not produced for sale but they have a price. This provides the basis for a critical analysis of capitalism. Treating money, nature and labour as objects whose price is determined by the market can result in indebtedness, dispossession, destruction and unequal inclusion (Burawoy, 2015). Fictitious commodities cannot be the foundation for a moral economy, because they are an assault on life itself, especially a life worth living, 'a life in which people could develop their potential, fulfil their social roles with dignity, and affirm their value in the rituals of living (birth, puberty, marriage, childrearing, anniversaries, public festivals, close friendships, and death)' (Silva, 2012: 24).

Second, dominant global powers drive the expansive and global nature of capitalism through ideology, institutions and violence. As with the C19th *laissez-faire* movement, the neoliberal wave of commodification was accomplished though the delegitimation of previous economic systems, the imposition of an instituted market process, and ultimately violent dispossession and exploitation (Harvey, 2005; Satgar & Williams, 2019). Social groups in favour of marketisation depend on powerful international institutions, and invoke their authority whenever countervailing groups demand social protection. The pro-market movement claims that reforms are necessary for economic development, and international rules would not sanction demands for social protection (Block, 2008).

Third, Polanyi's dictum '*laissez-faire* was planned' meant that the state needed to manage the supply and demand of fictitious commodities to ensure critical inputs to the production process (Block, 2008). For instance, private property was not self-reinforcing, but required state institutions, such as the judiciary and the police, to interpret and enforce owners' rights and responsibilities. In the neoliberal wave of marketisation, global and national legal and judicial mechanisms (e.g. international investment treaties and courts) often promote and protect property rights to the detriment of wider societal interests (Schneiderman, 2008).

The state plays a central role in the double movement, because it can create, facilitate and regulate markets. It is a key site of social contestation, and political struggles occur over state control. Regulation is never neutral, but an outcome of unequal social forces over the nature of the capital reproduction. Political actors negotiate contradictory demands, privileging some groups and interests over others, thereby enabling and constraining market and countervailing forces in society.

Fourth, after being exposed to destructive market forces, societies respond with protective countermovements, which aim to re-embed economy in social relations. This highlights social movements' normative dimensions. Social movements emerge from people's dissatisfaction with an unequal world, and their longing for a better one (Burawoy, 2015). Social movements are not merely assessed on the basis of their longevity or transformative powers, but their concerns and aspirations.

The neoliberal commodification threatens a wide range of social groups, including the middle class, as well as increases the salience of locality, community and production sites as fields for the emergence of countermovements. For instance, the commodification of money, land, labour and basic services (such as education and health) can be a source of multiple grassroots movements, galvanising a wide range of protesters from rural migrants, farmers and pensioners to public sector workers and urban mortgage-holders. But this very diversity can produce divisions within and between social movements, preventing the formation of a broad-based countermovement capable of exerting effective pressure on the state.

Many Polanyian scholars observe countermovements are 'stymied by a cacophony of voices and divergent interests' (Sandbrook, 2014: 12). In some cases, movements fail to materialise, suggesting that societal reactions to markets are not inevitable. The complexity of social responses requires sensitivity to countermovements' protective aspirations. Goodwin (2018) conceptualises decommodifcation as a gradational process to differentiate countermovements. Defensive countermovements aspire to limit market forces, while offensive ones seek to prevent or reverse them.

Decommodification and re-embedding are two analytically distinct processes (Goodwin, 2018). Countermovements are unlikely to result in economic re-embedding. Polanyi himself viewed re-embedding not as regulation of markets, but radical supersession of capitalism through socialism. An embedded economy only succeeds if it subjugates economic processes to democratic control by society, something as yet no country has managed to do.

Several Polanyian scholars examine the complex interactions between countermovements and the state (Block, 2008; Goodwin, 2018). In general, social groups that seek protection from market forces are at an economic and political disadvantage vis-à-vis pro-market groups. Opportunities to influence the state can arise during an economic crisis, when political and economic elites are bitterly divided over its resolution (Block, 2008). Depending on the context and the balance of social forces at specific moments, political regimes can respond by weakening, neutralising or crushing social movements. The state-countermovement relationship is not unidirectional, but multidirectional (Goodwin, 2018).

The State as a Site of Social Struggle

The state is not a thing that possesses power, but an ensemble of social forces acting in and through state institutions (Jessop, 2002). It mediates and organises social relations of power. The state is a site of social struggle over the institutionalisation and enforcement of property relations, and the appropriation and distribution of surplus value, in particular economic rent. Depending on the balance of class forces at specific moments, the state can facilitate rentierism.

Andreucci et al. (2017) introduce the notion of 'value grabbing' to render visible and politicise the processes at work by which rent is distributed unevenly between different classes and fractions of classes. Value grabbing involves two related but analytically distinct moments. First, class struggles unfold over the creation and regulation of property rights and entitlements that institutionalise rent relations. Second, social tensions and conflicts occur over the appropriation and distribution of surplus value generated by rent relations.

The state plays multiple roles in these processes. First, the state institutes property rights and regimes that enable the conditions for value grabbing (Andreucci et al., 2017). The privatisation, deregulation and liberalisation of economic sectors created a powerful class of rentiers to be free to extract rent without state control. The neoliberal property regime justifies and legitimises rent relations in a 'free market' economy (Hudson, 2017).

Second, the state is a regulator, setting and enforcing the distribution of titles, their conditions of use, and so forth. Class struggles over property and rent relations can cause the state to be selective about what and when to enforce the law. The state shapes the specifics of value grabbing; i.e. who captures rent and who pays (Andreucci et al., 2017). In the neoliberal context of lax regulatory oversight, rentiers operate with relative ease and little scrutiny.

Third, the state can act as a property owner, controlling access to state-owned assets and their use-values and exchange-values (Parenti, 2015). Although neoliberalism has considerably reduced the scale of state ownership in transition economies, the state still possesses significant assets, whose access and flow of rent have political implications. Popular protests can directly address the state-as-owner to renegotiate contracts to extract more or less rent. Rent-seeking state officials usually provoke a public outcry, if illicit payments are exposed.

Rentierism is not to be understood simply as a story of deregulation, but as the state's role in the creation and maintenance of rent relations. Rentiers, led by financiers and property developers, built institutions and regulations to create and facilitate rentier capitalism (Standing, 2016). New property rights removed restrictions on speculation and unearned income. The privatisation of valuable assets established a powerful class of rentiers. International legal conventions, investment treaties and arbitration tribunals protected investors' rights against attempts by states and social movements to change contracts (Schneiderman, 2000).

The massive and rapid concentration of wealth in capitalist and transition economies is both a cause and a consequence of a shift in political power to the rich (Sayer, 2016). As governments are dependent on the capitalist class to deliver economic growth, the latter has structural power to shape policies that suit its interests. Capitalists andrentiers have the wealth to lobby, dominate the media, make political donations, and infiltrate government (Standing, 2016).

The wealthy have an abundance of political capital (Rothe & Kauzlarich, 2016). Their political power can be manifested in multiple ways. They can have considerable decision-making and participatory powers in state and regulatory bodies; can possess a significant capacity to set agendas and raise issues in public forums; and can exercise powerful ideological and moral influence on people's interests and ideas (Lukes, 2005).

The immense political capital of the rich represents a victory for plutocracy over democracy. As Sayer (2016) notes, democracies are increasingly operating in the shadow of plutocracy. The rich are able to control many aspects of economic life and dominate politics, so their special interests, view of the world and moral justifications come to restrict what democracies can do (MacLean 2017). A plutocratic mode of local and national governments can shape the provision of goods and services to benefit elites allied to rentier capitalism.

New Constitutionalism

According to neoliberalism, the rule of law offers an effective way to secure justice. It protects individual rights and freedoms, including private property rights, and restrains the coercive capacity of the state (Gill, 2002). The institution of private property is a necessary condition for liberty, and the rules of justice are designed to prevent the infringement of private property. Liberals assert that the right is prior to the good, meaning that individual rights cannot be sacrificed for the sake of the general good (Sandel, 1984).

The rule of law also addresses the key economic problem, which is not of scarcity and choice, but rather of identifying sets of binding rules and procedures that can facilitate a creative market process (Gill, 2002). Whereas orthodox economics concentrates on how individuals make choices *within* constraints that are externally imposed on them, Buchanan (1990) argues that constitutional political economy examines the choice *among* constraints. The analytical shift to the latter means that rules and institutions can be controlled in the interest of all individuals.

Constitutional rules can ensure the stability of expectations for economic actors, including long-term investors. Hayek (1944: 76) explains that rules 'make it possible to foresee with fair certainty how the authority will use its coercive powers in given circumstances, and to plan one's individual affairs on the basis of knowledge.' Under the rule of law, governments cannot exercise arbitrary actions to stultify individual efforts. Formal rules are instrumental for achieving people's own individual goals, and creating credibility and confidence in the economy.

While constitutional rules can be created through democratic procedures, Buchanan (2008) argues that the democratisation of constitutional politics must be limited by quasi-permanent rules. Public choice theory drops any presumption that political actors are naturally benevolent. Rather they are represented as seeking to secure collectively their own private interests. Specifically, government and other public agencies are viewed as rent-seeking monopolies, who enlarge their revenues and power at the expense of the public (Maclean, 2017). For public choice theorists, quasi-permanent rules are necessary to prevent future governments from making decisions that can produce economic inefficiency and injustice for the population.

Critically, the rule of law depoliticises economic institutions by separating them from political influence of elected politicians and the wider public (Gill, 2002). Many central banks have independence from political control to ensure 'sound' money and macroeconomic stability. Trade and investment agreements protect capital from expropriation and nationalisation. Transnational corporations can go to international arbitration over national laws that threaten their interests. If democratically elected parliaments legislate in the public interest, their laws and regulations are likely to be judged as 'takings', so tantamount to indirect expropriation or nationalisation (Schneiderman, 2008).

Neoliberalism represents wealthy owners and investors as an exploited minority in need of protection from arbitrary political decisions, such as expansionary fiscal policy and strict environmental regulations (Sayer, 2020). By limiting government powers, constitutional rules lock in property owners' rights and interests, and lock out vulnerable and propertyless groups. Neoliberal constitutionalism does not merely establish unequal representation of the propertied class within the state, it legitimises and promotes rentierism and unearned income. Major owners of improperty are de facto constitutionalised under the neoliberal notions of liberty, justice and democracy.

Neoliberals ignore private corporations' rent-seeking behaviour. Corporations are assumed to operate in an idealised model of competitive markets, rather than in actually existing markets where monopoly power and rent-seeking are common (Sayer, 2020). Neoliberalism elides the moral economic distinction between unearned income based on power, and earned income based on productive work (Sayer, 2015a). Another vital difference overlooked is between unearned income and transfers, which are based on recognition of need and democratically approved taxation.

While private-sector rentierism is unchallenged, neoliberals criticise the state as a rentier. Rent-seeking is depicted as any collective action by voters, interest groups and public officials that prompts government action to extract money from economic producers through taxes (Maclean, 2017). Individuals are assumed to advance their personal self-interests, rather than collective goals or the common good. In effect, neoliberalism promotes private rentierism, but restricts alleged public rent-seeking through constitutional and undemocratic mechanisms (Sayer, 2020).

Despite neoliberal attempts to undermine its importance and power, the modern state is crucial for capital accumulation (Jessop, 2002). In relation to nature, the state controls nature's use-values, and delivers its exchange-values, mostly rent, to capital (Parenti, 2015). Social struggles over property and rent relations can cause the state to be selective about what and when to enforce the law. The state shapes the specifics of value taking.

The Production of Crimes

Tombs (2012: 177) observes, '[F]or just as states create and sustain markets, so too can and do they create and sustain criminogenic markets, that is, markets that are conducive to, or facilitate, the production of harms and crimes.' What appear to be discrete corporate crimes (such as illicit payments, tax evasion, market rigging, illegal trading practices and environmental damage) are better understood as state complicity of them. Crimes are not simply a result of lack of success of state regulation and enforcement, but are an outcome of regulatory settlements. These settlements are a product of struggles between social classes and within corporate and state elites at specific moments (Tombs & Whyte, 2009).

The neoliberal idea of a 'free market' did not merely promote rentierism, but facilitated weak government oversight, poor enforcement and near immunity from prosecution (Hudson, 2015). Neoliberalism undermined the state's regulatory capabilities, framing regulation as 'red tape', 'bureaucratic' and a 'burden on business'. Regulatory bodies are likely to minimise 'interference' in keeping with *laissez-faire* economics.

Black (2010, 2011) explains that mainstream neoclassical economics often rejects calls for extensive regulation, arguing that market discipline can prevent corporate crimes. Snider (2009: 182) cites Stenning et al. (1990: 12) to argue that a regulatory system has 'an essential faith in capitalism so obvious that it goes... unrecognised.' As the moral legitimacy of business organisations increased, their oversight diminished.

Regulatory bodies are not neutral, but are 'unequal structures of representation' (Mahon, 1979: 154). In capitalist and transition economies, rentiers and plutocrats successfully instituted lax regulatory regimes through state and regulatory capture (Hudson, 2015). Regulatory capture occurs when regulatory agencies come to advance the interests of the very industries they are charged with regulating. The rich dominate the politics of regulation through formal, covert and ideological means (Tombs & Whyte, 2009). While regulatory bodies tend to subordinate the interests of the least powerful, they are vulnerable to pressure from social movements.

Political will is often missing in pursuing white-collar and corporate crimes, so that regulators lack material, logistical and moral support to challenge powerful elites (Tombs & Whyte, 2020). A core feature of regulation is to reproduce the conditions under which capital can reproduce itself. A high degree of state capture by business elites ensures that local democratic politics does not interfere in regulatory matters to limit risk-taking and profit-making (Shaxson & Christensen, 2013). While some cases of corruption and fraud are investigated and controlled, or politicised, most are conventionalised and unexamined.

Regulatory capture by leading rent-extractive sectors can produce legally sanctioned corruption and fraud (Sayer, 2015a). In finance, oversight agencies are usually staffed with representatives of the banks they are supposed to supervise, thereby disabling regulatory protection (Hudson, 2015). Given that the construction industry supports government-sponsored building programmes, generates revenues and contributes to economic growth, its profitability and economic success are always juxtaposed with the 'burden' of regulation (Tombs & Whyte, 2009).

Deregulation, de-supervision and de facto decriminalisation can create criminogenic environments in banking and real estate sectors (Black, 2011). Criminogenic environments have perverse incentives to commit widespread crime, or control fraud. Control fraud occurs when a person controlling a seemingly legitimate corporation or government agency uses it as a weapon to commit fraud. Criminogenic environments facilitate a wide variety of corrupt but lucrative activities, including bribery and money laundering.

While criminogenic structures enable capitalists, rentiers and politicians to gain immense wealth and power, they have harmful and damaging effects on society, such as increased social inequalities and environmental pollution (Whyte & Wiegratz, 2016). But major harms are likely to be constructed as 'bad luck' or 'accidents', rather than as harms that are preventable and avoidable (Tombs & Whyte, 2009). To ensure accountability and responsibility, it is important to recognise and criminalise harms.

References

Andreucci, D., García-Lamarca, M., Wedekind, J., & Swyngedouw, E. (2017). 'Value grabbing': A political ecology of rent. *Capitalism Nature Socialism, 28*(3), 28–47.

Black, W. (2010, May). Neo-classical economic theories, methodology and praxis optimize criminogenic environments and produce recurrent, intensifying crises. *Creighton Law Review, 44*, 597–645.

Black, W. (2011, May 25). The two documents everyone should read to better understand the crisis. *HuffPost*. https://www.huffpost.com/entry/the-two-documents-everyon_b_169813. Accessed July 2020.

Block, F. (2008). Polanyi's double movement and the reconstruction of critical theory. *Revue Interventions économiques*, 38. https://doi.org/10.4000/interventionseconomiques.274.

Booth, W. (1994). On the idea of the moral economy. *American Political Science Review, 88*(3), 653–667.

Bourdieu, P. (2000). *Pascalian mediations*. Polity.

Buchanan, J. (1990). The domain of constitutional economics. *Constitutional Political Economy, 1*(1), 1–18.

Buchanan, J. (2008). Same players, different game: How better rules make better politics. *Constitutional Political Economy, 19*(3), 171–179.

Burawoy, M. (2015). Facing an unequal world. *Current Sociology, 63*(1), 5–34.

Clark, T. D. (2014). Reclaiming Karl Polanyi, socialist intellectual. *Studies in Political Economy, 94*(1), 61–84.

Fairclough, I., & Fairclough, N. (2012). *Political discourse analysis: A method for advanced students*. Routledge.

Gill, S. (2002). Constitutionalising inequality and the clash of globalisations. *International Studies Review, 4*(2), 47–65.

Goodwin, G. (2018). Rethinking the double movement: Expanding the frontiers of Polanyian analysis in the Global South. *Development and Change, 49*(5), 1268–1290.

Hann, C. (2016). Cucumbers and courgettes: Rural workfare and the new double movement in Hungary. *Intersections. East Europe Journal Society and Politics, 2*(2), 38–56.

Harvey, D. (2005). *A brief history of neoliberalism*. Oxford University Press.

Hayek, F. (1944). *The road to serfdom*. Routledge.

Hobson, J. (1937). *Property and improperty*. Victor Gollancz Ltd.

Hudson, M. (2015). *Killing the host: How financial parasites and debt bondage destroy the global economy*. CounterPunch Books.

Hudson, M. (2017). *J is for junk economics: A guide to reality in an age of deception*. ISLET.

Jessop, B. (2002). *The future of the capitalist state*. Polity.

Keat, R. (2000). *Cultural goods and the limits of the market*. Macmillan.

Lukes, S. (2005). *Power: A radical view* (2nd ed.). Palgrave Macmillan.

Maclean, N. (2017). *Democracy in chains: The deep history of the Radical Right's Stealth Plan for America*. Viking Press.

Mahon, R. (1979). Regulatory agencies: Captive agents or hegemonic apparatuses! *Studies in Political Economy, 1*(1), 162–200.

Marcuse, P. (1996). Privatization and its discontents: Property rights in land and housing in the transition in Eastern Europe. In G. Andrusz, M. Harloe, & I. Szelenyi (Eds.), *Cities after socialism: Urban and regional change and conflict in post-socialist societies* (pp. 119–191). Blackwell.

Mihalyi, P., & Szelenyi, I. (2017). The role of rents in the transition from socialist redistributive economies to market capitalism. *Comparative Sociology, 16*(1), 13–38.

Parenti, C. (2015). The environment making state: Territory, nature and value. *Antipode, 47*(4), 829–848.

Pettifor, A. (2017). *The production of money: How to break the power of bankers*. Verso.

Polanyi, K. (1944). *The great transformation: Economic and political origins of our time*. Rinehart.

Rothe, D., & Kauzlarich, D. (2016). *Crimes of the powerful: An introduction*. Routledge.

Sandbrook, R. (2011). Polanyi and post-neoliberalism in the Global South: Dilemmas of re-embedding the economy. *New Political Economy, 16*(4), 415–443. https://doi.org/10.1080/13563467.2010.504300.

Sandbrook, R. (2014). *Reinventing the left in the global south: The politics of the possible*. Cambridge University Press.

Sandel, M. (1984). The procedural republic and the unencumbered self. *Political Theory, 12*(1), 81–96.

Satgar, V., & Williams, M. (2019). Polanyi, nature and the international: The missing dimension of imperial ecocide. In A. Roland, B. Aulenbacher, U. Brand, F. Decieux, K. Fischer, & S. Birgit (Eds.), *Capitalism in transformation: Movements and countermovements in the 21st century* (pp. 198–2011). Edward Elgar Publishing.

Sayer, A. (2000). Moral economy and political economy. *Studies in Political Economy, 61*(1), 79–103.

Sayer, A. (2007). Moral economy as critique. *New Political Economy, 12*(2), 261–270.

Sayer, A. (2011). *Why things matter to people: Social science, values and ethical life*. Cambridge University Press.

Sayer, A. (2015a). *Why we can't afford the rich*. Policy Press.

Sayer, A. (2015b). Time for moral economy? *Geoforum, 65*, 291–293.

Sayer, A. (2016). Moral economy, unearned income and legalized corruption. In D. Whyte & J. Wiegratz (Eds.), *Neoliberalism and the moral economy of fraud* (pp. 44–56). Routledge.

Sayer, A. (2018). Welfare and moral economy. *Ethics and Social Welfare, 12*(1), 20–33.

Sayer, A. (2020). Rentiership, 'improperty' and moral economy. *Environment and Planning A: Economy and Space*. https://doi.org/10.1177/2F0308518X20908287.

Schneiderman, D. (2000). Investment rules and the new constitutionalism. *Law and Social Inquiry, 25*(3), 757–787.

Schneiderman, D. (2008). *Constitutionalising economic globalisation: Investment rules and democracy's promise*. Cambridge University Press.

Shaxson, N., & Christensen, J. (2013). *The finance curse: How oversized financial sectors attack democracy and corrupt economies*. Tax Justice Network. http://www.taxjustice.net/cms/upload/pdf/Finance_Curse_Final.pdf. Accessed July 2020.

Silva, E. (2012). Exchange rising? Karl Polanyi and contentious politics in contemporary Latin America. *Latin American Politics and Society, 54*(3), 1–32. https://doi.org/10.1111/j.1548-2456.2012.00163.x.

Smith, A. (1976 [1759]). *The theory of moral sentiments*. Liberty Fund.

Snider, L. (2009). Accommodating power: The 'common sense' of regulators. *Social and Legal Studies, 18*(2), 179–197.

Standing, G. (2016). *The corruption of capitalism: Why Rentiers thrive and work does not pay*. Biteback Publishing.

Stenning, P., Shearing, C., Addario, S., & Condon, M. (1990). Controlling interests: Two conceptions of order in regulating a financial market. In M. Friedland (Ed.), *Securing compliance* (pp. 88–119). University of Toronto Press.

Tawney, R. H. (1921). *The acquisitive society*. G. Bell and Sons.

Tombs, S. (2012). State-corporate symbiosis in the production of crime and harm. *State Crime Journal, 1*(2), 170–195.

Tombs, S., & Whyte, D. (2009). State and corporate crimes. In R. Coleman, J. Sim, S. Tombs, & D. Whyte (Eds.), *State, power, crime* (pp. 103–115). Sage.

Tombs, S., & Whyte, D. (2020). The shifting imaginaries of corporate crime. *Journal of White Collar and Corporate Crime, 1*(1), 16–23.

Whyte, D., & Wiegratz, J. (2016). *Neoliberalism and the moral economy of fraud*. Routledge.

PART II

Interrogating the Regime of Rent and Its Justifications

CHAPTER 4

Financial Institutions: Interest, Power and Moral Justifications

This chapter critically examines how banks and microfinance institutions justified their lending practices and income from interest in Kazakhstan and Kyrgyzstan. The lenders' myths, norms, discourses and obligations were central in legitimising and depoliticising the unequal social relationship between lenders and borrowers. Financial relations were particularly important in neoliberal economies, because they expanded rentierism beyond the traditional forms of rent-seeking in real estate and natural resources (Husdon, 2014). The chapter also evaluates two alternative forms of allocating credit (Islamic finance and a state-owned development fund) that aimed to minimise usury and finance productive investment.

The moral perspective of bankers and financiers is rarely explored in social science (Ho, 2012; Pelkmans & Umetbaeva, 2018). Social scientists have either avoided interrogating the issue, or have presumed financial activities to be already predefined immoral or amoral, even though social actors articulate moral claims to explain and justify them. Ho (2012) observes that social science is missing critical accounts of financiers' actual discourses of morality, and how they morally construe and legitimise their activities.

This chapter contributes to the literature on finance and morality in two ways. First, it offers first-person evaluations of lending as fair or

B. Sanghera and E. Satybaldieva, *Rentier Capitalism and Its Discontents*, https://doi.org/10.1007/978-3-030-76303-9_4

unfair, good or bad. Going beyond the usual focus on financial crisis, irrationality and fraud (Appadurai, 2012; Jessop, 2015; Whyte & Wiegratz, 2016), it examines the moral evaluations of taken-for-granted rights and practices underpinning debt (Graeber, 2011; Hudson, 2018; Sayer, 2015). It critically discusses the moral justifications and rationalisations of the basic features of the lender-borrower relationship, in particular the property rights of money, and what banks and debtors are allowed and required to do. It assesses how financial actors construe the moral influences on their practices, and evaluate their implications on society.

Second, it shows that power has a lot to do with the origins and maintenance of debt, and little to do with rational deliberations over its fairness and legitimacy (Hudson, 2014). Banks do not merely create credit money 'out of thin air', but extract rent by charging for it (Pettifor, 2017). Onceinterest has become an established practice, its validity is not questioned, only its amount. Lacking suitable options, individuals can normalise and acquiesce to it. Yet while debt is largely a product of power, questions of justice, fairness and well-being have to be raised and considered, otherwise there is little basis for criticising it (Sayer, 2016).

This chapter is divided into four sections. The first section briefly examines what role banks and microfinance institutions play in contemporary economies, and how they have developed in Kazakhstan and Kyrgyzstan. Section 'Moral Justifications of Lending Practices' analyses how financial institutions in our first case study understood and evaluated credit relations and their outcomes. The third section offers a critical discussion on debt. Finally, the conclusion summarises the chapter's key findings and ideas.

The Financial Sector in Kazakhstan and Kyrgyzstan

Banks are an essential component of modern capitalism, in that they create and control token money, which is intrinsically worthless and is used as a means of final settlement of transactions (Graziani, 1989). They possess monopoly-like power to generate and honour promises to pay that facilitate market transactions (Pettifor, 2017). Extending credit to firms and households can create productive capacity for the economy that can later be used to service the debt (Keen, 2011). But as Minsky (1978) explains, banks are also responsible for causing excessivedebt growth, asset speculation and financial instability.

International financial institutions and donor organisations promoted the liberalisation of finance as one of the effective ways to combat poverty and stimulate entrepreneurial activity, following the model of the Grameen Bank in Bangladesh (Bateman, 2010). In the early stages of private banking in transition economies, money came to domestic banks and microfinance institutions through investment by foreign banks, international financial institutions and Western development agencies, rather than household savings (Ruziev & Dow, 2013). Development agencies stipulated social missions, such as poverty reduction and rural development, as their lending criteria, and expected a return on equity.

The liberalisation and deregulation of the banking sector in post-Soviet countries in the 1990s aimed to increase competition and choice in the market, in the hope of injecting much-needed foreign-backed investment in fledgling economies after the collapse of the Soviet Union (Ruziev & Dow, 2013). The number of retail banks, microfinance institutions and pawnshops increased in Russia and Central Asia. They provided loans not only to business and middle class groups, but to more risky and vulnerable working class and poor individuals (Guseva, 2005; Ruziev & Midmore, 2014).

In the 1990s and 2000s, US and other Western financial institutions invested into Kazakhstan's and Kyrgyzstan's banking and non-banking sectors to fund a rapid expansion of credit, largely concentrated in petty retail trading, real estate and consumption. Kazakhstan's banks actively borrowed from abroad through syndicated loans, securitisation and issuance of bonded debt. By 2007, they amassed external debt of 46 billion USD, or 44% of GDP (International Monetary Fund, 2010). In the 2000s, Kazakhstan's banking sector was the second fastest-growing sector in the economy after the oil industry (Asian Development Bank Institute, 2014). Before the 2007–2008 global crisis, the banking sector consisted of privately owned financial institutions (Orazalin, 2019). The crisis caused the bankruptcy of three major commercial banks. The government responded by injecting funds into troubled banks, and refinancing loans to stabilise the sector. Currently, the sector has a mix of commercial private banks, state-owned banks and foreign-owned banks.

During 2002–2007, Kyrgyzstan's banking sector expanded strongly, with an average annual asset growth and loan growth of 22% and 57%, or 40% in real terms, respectively (Asian Development Bank, 2011). The total banking assets increased from 7.9 billion soms in 2002 to 178 billion soms in 2015 (National Bank of the Kyrgyz Republic, 2016). Global and regional financiers benefitted from lax regulation on interest rates and debt collection, enabling them to achieve high returns on equity. In Kyrgyzstan, the average interest rate on microfinance loans was about 34% in 2014 (National Bank of the Kyrgyz Republic, 2014). In 2014, there were 24 commercial banks, of which two were controlled by the state, and the rest were either private or foreign banks (International Finance Corporation, 2016). Sixteen commercial banks had foreign share capital, of these ten had foreign shareholdings of more than 50%.

Most of the bank clients consisted of middle and working class individuals. A significant share of the total bank loan portfolio consisted of dollar-denominated mortgages, which were issued to borrowers to purchase apartments (Ruziev & Majidov, 2013). During the 2001–2007 housing bubble in Kazakhstan, the middle class dream of homeownership enabled banks to extract rent through mortgage rates. But repayments became unmanageable for many borrowers, because of inflated property prices and the depreciation of the national currency against the dollar, especially after the 2007–2008 global financial crisis. In Kazakhstan and Kyrgyzstan, rising debt and repossessions sparked waves of protests against banks and governments, as will be discussed in Chapter 8.

By contrast, rural households usually borrowed small amounts (less than 1000 USD) from microfinance institutions, which charged higher interest rates than commercial banks (Angioloni et al., 2018). During the 2000s, microfinance was the main source of credit for rural borrowers, especially in Kyrgyzstan. Many of them were issued loans to start a business venture, enticed by the hope of becoming successful entrepreneurs. But high interest rates and low-entry barriers meant that most of them struggled to survive and make a profit (Bateman, 2010).

Moral Justifications of Lending Practices

Social Mission and Market Ethics of Lending

One of the abiding myths of micro-loans is that they fulfil the social mission of serving the poor (Bateman, 2010). International agencies view micro-loans as a catalyst for a sustainable 'bottom-up' economic and social development. They channel credit to local banks and microfinance companies to disburse to poor and disadvantaged groups to establish and expand microenterprises and self-employment (e.g. cross-border shuttle trade), and promote gender empowerment and community solidarity.

Several banks described how donors worked in partnership with them to support women microenterprises, poverty reduction and rural development. For instance, Tanya, a senior manager at a Kyrgyzstan's bank, explained:

> We've a partnership with the Asian Development Bank, and it's a programme for women entrepreneurs. . . . During our history, we've had special programmes with the International Finance Corporation and have started to work with KIVA social lending platform. . . . Most of our social investors have special social targets. In our portfolio, we've more than 46% women borrowers. It's our social target.

Tanya's bank had received a significant amount of credit from international agencies, including the US Agency for International Development (USAID), to target specific vulnerable groups, in particular female entrepreneurs in rural areas. Special loan programmes shaped banks' lending criteria to satisfy donors' social mission and values. In the context of patriarchy in developing countries, providing opportunities for women to participate in the business sector is an important development goal for donors (Bateman, 2010). Micro-loans can improve women's confidence and business acumen, thereby empowering them in society. As agents of social change, banks and microfinance companies can develop an enterprise culture, and can tackle gender inequalities.

But there is growing evidence of 'mission drift' in the micro-lending sector (Bateman, 2010). Commercialisation veers organisations away from their original mission to reduce poverty towards strategies to maximise profit. In Kyrgyzstan, three major NGO microfinance agencies, Bai Tushum, Finca and Companion, became commercial private banks (Hasanova, 2018). They were lured by the potential to expand their loan portfolio beyond donor-sponsored micro-loans, and pursue more lucrative markets, such as middle class consumer loans. Some participants in the study explained the tensions between social and economic goals, as Tanya, whose bank used to be an NGO microfinance agency, observed:

> As we're a commercial organisation, we should make a profit but . . . also we've social goals and we've special programmes with international organisations. . . . Of course, we've to be profitable. Of course, we should be profitable!

Tanya's organisation had moved away from being merely a vehicle for donors to achieve their social goals. As a commercial enterprise, it was imperative to make a profit. The social mission had become secondary to maximising profit. As Sayer (2007), notes, social and moral values can be compromised or overridden by economic pressures and interests.

Markets can be a benign force that tames wild passions, and liberates society from traditional bonds to achieve material improvements (Hirschman, 1982). But equally, ascriptive relationships and customs can limit the beneficial effects of markets. Several interviewees described how banks and microfinance companies were trying to civilise and discipline borrowers by tackling cultural attitudes and practices. Jyldyz, a senior manager at International Finance Corporation, maintained that market virtues of prudence and punctuality were important for the financial sector, but were difficult to cultivate among the Kyrgyz population:

> We've developed a calendar for [borrowers] . . . this teaches them to consider many issues like seasonality of business, of harvest and expenses. Our main message is saving, say to the people that you should save. . . . You know, Kyrgyz people spend a lot of money on marriages, funerals and births because they' re driven by traditions. . . . It's a mindset, it's a cultural thing, we're nomadic. . . . Historically we didn't have clocks and we're not strict on time and that's why Kyrgyz people aren't disciplined in repaying because it goes back to the roots plus cultural ceremonies.

Jyldyz felt that banking operations were shackled by lack of clock time discipline and traditional obligations of lavish life-cycle ceremonies, resulting in many families struggling to save and repay loans. Jyldyz's organisation ran educational and media campaigns, especially in rural areas, to warn people of the dangers of extravagant and carefree spending, and promote market virtues, such as prudence and punctuality.

Most financial elites construed banks and microfinance companies as civilising and moralising agents. Lenders tried to educate and regulate borrowers to become industrious, honest and disciplined, so as to avoid damaging their trust- and credit-worthiness. In their research, Pelkmans and Umetbaeva (2018) also found that informal moneylenders saw themselves as pioneers on a civilising mission to tame chaotic spaces on the capitalist frontier.

Furthermore, liberal markets can foster moral values, including formal equality, autonomy, and freedom (Booth, 1994). Market actors are free from hierarchal and ascriptive relationships, and they can formally access resources in pursuit of their projects. In our research, several banks favourably evaluated and compared the market mechanism of allocating credit to alternative arrangements, such as Islamic banking and rotating savings and credit associations. Islamic values and finance were characterised as opposing women's economic participation, freedom and equality.

> Our women don't wear burkas. 55% of our employees are women, and 51% of our clients are women. They're working or have a business. . . . Women in Kyrgyzstan are very independent, and traditional Islam is not practised here.
>
> Elnura, a bank director in Kyrgyzstan

> All banks operate on [market principles], and there's only one bank that operates according to Islamic finance. . . . Islamic principles aren't suitable for us. We don't have such fanatical beliefs. We've to defend the values of our country and the market.
>
> Gulmira, a bank director in Kyrgyzstan

For Elnura, the market system had expanded women's freedoms and autonomy. Gulmira construed liberal markets as beneficial for society, and believed Islamic principles to be harmful. Most participants evaluated market-based lending to be fair, in that a vast majority of the population could access credit (see Pettifor, 2017). Islamic banking had limited presence in Central Asia, and was seen as diminishing women's economic autonomy (cp. Botoeva, 2018; Hoggarth, 2016). Rotating savings and credit associations in Central Asia were exclusionary organisations, because members were selected on the basis of high income and social status (Kuehnast & Dudwick, 2002).

But markets can equally undermine moral values essential for their success (Hirschman, 1982). The pursuit of profit can foster a culture of dishonesty and corruption (Wiegratz, 2016). Bateman (2010: 55) observes that competitive commercial pressures can force moneylenders to 'pressure and hoodwink their clients in order to obtain new business', calling this 'a very serious case of "mission drift"'. Several banks framed incidents of negligence, dishonesty or fraud as aberrations committed by a few poorly educated or greedy individuals, rather than as widespread and routine phenomena. It was an article of faith that markets had largely civilising and beneficial effects on people and society.

In one complex case of malfeasance, several employees at a Kyrgyzstan's bank branch were accused of unlawful financial dealings. They had authorised loans to sub-prime borrowers, whose applications should have been denied because they had bad credit records. Recognising the damage to its reputation and business, the bank tried to blame a junior employee for the fraud, and dismiss the incident as an anomaly, as Asel, one of the bank directors, claimed:

> There was a case of fraud with one of our employees. . . But the borrowers must also accept responsibility because they signed contracts knowing that the employee's scheme was fraudulent. . . . The incident of fraud was uncommon. . . . The bank has made concessions to the borrowers, and their loans have been prolonged for 6-8 months and the interest rates have been reduced from 32% to 18%.

In explaining the fraud, Asel pointed to an individual employee's wrongdoing, and criticised the borrowers' moral character. Asel's narrative preserved her belief in the efficacy and efficiency of the market, and justified the revised loan repayments. Wiegratz (2016) argues that business leaders are likely to construe fraud as greed, individual freedom and self-interest gone too far, rather than as something that is systemic and pervasive in a neoliberalising society. Erturk et al. (2007) observe that financial problems are usually attributed to market actors' lack of skills, knowledge and discipline, rather than arising from commercial pressures.

The neoliberal ideal of a 'free market' can defend economic power against calls for regulation, and can weaken state regulatory bodies in favour of self-regulation. Neoliberalism promotes 'free markets' as a way to ease doing business, and spur creativity, entrepreneurship and economic growth. Most financial elites in our study believed that lenders should be free to regulate their own affairs. While financial malpractices can occur, market integrity and honesty would prevail, as Maxim, a director of an association of microfinance companies in Kyrgyzstan, observed:

> Microfinance institutions are aware of aggressive marketing, threats, intimidation and shaming people to pay back loans. . . . They need to self-regulate their activities, and don't need external regulations to monitor

> their activities. They can be motivated to be self-responsible because they can be motivated by international standards and recognition by international agencies. They can also be motivated by our association to ensure better practices. There's no need for regulations by the National Bank, rather we must rely on self-regulation to ensure good practices.

Maxim acknowledged that the microfinance sector had problems of predatory lending and illegal debt collection methods, but believed that market reputation and code of practice would motivate microfinance institutions to alter their business practices. But in practice, deregulation and de-supervision created a criminogenic environment in the industry (Black, 2011; Tombs, 2012). Allowing lenders to regulate themselves had failed to tackle financial fraud and malpractices, as will be discussed in Chapter 8.

Maxim's belief in a 'free market' and self-regulation also meant having markets free of government control so that lenders could extract rent uninhibited. His association lobbied the government to repeal a new legislation that required microfinance institutions to have a higher minimum starting capital, and capped lending rates above the central bank's base rate:

> For the last two years we've been fighting against the new legislation which has tightened microfinance activities. In particular, we're fighting against the regulation of interest rates on microfinance agencies, where interest rates have been reduced to 15%. We're fighting against the Central Bank which is trying to control and regulate the sector.

As a result of a long and sustained campaign by a grassroot movement against usurious interest rates and other financial malpractices, the Kyrgyzstani government capped interest rates. Banks and microfinance institutions saw this as a restriction on their economic practices, or rather rent-seeking activities. As Hudson (2014) explains, neoliberal supporters imagine free markets to mean markets free for rentiers to extract income free of government regulation. This reversed the classical political economy's idea of freeing markets of income extraction.

Cultural Norms and Liberal Discourses of Lending

The culture and morality of the financial sector can be complicit with, not antithetical to, mainstream cultural assumptions and norms (Ho, 2012). Financial understandings of morality can connect with larger cultural narratives of economy and society. Although money is a fictitious commodity, most financial elites understood it to be part of a general narrative that commodities could be bought and sold for profit. They emphasised that moneylending reflected a general norm and acceptance of commodity exchanges to make a profit. Alima, a senior manager at a Kazakhstan's bank, countered accusations that banks overcharged for loans by noting that they also had to attract funds:

> Banks have not only to give credits, but also get deposits. The difference between credit and deposit interest rates is the bank's income. Banks also have additional costs. This is fair.

Alima observed that banks' income was the difference between attracting and lending money. It reflected a wider economic culture of trading and marking-up products to cover costs plus more to make a profit. Tanya compared lending with other forms of buying and selling, such as livestock trade:

> One person buys a cow and then sells it. Then another person re-sells it. Re-selling is very common in our economy, it's our mentality of buying and selling, and reselling.

Moneylending and cattle trading were both examples of a generalised form of commodity exchange. Moneylending was construed as normal and natural, and as indistinguishable from other forms of buying and selling. When the Soviet Union collapsed, property rights were re-bundled to permit the right to dispose at a profit (Marcuse, 1996). This legalised and justified speculation and unearned income (rent, interest and capital gains). Commodity exchanges and the associated transfers of property rights and money have been widely accepted and practised.

International financial institutions have implemented economic and legal reforms to ensure that 'markets', defined narrowly in terms of routinised buying and selling under competitive conditions, have become an established economic institution (Ferguson, 2009). Sayer (2016) argues that while powerful actors may ensure that their economic activities are described in legitimising ways, it is the established order of things that largely ensures their acceptance. As Bourdieu (2000) notes, submission is less a product of conscious consent or force of ideas than a tacit and practical belief that becomes self-evident and common sense in the context of bodily habituation and lack of alternatives.

Although moneylending can be complicit with neoliberal cultural norms of making money (Wiegratz, 2016), it is qualitatively distinct from most forms of economic activity. Money is not like other commodities, which are produced for sale on the market and their prices equilibrated by supply and demand. It is a pretence that money, land and labour can be self-regulated as if they are true commodities. Polanyi (1944) argues that to allow the market mechanism to determine their allocation and prices would result in social misery and the demolition of society.

Whereas neoclassical economics treats a loan as simply a transfer of spending power from a saver to a borrower, and banks as mere intermediaries in the process, Keen (2011) argues that banks do not need deposits in order to lend, because by issuing a loan they can endogenously create new spending power (i.e. new deposits) without reducing savers' spending power. According to Post-Keynesian theory, 'banks create money simply by an accounting operation: a loan is extended to a borrower creates both debt and spending power "out of nothing"' (Keen, 2011: 155).

Lending simply transfers wealth from one person to another, allowing lenders to collect interest, and contribute nothing to the economy. No good or service is produced. Lenders' income is extractive, meaning that they are dependent on borrowers to produce goods and services, and generate a surplus, which is partly siphoned off through interest. Several banks described how their income was derived from others' enterprise and labour.

> Entrepreneurs make a profit, and we take a small part of their profit. If an entrepreneur makes five tenges [national currency] on a notebook, and we took five tenges, it makes no sense for him to take out a loan. But profits of our clients are quite high, their profits are more than our interest rate.
>
> Dina, a bank director in Kazakhstan

> It's clients' problem to find markets [for their products]. For them, to find a market is the most important thing. . . . If they get a loan, they feed us.

> . . . I tell them 'Thanks to you, we exist!' Honestly how much profit we have is only thanks to our clients.
>
> Medina, a bank director in Kyrgyzstan

Dina and Medina explained how banks extracted income produced by entrepreneurs and traders, while contributing nothing or very little to the production and distribution of goods and services. Having property rights entitles banks and microfinance companies to create and control money and charge rent on it—i.e. interest (Sayer, 2015). Their income is based on power, rather than on deliberations on what might be morally justified, 'deserving' or 'earned'. By contrast, waged and salaried workers and self-employed people directly or indirectly contribute to the provision of goods and services that others use, and can be said to 'earn' their income.

The discourse of consumer choice and individual autonomy is central to liberal celebrations of 'the market'. Markets allow people to exercise judgement and decision without being gullible or deferential to authority (O'Neill, 1998). Drawing on the discourse, several participants argued that borrowers had to take responsibility for their choices.

> It's a choice. Nobody forces a person to take a loan. A borrower himself agrees with all the conditions. So it's absolutely unfair to blame somebody else because he agreed with all the conditions.
>
> Alima

In emphasising borrowers' freedom and consent, Alima rejected accusations that loan contracts were unfair. The liberal discourse defends the market as a sphere of voluntary uncoerced contracts between free, equal and autonomous agents (O'Neill, 1998). Moreover, in the transition from the Soviet command economy to a market economy, liberals celebrated 'the market' for shifting decision-making powers from central planning authorities to individual market actors. Paternalism and elitism were rejected in favour of market choice and autonomy that allowed individuals to shape their own lives.

In the abstract, markets can operate according to liberal principles of equality and freedom, but in concrete situations, contracting parties are likely to be unequal in power, resulting in exploitation and injustice (O'Neill, 1998). Some participants explained that high interest rates and strict enforcement reflected banks' power over borrowers in Central Asia.

Nurlan, a senior manager of a regional development bank, observed that Kyrgyzstan's borrowers had no choice but to accept market rates:

> It's good for banks and bad for people. Banks earn the money, people are losing. People don't have a choice, and practically all the banks are charging the same high interest rate. People don't have a choice, they go to microcredit and are charged 60% or maybe 90%. It's terrible. It's a robbery.

Nurlan maintained that banks had market power to control interest rates, and they received considerable income by siphoning interest from debt. The banks' ownership and control of money allows them to take advantage of borrowers' dependence, and extract unearned income. Unable to be autonomous individuals or free choosers, borrowers are likely to act under duress within their unequal and dependent relationship with banks.

Sanctity and Myths of Lending

The modern understanding on the morality of debt involves accepting one's responsibilities, fulfilling one's obligations to others, and paying one's debt (Graeber, 2011). Immorality consists of shirking one's responsibilities, reneging on a promise, and refusing to pay a debt. The financial elites believed that borrowers had to honour their contractual promise, and threatened legal action against those who failed to do.

> The government will never forgive loans. It's people's obligation [to pay back], it's their responsibility. They can take the loan, but they've to be responsible.
>
> Jyldyz

> If [borrowers] delay repayments or don't make payments, we'll take them to the court. We'll make sure that they will pay their debts.
>
> Asel

Jyldyz and Asel believed that borrowers had a personal ethic of responsibility. Paying one's debt was construed as moral behaviour (Graeber,

2011). When borrowers reneged on their promise, the courts adjudicated against them, forcing them to comply. In cases of contract violation, Central Asian judges tended to uphold powerful owners' property rights against disadvantaged groups' needs and well-being (Sanghera, 2020). The rule of law and the security of private property are used to promote the sanctity of contracts and debt claims (Hudson, 2017).

But the morality of paying debts is not necessarily justice, if powerful creditors become enriched at the expense of impoverishing debtors, who have to cut back on necessities, migrate or possibly revolt (Hudson, 2017). Rather than construing debt repayments as a moral imperative (i.e. the sanctity of debt claims and the obligation to repay), the overall consequences can be morally evaluated. Several participants recognised the negative effects of repayments on people's well-being. For instance, Maxim observed:

> The [borrowers] are very disciplined to pay back the loans because they've a particular mentality and tradition, but at the cost sacrificing their food security, education and health. . . . [P]eople are making their repayments on time, but are cutting back on essential goods. This obviously causes them immense misery.

Maxim explained how borrowers felt obligated to honour their promises under a threat of legal action. As a consequence of reducing household expenditure to repay loans, people's well-being was damaged. Accepting one's responsibilities and fulfilling one's obligations can result in harm and suffering for most of the population (Graeber, 2011). Moreover, as repayments come from those who have less money to those who have more money than they need, social inequalities can be exacerbated. Interest rate is a regressive, unjust and hidden form of redistribution of income (Hudson, 2015; Kennedy, 1995; Tawney, 1921).

In addition, high interest rates can deter productive investment, and can have deflationary effects on the economy (Hudson, 2014). To achieve sustained economic growth, businesses and households require credit to cover temporary gaps between outgoings and revenues to prevent disruptions to the circuits of production and exchange (Sayer, 2015). While credit is useful for the economy, interest is damaging. Many banks explained that high costs of borrowing discouraged productive capital investment.

> Some of our customers wanted to build brick-making factories and processing plants for agricultural products, but the returns were over a long term and we've very high interest rates, so we weren't interested.
>
> Medina

Medina understood that it was unprofitable for businesses to borrow at high interest for long-term productive investments. Hudson (2014) explains that interest can cause debt deflation, as loan repayments reduce aggregate demand and productive capacity in the economy. The higher the interest rate, the lower the beneficial consequences for the population.

Banks and neoclassical economists often articulate a popular myth that a loan is a transfer of money from a saver to a borrower, and banks are merely intermediaries in the process (Keen, 2011; Pettifor, 2017). This justifies interest as a reward for savers' abstinence, and as revenue to cover banks' operating costs (Sayer, 2015). Several banks in the research described how savers' deposits became loans.

> Grandmothers and retired people entrust us with their money. . . . They come here with their good money, worked all their life, and want a worthy pension. . . . If [a borrower] doesn't pay off the loan, we can sell the collateral and refund the money to the grandmother. . . . We must meet our obligations to the grandmother.
>
> Medina

Medina characterised banks as brokers between savers and borrowers. They also had a moral obligation to return money with interest to savers, who were viewed as vulnerable and needy individuals. This representation of savers as a 'deserving' group helped to justify and depoliticise high interest rates and intimidating debt recovery tactics.

In reality, development agencies (e.g. the European Bank of Reconstruction and Development and the Russian-Kyrgyz Development Fund) as well as foreign banks have invested significant capital in the financial sector in the region (Charman, 2007). For instance, Jyldyz explained that International Finance Corporation, a member of the World Bank Group, had provided direct financing to major banks in Kyrgyzstan:

> We've been investing in commercial banks and microfinance organisations. Half of our investment has gone to the financial sector. Among our clients are KICB and Demir bank. . . . We've also invested in Bai Tushum, Finca and Companion.

International Finance Corporation provided both capital and technical support to establish and develop the financial sector. It is a misconception that commercial banks wait for ordinary savers' deposits to come in to lend out. They can attract funds (often denominated in US dollars) from institutional and foreign investors. They can also create money by electronically typing money into borrowers' accounts, thereby generating both liabilities and assets in equal amount (Keen, 2011). Banks are only limited by the viability of applicants' business plan in creating money.

In our study, banks and microfinance companies used popular myths, norms and discourses to deflect criticisms of their practices. They evaded critical scrutiny of how money was obtained and created, how it was 'invested' in the economy, and how they were 'rewarded' for controlling it. The lenders' moral construals rationalised and concealed the power and domination that creditors had over money, the economy and the population.

Alternative Methods of Allocating Credit

Given that interest contributes to economic inequality, unearned income and deflation, it is not surprising that alternative systems of allocating credit have been proposed that either eliminate or minimise usury. Some participants discussed Islamic finance and state-owned development loans as alternative systems to the dominant neoliberal financial system.

Islamic finance offers a religious critique of usury (Lewis, 2007). It prohibits lending at interest. It also supports sharing gains and losses between lenders and borrowers, and investment for the public good in compliant with Sharia law. Salamat, a director of an association of Islamic finance in Kyrgyzstan, explained that profit through useful activities was permissible, butinterest was sinful (or 'haram'):

> A profit in itself is not sinful, it's normal thing, it's a necessary thing without it the whole economy will fail. But the question is, how does the person get the profit: through interest or by means of healthy transactions, trade or investment? In the writings of Karl Marx and Engels, interest is a waste, but I also tell you interest is wasteful in Islam, in Kyrgyz 'sutkorchuluk', in Arabic 'riba'. It's forbidden not only in Islam, it's forbidden in all Abrahamic religions, beginning with Christianity, Judaism, Orthodox Christianity, Catholic, everywhere it's prohibited.

Salamat's opposition to usury was inspired by his faith and belief in the Koran as divine authority. He noted that Islamic finance does not object to market forces, the profit motive or private ownership. When money-making originates from useful activities (including production and trade), profit is earned and morally permissible. But usury is forbidden, because money is both the means and the end, and nothing of real utility is created to promote people's welfare (Tag El-Din & Hassan, 2007). Islamic finance treats money only as a medium of exchange, so there is no scope for making profit through dealing in money.

The presence of Islamic finance and investment is quite small in Central Asia (Botoeva, 2018; Wolters, 2016). There are currently only two small banks that operate according to Islamic banking principles: Kyrgyzstan's EcoIslamicBank, and Kazakhstan's Al Hilal Bank, which offers only corporate banking services. In 2014, Islamic finance accounted for only 2% of the total banking sector by assets in Kyrgyzstan, and there was no retail presence in Kazakhstan (International Finance Corporation, 2016). EcoIslamicBank's branch network is sparse and concentrated in economically important provinces, and people in rural areas do not have easy access to Islamic finance. Moreover, several borrowers in the study reported that the bank did not always operate according to Islamic principles, imposing high interest on loans as well as excessive administrative and late penalty charges.

Whereas Islamic finance uses divine authority to restrain usury and lenders' activities, state-owned development banks can employ a secular critique of commercial lenders based on criteria of productive efficiency and human well-being (Stiglitz, 1994). In 2015, Russia and Kyrgyzstan established the Russian-Kyrgyz Development Fund (RKDF) to modernise the Kyrgyzstani economy after its accession to the Eurasian Economic Union. One of RKDF's aims is to investment in production and export-orientated sectors, so that the economy becomes competitive within the EEU, and does not experience high unemployment.

RKDF operates in two ways. First, it provides large investment loans to businesses on a direct financing basis. Second, it provides finance to banks and microfinance institutions to be lent to small and medium businesses under concessional terms (Russian-Kyrgyz Development Fund, 2015). There are several priority sectors, including agri-business, and interest rates are capped. RKDF differs from other international financial institutions, because it recognises an important distinction between productive and unproductive investment, and the need to cap interest rates for borrowers.

In addition, RKDF is critical of commercial banks' 'free market' approach to lending. It works in partnership with banks to offer cheap credits on the strict condition that credit is disbursed for investment in the productive sector. It penalises lenders who allocate its funds for trade and unproductive purposes. Kuban, a top official at RKDF, explained that banks were still able to get unearned income, though much lower:

> Some banks have very easy access to international financial institutions and get money for like 5% and they will give this money for 20% so their margin is 15%. . . . So now we came onto the market and . . . we give money at 1%, and [the banks] charge additional 4%, of course it's not 15% margin.

While RKDF offers credit at 1% (which reflects its operational costs) and has helped to reduce market interest rates, banks and microfinance companies can still extract wealth. RKDF undertakes pragmatic interventions to restrict lenders' activities, otherwise self-interested elites would continue to govern banks for their own gain with damaging economic and social outcomes.

Critical Discussion on Debt

The financial elites articulated moral discourses, norms and myths to counter accusations of usurious and predatory lending. But critically, the moral construals and myths depoliticised and normalised the unequal relationship between lenders and borrowers. Their accounts of credit disregarded power and class by abstracting market actors from their social context, and assigning them individual rights and obligations. The nature of debt belied the neoliberal rhetoric of consumer choice, market freedom and enterprise culture.

Debt is a social relationship that involves economic dependency and power (Sayer, 2016). Borrowers lack and need money, which lenders have ownership and control of. Several participants recognised that lenders took advantage of borrowers' dependence to impose onerous contracts. Debtors had little choice but to accept exorbitant charges and collateralise assets. They also bore most of the risks. Repayments were fixed irrespective of a change in personal or economic circumstances, and creditors threatened to seize and dispose of collateral in cases of default.

Lenders' income is unearned, meaning that they can siphon interest from debt without contributing to wealth creation (Sayer, 2015; Tawney, 1921). Their mere ownership of money produces nothing, but the power and sanctity of property rights and debt claims allow them to extract income (Hudson, 2017). Several interviewees described how creditors profited from debtors' labour, enterprise and austerity. The debt relationship became regularised, normalised and accepted in the context of inadequate options, establishing itself as part of the order of things without much ethical scrutiny (Bourdieu, 2000).

Interest is a net flow of income from debtors to creditors, from the relatively poor to the relatively rich (Kennedy, 1995). Although donor-sponsored micro-loans sought to address social goals, debt involved a transfer of income from the asset-poor to the asset-rich. Some participants explained how poor families experienced social misery, because household expenditure was reduced to make repayments. As a hidden redistributive mechanism,interest was responsible for exacerbating social inequalities and suffering.

Conclusion

This chapter provided a critical and qualitative research on how banks and microfinance institutions morally construed and legitimised their rentier activities. Their moral evaluations justified and normalised exorbitant interest rates and unearned income, and depoliticised social inequalities and suffering (Hudson, 2017; Sayer, 2015).

The financial elites often understood and evaluated the lender-borrower relationship using abstract liberal market principles and ethics in three ways. First, many participants construed themselves as civilising and moral agents, who fostered liberal values of equality, autonomy and freedom (Booth, 1994; Hirschman, 1982; Pelkmans & Umetbaeva, 2018). The market mechanism was favourably compared and evaluated to alternative arrangements of allocating credit. The market allowed people to formally access credit in pursuit of their projects. By contrast, rotating savings and credit associations involved hierarchal and ascriptive relationships that excluded marginalised and poor groups, and Islamic banking was seen to diminish women's economic autonomy.

Second, most financial elites celebrated the credit market as an arena of consumer choice and freedom (O'Neill, 1998). Middle class groups tended to perceive the post-Soviet transition to a market economy as a shift of decision-making powers from central authorities to individual actors. People were free from paternalistic state planning controls. Borrowers were characterised as free choosers, who exercised personal liberty and responsibility in taking out a loan. Their contractual relationship with lenders was voluntary and consensual. Market loans allowed borrowers to shape their own lives.

Third, most participants rejected the idea of debt forgiveness, and promoted the sanctity of contracts and debt claims (Hudson, 2017). Despite the negative consequences on their families' well-being, borrowers were expected to fulfil their obligations and pay their debts (Graeber, 2011). When borrowers had reneged on their promise to repay, the use of intimidating and threatening debt recovery tactics was rationalised to defend the rule of law. The courts were duty-bound to protect creditors' property rights over money, and correct contractual violations (Weinrib, 2002).

But upon critical scrutiny, the financial elites' moral construals and justifications were weak. They were often based on myths, deceptions and misrecognitions around the creation of credit money, money as a commodity, 'free markets' and economic individualism (Keen, 2011; Polanyi, 1944). They also elided distinctions between earned and unearned income, and productive and unproductive investment.

The neoliberal regime of private property rights and the judiciary legitimised and protected unequal power and income extraction (Marcuse, 1996; Sanghera, 2020). Frederic Bastiat (1996: 130) describes how wealth extraction involves legal and moral resources, 'When plunder has become a way of life for a group of men living together in society, they create for themselves in the course of time a legal system that authorises it and a moral code that glorifies it.'

This chapter also critically examined the role of financial institutions in creating post-Soviet economies, in which economic rent became a significant form of obtaining income, alongside earning income through production and wealth creation (Mihalyi & Szelenyi, 2017). Neoliberalism did not merely promote privatisation and marketisation in post-Soviet economies, it re-bundled property rights, created unequal ownership and control of scarce assets, and expanded the role of rent.

References

Angioloni, S., Kudabaev, Z., Ames, G., & Wetzstein, M. (2018). Household allocation of microfinance credit in Kyrgyzstan. *Post-Communist Economies, 30*(1), 78–98.

Appadurai, A. (2012). The spirit of calculation. *Cambridge Anthropology, 30*(1), 3–17.

Asian Development Bank. (2011). *Sector assessment (Summary): private sector and finance*. Bishkek: Asian Development Bank Report. https://www.adb.org/sites/default/files/linked-documents/41544-082-kgz-ssa.pdf. Accessed July 2020.

Asian Development Bank Institute. (2014). *Connecting Central Asia with economic centers*. Asian Development Bank Institute. https://www.adb.org/sites/default/files/publication/159307/adbi-connecting-central-asia-economic-centers-final-report.pdf. Accessed July 2020.

Bastiat, F. (1996). *Economic sophisms* (A. Goddard, Trans.). Foundation for Economic Education.

Bateman, M. (2010). *Why doesn't microfinance work? The destructive rise of local neoliberalism*. Zed Books.

Black, W. (2011, May 25). The two documents everyone should read to better understand the crisis. *HuffPost*. https://www.huffpost.com/entry/the-two-documents-everyon_b_169813. Accessed July 2020.

Booth, W. (1994). On the idea of the moral economy. *American Political Science Review, 88*(3), 653–667.

Botoeva, A. (2018). Islam and the spirits of capitalism: Competing articulations of the Islamic economy. *Politics and Society, 46*(2), 235–264.

Bourdieu, P. (2000). *Pascalian mediations*. Polity.

Charman, K. (2007). Kazakhstan: A state-led liberalized market economy? In D. Lane & M. Myant (Eds.), *Varieties of capitalism in post-Communist countries* (pp. 165–182). Palgrave Macmillan.

Erturk, I., Froud, J., Johal, S., Leaver, A., & Williams, K. (2007). The democratization of finance? Promises, outcomes and conditions. *Review of International Political Economy, 14*(4), 553–575.

Ferguson, J. (2009). The uses of neoliberalism. *Antipode, 41*(S1), 166–184.

Graeber, D. (2011). *Debt: The first 5,000 years*. Melville House Publishing.

Graziani, A. (1989). *The theory of the monetary circuit*. Thames Papers in Political Economy, Thames Polytechnic.

Guseva, A. (2005). Building new markets: A comparison of the Russian and American credit card markets. *Socio-Economic Review, 3*(3), 437–466.

Hasanova, S. (2018). *Financial inclusion, financial regulation, financial literacy, and financial education in the Kyrgyz Republic* (ADBI Working Paper Series No. 850). Asian Development Bank Institute.

Hirschman, A. (1982). Rival interpretations of market society: Civilising, destructive or feeble? *Journal of Economic Literature, 20*(4), 1463–1484.

Ho, K. (2012). Finance. In D. Fassin (Ed.), *A companion to moral anthropology* (pp. 413–431). Wiley.

Hoggarth, D. (2016). The rise of Islamic finance: Post-colonial market-building in central Asia and Russia. *International Affairs, 92*(1), 115–136.

Hudson, M. (2014). *The bubble and beyond* (New). ISLET.

Hudson, M. (2015). *Killing the host: How financial parasites and debt bondage destroy the global economy*. CounterPunch Books.

Hudson, M. (2017). *J is for junk economics: A guide to reality in an age of deception*. ISLET.

Hudson, M. (2018). . . . *and forgive them their debts: Lending, Foreclosures and redemption from bronze age finance to the jubilee year*. ISLET.

International Finance Corporation. (2016). *Islamic banking and finance: Opportunities across micro, small and medium enterprises in Kyrgyz Republic*. International Finance Corporation.

International Monetary Fund. (2010). *Republic of Kazakhstan: 2010 Article IV Consultation* (IMF Country Report No. 10/241). International Monetary Fund.

Jessop, B. (2015). Hard cash, easy credit, fictitious capital: Critical reflections on money as a fetishised social relation. *Finance and Society, 1*(1), 20–37.

Keen, S. (2011). Debunking macroeconomics. *Economic Analysis and Policy, 41*(3), 147–167.

Kennedy, M. (1995). *Interest and inflation free money*. Seva International.

Kuehnast, K., & Dudwick, N. (2002). Better a hundred friends than a hundred rubles? Social networks in transition—The Kyrgyz Republic. *World Bank Economists' Forum, 2*, 51–88.

Lewis, M. (2007). Comparing Islamic and Christian attitudes to usury. In M. Hassan & M. Lewis (Eds.), *Handbook of Islamic banking* (pp. 64–81). Edward Elgar.

Marcuse, P. (1996). Privatization and its discontents: Property rights in land and housing in the transition in Eastern Europe. In G. Andrusz, M. Harloe, & I. Szelenyi (Eds.), *Cities after socialism: Urban and regional change and conflict in post-socialist societies* (pp. 119–191). Blackwell.

Mihalyi, P., & Szelenyi, I. (2017). The role of rents in the transition from socialist redistributive economies to market capitalism. *Comparative Sociology, 16*(1), 13–38.

Minsky, H. (1978). *The financial instability hypothesis: A re-statement*. Thames Papers in Political Economy: Thames Polytechnic.

National Bank of the Kyrgyz Republic. (2014). *The financial sector stability report of the Kyrgyz Republic*. The National Bank of the Kyrgyz Republic.

National Bank of the Kyrgyz Republic. (2016). *The financial sector stability report of the Kyrgyz Republic*. The National Bank of the Kyrgyz Republic.

O'Neill, J. (1998). *The market: Ethics, knowledge and politics*. Routledge.

Orazalin, N. (2019). Corporate governance and corporate social responsibility (CSR) disclosure in an emerging economy: Evidence from commercial banks of Kazakhstan. *Corporate Governance, 19*(3), 490–507.

Pelkmans, M., & Umetbaeva, D. (2018). Moneylending and moral reasoning on the capitalist frontier in Kyrgyzstan. *Anthropological Quarterly, 91*(3), 1049–1074.

Pettifor, A. (2017). *The production of money: How to break the power of bankers*. Verso.

Polanyi, K. (1944). *The great transformation: Economic and political origins of our time*. Rinehart.

Russian-Kyrgyz Development Fund (2015). *Annual report*. Russian-Kyrgyz Development Fund.

Ruziev, K., & Dow, S. (2013). *A review of banking sector reforms in transition economies* (Working Paper 03/13). Centre for Global Finance, University of the West of England.

Ruziev, K., & Majidov, T. (2013). Differing effects of the global financial crisis on the Central Asian countries: Kazakhstan, the Kyrgyz Republic and Uzbekistan. *Europe-Asia Studies, 65*(4), 682–716.

Ruziev, K., & Midmore, P. (2014). Informal credit institutions in transition countries: A study of urban money lenders in post-communist Uzbekistan. *Post-Communist Economies, 26*(3), 415–435.

Sanghera, B. (2020). Justice, power and informal settlements: Understanding the juridical view of property rights in Central Asia. *International Sociology, 35*(1), 22–44.

Sayer, A. (2007). Moral economy as critique. *New Political Economy, 12*(2), 261–270.

Sayer, A. (2015). *Why we can't afford the rich*. Policy Press.

Sayer, A. (2016). Moral economy, unearned income and legalized corruption. In D. Whyte & J. Wiegratz (Eds.), *Neoliberalism and the moral economy of fraud* (pp. 44–56). Routledge.

Stiglitz, J. (1994). *The role of the state in financial markets*. The World Bank. http://documents.worldbank.org/curated/en/239281468741290885/pdf/multi-page.pdf.

Tawney, R. H. (1921). *The acquisitive society*. G. Bell and Sons.

Tag El-Din, S., & Hassan, M. (2007). Islam and speculation in the stock exchange. In M. Hassan & M. Lewis (Eds.), *Handbook of Islamic banking* (pp. 240–255). Edward Elgar.

Tombs, S. (2012). State-corporate symbiosis in the production of crime and harm. *State Crime Journal, 1*(2), 170–195.

Weinrib, E. (2002). Corrective justice in a nutshell. *University of Toronto Law Journal, 52*, 349–356.

Whyte, D., & Wiegratz, J. (2016). *Neoliberalism and the moral economy of fraud*. Routledge.

Wiegratz, J. (2016). *Neoliberal moral economy: Capitalism, socio-cultural change and fraud in Uganda*. Rowman and Littlefield.

Wolters, A. (2016). Islamic finance and the state in Central Asia. *Central Asian Affairs, 3*(4), 360–384.

CHAPTER 5

Property Development: Improperty, Plutocracy and Criminogency

This chapter examines how property owners and developers gained wealth and political power in Kyrgyzstan and Kazakhstan. Along with other scarce assets, land and real estate were key sources of economic and political capital. The unequal ownership and control of real estate properties enabled wealthy elites to extract income by mere virtue of having property rights (Sayer, 2015). Business and political elites engaged in violent and criminal struggles to control lucrative real estate. Moreover new retail development projects involved elite struggles over the specifics of value grabbing; i.e. who pays rent to whom (Andreucci et al., 2017). Wealthy rentiers sought to capture the state through lobbying, donations, the media and elected office (Standing, 2016). The blurring of state and corporate interests created criminogenic environments, in which the crimes of the powerful and their harmful effects became endemic features of neoliberalisation (Rothe & Kauzlarich, 2016; Tombs, 2012).

In the Soviet Union, there was a definite set of property rights that people could rely on, and the state would respect and implement. The bundle of rights included rights to land and housing, and rights to occupancy and use for tenants and their families. Rent, interest and speculative gains were 'non-labour' income, and were not allowed (Maggs, 1961). Marcuse (1996: 136) observes, 'That part of the bundle of rights that is the right to dispose at a profit, or the right to speculate, did not exist in Soviet law.'

B. Sanghera and E. Satybaldieva, *Rentier Capitalism and Its Discontents*,
https://doi.org/10.1007/978-3-030-76303-9_5

After the collapse of the Soviet Union, the transition to a market economy expanded the role of rent and improperty in post-socialist countries (Mihalyi & Szelenyi, 2017). International financial institutions and donors (such as the International Monetary Fund and the World Bank) demanded property rights reform in post-socialist countries. Constitutions and legislations provided the protection of private property and its disposition by its owners free of state control (Schneiderman, 2000). The privatisation of housing allocated more rights to owners and mortgage lenders, with new rights to evict and foreclose (Hatcher, 2015a). The right to housing was still constitutional, but was rhetorical with the end of state subsidies.

The re-bundling of rights to allow property owners to dispose of their assets without state restrictions was explained and justified by international financial institutions as how 'free markets' work. The neoliberal Washington Consensus did not merely oppose socialist ideas about property and income, it reversed classical liberalism by favouring rent extraction, unearned income and deregulation (Hudson, 2017).

The chapter is divided into six sections. The section 'Soviet and Post-Soviet Housing' briefly discusses how housing has been a significant social issue for many decades in Central Asia. Drawing on our second case study, the sections 'Housing as Improperty' and 'Struggles Over Income Extraction in Retail and Industrial Sectors' analyse how property developers and state officials interpreted and shaped residential property, and then explore how owners struggled to control and extract rent from real estate properties. Section 'National, Regional and Local Plutocratic Structures' examines the nature of plutocracy, the rule of the rich, in Kyrgyzstan and Kazakhstan. The section 'Criminogenic Environments in Public and Private Sectors' investigates crimes and violations related to land and real estate. Finally, section 'Conclusion' summarises the chapter's key findings and ideas.

Soviet and Post-Soviet Housing

Housing was an acute social problem in the Soviet Union. Despite large-scale construction campaigns in the 1960s and 70s, people's needs and expectations greatly exceeded the housing stock (Morton, 1980). In 1987, 22.3% of all Soviet households were waiting to be rehoused (Andrusz, 1990a). The percentage of households waiting varied considerably between cities. It was 12% in Moscow, 15 in Almaty, 17% in Frunze

(Bishkek) and 26% in Kiev (Andrusz, 1990b). The waiting period for a new apartment could have been as long as ten years.

Moreover, many people lived in overcrowded and poor quality housing. The fact that living conditions had improved as a result of increased construction was of little comfort to those still living in inadequate conditions (Morton, 1980). In 1986, the average per capita living space in urban areas was 14.3 square metres (Andrusz, 1990b). There were variations across the Soviet Union republics. The average per capita urban living space in Estonia was 17.8 square metres, in Russia 14.5 square metres, in Kazakhstan 12.6 square metres, and in Kirghizia 11.3 square metres.

The Soviet housing allocation system was largely corrupt and unfair, and was more egalitarian in theory than in practice (Gentile & Sjoberg, 2013). Housing was used to increase labour productivity, and to ensure political support and loyalty. It was also highly stratified (Szelenyi, 1987). Members of elite professions and the nomenklatura often received superior quality apartments. A system of social privileges and connections allowed powerful and influential individuals to avoid formal regulations and norms of distribution (Sharipova, 2015). The shortage of housing incentivised queue-jumping through bribery and influence (Morton, 1980).

After the collapse of the Soviet Union, states shifted the responsibility of housing to the private sector. It was expected that market reforms would alleviate housing scarcity, as people acquired the rights to sell, rent and lease apartments for profit (Sharipova, 2015). New owners dissatisfied with their apartments were expected to sell them and buy better ones. The assumption behind shock therapy was that once price and rent controls were removed, property developers, mortgage lenders and real estate agencies would emerge to meet people's housing needs (Zavisca, 2008).

While the market-based system delivered better-quality housing with more variety and choice for consumers, it excluded most households from access to it (Tsenkova, 2014). The Soviet shortage of housing was replaced by a post-Soviet shortage of affordable housing. New housing inequalities and power dynamics appeared (Zavisca, 2008). The state and the market promoted and attended to elites' property rights, interests and preferences, but largely neglected and exploited poor and migrant groups' housing needs (Hatcher, 2015a).

The introduction of the market economy indirectly reduced ethnic residential segregation in Central Asian and Baltic republics (Gentile & Tammaru, 2006). Titular ethnic groups (such as Kazakhs and Estonians) improved their housing conditions relative to Russians. Since independence, the status of titular ethnic groups improved in the labour market, especially in public administration, where knowledge of titular languages became important. In gaining economic power, titular groups obtained better-quality housing than during the Soviet Union.

The market reforms produced mixed results in Kyrgyzstan's capital Bishkek. The rental housing market significantly increased. Families who received more than one property during the initial privatisation programme often made one or more apartments available for rent (Hatcher, 2015a). The purchase of property as an investment also contributed to the growing number of rental properties. Rent became an important source of income for the post-Soviet propertied class.

Property developers in the region focused on building elite housing and targeting affluent families. In 2010, the average selling price was 800–1000 USD per square metre in Bishkek, about 6–8 times the average monthly salary (Osenov, 2011). Between 2005 and 2011, Kazakhstan's average price of newly constructed housing per square metre increased by 66% (Sharipova, 2015). Buying a spacious apartment was often unaffordable for low- and middle-income households, forcing some of them to rent or build adobe houses in informal settlements on the outskirts of the city (Hatcher, 2017; Sanghera et al., 2012). In response to housing inequities, social movements emerged to decommodify land and housing, as will be discussed in Chapter 7.

Housing as Improperty

Property Developers' Construals of Housing

In capitalism, the provision of useful goods and services is not the prime goal, but a common, though not universal, by-product of the pursuit of profit. Effective demand, not needs, typically shapes what commodities are produced. In our study, most property developers catered to the wants and desires of wealthy and upper middle class families, because the profit margins were greater than for working class or lower middle class families. Aibek, an executive director of a construction company in Kyrgyzstan, explained that most of his apartment complexes targeted customers at the high end of the market:

> The market is divided into four sections: the economy class, comfort class, business class, deluxe, or luxury, premium class. We construct comfort class and premium class complexes, we're not building business class or economy class. . . . What defines premium class is first and the most important thing the location, and second the materials used.

In satisfying the wants of the affluent and wealthy, Aibek was able to generate profits. These elites had the money to pay for exclusivity, elegance and extravagance that property developers provided. Apartment complexes were located on prime sites, such as near nature reserves or gentrified and leafy districts of the capital. Many middle and working class families were financially excluded from the primary housing market, and were forced to buy or rent in the secondary market (Sharipova, 2015). Some resorted to building their own houses on the outskirts of the city.

Hudson (2014) observes that real estate is one of key ways to extract income. Rentiers hold assets for acquisition, not for productive or personal use (Tawney, 1921). The property developers believed that buying and selling luxury apartments was an effective way to make capital gains.

> Many perspective buyers are thinking to buy new apartments, and then will try to sell it in a short of period of time. They sell it to get profits easier and faster. You buy a property, and in two years you sell it and you get 30% profit. It's about reselling it. . . . It's better to invest 2 million USD in two years and get 30% profit and then just leave.
>
> Emil, a marketing director of a construction company in Kyrgyzstan

> Investment is always evaluated on how long it takes to be converted into money, right? Our real estate is one of the best in the secondary market, that is our apartments can be re-sold. . . . It's not necessary that investors should live in them, so they remain in the primary market.
>
> Tima, a senior manager of a construction company in Kyrgyzstan

Emil and Tima observed that reselling new luxury apartments was a lucrative business. Many of them were not used or occupied before they were re-sold. The property developers appeared to contribute to the production of use-value, but in fact they were dependent on and catered for the rentier class. By building new apartments merely for exchange-value, the property developers created instruments for wealth and power, expanded the sources of income extraction, and were rentiers at one removed (Sayer, 2015).

Whereas property is used to aid useful work that produces earned income, improperty is an alternative to work that results in unearned or non-labour income (Tawney, 1921). Some property developers characterised real estate investment as passive, in that affluent buyers were able to make money with little or no productive effort, as Aibek noted:

> [Many of our buyers] have new apartments as second or third apartments, maybe used for rent like investment or maybe for their young children for the future. . . . This is called lazy or sleep investment. It's different from active investment, when you have factory . . . all time it's a working company. Here you just put the money into apartments, like putting money in the bank.

Crucially, Aibek distinguished between two forms of investment in terms of labour. Affluent landowners were deemed to be 'lazy' or 'sleepy' investors. They did not work or invest in the provision of useful commodities, but bought an entitlement to a stream of unearned income in the form of rent.

The property developers helped to produce a shift from Soviet-era housing as a form of property that owners used for personal use to a form of improperty in post-Soviet Central Asia. This shift was highlighted by the rise of informal settlements on the outskirts of the capital. Many rural migrant families were forced to build adobe homes, because private apartment rents were too high (Hatcher, 2015b).

Buy-to-let housing allowed better-off families to meet their own security and welfare needs based on property ownership. Since the collapse of the Soviet Union, Central Asian welfare provisions have significantly diminished, leaving most families to fend for themselves. In the above interview quotation, Aibek observed that taking care of family members partly motivated buyers to acquire one or two apartments. Acquiring improperty and hence sources of unearned income enabled families to meet family needs, and sustain living standards. But this neoliberal form of welfare tends to favour the well-off and asset-rich at the expense of the less fortunate and asset-poor, whose income is extracted by the latter through rent.

Once basic economic institutions and relationships have become established, there is less attention on normative questions, as the focus moves to normalisation and acceptance, and questions of validity turn into questions of behaviour (Sayer, 2016). Re-selling and renting apartments scarcely needed moral deliberations and justifications, having become depoliticised and naturalised, and treated as 'a fact of life'. Bakyt, a senior manager of a construction company in Kyrgyzstan, accepted that new apartments were often mere assets:

> We certainly don't like [buyers re-selling apartments], but on the other hand we can't prohibit it, the investment. They're the customers of our business. We know that in the end someone will get a decent quality housing. Economically, it's not advisable for an apartment just to stay empty. It's possible to keep it empty for a month or two, a year maybe.

Bakyt wanted apartments to be used for their intended purpose, rather than as an instrument to make money. Unused and empty apartments frustrated him. But he was resigned to the established order of things. The property developers were economically dependent on affluent buyers, and their relationship was normalised without much ethical scrutiny. Acceptance and submission are a product of a tacit and practical belief that becomes self-evident and common sense in the context of lack of alternatives (Bourdieu, 2000).

Improperty is functionless, and creates social inequalities and tensions (Tawney, 1921). Whereas personal use can limit individual ownership of apartments, rentiers' ability to acquire and hold apartments seems unrestrained. Some property developers accepted and justified a high concentration of apartment ownership, and normalised foreign rentiers.

> I know some people who have maybe thirty apartments, maybe fifty apartments. . . . If they can, why not! If you didn't steal the money, it's your right.
>
> Aibek

> Foreigner buyers invest money here. . . . If our country represents a commercial opportunity for them to make money, why not! So it should be!
>
> Tima

As Aibek and Tima attested, improperty has no practical limits, so that the better-off can accumulate assets on the basis of power without regard to need or purpose. Aibek depoliticised improperty, explaining that buyers were acting according to the law. As Marcuse (1996) observed, property rights were re-bundled after the collapse of the Soviet Union to liberalise and deregulate state controls on private property, and legitimise speculation and unearned income.

Moreover, Tima justified improperty noting that buyers were enacting the cultural norm of making money (Wiegratz, 2016). He and other property developers expressed satisfaction that Central Asia offered investment and money-making opportunities in real estate to wealthy foreign investors. By viewing real estate properties as commodities to be bought and sold, housing was indistinguishable from other forms of exchange for profit. The housing market was characterised as open and free for all. Any restriction on trade was seen as limiting economic freedom, choice and prosperity. But such evaluations elided vital distinctions between genuine and fictitious commodities, property and improperty, and productive and unproductive investment. 'Investors' made money based on power derived from liberal property rights over assets, unrelated to effort, desert or the production of use-values.

But the commodification of real estate properties resulted in social inequalities and misery (Polanyi, 1944). Some property developers were concerned to manage acquisitions without causing social discontent about asset inequality. In certain circumstances, they hid or obscured the full details of their wealthy clients' purchases. Aibek described how affluent buyers could register apartments under their family or friends' names to conceal property holdings:

> [Some owners] have registered apartments under different names. . . . If people knew that they had a lot of apartments, of course it would cause resentment. The people love to envy, you know, the rich. If they knew the real situation, it would cause a scandal, an uproar. So we keep it a top secret, the names of clients who have a lot of apartments. We don't say who owns how many.

In the context of high rent and lack of affordable housing, Aibek was aware that public knowledge of concentrated ownership could trigger dissatisfaction and protests. His accusation that most people were engaged in a politics of class envy served to deflect arguments and evidence about improperty, inequality and injustice. By masking real ownership, Aibek was complicit in facilitating rentiers' acquisitions, reducing their exposure to risk, and containing public anger over the commodification process. Professional intermediaries (such as lawyers, creative accountants, brokers, tax avoidance consultants, banks and marketing experts) use their superior knowledge and power to assist active rentiership (Sayer, 2015). As major beneficiaries of rentier activities, they willingly provide services to promote and protect the rich.

Income Extraction Through State Mortgage Schemes

The modern state plays a significant role in creating rent relations (Andreucci et al., 2017; Parenti, 2015). It is at the centre of social struggles over use-value and exchange-value of land and property. During the transition to a market economy, Central Asian political regimes changed its constitution and legislations to re-bundle property rights. The changes protected investors' ownership of assets free of state control, and their rights to speculate and dispose at a profit. Nurlan, a senior official at the City Department of Architecture in Kyrgyzstan, explained how the urban real estate shifted from Soviet social housing to private housing market that promoted investors' economic interests over others' needs:

> Under the Soviet system the society was planned for people to live and work comfortably. Now cities are based on making money only. . . . We're a free market, a capitalist country. The money investors give must be paid back, they're not doing it just for the people. . . . They pursue only money, they don't think about the people.

In transition economies, property rights were liberalised and deregulated to institute a 'free market' ideology. As Nurlan noted, this meant that investors were free to make income without regard to social needs. Hudson (2017) observes that whereas classical political economy understood 'free market' to mean an economy free of economic rent, neoliberal reforms have allowed investors to extract income free of state regulation.

The financialisation of the mortgage market originated from the US, and then spread to other parts of the world (Aalbers, 2008). In the 2010s, Kazakhstan and Kyrgyzstan created legal frameworks to securitise mortgage debt. Their state mortgage schemes were a response to lack of affordable housing, and the need to increase people's access to cheap mortgage loans. Borrowers could use state subsidised loans either to purchase apartments at primary or secondary housing markets, or to build their own houses (Auyezkhanuly et al., 2019). Ulan, a senior official at the state agency for strategic research in Kyrgyzstan, explained that public sector employees (such as doctors, teachers and civil servants) were particularly targeted by the scheme to satisfy their housing needs:

> We're not just giving apartments to public sector workers, but we give them an opportunity to get one. The State Mortgage Company can give credit to them and they can buy one. . . . It operates through the market instrument, and it's more sustainable.

Given that the post-Soviet states can no longer build or guarantee housing for all their employees, they created market-based schemes for them to buy an affordable apartment. The schemes aimed to solve a housing crisis that had been developing for over two decades, having the consequence of eroding the legitimacy and authority of the state and the legal system.

Under the state mortgage schemes, individuals had to meet strict conditions to be eligible for a loan. It excluded people with more than one apartment, or a recent record of transactions in the housing market. Kuban, a senior official and one of the architects of the scheme at the Ministry of Economy in Kyrgyzstan, stated:

> We set a requirement that it should not be their second or third home, but their first home. Plus we require a certificate that the person has had no real estate transactions during last three years. . . . This was done in order to avoid some people selling their apartments to obtain an additional apartment. Then we have limited the value of the apartment to 600 USD per square metre up to 70 square metres.

Kuban believed that his country's scheme would benefit families, who wanted to buy apartments for personal use. It was designed to prohibit rentier activities, such as buy-to-let or real estate speculation. On the one hand, post-Soviet states legitimised and justified rentiers' property holdings for acquisition as a 'free market' operation, but on the other hand, they aimed to make housing affordable for the less well-off, so as to avert a political and social crisis. As Jessop (2002) argues, the state in a capitalist society invariably has contradictory state goals and projects.

The financialisation of the mortgage market facilitated income extraction through financial relations. Kazakhstan's and Kyrgyzstan's state mortgage companies were established to issue mortgage credit, and to collect and sell debts to investors as mortgage-backed securities. This allowed the state mortgage schemes to raise revenue to issue more loans. Kuban was confident that investors would buy the securities because they were a safe investment:

> We think the mortgage-backed securities will be sold well. Because they're state guaranteed bonds. . . . Everybody purchases them as investment to diversify their portfolio. They're considered to be without risks. . . . It will be very attractive for investors because each month they will get a guaranteed stable flow of income.

Kuban stated that mortgage-backed securities were guaranteed by the state, entitling investors to a stream of risk-free dividends. Investors could also sell securities in the secondary market in pursuit of capital gains. In case of default, borrowers lost their homes, which could be sold or remortgaged. Critically, the state mortgage schemes enabled a transfer of income from borrowers to investors. Whereas the state and borrowers bore the risk of loss, investors received unearned income on the basis of mere ownership of assets, without working or risking (Sayer, 2015). The social rights and guarantees enjoyed by working families during the Soviet system were replaced by new arrangements and relations that transferred rights and guarantees to rentiers.

The state mortgage companies partnered with several domestic retail banks. The former were mortgage lenders, and the latter were mortgage servicers. Kuban explained that Kyrgyzstan's state mortgage scheme was administered through an existing network of bank branches, thereby significantly reducing infrastructural costs:

> Commercial banks were selected as partners for the State Mortgage Company. . . . It was calculated that it was profitable to have commercial banks as loan servicers because they have branches throughout the country. . . . Banks get 5% commission. It's a lot! We met and discussed this, and they persuaded us.

The partner banks had superior capabilities that allowed the processing of loans, including tracking loan payments, sending reminder notices and filing foreclosure documents, to be effectively managed. They used their infrastructural monopoly power to charge a large fee, thereby extracting income because they could, not because they deserved it (Hudson, 2014).

Higher bank fees meant higher mortgage interest and payments, which borrowers bore. By accepting the banks' terms of service, the Central Asian states created, legitimised and normalised the extraction of income from borrowers to banks. They facilitated the appropriation and distribution of rent in favour of landowners, investors and banks (Andreucci et al., 2017).

When the state mortgage schemes were launched, middle class families were targeted, because they were likely to have adequate savings to pay an initial deposit. Ermek Kambaraliev, a state official at Kyrgyzstan's state mortgage company, said at a roundtable, 'Rich citizens can buy premium class housing. Poor people don't have money at all, we don't target them either. We are targeting the middle class, they have some savings' (Central Asian News Service, 2016). The schemes focused on professional groups, such as teachers, doctors and social workers.

It was also believed that middle class homeownership would contribute to social and political stability, as Azat, a senior manager of House Construction Saving Bank in Kazakhstan, explained:

> The bank's key role is to help people to get their own housing and contribute to stability in the country. Our role is to promote the formation of the middle class. . . . Housing is often considered as an important quality of the middle class. . . . One of characteristics of the middle class is an ability to plan life, and our bank teaches people to develop a middle class discipline.

Azat's state bank was responsible for managing Kazakhstan's state mortgage scheme, and expanding the number of middle class families owning their homes. He believed that the scheme would inculcate individuals with economic values of rationality and discipline to make monthly payments for homeownership. Mortgage debt can be an instrument of political and economic control to make the property-owning middle class autonomous, self-responsible and disciplined citizens. These individuals can reject welfare rights and social solidarity in favour of market freedom and individual choice, thereby shoring up neoliberalism in the country.

But many middle class people complained that the schemes' terms and conditions were too prohibitive (Sharipova, 2015; The Times of Central Asia, 2017). In Kyrgyzstan, politicians raised concerns that public sector employees could not afford interest rates of 10–12%, and that their total repayment would be double of their initial loan. Nurgazy Nishanov, an oppositional parliamentarian, claimed that teachers' salaries were insufficient to pay the mortgage, and that 25,000 teachers were in desperate need of housing (Central Asian News Service, 2017).

In Kazakhstan, many people who acquired housing through state programmes rented their apartments (Sharipova, 2015). The relatively affluent families used the opportunity of state subsidised interest rates to buy additional apartments to lease to poorer families, who could not raise the required deposit or have adequate regular income to be eligible for the affordable housing scheme. The financialisation of the mortgage market largely entrenched existing economic inequalities.

Housing affordability has remained quite modest in Kazakhstan and Kyrgyzstan, reflecting low levels of incomes among the population and high costs of commercial and subsidised mortgage lending. In light of social movements' demands for affordable housing and better financing, the political regimes recently lowered interest rates, so reducing value appropriation by investors and banks. The state can be targeted by social struggles over who captures rent and who pays, and its regulation depends on class balances at specific moments (Andreucci et al., 2017).

An unequal society is prone to political instability and uprisings. Since its independence, Kyrgyzstan has had three political uprisings in 2005, 2010 and 2020. The police and security forces played an important role in the development of these uprisings. In order to maintain political authority, the state tried to strengthen its social contract with the police and military. In exchange for extra resources, including free apartments, police and military officers were expected to show loyalty to the state.

By 2016, about 800 state-owned apartments were built for law-enforcement and military officers, and another 1000 new apartments were planned (The Times of Central Asia, 2016). The state, as a property owner, used its assets for strategic and political purposes. It controlled which segments of the population were removed from rent relations, thereby shaping the specifics of value grabbing (Andreucci et al., 2017).

Struggles Over Income Extraction in Retail and Industrial Sectors

After the collapse of the Soviet Union, buildings and urban spaces were privatised to become rent-generating properties. In particular, retail development provided owners with a significant opportunity for unearned income. In 1989, Kazakhstan and Kyrgyzstan had about 400 and 100 marketplaces respectively, by 2005 their numbers rose to 950 and 400 respectively (Spector, 2006, 2008). Marketplaces were built on empty or unused land, territories of Soviet-era factories and warehouses and car parks. While some shopping malls were converted factories and warehouses, others were purpose-built to represent the allure of a modern, orderly and civilised consumer world in contrast to traditional bazaars (Karrar, 2020).

Some owners had substantial retail properties. For instance, Askar Salymbekov is one of the top ten richest people in Kyrgyzstan, and a long-serving parliamentarian (Central Asia and Caspian Intelligence, 2008). His family company, Dordoi Corporation, largely owns Dordoi Market, which is one of the largest retail and wholesale marketplaces in Central Asia, located outside of Bishkek city. It operates twenty different marketplaces, including a highly profitable one for auto parts, Alamedin retail market and Dordoi Azia wholesale market, which specialises in household appliances, office supplies, rugs and everyday hygienic products. Dordoi Corporation also owns other rent-generating businesses, including shopping malls and a retail bank.

Business and political elites sometimes engaged in violent and criminal struggles over the ownership and control of lucrative rent-generating retail properties (McGlinchey, 2011). The Karasuu Bazaar is one of the largest Central Asian marketplaces, located in southern Kyrgyzstan. In 2000, Bayaman Erkinbaev, a notorious criminal businessperson turned parliamentarian, seized control of the marketplace, and captured its rent. Bazarbai, a businessman in Beshkoshkon village near the Karasuu Bazaar explained:

> There were about fourteen people who had the legal rights to parts of the market. Bayaman didn't care about that, and he claimed to be the sole owner and managed to keep other people quiet!

Erkinbaev used violence and intimidation to become the sole owner of Karasuu Bazaar. In 2005, many market traders demonstrated against steep hikes in licence fees, demanding Erkinbayev give up his control of the marketplace (International Crisis Group, 2005). After a brief power struggle, Abdalim Junusov, a competing businessperson, was installed as the new owner. But a few months later, he was assassinated, which was blamed on Erkinbayev's network. Erkinbayev restored his control over the marketplace, though a couple of weeks later he was shot dead.

After his assassination, Karasuu Bazaar was divided between Beshkoshkon village council (*ayil okmotu*) and twelve private owners. The marketplace contributed a significant flow of revenue to the village council. Its budget rose from around 7 million soms in 2005 to 200 million soms in 2008 (Satybaldieva, 2011). The council funded an ambitious programme of social and physical infrastructure spending, rebuilding local schools, sport centres and kindergartens, and improving roads, electricity and pathways. Unlike private ownership of scarce assets, state ownership can generate substantial gains for the population.

In some cases, new retail development projects involved elite struggles over the specifics of value grabbing; i.e. who pays rent to whom (Andreucci et al., 2017). In Kazakhstan, Almaty City Council desired civilised, hygienic and modern forms of retail trade. New shopping malls, supermarkets and big stores were built, and some marketplaces were either closed or transformed. The number of marketplaces in the city fell from 83 in 1999 to 71 six years later (Spector, 2008). But the urban redevelopment did not merely attempt to project a modern image of the city, it changed rent relations in favour of different sets of economic and political elites. For instance, Baian Aul Market was closed down, and the market traders were moved to new marketplaces with different owners.

At its peak, Baian Aul Market had about 1000 shipping containers, out of which market traders sold spare car parts, and it sold about 200–300 cars on good days (Spector, 2008). In 2005, the city council ordered the marketplace to be shut for violation of sanitary norms. The market traders protested, and challenged the closure through the courts. Despite losing their legal battle, most traders refused to leave for a year until the police came to enforce the eviction. Over a thousand police officers were deployed to evict them, resulting in violent clashes and severe injuries. Traders faced frequent violent assaults until most of them moved to new marketplaces, or exited the business.

The new car marketplace, Baris III, was a huge complex with restaurants, hotels and other conveniences for customers. The owners and investors of Baris III were senior state officials and their family members, including several regional governors and the brother of then President Nazarbayev's, Bolot Nazarbayev (Spector, 2008). A new spare parts marketplace, Zhibek Zholu Market, was also owned by senior members of the ruling elite. Local governments, courts and elites used legal, judicial and coercive measures to redistribute rent-generating retail properties. Retail development did not merely promote and enhance rent extraction, it sustained plutocratic control on wealth and power.

The demolition and reconstruction of retail properties often bolstered the predatory power of landowners over tenants. For instance, in the 2010s there were several fires at Barakholka marketplace in Almaty. The fires (accidental or intentional) endangered traders' lives, destroyed their stocks, and ruined their businesses (Karrar, 2020). The fires helped to clear the old marketplace of disorderly shipping containers for a modern multistorey shopping mall, which had more rental units. While the city council framed the transition as civilising the urban landscape, the retail upgrade increased the owners' capacity to extract rent. The creation of clean and orderly retail trade involved socio-spatial dispossession and violence.

The neoliberal commodification of retail properties produced unregulated markets, in which tenants were resigned to pay excessive rent to powerful rich owners. In our interviews with market traders in Bishkek and Osh, they explained that owners could easily replace traders struggling with high rent with new ones.

> If market owners don't get their money, they'll just evict the traders, and write 'For Rent' on their stalls. And another one will come and get it. . . . Recently the owner came and said to me, 'If you don't want to pay the rent, I'll take all your stuff and throw you out!'
>
> Nargiza, a female trader at Dordoi Market, Kyrgyzstan

> Of course, rents are high. . . . We don't have a choice! The owner says, 'If you don't like it, leave and go to another place'.
>
> Jamilya, a female trader at Karasuu Bazaar, Kyrgyzstan

Nargiza and Jamilya believed that market traders did not have enough power to negotiate lower rent, so that they either accepted the situation, or left. Many traders dismissed the associations of market traders as ineffective for fighting on behalf of the members' interests, partly because the leaders of the associations were co-opted to manage and administer the marketplaces. Traders normalised high rent and lack of power, and aimed to make the best of a bad situation.

Lacking social solidarity and collective action, the market traders privatised and individualised their problems. In some cases, they took out loans to pay high rent, exacerbating their economic situation, as Nargiza explained:

> [My partner and I] need to pay the rent, and have to find the money. . . . We went to the pawnshop, and gave them our gold earrings and rings. . . . And then we went to Halyk Bank – it's very bad bank. They'll just eat you up. People have lost their homes. . . . We come to work every morning at six. We're feeding the banks. . . . The banks and market owners have a good life, and we're suffering.

Because trade was low, Nargiza and her partner had to borrow money from a bank and pawn their jewellery to make rental payments. While Nargiza and other traders made sacrifices, rose early to work, and took risks, market owners and banks extracted income from them without much effort or taking risks.

Industrial property development usually involved intense struggles between rentier and productive classes. After 1991, Kyrgyzstan experienced deindustrialisation as its light industry sector collapsed. Factories, warehouses and other industrial buildings were transferred to Soviet-era directors. Some of these buildings became valuable assets, because they were centrally located in Bishkek, and were integrated into a power grid (Spector & Botoeva, 2017). Whereas large parts of the city frequently experienced electricity blackouts, these buildings received uninterpreted electricity flows, making them highly sought after by businesses. Building owners took advantage of their monopoly power by charging high rents.

Some small and medium-sized apparel manufacturers rented expensive units in the Soviet-era buildings to access resources, including stable power supply, essential for production (Spector & Botoeva, 2017). Whereas the manufacturers used the property as an aid to productive work, the owners were passive and idle, devoid of any creative spirit (see Tawney, 1921). The latter partly appropriated the surplus value generated by the former on the mere basis of having private property rights. The owners were often senior state officials, or closely connected to the political regime.

The owners undermined the manufacturers' productive capacity in two ways. First, by extracting significant rent, they deprived the manufacturers of much-needed investment to modernise production, and so constrained the apparel sector's productive capacity and international competitiveness. Second, they failed to repair or renovate dilapidated buildings. Unable to pressurise the powerful owners, the manufacturers often undertook their own interior repairs at their own expense. They were angry and bitter that the owners imposed high rents without doing much to the buildings (Spector & Botoeva, 2017).

The effect of the neoliberal regime of private property was to transfer wealth from creative producers to functionless owners, and deplete industrial competitiveness. In the case of Bishkek's apparel industry, many small and medium-sized manufacturers dreamt of setting up workshops in cheaper parts of the city. But the lack of reliable electricity elsewhere meant that they were resigned to their present exploitative circumstances.

National, Regional and Local Plutocratic Structures

Politicians' Wealth in Kyrgyzstan

State capture by the rich has been a significant feature of the post-Soviet political landscape (Braguinsky, 2009; Mihalyi & Szelenyi, 2017). Economic and political elites merged to become plutocrats, as economic capital converted into political capital, and vice versa. Elected office has been a popular route for the rich to dominate politics. In entering politics, business elites sought to legitimise their wealth, evade potential prosecution, shape policies, and amass extra fortune through licit and illicit practices (Cooley & Heathershaw, 2017).

Political elites have often been allied to rentier interests, owning and controlling valuable assets. In Kyrgyzstan, the richest twenty individuals engaged in various forms of rentierism, as discussed in Chapter 2. They typically extracted rent based on wholly or partly owning multiple companies operating in a range of economic sectors, including banking, real estate, minerals and mobile telephony. All but two individuals occupied senior political positions. Omurbek Babanov and Almazbek Atambaev were former Prime Ministers. Atambaev was also an ex-President. Nariman Tuleyev, Isa Omurkulov, Askar Salymbekov, Melis Myrzakmatov and Dinara Isaeva's husband were former city mayors.

Using a range of open sources, the significance of rentierism can be ascertained among Kyrgyzstan's parliamentarians and Bishkek city councillors. Table 5.1 shows the nature and extent of parliamentarians' business interests in 2015 according to Tazabek, a business news agency. It is based on a sample of 71 out of 120 parliamentarians. Information on parliamentarians' business interests, which included their property as well as assets and companies transferred to trust management, was provided by the State Personnel Service, the Ministry of Justice, the National Bank of Kyrgyzstan and the Parliament's official website.

Rent extraction, and hence unearned income, occurred in two ways: shares in companies entitled owners to dividends, profit and capital gains; and companies extracted specific forms of rent (e.g. land rent, interest, fees and commissions) depending on the economic sector. Of the 71 parliamentarians, forty-one had business interests in two or more sectors. Most business politicians were involved in several forms of rent.

First, land rents comprise ground and housing rent and capital gains based on the ownership and control of land and real estate. Thirty parliamentarians possessed residential apartments, office buildings and land plots that were either rented or re-sold. Thirteen business politicians facilitated rentier activities through property development and housing construction.

Table 5.1 Parliamentarians' ownership and control of assets by economic sectors in 2015

Real estate and land—30	Construction—13	Hotels—2
Energy—5	Building materials—6	Restaurants and cafes—3
Minerals—1	Furniture—2	Tourism—4
Finance—6	Manufacturing and engineering—4	Sports—5
Private equity—12	Agriculture and fishing—8	Hospitals and education—2
Shopping malls and marketplaces—4	Air transport—3	Advertising and consultancy—2
Wholesale trade and commerce—16	Transport—3	Security—3
Entrepreneurs—4	Food and drinks—5	Others—4

Source Adapted from Tazabek Business News, 20 July 2015, available at http://www.tazabek.kg/news:732021/?embed&pack=one

Second,financial rents consist of interest, dividends and capital gains derived from financial assets. Six parliamentarians siphoned off interest and other charges based on the ownership and control of credit money through banks and microfinance institutions. For twelve politicians, profits and capital gains were obtained through private equity.

Third, natural resource rents involve extracting income based on naturally occurring resources. Six business politicians wholly or partly owned companies that had leasing rights to extract and/or distribute energy products and other minerals, including oil, gas, coal and gold. Controlling the fuel trade allowed some politicians to obtain local monopoly rent.

Fourth, natural monopoly rents occur when natural monopolies can charge excessive prices for their commodities because they are spatially free from competition (Christophers, 2019). Four parliamentarians collected rent based on their ownership of shopping malls and marketplaces. Two business politicians owned hotels, which enabled rent extraction based on a degree of spatial monopoly power. Owning and controlling the country's airports and airlines allowed three individuals to obtain economic rent. Sixteen politicians had interests in retail and wholesale trade, and through their ownership of retail chains and exclusive licences had a degree of monopoly power over specific goods.

Table 5.2 shows the nature and extent of Bishkek elected city councillors' main occupation by economic sectors in 2016. The data was formed using various open sources, including Akipress news agency. Of the 45 city councillors, all but five were company directors, most of whom operated in the private sector. Many of them also wholly or partly owned

Table 5.2 Bishkek city councillors' occupation by economic sectors in 2016

Construction—14	Media—1	Engineering—1
Engineering surveys—3	Pharmaceutical—1	Sports and charities—3
Legal services—3	Public utilities—3	Education—1
Finance—1	Food and drinks—1	Municipal company—1
Fuel and minerals—4	Wholesale trade—1	Unknown—2
Entrepreneurs—3	Transport—2	

Source Adapted from Akipress News, 26 December 2016, available at http://kg.akipress.org/news:1353644&f=cp

their companies, and had multiple business interests. The other councillors comprised one senior manager, one senior union official, one advisor, and two with unknown occupations.

Like the parliamentarians, most councillors engaged in different forms of rentierism. First, a significant minority of councillors' companies were an essential part of the rentier ecology. Fourteen councillors were directors and owners of construction companies, many of them involved in developing and managing real estate. As already discussed, apartments often served as an instrument for landowners to acquire wealth without doing creative work. While not rentiers themselves, the construction companies were intermediaries, actively assisting rentierism (Sayer, 2015).

Some councillors were beneficiaries of the rentierisation of the local economy. Three councillors were directors and owners of engineering surveying companies, which played an important role in designing, planning, and monitoring construction projects, including apartment complexes. Some companies benefitted from asset trading through value-skimming. Two councillors were directors and owners of law firms, and another was a legal advisor. As lawyers, they acted as intermediaries in the real estate market.

Second, another significant group of councillors' companies were rentier organisations. Five councillors owned and controlled a micro-finance institution, a gas company, two coal companies and a mining firm, thereby obtaining financial and natural resourcerents. One councillor was a director of a television broadcasting company, which extracted spectrumrents based on exclusive rights to use certain frequencies of electromagnetic energy for communication (Christophers, 2019).

Natural monopoly rents were significant for three councillors' companies, which had a degree of local monopoly power. One company had the ownership and control of the city's airport. Another firm possessed exclusive licences to a range of branded natural water and soft drinks. The third councillor's company operated a regional pharmacy chain.

A construction-dominated plutocratic mode of local government emerged in Bishkek. In 2018, Aziz Surakmatov was elected Mayor of Bishkek. He and his family owned several construction companies and considerable real estate (Sputnik, 2019). Of the fourteen councillors who owned construction companies, twelve of them were part of the coalition majority in the council, making up almost a half of the coalition (24.kg, 2020).

The construction-dominated coalition of councillors was an influential group, resulting in accusations of state and regulatory capture (24.kg, 2020). They sat on key strategic committees. Four of them were on the committee on municipal property, land issues, urban planning and architecture; four on budget and finance; three on housing and communal services, fuel and energy complex, transport, communications and investments; two on social issues; and one on local self-government and work with public organisations.

The construction-dominated coalition was responsible for pushing through regulations to confiscate private property for urban development and construction (24.kg, 2020). This was adopted without a full council discussion, because the coalition believed that it had already considered the matter. Some Bishkek residents and activists feared that Soviet-era apartment buildings, old houses and low-end retail stores in prime locations would be seized to build luxury apartments for the rich, resulting in social cleansing (24.kg, 2019).

Politicians' Wealth in Kazakhstan

Kazakhstan's political elites were often allied to business and rentiers interests, sometimes indirectly through family businesses. Using a range of open sources, the extent of politicians' business interests can be established among regional governors (*akims*) and candidates for the lower house of the bicameral parliament (Mazhilis deputies). Table 5.3 shows the nature and extent of the regional governors' family companies in 2019

Table 5.3 Regional governors' family companies by economic sectors in 2019

Construction—4	Media—1	Freight and transport—2
Real estate—2	Agriculture and food processing—5	Car rental and leasing equipment and machineries—2
Gas—2	Tourism—1	Geological exploration—1
Financial management—3	Fashion—2	Entrepreneur—1
Banking—1	Hairdressing—1	

Source Adapted from Baige News, 26 December 2019, available at https://baigenews.kz/news/dela_semeynye-_kto_est_kto_sredi_rodstvennikov_akimov_v_kazakhstane/

according to Baige News, an online news agency. Family companies were often managed by spouses, children and siblings. The table is based on a sample of twelve out of fourteen regions and three municipalities of Nur-Sultan, Almaty and Shymkent.

Although information on regional governors' wealth is difficult to access, the table offers a reasonable understanding of the range of economic sectors they operate in. Rentierism was significant for ten of the fifteen governors, arising from their family companies' involvement in residential and non-residential construction and property development, real estate rental and management, gas exploration, engineering and distribution, financial investment management, banking, car rental and leasing equipment and machineries. These companies were either rentier organisations, or facilitated others to extract income. Real estate properties, financial assets and natural resources were major instruments for acquiring wealth.

For three regional governors, agriculture, farming and food processing were significant source of family income. Another governor's family business was solely involved in freight and transport. In one case, it was not possible to identify the nature of a governor's business.

Business elites often seek to convert their wealth into political power, and have influence over state resources and capacities. They actively participate in national and local elections, standing as candidates for the national parliament and regional councils. Table 5.4 shows candidates' economic occupation by political party for the 2021 parliamentary elections according to Forbes Kazakhstan. It is based on a sample of 293 out of 312 candidates, who applied for 98 seats, on average about three candidates for each Mazhilis deputy.

Nur Otan is the dominant political party, linked to the ex-President Nursultan Nazarbayev and the current President Kassym-Jomart Tokayev. In the 2021 general election, it obtained over 71% of the total votes, and won 76 of the 98 seats. It had the most candidates standing in the general election. Many of its candidates were existing parliamentarians, councillors or senior members of the party. Many incumbent parliamentarians owned business companies involved in a range of economic sectors, including finance, real estate, natural resources, the media and agriculture (Inform Buro, 2017). Business owners and directors represented about 25% of the party's list of candidates. Professionals and senior state officials also constituted a large share of the party's list.

Table 5.4 Candidates' economic occupation by political party for the 2021 parliamentary elections

	Nur Otan	*People's Party of Kazakhstan*	*Ak Zhol*	*Adal*
Business owners and directors	31	13	21	3
Scientists, doctors, lecturers, teachers, artists	18	27	3	2
Journalists, publishers, broadcasters	3	6	1	2
Sports athletes	1	6	–	1
Senior state officials	16	12	–	–
Parliamentarians, councillors, political party members	42	23	7	3
Officials of trade associations	4	4	2	3
Officials of non-trade associations	8	15	1	1
Employees in the private sector	–	9	3	1
Others	3	–	–	–
Total	126	113	38	16

Source Adapted from Forbes Kazakhstan, 10 December 2020, available at https://forbes.kz/process/tri_cheloveka_na_mandat_kto_ballotiruetsya_v_majilismenyi_polnyiy_spisok_kandidatov/

People's Party of Kazakhstan was formerly called the Communist People's Party of Kazakhstan. Its share of the total votes in the general election was over 9%, obtaining 10 seats. Its list of candidates reflected a broader cross-section of society than any other party. It also had more non-trade association officials, employees in the private sector, sports athletes and professionals standing for public office. Its share of business owners and directors (about 12%) was the lowest of all the parties. Some party parliamentarians had business companies involved in lending, mineral extraction, advertising, the media and distribution of goods (Azattyq Ryhy, 2020a).

Ak Zhol is viewed as the pro-business party. Its share of the total votes was about 11%, winning 12 seats in the Mazhilis. Over 55% of its candidates were business owners and directors. Most of incumbent deputies had considerable business interests, including food processing, business consultancy, legal services, wholesale trade, leasing agricultural machineries, real estate, machine repairs and transport (Azattyq Ryhy, 2020b).

Adal is a small party, and largely represents middle class interests. It failed to win any seats in the general election. Its list of candidates consisted of business owners, academics, journalists and officials of trade associations.

Tables 5.3 and 5.4 show the nature and extent of plutocracy in Kazakhstan. While some politicians used their influence and connections to become rich, many were already affluent prior to holding public office. Once in office, most businesses were placed in trust or transferred to family members. Many of the plutocrats' companies belonged to the rentier ecology, either as rentier organisations or intermediaries. Some business owners and directors seeking to be elected were also engaged in rentierism, usually operating in key economic sectors, such as finance, real estate and natural resources.

The tables also suggest how Kazakhstan's legislative andstate structures were never neutral, but were constituted by social forces that favoured specific economic and political interests over others (Jessop, 2002). Rentier and business interests featured strongly in the country's state governance and political parties. While the state was a site of contestation of social forces, in which electoral and legislative struggles occurred over state goals and strategies, the outcomes invariably favoured rentier and capital interests over human flourishing. It was in this context that many disadvantaged and marginalised groups viewed the formal political institutions and processes as being unsympathetic to their interests and needs, and why some of them engaged in contentious forms of politics, as will be discussed in the third part of the book.

Criminogenic Environments in Public and Private Sectors

Crimes in the Bishkek Mayor's Office and the Construction Sector

Neoliberalism did not only promote rentierism and plutocracy, it also facilitated weak regulatory settlements, criminogenic environments and corruption (Hudson, 2015; Tombs & Whyte, 2009). Operating in the shadow of plutocracy, democracies tended to undermine states' regulatory powers, so that white-collar and corporate crimes became routine and endemic.

Information from a range of open sources, including newspapers and media platforms (e.g. Kloop, Sputnik, 24.kg, Azattyk and Kaktus Media) was gathered on Bishkek mayors' fraudulent and corrupt practices. Table 5.5 shows the wealth and political positions of the last nine Bishkek mayors, and corruption charges against them. It excludes Balbak Tulobayev, who was appointed as acting mayor after the October 2020 uprising.

Before occupying the mayoral position, all nine individuals possessed considerable wealth. According to the 2013 ranking of the top 100 richest people in Kyrgyzstan, three former mayors, Askarbek Salymbekov, Nariman Tuleyev and Isa Omurkulov, were in the top twenty, as was Daniar Usenov's then wife. It is common for close family members to hold assets as a way to conceal wealth.

Like the parliamentarians and Bishkek city councillors, the mayors engaged in rentier activities. Eight of them owned substantial assets in several economic sectors, obtaining two or more forms of rent. Eight mayors received land rents from real estate and land. Four extracted income based on financial assets. Four obtained rent based on wholly or partly owning shopping malls and marketplaces. Four mayors owned construction companies, partly creating improperty for the rich. Six were involved in wholesale and retail trade, extracting economic rent based on branded goods and control of distribution channels.

Most mayors amassed political capital to develop their political career. Three of them entered Parliament. Arguably, they hoped to enjoy parliamentary immunity, though Nariman Tuleyev was prosecuted for corruption after the 2010 political uprising. Three mayors became government ministers. Arstanbek Nogoev and Daniar Usenov were prosecuted for abuse of power, and they went into exile to escape custodial sentences, taking up political and corporate positions in Russia and Belarus.

Rather than viewing white-collar, state and corporate crimes as discrete and marginal phenomena, they are better understood as products of state capture by the rich and unequal social powers (Tombs, 2012). The Bishkek mayoral office developed a criminogenic culture, partly arising from its considerable power over privatising municipal land, granting planning permissions, and awarding council contracts. Of the past nine Bishkek mayors, seven were accused or charged with corruption, fraud or abuse of power.

The case of the second largest park Ataturk Park in central Bishkek was the most glaring example of abuse of office (Kloop, 2019a). While the

Table 5.5 Bishkek mayors' wealth, political positions and corruption charges

Mayors of Bishkek	*Major assets by economic sectors*	*Key political positions*	*Corruption charges*
Medetbek Kerimkulov, August 1999–March 2005	Real estate and land	First Deputy Prime Minister	Accused of illegal privatisation of municipal land; never charged
Askarbek Salymbekov, April–August 2005	Retail and wholesale marketplaces, shopping malls, real estate, retail trade, construction and insurance	Parliamentarian	Unknown
Arstanbek Nogoev, August 2005–November 2007	Finance, wholesale and retail trade, catering and agri-business	Minister of Agriculture; First Deputy Prime Minister, Penza Region, Russia; Vice-Mayor of Kashira, Russia	Convicted in absentia of corruption, state embezzlement and illegal privatisation of state property and municipal land
Daniar Usenov, November 2007–July 2008	Banking, agri-business, tourism, chemicals, furniture, real estate, private equity, advertising and security	Parliamentarian; Prime Minister; Director of the Belarusian National Biotechnology Corporation, Belarus	Convicted in absentia of corruption, state embezzlement, illegal privatisation of municipal land, and complicity in murder and attempted murder; property confiscated
Nariman Tuleyev, July 2008–April 2010	Banking, real estate, shopping malls, retail, construction, telecommunications and tourism	Parliamentarian	Convicted of corruption, money laundering and illegal privatisation of municipal land; imprisoned and property confiscated
Isa Omurkulov, April 2010–December 2013	Shopping malls, real estate, catering, retail and livestock	Parliamentarian; Assistant Vice President, First Vice Prime Minister	Acquitted of illegal privatisation of municipal land

(continued)

Table 5.5 (continued)

Mayors of Bishkek	*Major assets by economic sectors*	*Key political positions*	*Corruption charges*
Kubanychbek Kulmatov, January 2014–February 2016	Real estate, land, construction, hotels, engineering surveys, wholesale trade, tourism, restaurants and salons	Advisor to the President	Convicted of corruption and state embezzlement; fined
Albek Ibraimov, February 2016–July 2018	Real estate, land, banking, farms, agriculture and trade	Deputy Head of the Office of the President	Convicted of corruption, state embezzlement and illegal privatisation of state property; imprisoned and property confiscated
Aziz Surakmatov, August 2018–October 2020	Construction, real estate, real estate agency, law firm, furniture, home improvements, wholesale trade, food production, business consultancy, shopping malls and security	Parliamentarian	Accused of building without planning permissions and land lease agreements, poor quality, financial irregularities and conflict of interests

Source Adapted from Stan Radar, 27 August 2016, available at https://stanradar.com/news/full/21936-10-eks-merov-bishkeka-kakim-biznesom-vladejut-byvshie-gradonachalniki.html

country's land code allows for small parcels of unused public land to be granted to needy and vulnerable individuals, over a hundred land plots of prime land were privatised and distributed to wealthy and influential citizens between 2000 and 2010 (Kloop, 2019b). Moreover, in 2002 the state declared that Ataturk Park was a historical site, and this was supposed to stop any construction of private housing in the park.

Nevertheless land plots were secretly distributed to the rich and powerful in violation of multiple laws and regulations. Most of the owners sold their newly acquired land to make a quick profit, thereby obtaining unearned income. Four mayors were involved in the Ataturk Park scandal. Although three of them were arrested and sentenced for corruption and abuse of office, only one was convicted for violations relating to Ataturk Park.

In 2000, Mayor Kerimkulov started to give away land plots in Ataturk Park, mostly to political and social elites. More than eighty plots were privatised, though he was never charged (Kloop, 2019b). In 2005, Mayor Nogoev gave away two plots of land, one to a business person. Later as Minister of Agriculture, he attempted to illegally sell the national hippodrome. In 2014, he was charged for this, but he fled the country before the trial. He was convicted in absentia for corruption and embezzlement.

Between 2007–2008, Mayor Usenov illegally allocated eleven hectares of parkland to affluent individuals for the construction of private apartments (Kloop, 2019b). Later as Prime Minister, he was embroiled in state embezzlement that eventually led to the overthrow of the government in 2010. He fled the country, and was convicted in absentia for misappropriating Ataturk Park, and for the complicity in murder, attempted murder and abuse of office during the 2010 uprising.

Mayor Tuleyev was the last person to misappropriate Ataturk Park that his predecessors began. He privatised and distributed twenty-one land plots, including land for a hotel construction (Kloop, 2019c). After 2010, he entered Parliament. But in 2012, he was arrested for fraud committed during his mayoral tenure. The charges were unrelated to Ataturk Park. He was sentenced for eleven years.

Land plots in other parks in Bishkek were also illegally granted to elites. According to a parliamentary commission, wealthy and powerful individuals unlawfully acquired over a half of Karagacheva Roshcha, the biggest park in Bishkek, which is also a historical and cultural monument (Kloop, 2019c).

Other mayors were also accused of misappropriation and embezzlement (Sputnik, 2018). Mayor Omurkulov was prosecuted for redrawing the borders of Victory Park in central Bishkek to accommodate the existence of illegal constructions, and allowing new buildings in the park. He resigned as mayor, and was acquitted in 2014. After leaving his mayoral office, Kulmatov was accused of embezzling the state that involved redirecting 2 million USD in Chinese grants. He was convicted and fined. While in office, Mayor Ibraimov was charged with embezzlement and illegal allocation of municipal land. He was convicted and imprisoned.

Corruption prosecutions in Kyrgyzstan are often politicised (Aidar, 2018; The Diplomat, 2018). Specific individuals are targeted because of political expediency, rather than the pursuit of justice. For example, Daniar Usenov was prosecuted because as Prime Minister, he was very close to President Bakiev, and was partly responsible for deploying armed forces to squash protests during the 2010 revolt. The arrests of Kubanychbek Kulmatov and Albek Ibraimov were part of an acrimonious rift between the ex-President Atambaev and the incumbent President Jeenbekov.

Regulatory capture by business elites can restrict local authorities' attempts to regulate and monitor risk-taking and profit-making (Shaxson & Christensen, 2013). Regulation is often negatively framed as a 'burden on business' (Snider, 2009). The justifications for minimising regulation include the ease of doing business, economic growth and employment and state corruption.

With the support of International Finance Corporation, Kyrgyzstan almost halved its business inspections from 21,000 in 2011 to 13,500 in 2012 (International Finance Corporation, 2013). At the time, the Minister of Economy, Temir Sariev who was one of the top twenty richest individuals in Kyrgyzstan, remarked, 'We can see the positive impact. In 2012, the number of inspections decreased by 45%. Fewer inspections mean less corruption, which helps create a better environment for business' (International Finance Corporation, 2013). More than seventy-two types of licenses were abolished, and the number of civil servants was reduced by 15% (Transparency International, 2013).

State and regulatory bodies introduced a number of reforms to ease doing business in the country. To ease the process of getting construction permits, a risk-based system of approval and building control was introduced, low-risk projects were allowed to conduct an internal building control process, and obtaining utility connections were simplified (World Bank, 2014). Surveying and notarisation requirements were made optional for property registration. The tax burden on businesses was eased by reducing the rates for several taxes. Requirements relating to redundancy dismissals and worker reassignment were relaxed.

The construction sector in Kyrgyzstan possessed considerable economic and political power to press for minimal regulation and enforcement, and flout existing rules and norms (see also Tombs & Whyte, 2020). It has been a significant part of the economy, contributing to 9.7% of the gross domestic product in 2019 (Cabar, 2020). It has had close relationships with central and local government, as Tables 5.1, 5.2 and 5.5 showed. In addition to strong vested interests, the neoliberal idea of a 'free market' justified minimum state 'interference' in the sector.

According to the World Bank's *Doing Business* reports, Kyrgyzstan reduced the procedures, time and cost of dealing with construction permits. Using an illustrative case of building a warehouse, the time to deal with construction permits declined from 332 days in 2008 to 155 days in 2015, and the number of procedures dropped from twenty-two to ten over the same period (World Bank, 2009, 2014). Kyrgyzstan's score for ease of dealing with construction permits was higher than the European and Central Asian regional average score.

But deregulation and de-supervision created a criminogenic and harmful environment in the construction sector (Tombs & Whyte, 2009). The sector was criticised for violating building codes and general legislation, mis-selling to customers, bribery, corruption, illegal labour practices and environmental damage (Tazabek, 2019). In 2014, there were 235 known cases of illegal construction projects in the capital, though this was a conservative figure collated by the Bishkek Mayor's Office (Eurasianet, 2014).

One such illegal project was an apartment complex in central Bishkek (Azattyk, 2014). Its construction began despite protests from local residents. The construction company was fined a paltry sum of 160 USD for destroying green space for the building. The state inspection agency ordered the company to stop construction. But the company owner, who was an influential person, refused, and continued building.

The construction sector has been a dangerous place of work, and many fatal injuries have occurred (Akipress, 2016). In the first nine months of 2016, there were 94 incidents at construction sites in Kyrgyzstan that resulted in 48 deaths and 68 serious injuries. Due to pro-business reforms, the State Inspection for Environmental and Technical Safety lacked resources to monitor and prosecute occupational health and safety violations and incidents. Since 2012, the number of full-time labour inspectors fell from 62 to 23 (Solidarity Center, 2019).

Official statistics on occupational health and safety violations and incidents tend to under-report the nature and extent of violations and incidents, because informal sector workplaces are excluded from official statistics. Over 70% of workers are informal, leaving them with inadequate trade union and labour law protection (Equal Times, 2017).

Crimes in the Almaty Mayor's Office and the Housing Sector

Similar to the Bishkek Mayor's Office, rentierism in the real estate sector created a criminogenic environment in the Almaty Mayor's Office. The scale of public corruption was larger in Almaty than in Bishkek, because the former had more opportunities for rent extraction. The city was the financial and business centre of Kazakhstan, and land and property prices were very expensive.

Between 2004 and 2008, a state-owned company Almatyjer seemingly acted on behalf of the Almaty City Council to seize land plots under eminent domain. The legal basis for its actions was the power of attorney from Mayor Imangali Tasmagambetov, who issued the document. But Mayor Tasmagambetov acted alone without the authority and support of the city council. This violated the Land Code, which required that the city council to collectively decide and authorise the confiscation of property (Kazakhstan Today, 2008). Hundreds of illegal forced evictions occurred, as Almatyjer confiscated real estate and land properties without the council's approval. By 2006, Almatyjer seized 810 buildings in the city.

Mayor Tasmagambetov abused his public office in directing Almatyjer to confiscate and sell properties to private developers and construction companies. Sergei Utkin, an Almaty-based lawyer, remarked, 'Tasmagambetov made all the decisions on confiscations unilaterally, and this is a serious crime. Almatyjer had no legal powers to confiscate land' (Kn.kz, 2008).

Mayor Tasmagambetov and Almatyjer acted in the interests of private developers and construction companies, which underpaid for lucrative assets. Utkin explained that the criminogenic nature of the confiscations advanced business interests over social needs (Kn.kz, 2008):

> The most important violation is that the land was seized not for state needs but for private construction companies. We saw contracts that [Tasmagambetov] signed with private construction companies. He entered into a contractual relationship with them. The contract states that the mayor will confiscate land plots from citizens under the guise of state needs, and then will transfer them to private companies so that they could make money.

Utkin found that the pretext of eminent domain was illegally used to transfer land to wealthy and powerful rentier groups. At the trial of Almatyinveststroi, one of the construction companies which acquired a land plot, its director Dmitrienko said, 'Do you have any idea how much I had to give [as a bribe] to get this land?' (Kn.kz, 2008). The suggestion was that the mayor and senior Almatyjer officials were paid bribes to sell lucrative properties to private companies. Mayor Tasmagambetov was never prosecuted for abuse of office. Instead, he was transferred to Nur-Sultan, where he became the city mayor.

Rentierism in Kazakhstan's housing sector also created a criminogenic environment. The nature and size of corruption and fraud in the sector became apparent after the 2008 financial crisis when the speculative property bubble burst. For instance, in Nur-Sultan a construction company Azbuka Jil'ya, owned by Yerkanat Taijanov, a former parliamentarian, failed to build eight housing complexes in 2008. Taijanov deceived about 2100 shareholders (*dol'shiki*), who had made monthly payments to own apartments under construction. He absconded the country with more than 40 billion Kazakh tenge (over 100 million USD). He currently lives in Austria pending extradition. In another case, Amangeldy Ermegiyaev, who at one time was the deputy chairperson of the ruling Nur Otan political party, established several construction companies, such as Almaty Kurylys and Sert. In 2009, his companies failed to build apartment complexes, cheating about 800 shareholders, who paid for unfinished apartments (Today, 2009).

Conclusion

The chapter examined how rentierism in real estate development involved improperty, morality, plutocracy, criminogency and other harms. Neoliberalism created and promoted rentiership in the real estate sector, in which property developers and rich owners viewed residential, retail and industrial holdings as instruments for acquiring wealth rather than to aid productive work; i.e. improperty (Tawney, 1921). The property developers construed and justified unearned income as part of the neoliberal 'free market' ideology (Hudson, 2018). They elided vital moral economic distinctions between wealth creation and rent extraction, and true and fictitious commodities. Wealthy rentiers were often seen as engaging in the cultural norm of making money, the common practice of buying and selling commodities, and conforming to the law.

Rentierism contributed to the emergence of plutocratic structures at all levels of the state. States were sites of contestation of social forces, in which the rentier class competed for access to state power and resources (Jessop, 2002). The rich dominated politics, and captured the state through elected office. Many elected politicians were part of the rentier ecology as a result of their family businesses operating as rentier organisations, or as beneficiaries or intermediaries of the rentierisation of the economy. In Kyrgyzstan, a construction-dominated plutocratic mode of local government emerged in Bishkek. Most of regional governors in Kazakhstan had rentier and business interests.

Central Asian states played a critical role in deregulating and facilitating property and rent relations. The pro-business regulatory regimes helped to create and sustain criminogenic environments in private and public sectors (Tombs & Whyte, 2009). The neoliberal ideology justified the reduction in state licenses, inspections and personnel. The construction sector became de facto decriminalised, allowing illegal practices to occur largely undetected and unpunished. The rentier class sometimes engaged in violent and criminal struggles to own and control lucrative assets. Corruption by plutocrats was routine and widespread. For instance, several wealthy Bishkek mayors had illegally privatised and distributed scarce municipal land that enabled new owners to extract significant rent.

Rentierism and criminogenic environments produced a wide range of harms (Sayer, 2015; Tombs, 2012). Our study on property development described the loss of green space as a result of illegal property development; fatal injuries at construction sites due to lack of safety regulations; accidental or deliberate fires in marketplaces that endangered lives and ruined businesses; bitter and angry manufacturers who paid excessive rent for dilapidated buildings; and entrapped market traders who took out loans to pay high rent. Corruption, illegal practices and harms were outcomes of emasculated regulatory regimes, which were largely shaped by the wealthy propertied class to favour their interests, and so it was difficult to bring the rich and powerful to justice.

In the context of unequal power relations and lack of alternatives, opposition and resistance against high rent were difficult to organise. Invariably, state officials, property developers and tenants defended, accepted and depoliticised rentierism as how things were and deserved to be. Nevertheless grassroots movements did emerge in response to the harms produced by the neoliberal marketisation of post-Soviet economies, as will be discussed in the third part of the book.

References

24.kg. (2019, October 15). *Building by the rules, or attempting to seize property*. https://24.kg/obschestvo/132225_stroitelstvo_ponbsppravilam_ili_popyitka_izyyat_sobstvennost_/.

24.kg. (2020, February 12). *The building lobby of the Bishkek City Council in the faces. They took the RAP*. https://24.kg/obschestvo/143277_stroitelnoe_lobbi_bishkekskogo_gorkenesha_vlitsah_oni_prinimali_pdp/.

Aalbers, M. (2008). The financialization of home and the mortgage market crisis. *Competition and Change, 12*(2), 148–166.

Aidar, S. (2018, October 22). What we know about alleged elite corruption under former Kyrgyz President Almazbek Atambayev. *openDemocracy*.

Akipress. (2016). *94 construction incidents including 46 deaths recorded in Kyrgyzstan in 9 months—State Technical Safety Inspection*. https://akipress.com/news:585654/.

Andreucci, D., García-Lamarca, M., Wedekind, J., & Swyngedouw, E. (2017). 'Value grabbing': A political ecology of rent. *Capitalism Nature Socialism, 28*(3), 28–47.

Andrusz, G. (1990a). A note on the financing of housing in the Soviet Union. *Soviet Studies, 42*(3), 555–570.

Andrusz, G. (1990b). Housing policy in the Soviet Union. In J. A. A. Sillince (Ed.), *Housing policies in Eastern Europe and the Soviet Union* (pp. 288–329). Routledge.

Auyezkhanuly, A., Manap, A., Akpanov, A., & Karshalova, A. (2019). The study of the residential real estate market in the Republic of Kazakhstan. *Journal of Real Estate Literature, 27*(1), 117–133.

Azattyk. (2014, August 28). *Bishkek. 13 floors of lawlessness*. https://rus.azattyk.org/a/26554594.html.

Azattyq Ryhy. (2020a, December 2). *What kind of business do the communists own?* https://rus.azattyq-ruhy.kz/politics/5350-kakim-biznesom-vladeiut-kommunisty.

Azattyq Ryhy. (2020b, February 6). *What kind of business do the defenders of businessmen—MPs from the Ak Zhol party own?* https://rus.azattyq-ruhy.kz/politics/5098-kakim-biznesom-vladeiut-zashchitniki-biznesmenov-deputaty-ot-partii-ak-zhol.

Bourdieu, P. (2000). *Pascalian meditations*. Polity.

Braguinsky, S. (2009). Postcommunist oligarchs in Russia: Quantitative analysis. *Journal of Law and Economics, 52*(2), 307–350.

Cabar. (2020, May 14). *Some residential construction projects may fail due to COVID-19 in Kyrgyzstan*. https://cabar.asia/en/some-residential-construction-projects-may-fail-due-to-covid-19-in-kyrgyzstan/.

Central Asia and Caspian Intelligence. (2008, February 25). *The Salymbekov Clan and the Dordoy Bazaar*. No. 28. https://wikileaks.org/gifiles/attach/177/177775_CACIA27.pdf. Accessed July 2020.

Central Asian News Service. (2016, February 12). *Commercial banks to quit from mortgage, consumer lending markets over National Bank's restrictions—Expert*. https://akipress.com/news:572629:Commercial_banks_to_quit_from_mort

gage,_consumer_lending_markets_over_National_Bank_s_restrictions_-_expert/.

Central Asian News Service. (2017, March 2). *Nearly 25,000 teachers in Kyrgyzstan need housing—State mortgage company*. https://24.kg/english/46362_25000_teachers_in_Kyrgyzstan_badly_need_housing/.

Christophers, B. (2019). The rentierization of the United Kingdom economy. *Environment and Planning A: Economy and Space*. https://doi.org/10.1177/0308518X19873007.

Cooley, A., & Heathershaw, J. (2017). *Dictators without borders: Power and money in Central Asia*. Yale University Press.

Equal Times. (2017, October 12). *Kyrgyz trade unions vow to protect labour rights ahead of Sunday's elections*. https://www.equaltimes.org/kyrgyz-trade-unions-vow-to-protect?lang=en#.X0AUri2ZPBI.

Eurasianet. (2014, July 22). *Kyrgyzstan: After the revolution came the cranes*. https://eurasianet.org/kyrgyzstan-after-the-revolution-came-the-cranes.

Gentile, M., & Sjoberg, O. (2013). Housing allocation under socialism: The Soviet case revisited. *Post-Soviet Affairs, 29*(2), 173–195.

Gentile, M., & Tammaru, T. (2006). Housing and ethnicity in the post-Soviet city: Ust'-Kamenogorsk, Kazakhstan. *Urban Studies, 43*(10), 1757–1778.

Hatcher, C. (2015a). Illegal geographies of the state: The legalisation of a 'squatter' settlement in Bishkek, Kyrgyzstan. *International Journal of Law in Built Environment, 7*(1), 39–54.

Hatcher, C. (2015b). Globalising homeownership: Housing privatisation schemes and the private rental sector in post-socialist Bishkek Kyrgyzstan. *International Development Planning Review, 37*(4), 467–486.

Hatcher, C. (2017). Making property in Kyrgyzstan: Bishkek's urban periphery as redistributive space. *Central Asian Affairs, 4*(2), 173–196.

Hudson, M. (2014). *The bubble and beyond* (New). ISLET.

Hudson, M. (2015). *Killing the host: How financial parasites and debt bondage destroy the global economy*. CounterPunch Books.

Hudson, M. (2017). *J is for junk economics: A guide to reality in an age of deception*. ISLET.

Hudson, M. (2018). *. . . and forgive them their debts: Lending, Foreclosures and redemption from bronze age finance to the jubilee year*. ISLET.

Inform Buro. (2017, January 22). *One seat in two chairs: When parliamentary business is not an obstacle to lawmaking*. https://old.informburo.kz/stati/odnim-mestom-na-dvuh-kreslah-kogda-deputatskiy-biznes-zakonotvorchestvu-ne-pomeha.html.

International Crisis Group. (2005). *Kyrgyzstan: A faltering state* (Asia Report No. 109). https://www.crisisgroup.org/europe-central-asia/central-asia/kyrgyzstan/kyrgyzstan-faltering-state.

International Finance Corporation. (2013). *In the Kyrgyz Republic: Cutting red tape*. https://www.ifc.org/wps/wcm/connect/news_ext_content/ifc_external_corporate_site/news+and+events/news/kyrgyz+icpackage.

Jessop, B. (2002). *The future of the capitalist state*. Polity.

Karrar, H. (2020). The bazaar in ruins: Rent and fire in Barakholka Almaty. *Central Asian Survey, 39*(1), 80–94.

Kazakhstan Today. (2008, November 24). *Proceeds from illegal monopoly activities of 'Almatyzher' should be collected into the city budget—Human rights activist*. https://www.kt.kz/rus/economy/dohodi_ot_nezakonnoj_monopoljnoj_dejateljnosti_almatizher_sleduet_vziskatj_v_bjudzhet_goroda_pravozashtitnik_1153469649.html.

Kloop (2019a, October 23). *The park that was lost*. https://www.occrp.org/en/public-land-private-hands/the-park-that-was-lost. Accessed July 2020.

Kloop. (2019b, October 23). *The officials who gave it away*. https://www.occrp.org/en/public-land-private-hands/the-officials-who-gave-It-away. Accessed July 2020.

Kloop. (2019c). *How mayors of Bishkek and officials distributed land in Ataturk Park*. https://kloop.kg/t/park-ataturk/kak-chinovniki-razdavali-zemelnyye-uchastki-v-parke-atatyurk/ Accessed July 2020.

Kn.kz. (2008, April 8). *Interview of lawyer Sergei Utkin to the agency Kazakhstan Today*. https://www.kn.kz/article/1201/.

Maggs, P. (1961). The security of individually-owned property under Soviet law. *Duke Law Journal, 1961*(4), 525–537.

Marcuse, P. (1996). Privatization and its discontents: Property rights in land and housing in the transition in Eastern Europe. In G. Andrusz, M. Harloe, & I. Szelenyi (Eds.), *Cities after socialism: Urban and regional change and conflict in post-socialist societies* (pp. 119–191). Blackwell.

McGlinchey, E. (2011). *Chaos, violence, dynasty: politics and Islam in Central Asia*. University of Pittsburgh Press.

Mihalyi, P., & Szelenyi, I. (2017). The role of rents in the transition from socialist redistributive economies to market capitalism. *Comparative Sociology, 16*(1), 13–38.

Morton, H. (1980). Who gets what, when and how? Housing in the Soviet Union. *Soviet Studies, 32*(2), 235–259.

Osenov, S. (2011). Real estate and construction: Market analysis in Bishkek and Kyrgyzstan. *Aki Press*. http://parfenon39.ru/novosti/novosti-20/novost-71.

Parenti, C. (2015). The environment making state: Territory, nature and value. *Antipode, 47*(4), 829–848.

Polanyi, K. (1944). *The great transformation: Economic and political origins of our time*. Rinehart.

Rothe, D., & Kauzlarich, D. (2016). *Crimes of the powerful: An introduction*. Routledge.

Sanghera, B., Satybaldieva, E., Rodionov, A., Serikzhanova, S., Choibekov, N., & Sultanmuratova, K. (2012). *Illegal settlements and city registration in Kyrgyzstan and Kazakhstan: Implications for legal empowerment*. Open Society Foundations.

Satybaldieva, E. (2011). *The nature of local politics in rural Kyrgyzstan: A study of social inequalities, everyday politics and neoliberalism*. Unpublished PhD Thesis, School of Politics and International Relations, University of Kent.

Sayer, A. (2015). *Why we can't afford the rich*. Policy Press.

Sayer, A. (2016). Moral economy, unearned income and legalized corruption. In D. Whyte & J. Wiegratz (Eds.), *Neoliberalism and the moral economy of fraud* (pp. 44–56). Routledge.

Schneiderman, D. (2000). Investment rules and the new constitutionalism. *Law and Social Inquiry, 25*(3), 757–787.

Sharipova, D. (2015). Who gets what, when and how? Housing and informal institutions in the Soviet Union and post-Soviet Kazakhstan. *Central Asian Affairs, 2*(2), 140–167.

Shaxson, N., & Christensen, J. (2013). *The finance curse: How oversized financial sectors attack democracy and corrupt economies*. Tax Justice Network. http://www.taxjustice.net/cms/upload/pdf/Finance_Curse_Final.pdf. Accessed July 2020.

Snider, L. (2009). Accommodating power: The 'common sense' of regulators. *Social & Legal Studies, 18*(2), 179–197.

Solidarity Center. (2019, March 8). *Kyrgyz unions find unreported worker death and injuries*. https://www.solidaritycenter.org/kyrgyz-unions-find-unreported-worker-deaths-and-injuries/.

Spector, R. (2006). *Who governs the marketplace? The politics of bazaars in Kyrgyzstan*. Institute of Public Policy.

Spector, R. (2008). Bazaar politics: The fate of marketplaces in Kazakhstan. *Problems of Post-Communism, 55*(6), 42–53.

Spector, R., & Botoeva, A. (2017). New shop owners in old buildings: Spatial buildings of the apparel industry in Kyrgyzstan. *Post-Soviet Affairs, 33*(3), 235–253.

Sputnik. (2018, August 8). *How not to turn from a mayor into a prisoner—Learning from the mistakes of ex-mayors*. https://ru.sputnik.kg/politics/20180808/1040543325/bishkek-mehr-ugolovnoe-delo.html.

Sputnik. (2019, November 21). *Surakmatov has 11 apartments, one of 318 square meters*. https://ru.sputnik.kg/politics/20191121/1046305365/kyrgyzstan-surakmatov-11-kvartir.html.

Standing, G. (2016). *The corruption of capitalism: Why Rentiers thrive and work does not pay*. Biteback Publishing.

Szelenyi, I. (1987). Housing inequalities and occupational segregation in state socialist cities: Commentary to the special issue of IJURR on east European cities. *International Journal of Urban and Regional Research, 11*(1), 1–8.

Tawney, R. H. (1921). *The acquisitive society*. G. Bell and Sons.

Tazabek. (2019, June 3). *Blacklist of construction companies: Who are they?* http://www.tazabek.kg/news:1549840.

The Diplomat. (2018, August 9). *Unopposed but protested: Bishkek gets a new mayor*. https://thediplomat.com/2018/08/unopposed-but-protested-bishkek-gets-a-new-mayor/.

The Times of Central Asia. (2016, January 16). *State mortgage company starts operating in Kyrgyzstan*. https://www.timesca.com/index.php/news/16215-state-mortgage-company-starts-operating-in-kyrgyzstan.

The Times of Central Asia. (2017, February 27). *'Affordable housing' unaffordable for most public sector employees in Kyrgyzstan*. https://www.timesca.com/index.php/news/17730-affordable-housing-unaffordable-for-most-public-sector-employees-in-kyrgyzstan.

Today. (2009, July 7). *Shareholders ask the president for help*. http://today.kz/news/kazahstan/2009-07-07/15961-sert/.

Tombs, S. (2012). State-corporate symbiosis in the production of crime and harm. *State Crime Journal, 1*(2), 170–195.

Tombs, S., & Whyte, D. (2009). State and corporate crimes. In R. Coleman, J. Sim, S. Tombs, & D. Whyte (Eds.), *State, power, crime* (pp. 103–115). Sage.

Tombs, S., & Whyte, D. (2020). The shifting imaginaries of corporate crime. *Journal of White Collar and Corporate Crime, 1*(1), 16–23.

Transparency International. (2013, January 9). *Overview of corruption and anti-corruption in Kyrgyzstan*. Number 363. https://www.transparency.org/files/content/corruptionqas/363_Overview_of_Corruption_in_Kyrgyzstan.pdf.

Tsenkova, S. (2014). The housing policy nexus and people's responses to housing challenges in post-communist cities. *Urbani Izziv, 25*(2), 90–106.

Wiegratz, J. (2016). *Neoliberal moral economy: Capitalism, socio-cultural change and fraud in Uganda*. Rowman and Littlefield.

World Bank. (2009). *Doing business 2010: Kyrgyz Republic*. The World Bank.

World Bank. (2014). *Doing business 2015: Kyrgyz Republic*. The World Bank.

Zavisca, J. (2008). Property without markets: Housing policy and politics in post-Soviet Russia, 1992–2007. *Comparative European Politics, 6*(3), 365–386.

CHAPTER 6

Natural Resources: Transnational Capital, Constitutionalism and Environmental Harms

This chapter examines how neoliberal reforms served to secure foreign investors' rights to valuable natural resources in Kazakhstan and Kyrgyzstan. Legal and judicial mechanisms of governance emerged to extend, deepen and lock in private property rights, enabling transnational corporations to extract resources and rent with confidence and certainty (Gill, 2008; Schneiderman, 2008). In conferring privileged rights and representation to investors, national economies became increasingly insulated from democratic rule and popular accountability. The process of instituting legal and judicial mechanisms to discipline states to market forces and values is referred to as 'new constitutionalism' (Gill, 2008).

The constitutional aspects of the economy did not merely promote the power and freedom of capital, they often prevented future governments from withdrawing or undoing commitments to the neoliberal regime of capital accumulation. In so doing, legal and judicial mechanisms tended to freeze existing distributions of wealth, and privilege the status quo (Schneiderman, 2008). The rule of law provided a moral underpinning to justify and normalise investors' wealth and power. It claimed that all are equal before the law, the state cannot infringe individual rights and freedoms, and the domain of private property must be protected from majoritarian politics (Gill, 2002).

International investment rules and procedures (such as multilateral investment agreements and bilateral investment treaties) are powerful

B. Sanghera and E. Satybaldieva, *Rentier Capitalism and Its Discontents*,
https://doi.org/10.1007/978-3-030-76303-9_6

mechanisms that have quasi-constitutional status (Schneiderman, 2008). They discipline host states to transnational capital, creating a stable and favourable investment climate, in which private property rights and profit flows are protected and guaranteed. The neoliberal investment rules regime binds governments to agreements signed with transnational corporations, thereby ensuring the rule of law and the sanctity of contracts. If agreements are violated, investors feel justified to take host states to international arbitration for damages.

According to international financial institutions, investment treaties can address the problem of lack of effective governance structures in the Global South, which is characterised in terms of a weak rule of law, corruption, poor transparency and political instability (Appel, 2019). Investment rules perform a signalling function to the investment community that domestic economic policy favours global capital, and that transnational corporations will receive a 'fair and equitable' treatment (Schneiderman, 2000). The global growth of bilateral investment treaties has been phenomenal. There are over 2850 bilateral investment treaties, most of which were signed during the 1990s and early 2000s (Transnational Institute, 2017).

But foreign investors' privileged status is problematic for three reasons. First, it can limit democratic decision-making and can produce a concentration of wealth and power in society (Gill, 2008). Adam Smith (1776: Book 5, Chapter 1, Part 2) notes that 'civil government, in so far as it is instituted for the security of property, is in reality instituted for the defence of the rich against the poor, or of those who have some property against those who have none at all.'

Second, private corporations operating in the natural resource sector can plunder the earth at ever-greater speed, contributing to global warming, pollution and environmental destruction (Sayer, 2015). Third, as natural resources already exist, investors receive income based on power and privilege, that is privatising scarce resources that nature has endowed society as a common inheritance. They do not create something useful from scratch, which usually justifies property, but profit from free gifts of nature. As Tawney (1921: 80) notes, 'Property is not theft, but a good deal of theft becomes property.'[1]

[1] In Russian, privatisation is sarcastically referred to as 'prihvatizatsiya' (grabification).

The chapter is divided into five sections. The first section briefly discusses the development of production agreements and investment treaties in Central Asia. Section 'Investment Disputes in Central Asia' investigates the nature of investor-state disputes in Central Asia, and how international tribunals adjudicated them. The third section examines two case studies of major foreign investments in oil fields in Kazakhstan. Section 'Foreign Investors' Dominance in Kyrgyzstan's Gold Mining Sector' analyses a case study of a prominent foreign gold mine in Kyrgyzstan. Finally, the conclusion summarises the chapter's key findings.

Production Agreements and Investment Treaties in Central Asia

When the Soviet Union collapsed, Central Asian economies with abundant natural resources lacked the technical expertise to efficiently exploit them (Pomfret, 2011). While existing oil and gas fields and mineral deposits continued to be extracted and exported with limited foreign involvement, new sites required partnership with transnational corporations with the state-of-the-art technology. Central Asian states negotiated production-sharing agreements (PSAs) with foreign investors to attract capital and expertise for energy and mineral exploitation.

PSAs emerged as a popular form of energy and mineral contracts in Central Asia and other resource-rich regions (Appel, 2019; International Institute for Environment and Development, 2012). Although their popularity has diminished, major oil and gas fields and mines are still developed under such arrangements. Whereas traditional colonial-era concession agreements relinquished national sovereignty over resources to foreign companies, PSAs are designed to share the extracted resources between the parties, and leave the title to unextracted resources with host states. Contracts are often signed for 25–30 years, though some can be longer.

Typically, PSAs grant transnational companies rights to explore, develop and extract resources. Foreign investors retrieve most of the initial capital expenditure and ongoing maintenance costs before revenue is shared in agreed proportions (Pomfret, 2011). Profits, taxes, bonuses and royalties are calculated on the basis of production, and they change over the duration of the contract. Companies often bear the high costs and risks of exploring and developing fields and mines. Contractual disputes are subject to international treaties and arbitration tribunals, so that host states cede some sovereign immunity.

Central Asian states' contracts with major Western companies occurred in the context of neoliberal globalisation. A series of bilateral, regional and multilateral agreements promoted and protected foreign direct investment that generated an interlocking web of rules and rule-enforcing structures that significantly limited state action (Schneiderman, 2008). Under the guidance of the International Monetary Fund, the World Bank, the World Trade Organisation and other neoliberal institutions, new constitutional rules were enacted to separate politics from economics, and maximise the power of global capital (Gill, 2008).

Since independence, Kazakhstan and Kyrgyzstan have pursued a stronger neoliberalising agenda than their neighbours. They have 51 and 37 bilateral investment treaties respectively, and have 12 and 9 treaties with investment provisions, including the Energy Charter Treaty, respectively (UNCTAD, 2020a). For two decades after independence, other Central Asian countries had limited foreign involvement (Pomfret, 2011). Nevertheless Uzbekistan, Turkmenistan and Tajikistan have 55, 28 and 39 bilateral investment treaties respectively, and have 5, 7 and 7 treaties with investment provisions respectively.

Bilateral investment treaties include provisions for the admission and promotion of conditions favourable to foreign investment, protection from expropriation and nationalisation, and mechanisms for settling or adjudicating disputes. Investment treaties are seen to be necessary because Central Asian states have serious problems with the rule of law, control of corruption and transparency (Muminov, 2019). Without international legal and judicial safeguards, public corruption and rent-seeking can motivate arbitrary and inconsistent applications of national laws.

Model investment treaties and production agreements were authored by capital-exporting states and transnational corporations, and were signed by transition and developing countries in conditions of unequal bargaining power (Appel, 2019; Schneiderman, 2014). In the first decade after independence, energy and mineral corporations were stronger relative to Central Asian states' position, resulting in agreements highly favourable to foreign investors (Orazgaliyev, 2018). Although governments substantially strengthened their relative position, transnational corporations managed to preserve their initial dominance, reflected in the ownership and control of energy and mineral projects, and resistance to state intervention.

While investment agreements were signed in the hope of attracting and protecting foreign investment, the risks and costs of signing them were underestimated. Central Asian states surrendered their sovereign right to regulate in the interest of people and the environment (Crude Accountability, 2013; Transnational Institute, 2017). Foreign investors can interpret treaties' vaguely worded protection clauses (such as the right to fair and equitable treatment, a stable investment climate and observance of the legitimate expectations of investors) to prevent governments enacting democratically-approved legislation that threatens current or future corporate profits.

Investment agreements purport to depoliticise investor-state disputes (Schneiderman, 2001). Disputes are adjudicated and settled before international tribunals, rather than mediated through inter-state diplomatic relations. But the process is biased in favour of investors. Only foreign investors are entitled to pursue litigation to enforce contracts, and submit disputes to binding arbitration. Moreover, they can bring disputes to jurisdictions with the most advantageous investment treaty protections. Many of the investor-state disputes involving Central Asian states were heard at tribunals of neoliberal institutions and capital-exporting states, such as the World Bank's International Centre for Settlement of Investment Disputes and the Arbitration Institute of the Stockholm Chamber of Commerce.

Tribunals have an incentive to decide in investors' favour, because arbitrators are commercial investment lawyers, who are paid commercial fees on a case-by-case basis. Investors cannot always win because states would then withdraw from the process, causing the system to collapse (Schneiderman, 2015). Though they do often win, sometimes with considerable awards. Expensive lawsuits mean less funds for public programmes. For small economies, the consequences can be quite damaging. In 2014, there were eight pending investment disputes against Kyrgyzstan, amounting to 925 million USD, which was double the annual education budget, or nearly five times the size of the annual health budget (Transnational Institute, 2017).

Investment Disputes in Central Asia

Central Asia's vast natural resources offer governments and transnational corporations rentier opportunities (Franke et al., 2009). Kazakhstan, Turkmenistan and Uzbekistan have significant reserves of hydrocarbons and minerals. From 2008 to 2016, Kazakhstan accounted for 70% of foreign direct investment into Central Asia, while Uzbekistan and Turkmenistan had 16% and 8% respectively (Samruk Kazyna, 2018). In 2015–2016, Kazakhstan's oil and gas industry received 17% of global investment in the sector. Historically, the natural resource sector has dominated foreign direct investment inflows, followed by financial services, retail trade and communications (Pomfret, 2019).

Social tensions and conflicts can occur over the appropriation and distribution of surplus value generated by rent relations (Andreucci et al., 2017). Opposition to foreign investors' rent or value grabbing can legitimate state attempts to change the specificities of rent relations. But foreign investors can invoke protection clauses under investment treaties to prevent direct or indirect expropriation. Table 6.1 shows the number of known international investment disputes by economic sector in Central Asia. To date, the region had 57 disputes, about 5.5% of the total in the world. The number is an underestimate, because it does not capture disputes that are not publicly known.

Kazakhstan and Kyrgyzstan had the most disputes with 19 and 15 respectively. Many of them arose in the natural resource sector, with nine

Table 6.1 Number of known investment disputes by economic sector in Central Asia

	Kazakhstan	*Kyrgyzstan*	*Uzbekistan*	*Turkmenistan*	*Tajikistan*	*Total*
Oil and gas	8	1	1		1	11
Minerals	3	4	2			9
Finance and banking	2	4				6
Real estate and hotels	1	4				5
Construction	1		1	8		10
Telecommunications	1	1		2		4
Retail (shopping malls)			1			1
Agriculture			3	2	1	6
Manufacturing	1					1
Electricity generation	1	1		1		3
Transport	1					1
Total	19	15	8	13	2	57

Source Adapted from UNCTAD (2020b), available at https://investmentpolicy.unctad.org/investment-dispute-settlement

in the oil and gas industry and seven in mining. Uzbekistan and Tajikistan had three and one disputes, respectively in the sector. Social struggles and disputes over property and rent relations were not surprising given the lucrative potential of natural resource rent. As commodity prices rose in the late 1990s, governments began to ascertain more power, seeking better terms and conditions to PSAs, which they had signed several years earlier (Orazgaliyev, 2018).

In addition, conflicts have occurred over other significant forms of rent, including financial, land and spectrum rents. The region's financial, real estate and telecommunication sectors had six, five and four investment disputes respectively, most of them in Kyrgyzstan. In the aftermath of the 2010 political uprising in the country, the new government took actions against banks with close links with the previous regime.

Other disputes related to the appropriation and distribution of natural monopoly and contract rents in the retail trade, transport, construction and electricity sectors. Turkmenistan had eight investment disputes related to construction projects. Investors' claims arose out of the government's termination of construction contracts, non-payment of fees and bonuses, unlawful expropriation of claimants' projects, and harassment of their employees.

Host states play a key facilitating and regulating role in establishing, modifying and enforcing rent and property relations with foreign investors (Parenti, 2015). When governments unilaterally amend or terminate production agreements and contracts, transnational corporations often seek compensation at international tribunals. Table 6.2 shows the types of claims pursued by foreign investors against Central Asian states.

Thirty-one investment disputes involved regulatory takings, which included outright takings or nationalisation of specific companies and incremental or 'creeping' expropriation through forced divestment of shares, excessive and arbitrary taxation and interference in the right of management (UNCTAD, 2020b). In Kyrgyzstan, disputes over nationalisation and creeping expropriation occurred in rent-extracting economic sectors: four in banking, three in mining, four in real estate and one in telecommunications. In Kazakhstan, claims of regulatory takings also involved rentier sectors: four in oil and gas, one in mining, two in banking, one in transport (airport) and one in electricity generation.

There were seventeen disputes involving wrongful termination of agreements, cancellations of licenses and withholding permits. Of these,

Table 6.2 Types of investors' claim in investment disputes in Central Asia

	Kazakhstan	*Kyrgyzstan*	*Uzbekistan*	*Turkmenistan*	*Tajikistan*	*Total*
Outright takings and incremental expropriation	9	12	5	5		31
Wrongful termination of contracts and withholding permits	9	2	1	4	1	17
Interference with the recovery of payment	1	1	2	3	1	8
Lack of fair and equitable treatment				1		1
Total	19	15	8	13	2	57

Source Adapted from UNCTAD (2020b), available at https://investmentpolicy.unctad.org/investment-dispute-settlement

nine were in Kazakhstan's rentier sectors: four in oil and gas, two in mining, one in telecommunications, one in real estate, and one in pharmaceuticals. There were eight investment disputes related to interference with the recovery of payment in different economic sectors across Central Asia.

Under neoliberalism, the judiciary becomes an important site of struggle for the ownership and control of existing assets, and the ability to extract economic rent (Sanghera & Satybaldieva, 2020). It neutralises and depoliticises conflicts by legitimising the legal process as an impartial and rational application of legal doctrines, which are recognised to have universal and logical qualities (Bourdieu, 1987). Table 6.3 shows international tribunals' judgements on investment disputes in Central Asia.

The judiciary's rhetoric of neutrality and universality masks its ideological neoliberal bias towards transnational capital (Bourdieu, 1987). International tribunals upheld investors' claims in sixteen disputes. Of these, thirteen were awarded in key rentier sectors: seven in the natural resource sector, one in finance and banking, four in real estate, and

Table 6.3 International tribunals' judgements on investment disputes in Central Asia

	Kazakhstan	*Kyrgyzstan*	*Uzbekistan*	*Turkmenistan*	*Tajikistan*	*Total*
Decided in favour of the investor	6	6	2	2		16
Decided in favour of the state	5		3	3		11
Settled	1	3		2		6
Decided in neither party or case discontinued	1	2		1	1	5
Pending	6	4	3	5	1	19
Total	19	15	8	13	2	57

Source Adapted from UNCTAD (2020b), available at https://investmentpolicy.unctad.org/investment-dispute-settlement

one in telecommunications. In making these judgements, tribunals sent a clear signal to transnational corporations and host states on the sanctity of private property. They did not merely secure investors' rights, they legitimised rentierism.

Although the tribunal process tended to favour investors, the latter did not always win (Schneiderman, 2015). Host states won in eleven cases, of these five were in major rentier sectors. Three of the five claims were dismissed because claimants failed to meet the qualifying criteria set by international investment treaties, rather than for reasons of endorsing state interference. In the case of Caratube v Kazakhstan (2008), the claimant did not qualify as an investor (Shmatenko, 2013). In the case of KT Asia v Kazakhstan (2009), the claimant's shareholding did not qualify as an investment (Lexology, 2014). In the case of Metal-Tech. v Uzbekistan (2010), the claimant's holding did not qualify as an investment because of corruption (CIS Arbitration Forum, 2013).

In rulings in favour of investors, tribunals obligated governments to compensate investors. To date, the total amount awarded in Central Asia was 879.8 million USD, of which 673.3 million USD was awarded against Kazakhstan, and 167.7 million USD against Kyrgyzstan. These awards meant reductions in state budgets for education, health and other social areas. For small economies like Kyrgyzstan, they had a severe impact on human development and well-being.

Foreign Investors' Rights and Power in Kazakhstan's Oil Sector

Unequal Oil Contracts

Following the disintegration of the Soviet Union, Kazakhstan experienced political turmoil and economic deterioration. Kazakhstan was in desperate need of foreign capital and technical expertise to exploit its abundance of natural resources. Under these difficult and weak conditions, the government signed PSAs with powerful transnational corporations (Palazuelos & Fernandez, 2012). In so doing, it locked in investors' interests, and limited its future interventions (Gill, 2008).

Kazakhstan's vast hydrocarbon reserves attracted major oil companies, including the US-based Chevron and ExxonMobil and European-based BG Group, Royal Dutch Shell, Total and Eni. In 1979, the Tengiz onshore field was discovered, estimated to contain nine billion barrels of recoverable light oil. It was the largest discovery since Alaska's Prudhoe Bay in 1968 (Yessenova, 2015). In 2000, the Kashagan offshore field was discovered, projected to hold thirteen billion recoverable barrels. It was the second largest oil field in the world after Saudi Arabia's Ghawar field (Friends of the Earth Europe, 2007).

In 1991, Kazakhstan initially proposed to Chevron a technical service contract for Tengiz. The contract would have excluded Chevron's equity in the project, allowing the state to claim all excess profits and maintain full control (Yessenova, 2015). Chevron rejected the proposal, and suggested a PSA. From a weak bargaining position, the government signed an oil contract with Chevron. It allocated 80% share of the production to the state and the remaining 20% share to Chevron. It seemed that the state negotiated an attractive deal that would develop the country's oil sector, and would benefit the population. But the terms and conditions favoured Chevron. The acquisition of Tengiz and Korolev oil fields increased the US-based company's oil reserves by 50% in just one day.

Chevron paid 800 million USD for its 45% stake in Tengiz. 400 million USD was to cover production costs, and the other half was to be paid to the state once TengizChevroil became a profitable enterprise (Yessenova, 2015). TengizChevroil's profitability threshold was linked to a gross production of twenty-three million tons a year. The state's 80% share of production was only triggered after TengizChevroil became profitable, which occurred in 2008, fifteen years after the contract was signed. Until then Chevron kept the state's share for itself.

The state was entitled to a 450 million signature bonus (Yessenova, 2015). But 420 million USD from this amount was only to be paid after the state had built a dedicated pipeline to carry Tengiz crude to a Russian port on the Black Sea. This meant that upon signing the contract in 1992, Chevron paid the state 30 million USD for assets valued at 1.66 billion USD, with dates for state's production share and bonus uncertain. Once signed,the state was legally prohibited from terminating or altering the Tengiz contract.

Furthermore, the state bore the costs of making the contract. The state paid all the debts of the Soviet company, which was responsible for developing Tengiz oil fields, and this amounted to 40 million USD (Yessenova, 2015). The state had to expand Tengiz's production capacities at the cost of over 200 million USD in time for TengizChevroil to take possession in 1993. In meeting these obligations, the state reallocated funds from depressed sectors of the economy, and borrowed money from the International Monetary Fund. The opportunity cost of using scarce resources to develop the hydrocarbon sector was high at a time of widespread economic and social dislocation and discontent.

In 1997, Kazakhstan and an international consortium, which included Royal Dutch Shell, ExxonMobil, Total and Eni, signed a PSA for Kashagan. The contract did not reflect traditional norms of giving the state a royalty (usually around 15%), or setting a limit of 40–60% on how much of the extracted oil can cover the investor's costs, thereby ensuring the state has some income (Friends of the Earth Europe, 2007). The Kashagan PSA did not include any royalty, and set the cost recovery limit at 80%.

Moreover, the state would hardly receive any revenue until the consortium achieved its healthy rate of profits and gross production target. Under the terms of the contract, 90% of the profits would be allocated to the consortium until its internal rate of return reached 17.5%, its receipts exceeded expenditure by a factor of 1.4:1, or its production exceeded three billion barrels, about 23% of the recoverable reserves (Friends of the Earth Europe, 2007). While the project was still being developed, the state only received 2% of the project's revenue, and the consortium took 98%.

The PSA allows the consortium to renegotiate terms in extraordinary circumstances, which causes the consortium economic hardship. The state does not have the corresponding right to renegotiate the contract to ensure for itself adequate revenue (Friends of the Earth Europe, 2007). The contract effectively serves to secure consortium profits from economic, legal and political changes at the expense of local communities, workers and the wider population (Appel, 2019). The consortium has legal stability and economic flexibility, in that no new laws or regulations can make the project less profitable, and the contract's terms and conditions ensure the consortium receives most of the revenue.

International financial institutions promoted and financed the Kashagan project. From 2003 to 2006, the European Bank for Reconstruction and Development provided loans to construct artificial islands and marine support base for oil extraction. In addition to almost direct funding, the bank funded infrastructure projects to improve road access and upgrade the regional airport that primarily benefitted the oil industry (Friends of the Earth Europe, 2007). In 2005, Japan Bank for International Corporation and mega Japanese private banks co-financed a private company, which has an equity stake in the consortium. Japan's energy needs and security motivated its involvement.

Struggles Over Contracts

In the second decade after independence, Kazakhstan experienced remarkable economic growth, attributed to increased oil exports, which coincided with high oil prices. Revenues from oil exports constituted a large part of the country's budget, making the state dependent on transnational energy corporations for economic and political stability (Orazgaliyev, 2018). In 2001, the government recognised the need to restore the balance of interests betweenthe state and transnational companies. The state sought to realign the power relationship, and assert its sovereignty over natural resources.

The government revised legislation to strengthen its control over the oil sector. The law stipulated that Kuzmunaigas, the national oil company, would have at least a 50% share in all new oil field development projects (Orazgaliyev, 2018). The state could also exercise pre-emption rights on any oil assets for sale in the country. From 2004 to 2005, the Tax Code was amended, specifically to target energy corporations. Royalty payments increased from 0.5% to 2–6%, oil revenue tax rose from 65% to 85%, excess profit tax jumped from 0–30% to 15–60%, and a floating rent tax for oil exports was introduced.

But the new Tax Code only applied to new contracts concluded from January 2004. It left the tax regime unchanged for existing contracts, such as those signed with TengizChevroil and Kashagan oil consortium. The state did not merely recognise tax stability provisions in existing PSAs, it was prevented by investment treaties from withdrawing or undoing commitments to foreign investors (Schneiderman, 2008). Legal and judicial mechanisms often froze unequal property rights and production and rent agreements, thereby constitutionalising inequality and rentierism to benefit transnational capital.

Kazakhstan's legislative changes caused widespread anger among Western investors, who saw the increasing state control as an infringement of their economic freedoms and rights (Ostrowski, 2010). The new regulations were perceived to contradict Kazakhstan's Constitution, Civil Code and other laws. Some foreign companies mobilised the support of their home governments to put pressure on Kazakhstan to cancel the new measures. In 2002, the ambassadors of the US, Canada and several EU countries sent a joint letter to the government to protest about the measures, asking for them to be annulled.

Some threats to foreign investors required high-level diplomatic interventions. In 2007, the state warned the Italian energy company Eni about the consequences of delays in the Kashagan oil field. Shortly afterwards, the Italian Prime Minister Romano Prodi visited Nur-Sultan to restore confidence (Orazgaliyev, 2018). In 2010, a row erupted between the state and TengizChevroil over illegal oil extraction from wrong depths that amounted to 1.4 billion USD worth of oil production. The US special envoy on Eurasian Energy immediately arrived on a business trip to dissipate the conflict with Kazakhstan's prime minister (Crude Accountability, 2013).

PSAs allow the government to intervene and terminate contracts in circumstances where oil operations threaten people's health and safety. To some extent, Kazakhstan has used environmental concerns to strengthen its national share in the oil sector, enhancing the role of Kuzmunaigas as a stakeholder, and obtaining greater income from production and oil exports (Palazuelos & Fernandez, 2012). In 2007, Eni announced a four-year production disruption and rising costs in the Kashagan field. The government was angry over a lengthy delay in revenues from the project. The government suspended the consortium's operations for three months on the pretext of environmental violations. After protracted negotiations, the consortium agreed to give Kuzmunaigas a greater stake in the project from 8.33% to 16.81%.

Although Kazakhstan increased its revenue and control in the oil sector, foreign investors enjoy a favourable position compared to their counterparts elsewhere in the world. Kazakhstan's government, Kuzmunaigas and local communities are estimated to receive 60% of long-run cumulative profits from major oil fields, and transnational corporations 40% (Palazuelos & Fernandez, 2012). In Middle Eastern and European countries, the national share is much higher, and in Norway, the ratio is 80-20% in favour of the state. Chevron's net profits from its stake in TengizChevroil from 1998 to 2012 exceeded 27 billion USD (Crude Accountability, 2013).

Using stability clauses in existing PSAs, major transnational corporations successfully resisted state attempts to impose higher taxes. Technological challenges to developing oil fields mean that international oil companies cannot be replaced. But the geopolitical competition has intensified for Kazakhstan's oil sector. Initially, Western transnational corporations largely gained access and control of hydrocarbon deposits, but later Chinese and Russian companies sought to increase their shares. This geopolitical rivalry enabled Kazakhstan to have alternatives to Western companies, and negotiate better contracts than those of the 1990s (Palazuelos & Fernandez, 2012).

Environmental Harms

Neoliberalism produces environmental harms: an ever-greater appropriation of natural resources, a criminogenic environment in extractive industries, damage to local ecosystems and local people's well-being, and increased carbon dioxide emissions from fossil fuels, leading to global warming (Sayer, 2015). The terms and conditions of PSAs provide transnational corporations and governments with strong incentives to hasten the development of oil fields (International Institute for Environment and Development, 2012). Seeking higher tax revenues, governments push corporations to quickly achieve greater revenue streams and profitability thresholds. In the process, environmental and health violations are often routinised and conventionalised (Tombs & Whyte, 2009).

According to government data, TengizChevroil is one of the leading environmental offenders in the oil and gas sector. As TengizChevroil strives for greater extraction and revenues, limits on emissions are routinely exceeded. During 2008 to 2013, the corporation had 720 cases of exceeding established emissions limits (Crude Accountability, 2013). From 1993 to 2011, it emitted more than one million tons of harmful substances into the atmosphere, causing irreparable damage to the environment and people's health in the region. Its open storage of large volume of sulphur can also result in acid rain over Europe. TengizChevroil regularly receives fines for environmental pollution.

The crude oil at Kashagan consists of very high levels of sulphur and other toxic pollutants, such as mercaptans. The Kashagan oil development has been linked to a drastic decline in Northern Caspian biodiversity. After the first offshore exploration started in 1999, marine animals, including seals, began to die in considerable numbers. Many migrating birds have died, experiencing breathing difficulty because of the high concentration of hydrogen sulphur in the air (Friends of the Earth Europe, 2007).

Local fishing communities have reported a decrease in fish stock, especially of sturgeon, and fish skin diseases. This has had a severe impact on the local economy, which employs many people in the fishing industry. Moreover, medical specialists have observed that local people's general bad health is related to the oil industry and its emissions of highly poisonous chemicals. People often complain of cardiovascular and respiratory illnesses, skin diseases, anaemia, leukaemia and high levels of premature births and stillborn babies. Thousands of people in surrounding villages have been relocated because of chemical emissions.

But deregulation and regulatory capture have enabled private corporations to escape scrutiny and punishment for environmental harms (Tombs, 2012). Lacking adequate public monitoring stations, public authorities have relied on TengizChevroil and the international oil consortium operating at Kashagan to provide them with information on their impact on the environment and local communities. Corporations' own measurements and commissioned environmental monitoring have often been inaccurate and unreliable.

TengizChevroil's commissioned contractors acknowledged that their findings were usually manipulated so as not to exceed the maximum allowable limits (Crude Accountability, 2013). The international consortium's monitoring stations were only operating at half capacity by 2007, recording merely two of the nine key pollutants released in the air

(Friends of the Earth Europe, 2007). It also refused to allow independent monitoring in the area. Through fraud, deception and wilful neglect, oil corporations have successfully negotiated for higher emissions limits and lighter fines.

Transnational corporations possess significant political capital to minimise and circumvent their responsibility and accountability for producing harmful pollutants (Rothe & Kauzlarich, 2016). In 2007, TengizChevroil contravened environmental laws on sulphur storage, and was fined 303 million USD (Crude Accountability, 2013). It used its connections with Kazakhstan's President Nazarbayev to repeal the fine. In 2009, Kazakhstan's Parliament decided that sulphur had an insignificant impact on the environment. The sulphur problem was tasked to a quasi-scientific council, whose staff were paid by TengizChevroil.

When the government announced a three-month moratorium of the Kashagan project for environmental violations, the international consortium received political support from Italy's Prime Minister. Moreover, the European Commission publicly supported the European members of the consortium despite their failure to meet basic environmental regulations (Friends of the Earth Europe, 2007). Though the consortium lacked sufficient influence over Kazakhstan's political regime, resulting in a partial sale of shares to the national oil company to resolve the dispute.

State-corporate symbiosis, self-regulation and criminogenic attributes contributed to predatory and destructive rent extraction. From 2002 to 2010, TengizChevroil drilled oil at unauthorised depths. This significantly reduced the cost of production, but it led to a severe drop in reservoir pressure, making half of Tengiz oil unrecoverable. The company used its diplomatic and political influence over the government to amend its PSA to include new depths, making what was previously illegal extraction permissible. While highly profitable, excessive extraction made Tengiz prone to earthquakes. The seismic station, which used to record changes, was dismantled after the arrival of TengizChevroil, so limiting data collection on the company's environmental impact (Crude Accountability, 2013).

Foreign Investors' Dominance in Kyrgyzstan's Gold Mining Sector

Rent Appropriation

Soviet geologists knew Kirghizia was rich in mineral resources, including gold, but deemed operations to be too costly and environmentally damaging to extract them. After independence, Kyrgyzstan sought to attract foreign investment to explore and develop its mineral deposits. With the aid of international financial institutions, Kyrgyzstan and other transition countries instituted a liberal regime of property rights, and adopted the rule of law agenda to signal their pro-investor credentials (Appel & Orenstein, 2018). Foreign investors were in a commanding position against weak post-Soviet countries (Orazgaliyev, 2018).

In 1994, a Canadian uranium corporation, Cameco, signed a PSA with Kyrgyzstan to operate its largest gold mine at Kumtor. The PSA established a joint venture, Kumtor Gold Company, whichthe state and the corporation owed two-thirds and one-third respectively. As is typical for a PSA, Cameco accrued revenues until its initial costs were recovered, and then revenue was more evenly shared with the state.

Cameco extracted income in two ways. First, after capitalising on Kumtor gold mine on the Toronto Stock Exchange, Cameco obtained unearned income from the sale of its stake. In 2004, Cameco created a new company, Centerra, which Cameco and the state owned two-thirds and one-third respectively. Five years later, Cameco divested its ownership when Centerra's share price doubled in value. It received about 821 million USD from the divestment (Proactive Investors, 2009).

Second, Cameco mined gold in large quantities. Since the mine started production in 1997, more than 12.6 million ounces of gold were extracted from the site by 2019. Cameco and Centerra benefitted from a boom in the world price of gold, rising from 260 USD an ounce in July 2001 to 2000 USD in August 2020. From 1997 to 2009, Cameco reported a net return of 727 million USD (Pomfret, 2011). From 2015 to 2019, Centerra generated a significant free cash flow of 1.11 billion USD from Kumtor, as a result of higher gold prices, greater extraction and lower costs.

The PSA prioritised the reimbursement of Cameco's upfront costs. In the early stages of the project, the government did not receive much income, causing public resentment towards the investor and suspicion of state corruption. The government was desperate to raise revenue for the state budget. Shortly after Centerra's initial public offering, the government sold half of its share to raise money for social expenditure. Later in the project, the government received more revenue. But it could have obtained more income if it had negotiated better terms in the initial PSA. Between 1997 and 2009, its net income from Kumtor gold mine was 543 million USD, or about 20% of government revenue over this period (Pomfret, 2018). The state viewed Kumtor gold mine as a way to finance important social expenditure, rather than as an asset to merely amass wealth.

Conflicts Over Surplus Value

Social conflicts can emerge over the distribution of rent. Despite making a substantial contribution to the gross domestic product, foreign investors tend to contribute very little to state revenues, especially at the start of the project. Opposition to foreign investors' value grabbing can legitimise state action to change PSAs' specificities. But foreign investors can invoke protection clauses under investment treaties to prevent direct or indirect expropriation (Schneiderman, 2008). Moreover, any attempt to renegotiate PSAs occurs under the shadow of international investment treaties, which threaten governments with costly lawsuits and arbitration. Investment treaties can have the effects of constraining democratic deliberations in favour of limited changes to PSAs.

In 2004, Cameco and the Kyrgyzstani state restructured the joint venture to create Centerra. The state's ownership dropped from 67% to 30% in return for larger payments to its budget (Gullette & Kalybekova, 2014). Then the government sold half of its share to raise money for social programmes. The non-transparent nature of negotiations and payments enraged the public, contributing to the overthrow of President Akayev in the 2005 Tulip Revolution. To address public concerns, President Bakiev put pressure on Centerra to sign a new agreement that would increase the state's share from 15% to over 30%. In 2008, a district court in Bishkek cancelled the company's mining licence, and the government suspended its bank account (Pomfret, 2011).

When Centerra threatened to take the state to the international tribunal, the Supreme Court reinstated its licence. Eventually, a new agreement was negotiated in 2009 that increased the state's ownership of Centerra to 33%, and levied tax at a 14% flat rate, replacing six separate duties. But Kumtor's financial arrangement again became a source of controversy, adding to other scandals that undermined the government's legitimacy. In 2010, President Bakiev was ousted following popular protests.

The new controversy over Kumtor sparked protests across the country. Protesters and opposition parliamentarians demanded greater control or nationalisation of Kumtor, and more effective state intervention to tackle social inequalities (Gullette & Kalybekova, 2014). While the new government under President Atambaev recognised that the existing share allocation with Centerra was unfair, it opted for limited intervention.

The government argued that expropriation would threaten the country's investment climate, and would contravene international treaties protecting foreign investors' rights. In Gullette and Kalybekova's (2014) survey of state bodies, professional organisations and international think-tanks, most deemed nationalisation to be a costly and risky strategy, involving lengthy lawsuits, international arbitration, hefty compensation damages and loss of production.

Nevertheless the government used anti-Kumtor sentiments to bargain with Centerra for a change to the 2009 agreement. It aimed to have greater control over the mine that fell short of nationalisation. In 2014, the government decided to trade 32.7% equity interest in Centerra for a 50% stake in Kumtor Gold Company. But its attempt to renegotiate a new deal created an acrimonious relationship with Centerra. The government threatened to withdraw the company's licence. A court fined Centerra about 98 million USD for mine waste, followed by a state lawsuit of 230 million USD (Pomfret, 2018). Security forces raided the company offices to confiscate documents. In response to creeping expropriation, including penalties, fines, staff harassment and interference in company management, Centerra pursued its own legal action, including international arbitration.

In 2019, Centerra and the government reached an agreement that ended mutual lawsuits, dropped environmental claims, and halted court proceedings. Centerra agreed to pay 50 million USD to a nature development fund to deal with environmental pollution caused by the mine, and make annual contributions of one million USD to the fund (Azattyk, 2019). It also agreed to allocate 10 million USD to a cancer care support fund, and 10 million USD to a regional development fund with extra annual contributions.

The 2019 agreement secured and enhanced Centerra's capacity to extract rent from the mine. The PSA's stability clauses and investment treaties enabled Centerra to prevent direct and creeping expropriation and termination of its licence. The tax rate was unaltered from the 2009 deal, and the expected life of the mine was extended from 2021 to 2026. But following the October 2020 uprising, the new government seized control of Kumtor mine, citing environmental damage and tax violations as its justifications. In May 2021, Centerra filed an international arbitration lawsuit against the government. The case is pending.

Environmental Damage

Neoliberalism promotes the view that natural resources are improperty, and owners can extract resources without limit (Sayer, 2015). Rent extraction trumps the interests of local communities and concerns over the environment. In order to ease doing business in the country, neoliberal reforms can weaken regulatory bodies' capacity to monitor and prosecute environmental violations (Tombs & Whyte, 2009). Moreover, regulatory capture by corporations can restrict attempts to regulate and monitor risk-taking and profit-making (Shaxson & Christensen, 2013). Attempts to introduce new environmental regulations can be impeded by foreign investors' threats to take host states to international arbitration if the changes violate PSAs' stability clauses (Schneiderman, 2008).

Kumtor gold mine has been developed in fragile conditions of permafrost, and in the vicinity of glaciers, which feed fresh waters into major rivers (Bankwatch Network, 2013). The mine's hot waste rock stored on top of ice has threatened the glacier environment, causing glaciers to melt faster. The waste chemicals have washed downstream, affecting the quality of drinking water and fish stock in the rivers.

At Kumtor, regulators cannot make unannounced audits, nor do they have adequate capabilities (such as staff and laboratories) to reliably oversee the water quality monitoring performed at the site. They also lack state financing for environmental protection, and the political support to perform independent and competent oversight (UNDP, 2010).

Often environmental harms were not 'natural disasters', 'bad luck' or 'accidents', but outcomes of regulatory settlements, which largely favoured corporate interests (Tombs, 2012). Several accidents at Kumtor were the results of poor self-regulation and lack of state regulatory and monitoring bodies. For instance, in 1998 a truck carrying 1762 kilogrammes of sodium cyanide fell into a river. Cameco did not immediately inform people living in a village downstream of its potential harm to health. Weeks after the spill, more than several hundred people required medical treatment, and nearly one hundred people were hospitalised (Radio Free Europe/Radio Liberty, 1998).

Centerra's actions point to a lack of environmental self-control and self-reporting. It controls the flow of information on the environment to the public and regulators. It pays for and directs the collection and distribution of technical reports on hydrogeology, water quality, aquatic resources, geochemical, metallurgical testing, and so on. But significant detailed technical reports are not available to regulatory bodies (Bankwatch Network, 2013). Technical reports are often prepared only in English, and have not been translated into either Kyrgyz or Russian.

Independent information has been unavailable to assess the mine owner's environmental impact. After the 1998 spill, Cameco downplayed the magnitude of cyanide poisoning. It also refused NGOs access to the mine site to ascertain the impact of the accident and assist with community support efforts. The company's failure to communicate environmental protection strategies with local communities, devise and share its emergency response plan, and cooperate with independent experts to monitor environmental problems galvanised local resistance to mining (Bankwatch Network, 2013).

Kyrgyzstan's system of environmental and biodiversity monitoring has failed to meet modern requirements that exist in North America and Europe (UNDP, 2010). It has not ensured that environmental impacts will be minimised, restored or mitigated. Existing punishments for environmental violations have not been effective to change behaviour. At Kumtor the mine's tailings (i.e. chemically polluted leftovers) has caused a natural lake to expand because of a melting glacier. Excessive extraction has destabilised the lake's natural dam. If it breaks, then the chemical waste would be washed downstream with catastrophic consequences (Bankwatch Network, 2013).

During the mine's summer operations, about five million cubic metres of wastewater from the tailings are treated and discharged into the rivers. Centerra does not publicise data on the quality of the discharged water. But the rivers have become polluted, affecting the fish population.

While local communities have received limited compensation for environmental pollution, public corruption and misappropriation of funds have exacerbated the problems of a weak regulatory and monitoring system.

Local communities have been alarmed at the rapid shrinkage of mountain glaciers at Kumtor. In the past, these glaciers had 700 million cubic metres of ice mass, but now only 200 million cubic metres are left (Bankwatch Network, 2016). Centerra has denied responsibility, blaming climate change for the loss. But environmental groups have highlighted that Centerra's mine blasts, storage of waste rock on top of ice and excavations of glacier masses have accelerated the rate of ice melt.

In 2015, civil society groups put pressure on the government to modify the country's Water Code that would have restricted Centerra's practice of moving ice. But the company argued that the prohibition would lead to an early closure of the mine, and its 2009 PSA's stability clauses exempted Centerra from new regulations that would damage its operations and profitability. Any restrictions would have been contested in international arbitration.

The government primarily views Kumtor gold mine of strategic economic importance that makes contributions to taxes and regional funds. Recent amendments to the Water Code have favoured Centerra. The company has been allowed to move ice, even though this would completely destroy some glaciers. Furthermore, it is protected from future litigation for environmental damage (openDemocracy, 2018).

Foreign investors can draw on political and symbolic capital to deny and evade their responsibility for environmental damage (Rothe & Kauzlarich, 2016). Among Kumtor's largest international public investors are the EU-owned European Bank for Reconstruction and Development and International Finance Corporation, a member of the World Bank Group. To divert attention from controversies connected with Kumtor, the European Bank for Reconstruction and Development and International Finance Corporation has engaged in projects to protect snow leopards in the vicinity of the mine (Bankwatch Network, 2013). They have also shielded Centerra from accusations of environmental damage.

Conclusion

This chapter examined how legal and judicial mechanisms of governance (such as investment treaties, PSAs and international tribunals) were established to secure and protect investor rights and transnational capital

(Schneiderman, 2008). Property and rent relationships in the natural resource sector were construed to facilitate unearned income and value grabbing, and prevent state infringement of private property. The chapter evaluated the consequences of rentierism on people's well-being and the environment. The pro-investor regulatory regime tended to limit local democracy, and produce environmental crimes and harms (Gill, 2008; Tombs, 2012).

The transnational corporations viewed natural resources as improperty, resulting in excessive and predatory extraction. Driven by economic considerations, such as profitability thresholds and contributions to state budgets, the foreign owners had an insatiable desire for unearned income. Their actions endangered people's lives, biodiversity and fragile local ecosystems, as human flourishing and sustainable development became secondary to income extraction.

Neoliberal notions of justice, liberty and democracy helped to maintain the US and European investors' favourable contracts in Central Asia by preventing host states from withdrawing or undoing commitments to investors (Schneiderman, 2008). The case studies showed how the investors mobilised significant political and symbolic capital to protect the sanctity of contracts and the rule of law. When PSAs were under threat or violated, they argued that economic liberty and justice were at risk, and felt justified to take Kazakhstan and Kyrgyzstan to international arbitration.

The case studies examined how neoliberal constitutionalism justified, normalised and regularised unequal relationships between capital-exporting and capital-importing countries, and foreign investors and host states (Gill, 2008). The transnational corporations used PSAs' stability clauses, investment treaties' prohibitions on direct and creeping expropriation and threats of international arbitration to resist state attempts to renegotiate more equitable rent-sharing agreements, or limit drilling and mining over concerns for the environment (Orazgaliyev, 2018).

But neoliberal constitutionalism did not merely establish and justify unequal representation and power, it legitimised and normalised natural resource rent and unearned income. While the popularity of PSAs has diminished, the case studies revealed that major oil fields and mines were still developed under such arrangements (Orazgaliyev, 2018; Pomfret, 2018). Under the protection of international investment treaties, the transnational corporations engaged in excessive extraction. Their diplomatic, financial and political connections often shielded them from regulation of their predatory practices. Most investor-state disputes related to rent-extracting sectors, and many arbitral tribunals adjudicated in favour of the investor.

The state can be viewed as an ensemble of social forces acting in and through state institutions, so that different state projects compete for strategic dominance and selectivity (Jessop, 2002). The case studies examined how after independence Kazakhstan and Kyrgyzstan instituted the rule of law as a legal and judicial regime that privileged transnational investors, while constraining the actions of parliamentarians, regulatory bodies, local authorities and civil society organisations (Bankwatch Network, 2013; Crude Accountability, 2013). By complying with the neoliberal investment rules regime, the governments often restricted local democratic forces.

State governance took place in the shadow of hierarchy (Jessop, 2002). While hoststates shaped the specifics of value grabbing, more powerful states (i.e. capital-exporting countries) structured the international rules and institutions in ways that suited their economic development (Schneiderman, 2008). Kazakhstan and Kyrgyzstan facilitated the transnational regime for the promotion and security of foreign investment, but struggled to enhance their fiscal and tax regimes or protect fragile local ecosystems. They failed to re-regulate major transnational corporations. The investment rules regime tended to undermine their political legitimacy and authority, sometimes forcing them to be inimical to foreign investment.

References

Andreucci, D., García-Lamarca, M., Wedekind, J., & Swyngedouw, E. (2017). 'Value grabbing': A political ecology of rent. *Capitalism Nature Socialism, 28*(3), 28–47.

Appel, H. (2019). *The licit life of capitalism: US oil in Equatorial Guinea*. Duke University Press.

Appel, H., & Orenstein, M. (2018). *From triumph to crisis: Neoliberal economic reforms in postcommunist countries*. Cambridge University Press.

Azattyk. (2019a, August 29). *Strategic agreement between Kyrgyzstan and Centerra: What did the parties agree on*. https://rus.azattyk.org/a/kyrgyzstan_kumtor_strategic_agreement/30134766.html.

Bankwatch Network. (2013). *Kyrgyzstan and the conflict over natural resources.* https://bankwatch.org/wp-content/uploads/2014/04/Kutmor-Kygryzstan-Jul2013.pdf. Accessed Sept 2020.

Bankwatch Network. (2016, April 20). *Mining company shirks blame for glacier damage in Kyrgyzstan.* https://bankwatch.org/bw_in_media/mining-company-shirks-blame-for-glacier-damage-in-kyrgyzstan. Accessed Sept 2020.

Bourdieu, P. (1987). The force of law: Toward a sociology of the *juridical field. Hastings Law Journal, 38*(5), 805–853.

CIS Arbitration Forum. (2013, December 16). *Metal-Tech v Uzbekistan: No jurisdiction because of corruption.* http://www.cisarbitration.com/2013/12/16/metal-tech-v-uzbekistan-no-jurisdiction-because-of-corruption.

Crude Accountability. (2013). *Republic of Chevron: 20 years in Kazakhstan.* https://crudeaccountability.org/wp-content/uploads/2013/06/20130604-Chevron20YrsInKazakhstan-en.pdf.pdf. Accessed Sept 2020.

Franke, A., Gawrich, A., & Alakbarov, G. (2009). Kazakhstan and Azerbaijan as post-Soviet rentier states: Resource incomes and autocracy as a double 'curse' in post-Soviet regimes. *Europe-Asia Studies, 61*(1), 109–140.

Friends of the Earth Europe. (2007). *Kashagan oil field development.* https://www.foeeurope.org/sites/default/files/publications/foee_kashagan_oil_field_development_1207.pdf. Accessed Sept 2020.

Gill, S. (2002). Constitutionalising inequality and the clash of globalisations. *International Studies Review, 4*(2), 47–65.

Gill, S. (2008). *Power and resistance in the new world order* (2nd ed.). Palgrave.

Gullette, D., & Kalybekova, A. (2014). *Agreement under pressure: Gold mining and protests in the Kyrgyz Republic.* Friedrich Ebert Stiftung.

International Institute for Environment and Development. (2012). *How to scrutinise a production sharing agreement: A guide for the oil and gas sector based on experience from the Caspian region.* https://pubs.iied.org/pdfs/16031IIED.pdf. Accessed Sept 2020.

Jessop, B. (2002). *The future of the capitalist state.* Polity.

Lexology. (2014, January 27). *Tribunal dismisses the ICSID case KT Asia v Kazakhstan for absence of an investment.* https://www.lexology.com/library/detail.aspx?g=cb52457a-df49-4708-94fc-5c8cd4b1c8c7.

Muminov, F. (2019). Protection of foreign investment in Central Asia. *Russian Law Journal, 7*(4), 125–150.

openDemocracy. (2018, April 3). *Gold and water.* https://www.opendemocracy.net/ru/kumtor/. Accessed Sept 2020.

Orazgaliyev, S. (2018). State intervention in Kazakhstan's energy sector: Nationalisation or participation? *Journal of Eurasian Studies, 9*(2), 143–151.

Ostrowski, W. (2010). *Politics and oil in Kazakhstan.* Routledge.

Palazuelos, E., & Fernandez, R. (2012). Kazakhstan: Oil endowment and oil empowerment'. *Communist and Post-Communist Studies, 45*(1–2), 27–37.

Parenti, C. (2015). The environment making state: Territory, nature and value. *Antipode, 47*(4), 829–848.

Pomfret, R. (2011). Exploiting energy and mineral resources in Central Asia, Azerbaijan and Mongolia. *Comparative Economic Studies, 53*(1), 5–33.

Pomfret, R. (2018). *Exploiting a natural resource in a poor country: The good, the bad and the ugly sides of the Kyrgyz Republic's gold mine* (IOS Working Papers, No. 372). Leibniz Institute for East and Southeast European Studies.

Pomfret, R. (2019). *The Central Asia economies in the twenty-first century: Paving a New Silk Road*. Cambridge University Press.

Proactive Investors. (2009, December 9). *Cameco sells 48.5% stake in Centerra Gold for C$872 million*. https://www.proactiveinvestors.co.uk/companies/news/71660/cameco-sells-485-stake-in-centerra-gold-for-c872-million-3205.html.

Radio Free Europe/Radio Liberty. (1998, May 9). *Kyrgyzstan: Kumtor spill signals further disasters*. https://www.rferl.org/a/1088758.html. Accessed Sept 2020.

Rothe, D., & Kauzlarich, D. (2016). *Crimes of the powerful: An introduction*. Routledge.

Samruk Kazyna. (2018). *Overview of investment attractiveness of Central Asian countries*. https://www.sk.kz/upload/iblock/05c/05cd94b6368a1aadd76795e999b7745d.pdf. Accessed Sept 2020.

Sanghera, B., & Satybaldieva, E. (2020). The other road to serfdom: The rise of the rentier class in post-Soviet economies. *Social Science Information, 59*(3), 505–536. https://doi.org/10.1177/0539018420943077.

Sayer, A. (2015). *Why we can't afford the rich*. Policy Press.

Schneiderman, D. (2000). Investment rules and the new constitutionalism. *Law and Social Inquiry, 25*(3), 757–787.

Schneiderman, D. (2001). Constitutional approaches to privatisation: An inquiry into the magnitude of neo-liberal constitutionalism. *Law and Contemporary Problems, 63*(4), 83–109.

Schneiderman, D. (2008). *Constitutionalising economic globalisation: Investment rules and democracy's promise*. Cambridge University Press.

Schneiderman, D. (2014). The global regime of investor rights: Return to the standards of civilised justice? *Transnational Legal Theory, 5*(1), 60–80.

Schneiderman, D. (2015). Constitutional property rights and elision of the transnational: Foucauldian misgivings. *Social and Legal Studies, 24*(1), 65–87.

Shaxson, N., & Christensen, J. (2013). *The finance curse: How oversized financial sectors attack democracy and corrupt economies*. Tax Justice Network. http://www.taxjustice.net/cms/upload/pdf/Finance_Curse_Final.pdf. Accessed July 2020.

Shmatenko, L. (2013). An overview of Kazakhstan's investment laws and its investor-state arbitral awards. *The International Law Quarterly, 30*(4), 25–33.

Smith, A. (1776). *An inquiry into the nature and causes of the wealth of nations*. https://www.econlib.org/library/Smith/smWN.html. Accessed Nov 2019.

Tawney, R. H. (1921). *The acquisitive society*. G. Bell and Sons.

Tombs, S. (2012). State-corporate symbiosis in the production of crime and harm. *State Crime Journal, 1*(2), 170–195.

Tombs, S., & Whyte, D. (2009). State and corporate crimes. In R. Coleman, J. Sim, S. Tombs, & D. Whyte (Eds.), *State, power, crime* (pp. 103–115). Sage.

Transnational Institute. (2017). *Kyrgyz Republic's experience with investment treaties and arbitration cases*. https://www.tni.org/files/publication-downloads/tni_pb_kyrgyz_republic_online_210717.pdf. Accessed Sept 2020.

UNCTAD. (2020a). *International investment agreements navigator: Kazakhstan*. https://investmentpolicy.unctad.org/international-investment-agreements/countries/107/kazakhstan. Accessed Sept 2020.

UNCTAD. (2020b). *Investment dispute settlement navigator: Kazakhstan*. https://investmentpolicy.unctad.org/investment-dispute-settlement/country/107/kazakhstan. Accessed Sept 2020.

UNDP. (2010). *Kyrgyzstan: The second progress report on the millennium development goals*. http://www.undp.org/content/dam/undp/library/MDG/english/MDG%20Country%20Reports/Kyrgyzstan/2010.pdf. Accessed Sept 2020.

Yessenova, S. (2015). The political economy of oil privatisation in post-Soviet Kazakhstan. In H. Appel, A. Mason, & M. Watts (Eds.), *Subterranean estates: Life worlds of oil and gas* (pp. 291–306). Cornell University Press.

PART III

Social Discontent Over Rentierism

CHAPTER 7

The Right to the City: The Land and Housing Movements

This chapter examines how rural migrants and propertyless groups struggled for land and housing in Kazakhstan and Kyrgyzstan. They mobilised to claim their right to the city, and resisted attempts by state and business elites to evict and exclude them. The neoliberal urban development largely benefitted rich and powerful groups, who privatised and commodified real estate for rent extraction, and constructed luxurious shopping and residential facilities to cater for their desires and wants (Harvey, 2013). But neoliberalism also spawned informal settlements, which offered poor residents an alternative to expensive homeownership and rental accommodation (Davis, 2004).

As land became ever more scarce and valuable, informal settlements were targeted for urban development. The residents of informal settlements demanded state protection against mass evictions, and appealed to moral norms and traditions to justify their construals of land and housing needs. They formed grassroots movements to counter the neoliberal commodification of land and its negative effects on people's well-being. Dispossession, exclusion, injustice and suffering motivated and stimulated land and housing movements (Burawoy, 2015). Post-Soviet political regimes had a complex relationship with social movements, sometimes embracing and tolerating them, but often weakening and crushing them (Goodwin, 2018).

B. Sanghera and E. Satybaldieva, *Rentier Capitalism and Its Discontents*,
https://doi.org/10.1007/978-3-030-76303-9_7

The chapter is divided into six sections. The first section examines the development of informal settlements in Kazakhstan and Kyrgyzstan. Section 'Asserting the Right to the City' draws on our fourth case study to discuss how informal residents, state officials and NGOs construed informal settlements and struggles for housing and land. The neoliberal nature of urban development is discussed in the third section. Section 'State Repression of Informal Settlement Protests in Kazakhstan' analyses the development of housing and informal settlement movements in Kazakhstan, and the state's responses to them. The fifth section examines how housing and informal settlement movements interacted with ruling and oppositional elites in Kyrgyzstan. Finally, the conclusion summarises the chapter's key findings and ideas.

Rural Migration and Informal Settlements

Land and housing struggles in Kazakhstan and Kyrgyzstan were rooted in multiple neoliberal policies, including the privatisation of the agriculture sector, lack of regional and rural economic development, the elites' appropriation of urban real estate and the financialisation of housing. The privatisation and fragmentation of farming accelerated labour migration to the cities as a result of low agricultural productivity[1] and rural unemployment. Kazakhstan's contribution of agriculture to Gross Domestic Product (GDP) fell from 34% in 1990 to 4% in 2014 (Bizhanova, 2018). In Kyrgyzstan, the agricultural sector fell from 43.9% of GDP in 1996 to 15.9% in 2015 (Mogilevskii et al., 2017). Despite this, the share of the rural population remains significant in Kazakhstan[2] and Kyrgyzstan, constituting about 47% and 64% respectively.

Development and investment policies have made a negative impact on agricultural and regional economic growth. Investment into agriculture has fluctuated between 0.5 and 2% of GDP (Bizhanova, 2018). Kazakhstan's current regional policy allocates the majority of public funds

[1] High cultivation costs forced many households to abandon farming (Mogilevskii et al., 2017; Steimann, 2011). In a privatised agricultural system, farmers cannot individually resolve problems of irrigation systems, fluctuating market prices, soil erosion, underdeveloped food processing, and weak certification and marketing institutions.

[2] The share of the rural population is higher in southern regions of Kazakhstan, constituting 77% for Almaty region, 62% for Turkestan and 58% for Zhambyl, these being particularly underdeveloped and poor.

towards 'dynamically developing cities and regions', the so-called 'growth poles'.[3] In 2018, funds for regional development fell from 513.3 billion tenge to 101.7 billion tenge (Turganbayev & Diener, 2018). Harvey (2013) notes that directing funds to the so-called 'entrepreneurial growth poles' is a spatial version of 'trickle-down' economics advocated by the World Bank, which sees such investment benefitting society in the long run.

Widespread rural poverty resulted in internal and external migration. In Kyrgyzstan, the rates of internal and external migration have been 60% and 40% of rural population respectively throughout the last 20 years (Fryer et al., 2014). In Kazakhstan, an average of 138,750 people per year engaged in inter-regional migration between 2000 and 2010 (Aldashev, 2011). The migration to 'growth poles' as a survival strategy reflected similar migration trends in other developing countries in the past 30 years.

In major cities, migrants faced problems of unaffordable accommodation, social exclusion, precarious employment and lack of access to public goods, because they did not have residence permits (*propiska*)[4] (Sanghera et al., 2012). A shortage of affordable urban housing drove thousands of rural migrants to seize land, or buy cheap vacant plots. The shortage, which existed during the Soviet period, was exacerbated by the withdrawal of state provision of free housing, and the adoption of mortgage-based housing policies, which indirectly increased house prices (Rolnik, 2011).

The post-Soviet housing policies privileged upper and middle class groups. The financialisation of housing led to house prices tripling in Nur-Sultan, and quadrupling in Almaty between 2001 and 2015 (Seitz, 2020). Housing for many local people was more unaffordable than in exclusive superstar cities, such as San Francisco and Vancouver. In 1991, the Kazakhstani state built 6.1 million square metres of public housing, by 1999 it was only 1.1 million square metres (Pchelyanskaya, 2016). Kazakhstan does not have an affordable rental market.

In Kyrgyzstan, the system of public housing collapsed after 1991. In 2010, only 2.7% of new apartments were built using state funds, in

[3] Kazakhstan's economic territories are categorised into cities of the first level (Nur-Sultan, Almaty, Shymkent and Aktobe); cities of the second level (regional centres, Semey and Turkestan), and cities of third level (small cities and single-industry cities).

[4] Without city registration, migrants lack adequate access to social services. In 2019, the rules of city registration tightened in Nur-Sultan and Almaty, limiting registration at the place of residence to 15 square metres per person.

contrast to more than 1 million square metres of housing built annually during the 1970s (Sanghera & Satybaldieva, 2020). Affordable housing programmes in both countries based on mortgages were aimed at middle class public sector workers (Sharipova, 2015).

As a result of neoliberal developments, class inequalities have spatially materialised. Almaty, Nur-Sultan, Bishkek and Osh are divided cities. The outskirts of these cities have undeveloped newly legalised and informal settlements, and city centres have shiny business offices, modern shopping malls and elite apartment complexes. The ongoing class struggle between rural migrants and a class alliance of banks, construction companies and state elites has focused on the city itself. Each city has its own specific history of resistance, which is ongoing and constitutes part of a broader class struggle.

In the past 10–13 years, Almaty had 29 informal settlements[5] with a population of 700,000, about one-third of the two million inhabitants (Yessenova, 2010). Almaty might have the largest informal settlements in Central Asia. The informal residents have been locked in legal struggles with local authorities, which have enacted brutal measures to eradicate the sites. The ongoing encounters with the city administration have turned the informal settlements into permanent sites of grassroots struggles for legality.

Zauresh Battalova, a leading activist on housing rights, believed that informal residents in Nur-Sultan constituted about 15% of the one million population. Ondiris, Kirpichnyi and Triangle settlements, which were established in the early 2000s, faced eviction threats. Koyandy, which emerged in the late 1990s and early 2000s through the repatriation of ethnic Kazakhs (*oralmans*), was the only legalised settlement in the city (Sanghera et al., 2012). In 2008, the state authorised its legalisation because *oralmans* had become a political embarrassment for the government, which had invited ethnic Kazakhs to migrate to their historic motherland, but when they came were denied full legal rights. Nur-Sultan's city administration tried to negate the existence of informal settlements located on the outskirts of the city. It segregated them by erecting two-metre high walls with images of forthcoming construction projects at the sites (Koch, 2014; Osmonova, 2016).

[5] Shanyrak is divided into nine sub-districts. There are other sizable settlements, such as Aigerim, Bakai, Ulzhan, Kurilisshy, Trudovik, Akbulak, Duman, Uzhet and Karasuu.

In Bishkek, the Ombudsmen Report (2017) suggested that there were 47 squatter-led settlements, with a population of 223,258, which was about 28% of the city population. Of these, twenty settlements were established before 2000, nine from 2000 to 2005, and eighteen from 2005 to 2010. In contrast to Kazakhstan's situation, most Bishkek-based settlements were legalised. According to the city administration, about 6382 houses were still listed as unauthorised constructions in 2017. Of these, 3598 houses will be legalised in the near future, but the remaining houses cannot be legalised because they were built in hazardous zones (i.e. territories under high voltage lines, underneath gas pipelines, or near public cemeteries and landfills). But the residents' struggles have been about demands for improvements in basic infrastructure and living conditions, rather than legalisation.

Due to the scarcity of land in and around Osh city, rural migrants were unable to occupy land, instead summer camps, abandoned or uncompleted buildings were seized. In 2013, the city administration estimated there were over 100,000 rural migrants, of which only 42,000 had the necessary documents to be on the official waiting list for housing. In addition to land and housing shortages, some residents were evicted from Soviet-era workers' dormitories. New property owners had privatised the buildings and hiked housing rent. Evicted residents, rural migrants and poor people came together and mobilised to demand land, housing and social protection.

Asserting the Right to the City

In his seminal work on Hong Kong's informal settlements, Smart (2001) argues that it is important to understand how they are legitimised and justified. There is an obvious tension between how informal residents and property laws conceptualise land. Sanghera and Satybaldieva (2012) argue that informal residents contested the discourse of 'land grabbing' that criminalised and demonised them. The discourse was a form of 'class othering' that reduced sympathy and compassion for them. In our study, land occupations were not usually spasmodic, irrational and visceral acts, rather informal residents were motivated by moral claims to necessity, basic rights and justice.

Rural migrants provided good reasons for their rights to habitat (Mitchell, 2003). They appealed to constitutional and human rights, traditional land-use practices, moral claims of fairness, land productivity and the right to subsistence. Moreover, since land is a fictitious commodity, institutional and normative forms of protection were required to limit the pursuit of economic gain and ensure human flourishing for all (Polanyi, 1944). But their attempts to embed the market in social relations beyond the legal notions of equality and justice were opposed by the powerful class alliance of business and state elites.

In Kazakhstan and Kyrgyzstan, rural migrants asserted their right to land on the basis of needing a place to eat, rest and sleep (Sanghera et al., 2012). They also stressed that most occupied land plots were previously idle, derelict and not used productively. In Almaty and Nur-Sultan, some informal settlements were built on swamp and waste lands. In Bishkek, several settlements (e.g. Ak Jar and Altyn Kazyk) claimed waste sites, or areas prone to floods. Some settlements grew around marketplaces, such as Dordoi Market in Bishkek or Barakholka Bazaar in Almaty, where many migrants worked. The informal residents turned vacant and waste lands into neighbourhoods for thousands of people.

The rural migrants' productive use of land for housing and human needs was contrasted with the wealthy elites' use of land for trivial and luxurious wants and desires. Zaure, an Almaty-based leader of the Kurlisshy informal settlement movement, explained how the elites used vast areas of land for conspicuous leisure when many local people were desperate for land:

> For instance, there's a golf-club on the uphill of the town, which takes up about 100 hectares. Is that land used well? Golf is not even a sport! Kazakh people don't care for it. So when [state officials] say that there is no land for social housing, why is there a 100-hectare land for golf? This is injustice! This is a violation of the law! This pushes us to act against the state!

For Zaure, land for housing to serve the needs of many was a superior claim to land for golf, which was a foreign and elite activity. Given the city's lack of land for housing, she judged the allocation and use of land for the entertainment of the rich as absurd, unjust and criminal. Such injustices reflected the tendency for private property rights to dominate the lived environment, and trump collective rights (Harvey, 2013). Mitchell (2003) argues that land's use-value rather than its exchange-value is the basis of a just city. When the state upholds that profit and rent are superior to housing needs, then homeless citizens can feel justified to protest. Human needs and suffering impose limits to land privatisation, since without access to land, poor and propertyless individuals are unable to sleep, rest, urinate or wash themselves. In a society where all land is privatised, they would eventually die.

Many informal residents also claimed their right to the city on constitutional grounds. For instance, many rural migrants in Bishkek legitimised their land occupations on the basis of the Kyrgyzstani constitution that obligates the state to provide housing (Sanghera & Satybaldieva, 2012). The right to housing has remained unchanged despite several revisions to the constitution. The constitution also enshrines citizens' rights to other basic goods, such as education and medicine, which are fundamental to human flourishing. While the state has a constitutional duty to protect private property, informal residents and settlement activists believed that the right to housing was a superior duty. Belek, an Almaty-based committee leader of the Bakai informal settlement, justified his claim for land and housing on the basis of his constitutional rights:

> I'm entitled to my share of land because our constitution guarantees 10 acres for each citizen. Kazakhstan is rich in land and ranks as the ninth largest country in the world. Surely, the state has the capacity and has an obligation to provide its citizens with land.

Belek explained that the state should give him and others land plots. He believed that there was no shortage of land in Kazakhstan, and the state was obligated to fulfil its duty. In citing the constitution, land occupations and settlements were seen as an act of rightful resistance (Sanghera & Satybaldieva, 2012).

Traditional norms and values were often invoked to oppose neoliberal market norms. After three decades of market laws, many informal residents recognised that the system benefitted the affluent propertied class. Belek argued that private land rights were alien to Kazakh traditions:

> Everything written in the law is aimed against us. Why should I respect the laws that don't protect my interests? These laws don't even reflect our traditions. We're nomads, born to be free and to move around. Nomads settled wherever they needed to. As far I as I'm concerned, I'm living the way my ancestors lived. . . . For instance, [President] Nazarbayev often said

> that democracy is not a Kazakh tradition and that we've our own way of doing things. But when it comes to people's land rights, the state suddenly begins to preach about property rights! But property rights aren't Kazakh traditions either!

Belek explained that Kazakhstan's traditional rights, customs and responsibilities emphasised the collective and social use of land. He opposed the privatised, individualised and monetised aspects of property rights. Cultural embeddedness promoted land's use-value over exchange-value, and restructured economic relations in ways that protected people and society from the harmful effects of market commodification (Polanyi, 1944).

Mitchell (2003) argues that the right to the city needs to be dissociated from the right to property, and returned to the right to inhabit. Many rural migrants drew on cultural discourses to undermine the dominant regime of private property rights, and assert their collective right to land to remake the city. As Harvey (2013: 4) notes, 'The question of what kind of city we want cannot be divorced from the question of what kind of people we want to be, what kind of social relations we seek, what relations to nature we cherish, what lifestyle of life we desire, and what aesthetic values we hold.'

Neoliberal Urban Development

The post-Soviet urban change has been marked by a loss of public spaces and the commodification of urban land (Frohlich, 2020; Nasritdinov & Schroder, 2017). Central Asian capital cities were shaped by elites for elites. Rather than *oeuvre* in which all citizens participate, capital cities became sites of capital accumulation through urbanisation (Harvey, 2013; Lefebvre, 1996; Mitchell, 2003). The polarisation of power politicised urban space, and activated housing struggles.

By the mid-2000s, informal settlements ceased to be tolerated in Kazakhstan as neoliberal urban policies came into full force. The oil boom and the expansion of the financial sector facilitated the development of new masterplans (*genplans*) for Nur-Sultan and Almaty. These cities were to become regional competitive investment hubs with entrepreneurial residents. Nur-Sultan stands out as a quintessential elite project of President Nursultan Nazarbayev. In 2019, the city was renamed after him to credit his role in shaping the capital.

President Nazarbayev spared no expense in creating the capital as a symbol of the country's capitalist development. By 2007, the construction costs of Nur-Sultan were estimated to be around 40 billion USD (Laszczkowski, 2011). In a short time, the city had erected various ostentatious buildings, which were designed by famous foreign architects, such as Kisho Kurasawa and Norman Foster. The city became a swanky playground for the rich, rather than a space for a communal living (Gawecki, 2013). Foreign visitors characterised the city as utopian, Disney-like and megalomaniac (Gawecki, 2013; Koch, 2012; Laszczkowski, 2011).

The list of expensive constructions included: the 97-metre tall Baiterek Tower with the mould of Nazarbayev's right hand that cost 6 million USD; a 77-metre high glass pyramid Palace for Peace and Reconciliation priced at 75 million USD; the Concert Hall, which resembled a jumble of glass shards, was built at a cost of 175 million USD; and a 150-metre tall Khan Shatyr shopping mall,[6] which was shaped like a yurt, cost 520 million USD (Millar, 2016). The city development came to define public space in terms of depoliticised consumption (Frohlich, 2020). The state only allocated about 331.3 million USD for the construction of affordable social housing units between 2005 and 2010 (Rolnik, 2011).

In 2017, 3–5 billion USD was spent on the construction of a futuristic city linked to Expo 2017 in Nur-Sultan. A Chicago-based team of architects built 28 buildings over 426 acres with an eight-storey globe dominating the site. The largely unpopulated site was supposed to be connected to a metro line launched in the same year, with a projected cost of another 2 billion USD (twice the amount spent in Almaty on the construction of a 8.5 km metro line). Many ordinary people ridiculed the state for spending billions on another prestige project when in 2016 only 46.3 billion tenge (about 104 million USD) was allocated for the country's industrial development (Fatyanova, 2017).

Speculative investments fuelled an unequal real estate market. While the wealthy benefitted from the construction of mega-projects in city enclaves, poor and working class groups were excluded and neglected (Rolnik, 2011). Koch (2014: 440) notes that Nur-Sultan's urban form

[6] The shopping centre has an area of ten football pitches, and features a beach with seawater, sand and palm trees imported from Maldives on the top floor. Andrea Bocelli, the famous operatic singer, gave a concert at its opening ceremony, and guests included presidents and heads of nine states (Koch, 2012).

was unique in its use of aesthetics and beauty 'as a subtle but highly effective mechanism of exclusion.' The capital alienated poor people, who felt 'out of place' (Laszczkowski, 2011; Osmonova, 2016). Urban development pathologised village-like and Soviet-era neighbourhoods as outdated and unsanitary spaces (Gawecki, 2013; Koch, 2014).

Inspired by Nur-Sultan's transformation, Almaty's elites attempted to rival its urban development by refashioning the city into a post-industrial financial capital of Central Asia. The Mayor of Almaty, Imangali Tasmagambetov,[7] the key architect of the city's new masterplan, noted that the city already had headquarters of thirty-three prominent banks, or 70% of all banking operations in the country. The masterplan commissioned the construction of 80 commercial buildings with a total area of 3 million square metres. In addition, from 2006 to 2010, the city allocated 496 hectares for the construction of elite housing.

The construction boom which ensued in Nur-Sultan and Almaty was driven by a class alliance of financiers, property developers and political elites. An estimated 70% of all Western bank loans (which by 2007 amounted to 46 billion USD) was linked to the luxury real estate sector (Seitz, 2020). Yessenova (2010) notes that 95% of all housing transactions were debt-financed at interest rates of 15–20%. The real estate market bubble grew exponentially,[8] and land in and around the city gained premium value. Seitz (2020) argues that such developments echo the dangers of the so-called 'superstar city' phenomenon, where living is like 'owning a scare luxury good'. Harvey (2013) notes that surplus capital flows build new cities for the upper class, redefining what cities are about, as well as who can live there and who can't.

Capitalist transformations in Bishkek and Osh were more modest for two key reasons. First, Kyrgyzstan's elites lacked capital and ambition to create utopian or modern cities. Suffering from power blackouts and poor roads, Kyrgyzstan prioritised infrastructural projects, which were often funded by international donors. Second, the economy did not attract large credit flows from the West into the real estate sector. Most major construction companies were established by domestic elites, and they did

[7] During his time as the Mayor of Almaty (2004–2008) and of Nur-Sultan (2008–2014), Imangali Tasmagambetov earned the reputation of being an aggressive advocate of neoliberal urban transformation.

[8] In Almaty between 2002 and 2006, prices for square metre went up 14 times from 250 USD to 3600 USD (Yessenova, 2010).

not have access to western financial institutions. Two political uprisings in 2005 and 2010 dampened the luxury real estate sector, which took off only in 2012. In 2020, Ilya Varlamov, a famous urban architect, viewed Bishkek as being 'stuck in the 90s' with nothing new to showcase or to be proud of.

But the city's lack of 'superstar city' phenomenon allowed rural migrants more freedom to use the space for socialising. They actively claimed public spaces, such as Ala-Too Square, the Kyrgyz Philharmonic Hall and the Bishkek Sports Palace, thereby diversifying the urban culture (Nasritdinov & Schroder, 2017). Nevertheless the commercialisation of Bishkek's and Osh's city centres resulted in some construction of shopping malls, business centres, elite apartment buildings and *toikanas* (grand restaurants).

Neoliberal urban policies created a criminogenic environment in local authorities. The effects included a significant loss of parkland and public spaces. In Kyrgyzstan, four Bishkek mayors illegally distributed over a third of Ataturk Park to rich elites. In 2002, Ataturk Park's status was raised to a category of special protection of historic and cultural monument to prohibit further elite land appropriation. But this did not stop the illegal distribution of parkland (Jumagulov & Li, 2019). From 2000 to 2008, the Bishkek City Council authorised the distribution of about 200 land plots to wealthy elites. Sooronbai Jeenbekov, the ex-president of Kyrgyzstan, received a parcel of parkland in 2003, when he was a parliamentarian. As one of the Bishkek activists noted, 'All those who received land in Ataturk Park already had housing. The Chief Justice of the Supreme Court, the Prosecutor General and others were not homeless' (Jumagulov & Li, 2019).

A parliamentary committee recommended an investigation into the illegal distribution of land plots in Ataturk Park. But the prosecutors' office only opened three cases, which were swiftly closed because of the statute of limitations. No one was held accountable for the illegal distribution, and no compensation was paid to the council.

In Almaty, elites illegally appropriated land in Medeo National Park, a home to endangered Tian-Shan pine trees, rare animals and old apple gardens (Yesenova, 2010). The public plea to investigate into illegal appropriation was opposed by Mayor Imagali Tasmagambetov. He owned a four-storey home in Medeo that was valued at over one million USD.

In 2006, the state passed an amnesty law that gave elite land-grabbers the right to legalise their mansions and other hidden assets, guaranteeing them complete anonymity. In return, the elites were obligated to compensate the state with a portion of the total value of their stolen and hidden properties. In practice, multimillion-dollar mansions were legalised without much cost, because their owners were permitted to assign their own value to their properties, which were grossly undervalued. This then minimised their compensation to the state. Yessenova (2010: 31) notes that 'it was quite possible that the owners of multistorey mansions declared 1% of their property value.' Valera, an Almaty-based lawyer, described the amnesty law as a laundry operation for the rich.

State Repression of Informal Settlement Protests in Kazakhstan

Opposition to Mass Evictions in Almaty

At the height of the construction boom and speculative investments in Almaty, the city's state and business elites clashed with informal residents. The public policy shifted from tolerating poor neighbourhoods and informal settlements to their removal. In 2006, the city council used eminent domain to order the residents to vacate their settlements. Mayor Tasmagambetov contracted Almatyjer company to seize buildings and lands in and around the city marked for eminent domain. Between 2005 and 2006, Almatyjer sold lands of Bakai and Shanyrak settlements to Investgroup and other eight property developers and investors (Yessenova, 2010). One of them wanted to build a water park.

Many informal residents tried to legalise their homes using the 2006 amnesty law, which had legalised illegal holdings of rich elites. But their applications were rejected. The law was not intended to legalise land plots seized by poor migrants. The first demolition took place in Bakai settlement on 21 February 2006, and then proceeded to Aigerim and Shanyrak settlements. Special police forces, court executives and demolition workers with bulldozers arrived at the informal settlements without warning or a court order. Offering no explanations, the police, armed with rubber bullets, noise grenades and truncheons, broke down doors, threw belongings on the streets, and permitted bulldozers to flatten homes. When some construction workers refused to demolish homes, the police and court executives used sledgehammers themselves to tear down the homes. Valera, who witnessed the demolitions, explained state actions as illegal and callous:

> The state officials didn't follow the laws on evictions. The court executives had to verify whether the people had appealed against the court orders and whether they had alternative accommodation. But nobody spoke to the people! It was obvious that they were in a hurry. They had no intentions to talk, listen or negotiate. They manhandled grandmothers, who were wailing and begging, 'Please don't do this!'

Velera was shocked by the officials' abuse and mistreatment of the residents, in particular, vulnerable groups. Bakai and Shanyrak residents fought back. People threw stones at the police, laid down before the bulldozers, and climbed onto the roofs of their homes. Their resistance forced the police to withdraw, but not for long. Between February and July 2006, Bakai and Shanyrak residents faced eight eviction operations. Each time many homes were destroyed, leaving residents with broken noses, legs, head concussions and other injuries.

Initially, the residents were surprised by the evictions, but then they began to mobilise resources to defend their homes. They had little option but to be contentious against a repressive political structure that constrained their ability to engage with formal institutions to make demands or ask for representation, as well as to hold peaceful protests and demonstrations. Some leading oppositional organisations, such as Azat and Alga, and most of the middle class urban population had little to no solidarity with the squatters' struggles, either fearing political repression, or lacking sympathy with their cause. The informal residents largely relied on their own resources to struggle against state power. They received some support from small left-wing and nationalist political movements, such as the Socialist Resistance in Kazakhstan and Kazak Memlekety (Kazakh Nationhood).

The residents formed a system of collective self-defence, by erecting barricades and lookout posts, and setting up combat and civil defence groups. In addition, they tried to draw the attention of parliamentarians and the wider public to the brutal evictions. In March 2006, many residents participated in hunger strikes and road blockades. In May 2006, some local activists and leaders of political movements, such as Zher Ana (Mother Earth) and Kazak Memlekety, travelled to Nur-Sultan to show a film of the land evictions and the 'battle scenes' at Bakai to parliamentarians. After the screening, about forty parliamentarians signed a letter demanding a temporary postponement of the demolitions. The president's daughter Dariga Nazarbayeva established a committee to investigate the incident. But the committee failed to hold an inquiry because the members went away to take their summer vacation.

A week after the film was shown, Mayor Tasmagambetov ordered urgent mass demolitions. On 7 July 2006, 500 houses were demolished in Bakai in a single day. A week later, over 1000 special armed forces came in the early hours to Shanyrak to do the same job, but faced stiff resistance. The residents fiercely defended their homes, showering the police with stones and Molotov cocktails. By 2 p.m., they gained an upper hand in the conflict and took four police officers hostage. The special forces promised to completely withdraw in exchange for the hostages.

But when the special forces received reinforcements, they abandoned the negotiations and led another attack. Angered by the uncompromising stance, the residents set alight a 24-year-old police officer, who later died. In the days following the tragic incident, the police arrested 108 Shanyrak residents, including organisers and activists. Four activists received lengthy jail sentences. The state blamed them for the events, singling out Aron Atabek as a key 'terrorist'.

Mayor Tasmagambetov had little sympathy for the Shanyrak protesters and residents. He was scornful of their aims and tactics, describing the killing of the young police officer as immoral. He also argued their land occupation as irresponsible and criminal (Torebaeva & Ivanov, 2006):

> There are two kinds of social stratums in the city. One, queues up for housing, saves up for a mortgage, and goes to work every day. Sometimes, they may even have to work in three or four places [to save for a mortgage]. And then, there's a social stratum that violates all laws, and makes claims through aggressive dependency, saying "Hey, I'm a Kazakh, I must take this land by force!"

He contrasted the informal residents' lack of work ethic and discipline with the orderly and honest conduct of most urban residents, who were patient and worked hard to get housing. The mass media and most of the middle class urban population framed informal residents in disparaging terms, such as 'invaders', 'grabbers' and 'barbarians' (see Schroder, 2010).

Shanyrak's combative resistance halted mass demolitions in Almaty, and deterred similar measures in Nur-Sultan. The Shanyrak events were a warning to the state that marginalised groups had the power to resist its rule and repression. But the outcome was achieved at considerable pain and loss. Mitchell (2003) states that the right to the city is not given, but comes from social struggle and violence that are often the only ways to be heard. After this watershed moment, the state realised that it could not destroy informal settlements, and instead it formulated plans for subtle forms of dispossession and exclusion. The 2007–2008 global credit crisis also helped to ease social and political tensions, because property developers could no longer finance their projects. The informal residents were left alone until the economic conditions improved for property developers.

Almaty's Informal Residents on Borrowed Time

In 2008, the state appeared to adopt a policy of inclusion, promising to legalise informal settlements. The policy shift was partly explained by the opposition of centre-right political parties, which began supporting informal settlements after the Shanyrak events. Aman, a local state official, explained the change of tactics towards the settlements:

> We read the pamphlets of the oppositional parties that urged their members to weaponise the anger of Shanyrak and Bakai residents. That's a risk for us. We [the state] know what the opposition wants to do. So we learnt to address the risk through legalisation without using force. We stopped chasing people with bulldozers.

Aman feared that the informal settlements would become a breeding ground of oppositional forces, which could challenge and undermine state legitimacy. But oppositional parties never capitalised on the residents' anger. They largely focused on middle class groups as their key constituency, and avoided antagonising the political regime. Nevertheless the fear of residents' radicalisation against the backdrop of the colour revolutions in post-Soviet countries compelled the state to take a seemingly compromising stance.

In 2008, the Almaty city administration established a new Alatau district to process the legalisation of Shanyrak and Bakai informal residents, who were framed by state officials as 'victims of the transition period'. But on 23 December 2008, the Alatau administration announced that they would only legalise 189 homes. After the residents protested, the administration amended the figure to 1600. In the summer of 2009, three years after the Shanyrak events, the administration resumed demolitions, destroying five houses in Shanyrak-2 micro-district. The renewed demolitions mobilised informal residents to unite 18 micro-districts of Alatau district, and set up an informal settlement movement, officially named the People's Committee for the Protection of Constitutional Rights to Land and Housing. The ongoing repressive state tactics reinforced the informal residents' perceptions of injustice, and reactivated their political mobilisation.

The social movement carried out its own inventory, and listed 8487 houses as undocumented. In our interview with Zaure, the leader of the movement, she explained that the figures did not include land plots of the former Kirov collective farm and Aigerim-1 micro-district. According to her estimates, there were at least 10,000 undocumented land plots in 2011. The Shanyrak residents claimed that the city administration deliberately underestimated the number of undocumented homes, so as to minimise the issue of housing demolition.

The movement's activities were limited by strict laws on protests and peaceful public gatherings. Holding pickets and protests in public spaces became very restrictive. Unable to protest, the movement activists tried to shame the state by announcing that they were going to apply for refugee status at the US Embassy. The activists argued that the government, the constitution, land codes and other regulations had failed to treat them as citizens in any meaningful sense.

By 2011, many leading oppositional leaders were in exile, dead, or left politics. Independent political organisations were largely absent. Many of them had reconsidered their previous anti-government rhetoric, and decided to be co-opted by the government (Niyazbekov, 2018). The informal settlement movement had access only to a pro-government NGO Shanyrak, which initially offered some legal and advocacy support.

The state also used other means to squash the settlement movement. The city administration decided to offer lease agreements to the informal residents, instead of issuing certificates to legalise their homes. NGO Shanyrak, which received about 2.8 million Euros from the Council of Europe to support the legalisation programme, advocated rental contracts as the residents' best outcome. Zaure criticised the NGO's role, and questioned its director's motivation:

> We later learnt that Kozhahmetov [the NGO Shanyrak director] initiated these lease contracts for the residents. He pressurised us to settle for these contracts, and worked to undermine our movement. He was splitting us up. We refused to cooperate with his NGO. He simply made money out of our problems.

Zaure was critical of some human rights organisations, such as NGO Shanyrak, which worked closely with the state to legalise the settlements. She later explained that the lease contracts offered an illusion of legality and security, because the state could reclaim the land after the lease had expired. The informal settlements were treated as 'borrowed places', tolerated 'for the time being' until the next speculative deal came for the land (Smart, 2001; Yessenova, 2010).

Many residents, who refused to sign the lease agreements, received threats from the National Security Committee and the Public Prosecutor's Office. The security forces pressurised some to give up. For example, Tilek, a resident at Bakai settlement, signed the lease agreement, but was worried by the contractual terms:

> My circumstances forced me to accept this. The contract says that the state has a right to take away the land at any moment without compensation. After all these years, I still have no right to my land. I'm now leasing the land for 10 years.

Lacking adequate alternatives and facing threats, Tilek signed the contract. But he recognised that he was in a precarious and vulnerable position. He had bought himself some time, but he was unsure what would happen afterwards.

In 2012, the movement members, who refused to sign lease contracts, took legal action to defend their right to land. Their litigation was a defiant act of citizenship. Their actions against the state fostered a sense of solidarity. The movement activists studied and researched land codes and court archives to find and exploit loopholes. Using her experience of a former civil servant, Zaure managed to access archival documents, which helped the movement win some court cases:

> The city was ignorant about its own decisions. For instance, the Department of Land issued 23 official land acts to residents of Akbulak settlement alone. One of the reasons being that their homes were demolished nine

> times. It was a real war. Earlier decisions could be persuasive [for a court]. Like that, we prepared 25 large files of appeals.

Litigation proved to be an effective form of contestation. At the time of the interview, the residents' movement fully legalised 3600 homes, and were working on appeals for another 1500 cases. Zaure explained that the legal action achieved some gains because the informal residents collectively pressed for their rights, and refused to back down. Formal titles represented an important victory, because the informal residents were not defined as criminals, but as citizens (Yessenova, 2010). Formal titles recognised their rights, including rights to build a house and have a place to raise a family, ensuring a degree of security and prosperity.

As the market value of land began to rise again, the Almaty city administration postponed the legalisation programme, and started to attract investors to develop the settlements. Aman admitted that property development at Shanyrak and Bakai could result in new mass evictions:

> We know that people aren't happy about our lease agreements. And yes, when the investor comes to the district, people might be evicted, but they will be compensated. They will be able to buy something in another area. Our future plan is to demolish these houses and build brand new ones. We wish to improve things. Nobody wants African slums here.

Aman acknowledged that the newly legalised residents could be removed, and located to the outskirts of the city. Poor residents did not have a future in the city. The informal settlements were disparagingly described as 'African slums', so that the administration could justify their demolition in pursuit of economic development, civilisation and modernity (see also Karrar, 2020). Since 2006, the state has agreed to rehouse only 200 families, who were living in dangerous zones. The residents' movement was aware of the city administration's urban development plans, and had lobbied without success for a moratorium on the sale of land to private developers in their micro-districts. After years of social struggles and legal contestations, Zaure concluded that only the abolition of private property could help ordinary people to fend off the predatory alliance of state elites, financiers and property developers. But this required radical activism, which was absent in the country.

Protests Against Gentrification in Nur-Sultan

In Nur-Sultan, many rural migrants faced evictions from 2005 after their informal settlements were sold to multiple private developers. Similar to Almaty, the city administration used eminent domain to dispossess many families. But after the Shanyrak events, the Nur-Sultan city administration avoided undertaking forceful mass demolitions, instead it evicted residents on an individual basis. The administration refused to provide data on the number of forced demolitions, and the number of individuals who became homeless as a result (Rolnik, 2011).

In 2005, the residents of Ondiris and Kirpichnyi settlements asked Zauresh Battalova, who was then a parliamentarian, to assist them to defend their housing rights. Led by Battalova, an NGO For Decent Housing (Za Dostoinoe Zhil'e!) was formed to stop evictions. Using legal resources, the Ondiris and Kirpichnyi residents sued the city administration for failing to meet the right to adequate housing under international law. The law had been ratified in Kazakhstan, and it obligated the state to guarantee adequate compensation or alternative accommodation for families made homeless by demolition (Rolnik, 2011).

In 2007, the Ondiris and Kirpichnyi residents won a court case against the city administration, which agreed to offer alternative accommodation to families affected by state demolition. But in 2008, Imangali Tasmagambetov moved from Almaty to become the Mayor of Nur-Sultan, and he refused to recognise the court decision. His appointment stalled the progress over alternative accommodation. In a blatant disregard of the court decision, Ondiris and Kirpichnyi lands were officially sold to fourteen commercial property developers in December 2008. Since 2008, the private developers have tried to evict the Ondiris and Kirpichnyi residents. The city administration shifted the responsibility of compensation and alternative accommodation to the private developers, who neglected to do so. Battalova exhausted the legal process and believed that any further legal action was futile, because the courts had interpreted housing, land and other properties as market goods, rather than as human rights or public goods that required social regulation and protection (see also Sanghera, 2020).

The city administration displaced hundreds of families from Slobodka and Polyanka *dachas* (summer houses). Most of the evicted families were not informal settlers, because they had legal property documents. Slobodka and Polyanka gained premium value when they were included in the city territory, and the land became particularly favoured for elite housing (locally referred to as either Rublevka or Tengovka). The city officials forced evictions with minimal compensations to families, who were often unable to purchase suitable accommodation.

The resistance to evictions in Slobodka and Polyanka was fragmented and sporadic, prompting an NGO expert to observe that evicted families were more disciplined and less aggressive than Shanyrak residents. Mostly women held small protests against the evictions. Some protesters stood in front of their homes with a portrait of President Nazarbayev. Others climbed demolition cranes and stayed there for days with little food and water. The protests failed to stop the evictions (Glushkova, 2013).

While the city administration mostly succeeded in suppressing the resistance of informal and *dacha* residents, it was unprepared for a popular campaign for housing that followed the death of five sisters, aged between 3 months and 13 years old in February 2019. The five sisters died in a fire in a thirty-square metre dwelling on the outskirts of Nur-Sultan. The tragedy mobilised widespread protests by marginalised groups against poor housing conditions. The day after the funeral, many mothers and elderly women occupied city halls across the country to demand adequate accommodation. Kanagat Shumenova, a single mother of two children, helped to organise the mothers' protests in Nur-Sultan on almost a bi-weekly basis until the Covid-19 national lockdown forced an end to them.

The city administration deflected criticisms by urging the protesters to participate in the state housing programme. Kanagat, who worked as a police investigator for 25 years, explained that her pension of 13,000 tenge (30 USD) a month would not be enough for a deposit or monthly mortgage payments under the programme.[9] Launched in the early 2010s to address the housing crisis, the mortgage-based model was unaffordable for poor households. Battalova explained there was no social housing programme in the country:

> The social housing program in Kazakhstan is non-existent. All construction is aimed at building elite accommodation, and no-one is building the

[9] Kazakhstan's state-owned housing stock decreased from 7.8 million square metres in 2004 to 6.4 million square metres in 2008. During this period, the state allocated approximately one billion USD to the construction of mortgage-based housing for priority target groups, such as middle class public sector workers (Rolnik, 2011).

economy category of housing. They're all commercial projects, which allow companies to generate high profits. Today nobody wants to construct social housing. The reason for this is simple. Land in the central Nur-Sultan is expensive. Social housing can only be built in the suburbs where there is no infrastructure. Nobody wants to build communications there because it is too expensive. Construction companies try to use existing infrastructure, such as central heating system, water-supply system and electricity.

Battalova observed how the commercial property development catered for elites' desires and wants for luxurious accommodation while overlooking people's basic housing needs. It was not profitable for property developers to build social housing without state investment into physical infrastructure.

The dominant housing financing model resulted in lower rates of construction of affordable housing (Auyezkhanuly et al., 2019). In Sharipova's (2015) survey on Kazakhstan's housing, a majority of the respondents believed that housing had become less accessible after 1991. The private sector had failed to address the social housing problem. Using data on seventeen countries from 1920 to 2013, Kohl (2018) argues that the extension of mortgage credit to households did not lead to higher homeownership rates. More mortgage debt merely served to inflate asset prices, making homeownership difficult (Hudson, 2014). Historically, government programmes were better in building affordable houses.

Currently, over 6 million out of 8.4 million economically active population in Kazakhstan cannot afford to buy a house through various state housing programmes. Many privileged civil servants acquired state housing and rented them to other groups, who were desperate and in need of housing (Rolnik, 2011; Sharipova, 2015). In the process, the former became rentiers, extracting unearned income. In 2016, there were about 2.3 million people waiting for social housing. This number continues to grow (Auyezkhanuly et al., 2019).

In 2018, Nur-Sultan city administration created the Baikonur district, which consists of 19 settlements, including Ondyrys, Kirpichnyi and 12 *dacha* communities in Koyandy. In 2019, there were over 233,300 residents in Baikonur district. The urban development plan for the district proposed demolishing undesirable and chaotic informal houses, and constructing new elite housing and modern business centres. The Department of Architecture and Urban Planning prioritised the demolition of houses near the old market and in residential micro-districts of Koktal,

Chubary, Yugo-Vostok, Ondiris and Kazgorodok, because they aesthetically do not correspond to the status of the capital. The city plan did not specify where and how families from these areas would be relocated. Civilising and modernising the city invariably meant that rich and powerful groups obtained valuable assets, whereas poor groups were dispossessed, dislocated and neglected (Karrar, 2020).

Grassroots Movements for Housing and Land Rights in Kyrgyzstan

Housing Struggles in Osh and the Tulip Revolution

The urban housing crisis in Kyrgyzstan produced grassroots resistance in Osh and Bishkek. The resistance was incorporated into the 2005 political uprising. Bishkek's informal settlements, which initially emerged through 'quiet encroachment' (Bayat, 2000), doubled in size as a result of the 2005 Tulip Revolution. The origins of the Tulip Revolution can partly be traced to the housing crisis and struggles in Osh. The opposition to President Akayev's 15-year rule took shape in southern Kyrgyzstan. Many protestors were rural migrants, who joined the uprising because of a shortage of adequate housing.

Osh, as the second largest city in Kyrgyzstan, was a destination for many rural migrants from neighbouring regions. Due to the scarcity of urban land, many of them rented rooms in dilapidated dormitories, in summer houses in nearby areas, and rooms in minority ethnic Uzbek neighbourhoods.[10]

In the early 2000s, residents living in Soviet-era dormitories received eviction orders from new owners, who had recently acquired the dormitories. During the Soviet Union, the dormitories had belonged to various public organisations, which often housed their workers until the state issued them with permanent housing. In 1997, Alimbek Saralaev privatised Kirgizkurulush, a construction company, and received six dormitories for free on the condition of housing Kirgizkurulush workers. But soon after the privatisation, the residents were informed of a drastic increase in rent. The owner wanted to use the rent to pay the interest on a large bank loan. Over 640 families in the dormitories faced evictions, because of their

[10] Housing problems acquired an ethnised dimension in the city where minority ethnic Uzbeks constituted almost half of the city's population.

objections to the rent hike. In another case, hundreds of former textile employees had lived in factory-owned dormitories since the 1970s. After the dormitories were privatised, the new owner ordered the residents to be evicted, including those who had title deeds to their rooms.

A group of older women emerged as key protesters against the mass evictions. Tamara, a retired textile factory worker, mobilised the dormitory residents to sue the new owners for illegal evictions, and urged the Osh city administration to reverse the privatisation. The women leaders together with rural migrants spent two years in legal battles, losing district and regional court cases. The regional court ruled in favour of the private owners, and this fuelled a sense of injustice among the residents. Their lawyer advised them against taking the case to the Supreme Court in Bishkek, because the regional court judge had told them that the legal framework privileged private property rights, and they had little to no chance of winning (see Sanghera, 2020).

During the course of their two-year legal struggle, the dormitory residents developed a place-related collective identity, and a property-related consciousness of rights. They learnt about the privatisation process of dormitories, and how the business elites undermined their housing rights. Frohlich (2020: 189) observes that protesters' social interactions can 'trigger a collective process of meaning-making regarding interpersonally shared grievances', leading to dissent and protests.

Dispossession and exclusion politicised the dormitory residents to take radical actions and occupy spaces. After losing their court case, Tamara mobilised 83 families to occupy a disused public building:

> I worked for the factory for more than 20 years and didn't get housing. Many Kyrgyz employees who worked for the factory were left with nothing. Just like me. . . . In 2004 we broke into this abandoned building and occupied the rooms. Then we started picketing in front of the mayor's office to demand housing.

Tamara was angry and upset at how unfair and unjust the situation was for her and others over eviction orders and lack of social housing. She mobilised other affected families to address the issues. Other women leaders recruited migrants, who lacked proper accommodation, so enlarging the movement. The women activists articulated their housing needs, and argued for a redistributive policy based on moral values on how poor Kyrgyz people ought to be treated.

In 2004–2005, the women activists organised numerous protests, including hunger strikes and sit-ins, and asserted their housing rights. They frequently stormed into the offices of senior state officials, including the city mayor and the regional governor, and blocked major roads, drawing attention to their cause and gaining access to public officials. Unlike Kazakhstan, Kyrgyzstan had a more open political structure that allowed dissent in public spaces. The women leaders erected a Kyrgyz yurt in the public square of the city as their meeting place.

Moreover, police officers were reluctant to batter, push or drag protesters, most of whom were older women, fearing public backlash. The activists' political tactics included sit-ins, occupations and picketing that aimed to force the political elites to understand their grievances, as Jarkyn, one of the women leaders, explained:

> We occupied the governor's office and refused to give his seat back. When we took over his office, we told him, 'Now you're just like us, an ordinary person! Can you now understand where we're coming from?' And we kept on coming back. They couldn't get rid of us. When they got tired, they began negotiating with us.

Jarkyn believed that senior officeholders were not emotionally moved by accounts of injustice and suffering, and were only pushed into negotiations because of the movement's perseverance and tactics. Local state officials, who were unable to resolve the issue of housing, were forced to give rent subsidies for targeted groups, who previously did not receive them. But this measure was a limited concession, because only a small minority of families benefitted.

In early 2005, oppositional elites began to recruit disaffected social groups against President Akayev's regime. Some of them approached the older women activists after hearing about their contentious tactics against senior state officials, as Tamara recalled:

> So our attack on the Mayor quickly became famous in Osh. After that attack, various people started to seek our attention. In 2005 I set up my yurt in the centre and was making fried bread and selling *kymyz* [mare's

milk] from my yurt. One day Bayaman[11] and his people came to my yurt and they asked me to set up a women's group for the upcoming uprising. During those days Bayaman and Tekebaev[12] often came to my yurt. . . . My housing situation led me to become active in the 2005 revolution. I participated wholeheartedly in the revolution.

Local women leaders agreed to support the oppositional leaders with the understanding and hope that the latter would resolve their housing problems. Kyrgyzstan's oppositional leaders capitalised on urban grievances, and integrated them into their broader political struggles. The local protesters forced the city mayor and the regional governor out of their offices in the run-up to the Tulip Revolution in March 2005. The older women's enthusiastic participation in the political uprising was motivated by their normative concerns about housing and broader social justice, rather than any affinity or loyalty to oppositional forces.

When President Akayev's regime was toppled and the new ruling elites came to power, the new president did not deliver on his promise of more housing and land in Osh. Tamara explained, 'After the revolution I met [President] Bakiev at least six times in the White House. But he didn't solve our housing problem.' While President Bakiev clearly recognised Tamara's legitimacy by accepting and talking to her on six occasions, he was not willing to prioritise resources to honour their deal.

Informal Residents' Demand for Land and Legalisation in Bishkek

The 2005 Tulip Revolution prompted thousands of rural migrants living in cramped and dilapidated conditions to seize land on the outskirts of Bishkek. They acted decisively, sensing that the window of opportunity was short. Within days they formed their own groups, divided land plots, swiftly laid foundations, and began demanding legalisation. One of such groups was formed in Kelechek by Kanykey, a 50-year-old rural migrant. After the closure of a mercury factory in Kadamjai district of Batken province, Kanykey moved to Bishkek in 1995. For ten years, she rented a

[11] Bayaman Erkinbaev was an infamous Kyrgyzstani nouveau riche, who privatised the Karasuu Bazaar and controlled drug trafficking in southern Kyrgyzstan. He also served as a parliamentarian for three terms. He was killed after the 2005 Tulip Revolution.

[12] Omurbek Tekebaev was the leader of Ata Meken political party and a parliamentarian. He was a leading oppositional figure during Presidents Akayev's and Bakiev's regimes.

room near Dordoi Market, where she sold bread. She acted quickly when she heard that people were taking land, 'On 11 April, we women got together and came to Kelechek. We didn't even know how to measure one *sotka* [100 square metres]. Every person in my group got thirteen steps of land.'

Kalys, another rural migrant, described her group's mood, 'No one cared about us for all these fifteen years, so now we took care of ourselves!' Bishkek's rural migrants capitalised on the uprising to redistribute resources and achieve some justice. In our study, many informal residents claimed that the Tulip Revolution was their revolution, and they deserved a small land plot after many years of deprivation. Hatcher (2017: 186) observes that the protestors were angry that 'the "trickle down" effects following years of shock therapy remained with the political elites', and now 'the people wanted a piece of it, too.' The interim government did not have the moral authority to condemn land occupations when they had just grabbed power. It was widely understood that oppositional elites promised to give rural migrants land around Bishkek in exchange for their support in overthrowing President Akayev.

The rural migrants' land seizures caused an outcry among Bishkek's middle class urban population. On 10 April 2005, about 3000–5000 residents of Bishkek and Chui oblast staged a rally in the central Ala-Too Square, demanding a moratorium on land distribution. Following the demonstration, the urban middle class residents formed a committee For Stability and the Rule of Law to prevent further land distribution around Bishkek. In response, the rural migrants established their own committee Coordination Council and grassroots initiative groups (such as Ai Bulak, Yntymak, Asanbai, Kaarman, Tynchtyk, Jashasyn, Dil Nur, Muras Ordo, Sovmin, Muras, Rukhiy Muras, Ordo Jer, Jygach, Beliy Sokol, Jetigen, Bakai Ordo, Dunuyo koomu) to pressurise the state to deliver on land promises. The Bishkek and Chui state officials had to navigate between these two opposing social groups.

The two groups clashed in Lebedinovka (near Tunguch micro-district) and Kok Jar during the summer and autumn of 2005. In Lebidinovka, the residents protested against the authorisation of fifty hectares of arable lands for individual housing construction for rural migrants. In Kok Jar, the confrontation between its residents and about 1500 land claimants lasted two days, resulting in injuries on both sides. The Kok Jar residents resisted the migrants' attempts to seize land by surrounding the field with horse riders.

Throughout the summer and autumn of 2005, the rural migrants held frequent protests in front of the city administration, demanding authorities to honour their promise of land allocation, and expedite the distribution process. Administrative delays were met with more land occupations. For instance, in September 2005 about 500 people, representing Asanbai and Altyn Kazyk grassroots initiative groups, occupied thirty-six hectares of land opposite the US Embassy. But in October 2005, the city administration declared that land allocation for individual housing construction was over, and that future housing claims would only be met through the construction of multistorey housing. The government retroactively legalised most settlements. It then asked the World Bank to support infrastructure improvements in the new settlements.

Some of the post-2005 informal settlements (e.g. Kelechek and Ak Jar) faced opposition from rich individuals, who had privatised the land upon which the settlements were built for commercial purposes, such as marketplaces. Raikan Alkanov,[13] who is one of the top 100 richest individuals in Kyrgyzstan, claimed ownership of land in Kelechek. He prevented the legalisation of Kelechek settlement for five years. On several occasions, laws enforcement officers threatened and removed some informal residents. But the residents refused to be intimidated, and Kelechek was eventually legalised. It was unclear whether Alkanov received another land site, or monetary compensation for surrendering his rights to Kelechek.

In Ak Jar, about 4000 households resisted Arslan Maliev, a former rich parliamentarian, who had privatised 134.5 hectares of farmland in 1997. According to the head of Alamedin administration, Ak Jar residents pressurised the Prosecutor's Office to sue Maliev, and return the land to the state. The legal dispute lasted six years, and in February 2011, the Supreme Court ruled in favour of the state, citing Maliev's failure to use the land for agricultural purposes and his failure to pay land taxes from 1997 to 2005. The court decision was based on the technicalities of private ownership, and it did not challenge the notion of private ownership (Hatcher, 2017). While the state prohibited land distribution to rural migrants, the Bishkek City Council illicitly authorised the distribution of Ataturk Park land plots to wealthy elites until 2010.

[13] Raikan Alkanov is the owner of Alkanov and Co Market adjacent to Dordoi Auto Market.

After the struggles over legalisation, the residents of new settlements demanded better infrastructure; e.g. electricity, paved roads and sanitation. In Kazakhstan, informal residents, who lacked basic infrastructure, did not petition the authorities to improve their settlements. Kazakhstani rural migrants were willing to improve the infrastructure on their own as long as the state legalised their land plots. But in Bishkek, the residents viewed improvements to their living conditions as the 'real legalisation'. The infrastructure was important for their well-being and recognition as citizens.

Land Struggles in Osh and Bishkek After the 2010 Uprising

In April 2010, President Bakiev's regime was toppled in a violent uprising, which resulted in 87 people killed, and over 1000 injured with gunshot wounds. The political conflict led to the ethnic violence between the majority Kyrgyz and minority Uzbeks a couple of months later in Osh that claimed hundreds of lives. The city became a site of a desperate power struggle between the interim government and a populist Mayor Melis Myrzakmatov. The former was keen to mobilise support among majority Kyrgyz for the upcoming parliamentary and presidential elections.

Several older women leaders used the opportunity of elite fragmentation and weak state legitimacy to demand housing. They successfully negotiated for resources with the interim government, which felt guilty and fearful in the post-conflict and pre-election context. Several months after the tragic violence in the city, they met the interim Prime Minister Atambaev. His belated appearance compounded the interim government's lack of legitimacy, giving the older women leaders further leverage in negotiations, as Jarkyn explained:

> When [Prime Minister Atambaev and other ministers] came here all they could say was that they hadn't anticipated how things would turn out. But we told them, 'Look at how many people have died! That means that you're responsible! Now after all the mistakes you made, why aren't you making compensation to the people? How can you be a real leader of the country?'

Jarkyn believed that the interim government had to be accountable for the violence and deaths in June, and make appropriate compensation. After the meeting, Atambaev, who was campaigning to become the next president, ordered the local authorities to immediately find and distribute land for housing to poor residents. He also instructed his ministers to make payments to families affected by the violence, and forgive affected families of their debts and tuition fees (see also Eurasianet, 2011).

When the local authorities delayed the process of land distribution, the older women leaders mobilised about 1000 rural migrants and seized 80 hectares of minority ethnic Uzbek-owned farmland in Karasuu district to put pressure on the authorities. Zeinep, one of the older women leaders, explained that the political elites were anxious not to reignite ethnic clashes, and expediated the allocation of 500 hectares of land from the neighbouring Karasuu district to about 45,000 applicants. After the presidential election, the authorities distributed a further 1124 hectares (see Ibraimov, 2011). Several older women leaders became members of a committee, which registered applicants for land allocation. They oversaw the registration of about 45,000 applicants, posting applicants' registration details on large window panels of the town hall, so that the process was seen to be transparent.

In Bishkek, residents of informal and legalised settlements also used the 2010 uprising as an opportunity to win concessions for their settlements and gain more land. About a couple of weeks after the uprising, hundreds of poor majority ethnic Kyrgyz marched to the village of Mayevka to seize land belonging to minority ethnic Meskhetian Turks, who fought back to defend their homes. In the ensuing violence, many homes were burnt, and several people died. The new interim government ordered the army to stop and shoot looters and 'land-grabbers' in an attempt to re-establish the rule of law and social order, and win the confidence and trust of the international investment community and local businesses. Nevertheless some existing informal settlements, such as Ak-Ordo and Tynchtyk, expanded with new arrivals of migrant families (Sanghera et al., 2012).

Between 2010 and 2013, internal migrants organised over 2000 protests in Bishkek, turning the city into a hotbed of civil activism (see also Nasritdinov & Schroder, 2017). Activism peaked during the 2011 electoral year, when residents from Ak Jar, Jumgal Ata, Archa-Beshik, Ak-Ordo and other settlements demonstrated outside state buildings and blocked main roads. They met senior state officials and politicians to demand basic utilities and services. In August 2011, the Ak Jar residents blocked the main road for the second time in the year, claiming that the city administration had failed to fulfil its earlier promise to provide electricity and water. Atambaev publicly reprimanded the mayor of Bishkek and the regional governor for their failures, and ordered the Bishkek City Council to take control of Ak Jar (Sanghera et al., 2012).

The Bishkek administration tried to improve infrastructure in the settlements. It built several schools and nurseries, and improved the provision of electricity and water.[14] Despite the official rhetoric of inclusion, the Bishkek administration stressed that its budget was limited, and urged the settlements to attract donor funds and mobilise their own resources. In one case, an NGO Arysh attracted donors to fund trainings on self-help, legal rights and microcredit entrepreneurship. Since 2006, it has established 130 self-help groups in the new settlements with the aim of developing road maps to improve infrastructure. The activities of Arysh and other similar NGOs reflected the neoliberal development ideology, which shifted the responsibility of social development to individuals, and discouraged political activism and mobilisation. In our interview with the director of Arysh, Talgat explained that self-help groups were trying to teach the residents 'not to block roads and scream', but develop their own strategies for improving life.

Conclusion

The chapter examined how the post-Soviet urban development in Kazakhstan and Kyrgyzstan produced grassroots resistance to the neoliberal commodification of land and real estate. City administrations and speculative capital tried to dispossess and exclude poor and migrant groups from the city in pursuit of acquisition and civilisation of urban spaces (Harvey, 2013). In our study, the informal residents opposed state and business elites' attempts to evict them, and asserted their right to the city. They objected to how neoliberal land and property reforms had prioritised the interests of the rich and powerful, resulting in spatial inequalities and social suffering. They construed land and real estate in terms of social needs and well-being, rather than as instruments to acquire wealth and power (Sanghera & Satybaldieva, 2012).

[14] According to the mayor's office, out of 47 settlements, 17 had schools with a total capacity of 20,000 children. In 2016, there were 46,066 school children in the settlements. There were only seven kindergartens with a total capacity of 2106 children. The Ombudsman Report (2017) found that drinking water provision in Bishkek settlements reached only about 67% of the residents.

The relationship between political regimes and countermovements was complex and multidirectional (Goodwin, 2018). The post-Soviet states had the capacity to accommodate, dilute and repress movements' demands for protection. The grassroots movements engaged in conventional and contentious forms of political action. The nature of housing and land struggles was partly shaped by country-specific political structures. Kazakhstan's political structures were restrictive that repressed, co-opted and removed oppositional leaders. Housing protests were limited to defending existing urban encroachments, rather than demanding new concessions (Bayat, 2000). Kyrgyzstan's relatively open political structures enabled the rural migrants to be proactive, and demand new concessions from state authorities. The open political structures created some opportunities to build alliances between oppositional elites and marginalised groups that expanded and improved informal settlements.

Speculative capital into the real estate sector in Kazakhstan affectedthe state's relationship with informal settlements. The state was captured by the rentier class to promote urban and housing strategies that facilitated rent extraction. Foreign and domestic capital fuelled the country's construction boom and real estate speculation. National and local authorities pursued repressive and exclusionary urban policies that involved denying informal residents full rights to their homes. Urban development plans proposed the demolition of informal settlements, and the construction of elite apartment complexes, shopping malls and business centres to increase revenues to state budgets and reflect the country's modern and global image (Karrar, 2020). The housing needs of poor migrants were secondary, and state concessions were extracted under considerable political pressure.

Kyrgyzstan's swift legalisation of informal settlements and their formal inclusion into the city were outcomes of grassroots resistance. The movement leaders and activists took advantage of political uprisings to distribute and legalise land for poor and migrant groups. The state elites were forced to make concessions to them, who had temporarily politicised poverty and lack of housing. There were no mass demolitions and eviction orders. In some cases, the state administrations acted on behalf of informal residents against the rentier class to ensure their political legitimacy and authority. Although the informal residents' gains were significant, they did not alter the nature of property rights, which continued to favour the asset-rich over the asset-poor, and rent extraction over social needs (Sanghera & Satybaldieva, 2020).

The neoliberal property regime was dominant in Kazakhstan and Kyrgyzstan, allocating rights, wealth and power to property owners, and shifting the responsibility of housing to the private sector. To address the housing shortage, the mortgage-based affordable housing model was adopted that favoured middle class families (Sharipova, 2015). Many working class and poor migrant families often had little option but to erect, buy or rent a house in informal or newly legalised settlements. These settlements were tolerated, because they served as a buffer to control public anger and demand for public housing (Smart, 2001). The housing and informal settlement movements wanted public housing provision or highly regulated housing market, but they struggled against a powerful class alliance of property developers, financiers and plutocrats.

References

Aldashev, A. (2011). *Determinants of internal migration in Kazakhstan* (Working Papers 301). Osteuropa-Institut Regensburg.

Auyezkhanuly, A., Manap, A., Akpanov, A., & Karshalova, A. (2019). The study of the residential real estate market in the Republic of Kazakhstan. *Journal of Real Estate Literature, 27*(1), 117–133.

Bayat, A. (2000). From 'dangerous classes' to 'quiet rebels': Politics of the urban subaltern in the global south. *International Sociology, 15*(3), 533–557.

Bizhanova, M. (2018). Can the Silk Road revive agriculture? Kazakhstan's challenges in attaining economic diversification. In M. Laruelle (Ed.), *China's Belt and Road initiative and its impact in Central Asia* (pp. 54–67). The George Washington University.

Burawoy, M. (2015). Facing an unequal world. *Current Sociology, 63*(1), 5–34.

Davis, M. (2004, March–April). Planet of slums. *New Left Review, 26*, 5–34.

Eurasianet. (2011, May 14). *Kyrgyzstan to pay Osh victims' families: Can it be done fairly*? https://eurasianet.org/kyrgyzstan-to-pay-osh-victims-families-can-it-be-done-fairly.

Fatyanova, U. (2017). *Eksperty poschitali skol'ko Kazakhstan potratil na EKSPO-2017*. https://the-steppe.com/novosti/eksperty-podschitali-skolko-kazahstan-potratil-na-ekspo-2017.

Frohlich, C. (2020). Urban citizenship under post-Soviet conditions: Grassroots struggles of residents in contemporary Moscow. *Journal of Urban Affairs, 42*(2), 188–202.

Fryer, P., Nasritdinov, E., & Satybaldieva, E. (2014). Moving toward the brink? Migration in the Kyrgyz Republic. *Central Asian Affairs, 1*(2), 171–198.

Gawecki, M. (2013). New urbanization of the steppe. Astana: A capital called the capital. *Studia Historiae Oeconomicae, 31*(1), 35–56.

Glushkova, S. (2013). Protest na krane prodoljaetsya vtorye sutki. *Azattyq*. https://rus.azattyq.org/a/protest-na-krane-vyselenie-nazarbayev-universitet/25165763.html.

Goodwin, G. (2018). Rethinking the double movement: Expanding the frontiers of Polanyian analysis in the Global South. *Development and Change, 49*(5), 1268–1290.

Harvey, D. (2013). *Rebel cities: From the right to the city to the urban revolution*. Verso.

Hatcher, C. (2017). Making property in Kyrgyzstan: Bishkek's urban periphery as redistributive space. *Central Asian Affairs, 4*(2), 173–196.

Hudson, M. (2014). *The bubble and beyond* (New). ISLET.

Ibraimov, B. (2011). *Kyrgyz plan grants land in South*. http://centralasiaonline.com/en_GB/articles/caii/features/main/2011/04/27/feature-01?mobile=true.

Jumagulov, M., & Li, A. (2019). Osobnyaki vmesto derev'ev. Kak vlasti Bishkeka unichtojili bol'she treti parka Ata Turk. *Kloop*. https://kloop.kg/t/park-ata turk/osobnyaki-vmesto-derevyev/.

Karrar, H. (2020). The bazaar in ruins: Rent and fire in Barakholka Almaty. *Central Asian Survey, 39*(1), 80–94.

Koch, N. (2012). Urban 'utopias': The Disney stigma and discourses of 'false modernity.' *Environment and Planning A: Economy and Space, 44*(10), 2445–2462. https://doi.org/10.1068/a44647.

Koch, N. (2014). Bordering on the modern: Power, practice and exclusion in Astana. *Transactions of the Institute of British Geographers, 39*(3), 432–443. https://doi.org/10.1111/tran.12031.

Kohl, S. (2018). More mortgages, more homes? The effect of housing financialization on homeownership in historical perspective. *Politics and Society, 46*(2), 177–203. https://doi.org/10.17/0032921875750.

Laszczkowski, M. (2011). Building the future: Construction, temporality, and politics in Astana. *Focaal—Journal of Global and Historical Anthropology, 60*(June), 77–92. https://doi.org/10.3167/fcl.2011.600107.

Lefebvre, H. (1996). *Writing on cities*. Blackwell.

Millar, J. (2016). Inside Astana, Kazakhstan: The 40 billion dollar city. *GQ*. https://www.gq.com.au/lifestyle/travel/inside-astana-kazakhstan-the-40-billion-dollar-city/news-story/1a3b7b9ac1c751efb23f827e456385d8.

Mitchell, D. (2003). *The right to the city. Social justice and the fight for public space*. The Guildford Press.

Mogilevskii, R., Abdrazakova, N., Bolotbekova, A., Chalbasova, S., Dzhumaeva, S., & Tilekeyev, K. (2017). *The outcomes of 25 years of agricultural reforms in Kyrgyzstan* (Discussion Paper No. 162). Leibniz Institute of Agricultural Development in Transition Economies, Halle. http://nbn-resolving.de/urn:nbn:de:gbv:3:2-69129.

Nasritdinov, E., & Schroder, P. (2017). Re/claiming Bishkek: Contestation and activism in the city of two revolutions. *Central Asian Affairs, 4*(2), 97–128.

Niyazbekov, N. (2018). Is Kazakhstan immune to color revolutions? The social movements perspective. *Demokratizatsiya, 26*(3), 401–426.

Ombudsmen Report. (2017). *Novostroiki g. Bishkek: pravo na dostatochnoe jil'e, i inye socialnye, ekonomicheskie i kulturnye prava*. https://ombudsman.kg/index.php?option=com_content&view=article&id=101&catid=52&Itemid=364&lang=ru. Accessed July 2020.

Osmonova, K. (2016). Experiencing liminality: Housing, renting and informal tenants in Astana. *Central Asian Survey, 35*(2), 237–256. https://doi.org/10.1080/02634937.2016.1146010.

Pchelyanskaya, I. (2016). *How much did housing cost 25 years ago?* Krishna. https://krisha.kz/content/articles/2016/skol-ko-stoilo-zhil-yo-25-let-nazad.

Polanyi, K. (1944). *The great transformation: Economic and political origins of our time*. Rinehart.

Rolnik, R. (2011). *Report of the Special Rapporteur on adequate housing as a component of the right to an adequate standard of living, and on the right to non-discrimination in this context.* UN Human Rights Council. https://www.ohchr.org/EN/HRBodies/HRC/RegularSessions/Session25/Documents/A_HRC_25_54_Add.2_ENG.DOC. Accessed July 2020.

Sanghera, B. (2020). Justice, power and informal settlements: Understanding the juridical view of property rights in Central Asia. *International Sociology, 35*(1), 22–44.

Sanghera, B., & Satybaldieva, E. (2012). Ethics of property, illegal settlements and the right to subsistence. *International Journal of Sociology and Social Policy, 32*(1/2), 96–114.

Sanghera, B., & Satybaldieva, E. (2020). The other road to serfdom: The rise of the rentier class in post-Soviet economies. *Social Science Information, 59*(3), 505–536. https://doi.org/10.1177/0539018420943077.

Sanghera, B., Satybaldieva, E., Rodionov, A., Serikzhanova, S., Choibekov, N., & Sultanmuratova, K. (2012). *Illegal settlements and city registration in Kyrgyzstan and Kazakhstan: Implications for legal empowerment*. Open Society Foundations.

Schroder, P. (2010). 'Urbanizing' Bishkek: Interrelations of boundaries, migration, group size and opportunity structure. *Central Asian Survey, 29*(4), 453–467.

Seitz, W. (2020). Urbanization in Kazakhstan: Desirable cities, unaffordable housing, and the missing rental market. *International Journal of Urban Sciences*. https://doi.org/10.1080/12265934.2019.1709534.

Sharipova, D. (2015). Who gets what, when and how? Housing and informal institutions in the Soviet Union and post-Soviet Kazakhstan. *Central Asian Affairs, 2*(2), 140–167.

Smart, A. (2001). Unruly places: Urban governance and the persistence of illegality in Hong Kong's urban squatter areas. *American Anthropologist, 103*(1), 30–44.

Steimann, B. (2011). *Making a living in uncertainty: Agro-pastoral livelihoods and institutional transformations in post-socialist rural Kyrgyzstan*. University of Zurich.

Torebaeva, M., & Ivanov, A. (2006). Imangali Tasmagambetov: Davaite vmeste rassmatrivat' etu problem. *Nomad*. https://nomad.su/?a=10-200607250314.

Turganbayev, Y., & Diener, A. (2018). Kazakhstan's evolving regional economic policy: Assessing strategies of post-socialist development. *Eurasian Geography and Economics, 59*(5–6), 657–684. https://doi.org/10.1080/15387216.2019.1586559.

Yessenova, S. (2010). Borrowed places: Eviction wars and property rights formalization in Kazakhstan. In *Economic action in theory and practice: Anthropological investigations, research in economic anthropology* (Vol. 30, pp. 11–45).

CHAPTER 8

Confronting the Power of Money: The Anti-Debt Movements

This chapter examines how the anti-debt movements emerged and developed in Kazakhstan and Kyrgyzstan. They protested over the harmful effects of the neoliberal commodification of money, which allowed lenders to extract income through interest. They demanded strong safeguards against usurious interest, financial malpractices and extrajudicial repossessions. The movement activists engaged in a reflexive process of interpreting and evaluating their situation, and attributing blame for their hardship (Crossley, 2002a). Over time, the movements moved from individualising and localising debt relations to politicising and internationalising them.

The anti-debt movements were weakened by internal social and class tensions as well as the state's repressive responses to their demands (Goodwin, 2018). Different groups of borrowers offered competing accounts of the debt relations, resulting in lack of class solidarity against a powerful class alliance of political, financial and legal elites. Whereas urban middle class borrowers wanted limited state interventions, rural working class borrowers campaigned for radical solutions. The state employed a range of discursive, legal, administrative and coercive tactics to disempower the movements.

The chapter is divided into five sections. Section 'The Debt Problem' briefly discusses the development of debt and its problems in Kazakhstan and Kyrgyzstan. The second section draws on our first case

B. Sanghera and E. Satybaldieva, *Rentier Capitalism and Its Discontents*,
https://doi.org/10.1007/978-3-030-76303-9_8

study to examine how borrowers emotionally experienced, interpreted and evaluated their indebtedness. Section 'The Anti-Debt Mobilisation in Kazakhstan' analyses the development and splintering of anti-debt resistance in Kazakhstan, and the state's complex interactions with movement leaders. The fourth section examines how the anti-debt movement struggled against the state and financial elites in Kyrgyzstan. Finally, the conclusion summarises the chapter's key findings and ideas.

The Debt Problem

When the post-Soviet countries gained independence in 1991, most of the population was free of commercial debt (Hudson, 2015). In the 1990s and 2000s, lending institutions in Kazakhstan and Kyrgyzstan borrowed from US and other Western financial institutions to finance a rapid expansion of credit. Loans were largely used for petty retail trade, real estate and household consumption. Central Asian commercial banks and microfinance institutions became integrated into the global circuit of capital.

Since independence, Kazakhstan's banks have actively borrowed from abroad, driving the domestic credit boom. Today, more than 80% of the economically active population are indebted (Panchenko, 2020). The banking sector accounted for 93% of the total loan portfolio. About 70% of loans were linked to the real estate sector that increased house prices at an unprecedented rate (Seitz, 2020). By 2007, 95% of housing transactions were financed at interest rates of 15–20%.[1] The state mortgage-based housing programme promoted and expanded the financialisation of the housing market (Yessenova, 2010). From 2004 to 2007, 200,000 mortgage loans were issued that amounted to 1.1 trillion Kazakhstani tenge (Pchelyanskaya, 2016). A significant share of the mortgage loans was US dollar-denominated, partly reflecting the appeal of lower interest rates of US dollar-denominated loans compared to those denominated in Kazakhstani tenge.

[1] A mortgage loan of 79,200 USD for a small studio at 15% interest rate over 30 years would amount to 249,880 USD in interest payments in addition to the principal (Azattyk, 2014).

Kyrgyzstan's financial sector also expanded quickly as a result of foreign capital flows.[2] In particular, Kyrgyzstan's microfinance sector grew rapidly with the support of Western donor and financial institutions. Global and regional financiers introduced commercialised microcredit lending to achieve high returns on equity. In Kyrgyzstan, the average interest rate on microfinance loans was about 34% in 2014. In 2019, Kyrgyzstan had the fifth highest real lending interest rate in the world (The Global Economy, 2020). High interest is a regressive form of income distribution (Hudson, 2015). From 1995 to 2012, microcredit enabled a transfer of up to 125 billion USD from poor communities in the Global South to financial centres in the Global North (Mader, 2015).

For Kazakhstan, the 2007–2008 financial crisis was compounded by a sharp decline in oil prices. The situation exposed domestic commercial banks' reliance and vulnerability to Western credit. The banking sector experienced a lack of liquidity, bad debts and huge losses. The devaluation of the national currency increased the domestic debt by 25–30% (Barisitz & Lahnsteiner, 2010). Esenbek Ukteshbaev, a leader of Ostavim Narodu Zhil'e! movement in Kazakhstan, argued that the financial elites violated Article 282 of the Civil Code by issuing US dollar-denominated loans because the law prohibited transactions in foreign currency within the country. Many households struggled to keep up with high mortgage repayments. The share of non-performing loans of the total loans increased from 7% in 2008 to a disquieting 38% in 2009 (Barisitz & Lahnsteiner, 2010).

Moreover, the financial crisis forced many construction companies in Kazakhstan to close, leaving about 450 projects unfinished. More than 62,889 shareholders (*dol'shiki*), who took out bank loans to participate in the housing construction, also suffered. Of these, about 16,000 shareholders lost their deposits to housing companies that left the country without completing their projects. Many shareholders were evicted from their unfinished apartments, because they were unable to make monthly repayments (Rolnik, 2011).

[2] In 2015, there were 24 commercial banks, including 16 with foreign share capital. Ten of these had foreign shareholdings of more than 50% (International Finance Corporation, 2016). There are only two state-owned banks, accounting for 18% of the total banking sector.

In Kyrgyzstan, the problem of indebtedness was significant among microcredit borrowers,[3] who were the most vulnerable members of society. Women were targeted for microcredit lending under the pretext of gender empowerment (Bateman, 2010; Fedirici, 2014). A global neoliberal strategy for debt-based growth viewed marginalised groups as a high-yielding investment opportunity. As Soederberg (2014: 202) explains, international finance targeted women 'as less risky investment choices because of innate gendered characteristics, such as the responsibility to nurture and work harder.' A study of over 90 microfinance institutions (MFIs) in Central Asia shows that targeting women improved the financial performance and profits of MFIs (Janda & Turbat, 2013). In Kyrgyzstan, by 2015 62% of borrowers were women, most of whom lived in rural areas (Sultakeev et al., 2018). The two leading MFIs in the country, Kompanion and FINCA, had very high rates of female borrowers, 85% and 67% respectively (Yale School of Management, 2011a). As a consequence, the regressive distribution of global wealth was clearly gendered, as female borrowers generated most of the surplus value, which was partly siphoned off to global financial elites (Fedirici, 2014; Keating et al., 2010).

The financial regulations in Kazakhstan and Kyrgyzstan minimised legal protections for borrowers, and removed limits on interest rates that facilitated predatory lending (Soederberg, 2014). The lack of financial regulations created a criminogenic environment in the financial sector (Black, 2011; Tombs, 2012). Pressurised to expand their loan portfolios, banks and MFIs offered loans to people on low income and with poor credit history. In some cases, sub-prime lending was operated informally by bank employees and managers, who appropriated borrowers' repayments. Sub-prime lending led to a high number of repossessions. In our study, many borrowers reported that banks had significantly undervalued their homes and other properties used as collateral, and sold them swiftly to insiders at below the market price.

Moreover, many borrowers were unaware of the terms and conditions of their loans. Ukteshbaev explained that many borrowers incurred excessive fines that had enlarged their debt: 'I took a loan of 12 million tenge,

[3] In Kyrgyzstan, the official estimate of microcredit borrowers reached 536,662 people in 2016 (Akchabar, 2016). In 2018, the number of people with credit loans in Kyrgyzstan had increased by 64.7%. Kyrgyzstan is predicted to have a full-blown over-indebtedness crisis, and is among the dangerously 'at-risk' countries (Bateman, 2018).

and the fine amounted to about 23 million tenge, exceeding the 10% limit of the principal' (Moskovka, 2010). Often borrowers did not know about the varied penalty charges, and were trapped in a spiral of debt. Until 2014, loan contracts in Kyrgyzstan violated banking and microfinance laws, because they were only available in Russian, rendering them incomprehensible to Kyrgyz-speaking borrowers (Mihailova, 2017). To prevent outside scrutiny of their business practices, banks and MFIs did not allow borrowers to share the details of their contracts with third parties.

Neoliberalised finance increased the pressure on social actors to circumvent regulations in pursuit of short-term profits (Whyte & Wiegratz, 2016). Such abuses were widespread in the financial sector (Paprocki, 2016). Most borrowers had little choice but to enter into an unequal social relationship with lenders, who often imposed terms and conditions on the former. While lenders justified loan contracts as voluntary and equal, in reality, debt involved an imbalance of power and exploitation, as discussed in Chapter 3. In Central Asia, borrowers confronted financial institutions without a significant level of state protection and rights that existed and was enjoyed by borrowers in developed countries (Keating et al., 2010).

The Affects and Effects of Indebtedness

Crossley (2002a) explains the importance of strain in precipitating social movement activity. Strain is defined as the effects of 'a negative mismatch between agents' habitual expectations, assumptions and ways of being-in-the-world' (Crossley, 2002b: 679). Strains can generate protests if they contribute to both affective elements (e.g. anger and shame) and cognitive effects of shocking agents out of their habitual engagement with the world. In particular, debt-related shame is a harmful emotion, causing a range of negative psychological outcomes, including low self-esteem, anxiety and depression (Engel, 2019).

In Kyrgyzstan, the strain of microcredit indebtedness was amplified throughdebt recovery technologies, such as the use of shame. MFIs actively deployed shaming techniques in order to maximise loan repayment rates (Karim, 2011). In our study, many borrowers felt an intense sense of shame and anger when credit collectors publicly humiliated them, and threatened them with legal action or bodily harm. They were in a constant state of fear and anxiety because debt collectors harassed them. Elisa, a female borrower in Kyrgyzstan, described her situation:

> You've to be made of stone to bear their insults and terror tactics. They came to my school and shamed me in front of my students and the school director.

Elisa explains how shaming was performed at her workplace to achieve significant impact. In the context where borrowers are expected to show moral character and discipline by paying off their loans, Elisa's honesty and integrity came under scrutiny, causing her to feel intense shame. The level of public humiliation and intimidation was a novel experience for many borrowers.

Fedirici (2014) explains that lenders and international agencies have studied various mechanisms by which different communities culturally enforce their social mores. Women have been deliberately subjected to shaming, because gendered norms of social reputation and honour make them sensitive to shame in a patriarchal culture (Engel, 2019). In Kyrgyzstan, local MFI employees often involved district state officials (*akims*) and the courts of elders (*aksakals*) to shame women for missing their repayments.

MFIs introduced group-based loans, which transformed communal relationships into a peer pressure mechanism for debt payment. This form of debt intensified shame and moral scrutiny in comparison to debt relationships between individual lenders and borrowers (Engel, 2019). When members of the family or social network turned into quasi-debt collectors, it personalised debt and discipline, exacerbating the sense of shame. Several female borrowers compared the shame of debt to being 'eaten' or 'swallowed' by it. Abusive mechanisms of shaming proved to be very effective, explaining the paradox of a high repayment rate among vulnerable women (Fedirici, 2014; Karim, 2011; Keating et al., 2010).

In addition to shaming, the financial sector undertook extrajudicial seizure of borrowers' properties (Kudryavtseva, 2016; Kushnareva, 2008). A delay in payment of over a 60-day period allowed banks and MFIs to seize the collateral without a court order.[4] Many borrowers did not anticipate that financial institutions would pursue foreclosures so aggressively, expecting concessions would allow them more time to repay

[4] According to a lawyer, Ruzelya Tranbaeva, banks and MFIs in in Kyrgyzstan forced borrowers to sign an agreement on extrajudicial seizure of property as a condition for obtaining credit (Kudryavtseva, 2016).

the loan. Instead, as Ainagul, a regional leader of the anti-debt movement in Kyrgyzstan, noted, 'people have lost homes simply because they couldn't pay a 1,000 USD loan.'

The shame of eviction caused some mortgage-holders (*ipotechniki*) to commit suicide. In 2011, Marat Nurkenov, aged 39, jumped off from a 9-storey building in Pavlodar, Kazakhstan because his bank and the court evicted him and his parents from the apartment. The same year, Kenzhegul Alinkulova, a mother of five children, set herself alight during a forced eviction in Almaty (Bocharova, 2014). In Kyrgyzstan, during 2011–2012, local activists documented the suicides of six women in Talas, and eleven suicides in Naryn.[5] All of them were driven to suicide because they faced repossessions. Suicides were a way to regain a sense of control in the face of overwhelming pain and shame (Engel, 2019).

Rojas and Stenberg (2016) examined the link between evictions and suicide based on 22,000 Swedish households. They found that people who had been evicted were nine times more likely to commit suicide. '[A]n eviction can be understood as a very traumatic rejection, that is, as an exquisitely shameful experience in which one's most basic human needs are denied. Merely the strain that comes with a threat of an eviction has been suggested to be sufficiently powerful for the individual to feel that it is unbearable, hence, the suicidal act' (Rojas & Stenberg, 2016: 411).

The process of commodification of money disembedded market relations from traditional values that had previously protected marginalised groups from harm (Polanyi, 1944). The female borrowers' shame and outrage were more intense in communities, where they had expected to be protected by norms and customs against market forces. Gulnaz, a Bishkek-based national movement leader, explained:

> Kyrgyz people never put mothers with kids on the streets before. We didn't even have the word *bomj* [homeless person] in our vocabulary.

Gulnaz observed that historically there were safeguards in place to ensure people had shelter, and were not abandoned to live on the streets.

[5] Debt-related suicide cases are difficult to document as they are often not registered as such by the police. According to a civic activist, Shamil Murat, six women, who had several small children, committed suicide in Talas. Erlanbek Omuraliev, the head of the public association Kutman-Zhol, documented eleven suicides in Naryn. There were no prosecutions, because it was not possible to prove that financial institutions were responsible, even though there were suicide notes blaming them (Vesti, 2012).

Most borrowers were shocked how traditional values of care and community had been trumped by market-driven rules of profit maximisation, 'ending the social world as they knew it' (Crossley, 2002b). Neoliberal finance can, as Graeber (2011: 14) contends, turn 'morality into a matter of impersonal arithmetic', and in the process justify behaviour that would otherwise 'seem outrageous and obscene'.

Local communities also struggled to understand why a borrower's death did not annul their debt. Thedebt was passed on to surviving family members, as Elisa described:

> What infuriates us the most is that banks don't make concessions when the borrower dies. They're shifting the debt to other family members, showing up at funerals and demanding payments. We had this case in Toktogul, when debt collectors came to the funeral, pulled aside the crying family members, and said, 'Make sure to give us the money that people have brought for the funeral.'

The lenders viewed repayments as the family's primary legal and moral responsibility, outweighing other concerns and obligations. Their blatant disregard to show respect, sympathy and concern for the grieving family, or to adhere to social customs at funerals shocked Elisa. Current banking and microfinance laws make family members responsible for loans that are secured against property registered under their names. Practically all loans, including group loans, are secured against property.

Debt-related suicide has become a major problem in the military in Kazakhstan. It was discovered that some military personnel had taken their own lives because of unpaid loans. In 2014, 27 indebted officers committed suicide. Kazakhstan declared 2015 as the year of suicide prevention in the army. The Ministry of Defence created a registry of heavily indebted military personnel, who were then placed under special protection (Prokopenko, 2015).

Another tragic feature of debt-related suicide was that some individuals had committed suicide having taken out loans on behalf of family members, colleagues and friends who had a poor credit history. For instance, in 2015 a school cleaner in Turkestan committed self-immolation in the school yard over a bank loan taken out for a work colleague. For almost ten years, the cleaner had struggled to pay off the loan because the penalty charges had enlarged the debt.

Neoliberal financialisation created a moral economy that celebrated and promoted money-making by any means necessary, often at the cost of human dignity and well-being (Wiegratz, 2016). Feelings of anger, shame and shock generated by the coercive financial system precipitated anti-debt protests and mobilisation in Kazakhstan and Kyrgyzstan.

The Anti-Debt Mobilisation in Kazakhstan

Resistance in Almaty

Crossley (2002b) argues that in order to restore the harmony between their habitus and the habitat, strains can either produce changes to agents' habitual expectations and ways of being-in-the-world, or the objective conditions of their lives. On the one hand, agents can attach the blame for problems to themselves, and/or define their situation as inevitable, thereby normalising and naturalising their circumstances. On the other hand, agents can blame structural factors and 'outgroups' as the cause of their hardship and suffering, viewing the former as mutable. Crossley (2002b: 681) refers to the process of agents interpreting their situation and attributing blame as 'situational definition'. It is an evolving process in which agents make reflexive and critical assessments of the responsibility, blame and possible solutions for their situation.

Initially, many grassroots initiatives (such as Ostavim Narodu Zhil'e!, El-Birligi, Za Dostoinoe Zhil'e!) in Almaty emerged to alleviate hardship on mortgage borrowers. The largest movement among them, Ostavim Narodu Zhil'e! (Let the People Keep their Homes!), was set up in 2008 by a group of Almaty residents, including Esenbek Ukteshbaev, a former engineer, Elmira Iskakova, a real estate agent, and Sania Niyazova, a former teacher. They mobilised struggling mortgage borrowers after banks refused to delay mortgage payments, and threatened to repossess their homes, as Elmira explained at a press conference (Aimbetova, 2008):

> My bank began to send notifications that it would put my apartment up for auction if I didn't pay off the debt. But I had nothing to pay with. And then I said to myself, 'It's not my fault that this crisis has come.' I realised that my housing rights must be defended. I saw that many people were in the same situation. So we got united.

At the early stage of mobilisation, there was a vague understanding that external factors were linked to the crisis, and the banks were being unfair.

There was little scrutiny of the causes of the crisis. The objective was to unite as many disaffected mortgage-holders as possible so as to collectively bargain for concessions with the banks. After the press conference, the grassroots group received calls from various parts of Kazakhstan wishing to join their movement. In a few weeks, Ostavim Narodu Zhil'e! had mobilised thousands of struggling mortgage-holders in Almaty, Astana, Shymkent, Taraz, Uralsk and Pavlodar.

But there were tensions among the movement members over different interpretations of the debt problem. The middle class members of the movement did not want to politicise indebtedness, or attribute blame to any actors. They sought 'pragmatic solutions' through constructive dialogue with the financial authorities. They wanted a moratorium on house repossessions, an extension to loan repayments, and mortgages to be restructured at a lower interest rate. Elmira Iskakova, who represented the business class of the movement, wanted the movement not to make any radical demands, such as debt forgiveness (Aimbetova, 2008):

> We're not asking to write off our debts. We'll pay all the money back. Before the crisis, we paid regularly. We're simply asking for a respite. After all, if banks now begin to take our apartments, an army of people will become homeless. For the government, this will be a more serious problem than the crisis of non-payment.

The middle class borrowers individualised and normalised debt, having internalised the market ethics of borrowing. The established banking practices were naturalised and treated as 'a fact of life' (Sayer, 2015). Believing that it was morally right to pay back the banks, they avoided interrogating the nature of financial capitalism, or the power inequality between lenders and borrowers. They framed themselves as honest and disciplined clients, and did not seek to change the existing power relations. Under Iskakova's leadership, the movement prioritised dialogue with the country's Association of Financiers, the National Bank of Kazakhstan and the Stabilisation Fund so as to restructure mortgage debts.

Low-income families, including large households on unstable or informal income, constituted about half of the members of the Ostavim Narodu Zhil'e! movement. In 2009, they demanded full or partial debt amnesty, and attributed blame for their situation to the financial sector.

The leader of the radical faction, Esenbek Ukteshbaev, defined mortgages as debt bondages, and argued for debt relief (Kalashnikova, 2015):

> Our eyes got opened to many things. All the agreements we signed with the banks were enslaving us. The banks borrowed from foreign investors at a rate of 1% to 3% per annum. . . . When the crisis happened, our banks got the state and international lenders to write off 80% of their debts and achieved a deferral of repayments. We now ask our banks to write off our debts. The same principle should be applied to us!

Esenbek attributed blame to the domestic financial elites, who borrowed cheaply overseas and issued loans to people under usurious conditions. He felt that the banks were obligated to offer some debt relief to people, who did not create the financial crisis. The banks were viewed as greedy and unjust for refusing to extend debt relief that they had benefitted from. The Kazakhstanistate spent around 18 billion USD to bail out banks so as to ensure liquidity and stability in the financial sector (Aliev, 2015). The radical faction explained that the bail out deteriorated the state budget, and diverted resources to private commercial institutions, rather than ordinary people, who ended up owing more debt because of the national currency devaluation.

The faction held many hunger strikes and protests in front of banks and offices of the ruling Nur Otan political party to draw attention to the financial and political injustices. But the state responded by arresting and fining radical members for organising and participating in unsanctioned protests. The state wanted to repress and crush any dissent in the country. While the state tolerated the middle class members of the movement, it weakened the radical faction (Goodwin, 2018).

Failed Alliances and Fragmented Movements

In 2009, the struggling apartment shareholders (*dol'shiki*) mobilised into various movements after they failed to get back funds invested in construction companies (Korneeva, 2009). Zauresh Battalova, the Nur-Sultan-based leader of the housing movement Za Dostoinoe Zhil'e! (For Decent Housing) explained that many shareholders were in a desperate situation. They were under pressure to continue making mortgage payments for homes that were not built. 'They've been paying for "empty air" all these years', said Battalova. After the financial crisis, a majority of construction companies declared themselves bankrupt, and offered no compensation, even though the shareholders won court rulings in their favour.

Crossley (2002b) argues that new situational definitions can be offered by groups or individuals who are already dealing with the 'problem', have their own interpretations, and will attempt to work with those affected by it. In 2009, Ainur Kurmanov, the leader of the Socialist Resistance in the Kazakhstan movement, helped to mobilise the struggling shareholders into a single movement Kazakhstan-2012, which aimed to challenge the established political regime in the upcoming parliamentary elections (Korneeva, 2009; Socialism.kz, 2016).

Kazakhstan-2012 was the first grassroots movement that openly pursued political goals with the slogan, 'Change your policies or we will change you!' Kurmanov offered the movement members a structural interpretation of the financial crisis and indebtedness. He attributed blame not solely to the domestic financial elites, but also tothe state and international lenders for creating and facilitating the privatisation and financialisation of the housing market. He explained how the state helped to create the housing/mortgage crisis (Regnum, 2010):

> The state bears complete responsibility for everything that happened. Did anyone regulate the mortgage lending? Did anyone control the banks? The state encouraged shared housing construction model and gave permits to dubious construction companies. Thus,the state is obligated to complete these projects. . . . We're creating a movement from below so that it can become a real political force in the future. . . . One of the strategies is to support one of the oppositional political parties if it agrees to include our candidates in the party list. Another option is to organise our own political party.

For Kurmanov, the state was a significant actor in the crisis, having the roles of facilitator and regulator of rent and debt relations (Andreucci et al., 2017; Parenti, 2015). He saw the movement as challenging the state and the status quo. The movement campaigned to nationalise private banks and construction companies, and demanded a relief package for mortgage-holders.

During 2008–2009, the government failed to adequately address thedebt problem, a situation exacerbated by skyrocketing food prices, job losses and salary arrears. Many people became disgruntled and politicised.

On 14 May 2009, Kazakhstan-2012, Ostavim Narodu Zhil'e! and Talmas formed an alliance in order to consolidate grassroots initiatives (Baitelova, 2009). The alliance openly challenged the political regime, and organised many protests at the end of the 2000s (see also Niyazbekov, 2018). It held a forum of opposition forces with the aim of forming a single oppositional party that would participate in the 2012 parliamentary elections. The forum was attended by the Democratic Party of Kazakhstan Azat, the National Social Democratic Party, the Communist Party of Kazakhstan and the unregistered party Alga! The forum agreed to unite under a single party.

But the single party failed to materialise, because the political regime responded swiftly to social forces that threatened its legitimacy. The state started to weaken and repress oppositional movements ahead of the elections. On 22 September 2009, Kurmanov received several blows to the head with a metal bar by two men at the entrance to his home. In 2011, he and Ukteshbaev, faced criminal charges under Article 327 Part 3 of the Criminal Code and fled to Moscow (Yuricyn, 2011). The removal of influential activists created tensions, divisions and disillusionment within the alliance[6] (see also Niyazbekov, 2018).

Nevertheless the politicisation of indebtedness in the run-up to the parliamentary elections had some impact. Fearing the consolidation of oppositional forces, the government allocated about 2.8 billion USD for the completion of housing projects, and offered some concessions on mortgage debts (Rolnik, 2011). The state sought to achieve popular consent for its rule with a range of targeted measures to pacify disaffected groups. Moreover, it signalled its willingness to address economic grievances as long as they were not politicised. State support was framed as an act of benevolence. For instance, Mayor Tasmagambetov of Nur-Sultan explained that the state should be praised for its assistance to apartment shareholders because their contracts signed with construction companies never stipulated state guarantees (Glushkova, 2011).

By 2012, Ostavim Narodu Zhil'e! split because some leaders of the movement wanted to distance themselves from oppositional politics, fearing for their own safety and believing that their objectives would be achieved quicker if their grievances were depoliticised. Iskakova and her pro-business middle class followers left the movement and joined the

[6] It is particularly noteworthy that the centre-right, pro-business oppositional parties, which had plenty of economic resources, failed to respond to social grievances.

Kazakhstan Nash Dom (Our Home Kazakhstan) movement, which was created by Talgat Akuov. Another leading activist, Sulubika Zhaksylykova, left the Ostavim Narodu Zhil'e! movement to set up its clone, named Obespech'te Narod Zhil'em! (Provide People with Homes) (Socialism.kz, 2009). Ukteshbaev, who returned to Kazakhstan in November of 2012, led what was left of Ostavim Narodu Zhil'e! The breakaway movements dissociated themselves from politics, and focused on pleading with the ruling elites, rather than challenging them.

The 2015 presidential elections offered another opportunity to negotiate new concessions on debt with the state. In the run-up to the elections, the government widely publicised its programme to refinance mortgage loans, and invited social movements to discuss the debt programme in Nur-Sultan. On their way to the debate, Ukteshbaev and other radical activists were arrested. The state-sanctioned gathering largely consisted of pro-government and middle class movements, which approved and legitimised the state programme of refinancing mortgages. By securing a seat at the negotiating table, these movements were co-opted by the government (see Niyazbekov, 2018). The strategy of co-opting the middle class was the basis of the political regime's stability. The regime ensured its hold on power in the face of pro-business opposition and coloured revolutions in neighbouring countries in the early 2000s (Ostrowski, 2009).

The government allocated 130 billion tenge (345 million USD) to refinance mortgage loans, but to be eligible applicants had to meet strict criteria, which favoured middle class groups. The refinancing programme accepted applications only from individuals who could demonstrate regular income. The programme also agreed to restructure loans issued from 2004 to 2009. It reduced the interest rate to 3% from an average of 15%, and extended the length of mortgage period to 20 years. Only a very small category of socially vulnerable individuals had the right to refinance loans at 1% for a period of five years (Forbes, 2019). The programme approved about 28,000 applicants.

But a majority of applicants were rejected. They were unsuccessful in reducing the mortgage rate or debt. Most low-income groups found the refinancing terms unaffordable. The 3% interest rate over a 20-year period still amounted to a significant monthly repayment relative to their monthly income, and the revised contract would have enlarged the total repayment on the loan. The refinancing programme had bypassed the vulnerable groups of borrowers to favour middle class borrowers. Djarlygapova (2017) argued that 'under the guise of protecting citizens,the state helped to bail out selected banks and better off borrowers.'

By 2016, protests over mortgage debt declined significantly. Some protests organised by Zhaksylykova, the leader of Obespech'te Narod Zhil'em!, were tolerated by the political regime. Whereas previous rallies were highly political and radical, the new protests were largely performative that aimed to shame the financial elites. On one occasion, the protesters organised a procession with a coffin, which was placed at the front entrance of a bank. Then they threw copies of their mortgage agreements into the coffin, and mourned aloud. On another occasion, they broke into several bank buildings, and threw underwears at bank employees, shouting, 'Take our last pants!', implying that the banks had stripped them naked (Mun, 2016). Other rallies involved banging pots and walking with black plastic bags placed over their heads. At one event, they dressed in grey cloaks, chanting, 'We're not a grey mass!', implying they were human beings (Eurasianet, 2016).

The political regime's relationship with the anti-debt movements was not neutral, rather it privileged the financial elites and pro-business social movements (see also Jessop, 2002). Its powers and resources were more accessible to the rentier class and middle class organisations than to radical and working class movements. The regime weakened and neutralised oppositional forces and social movements that demanded strong protections against market forces. By 2018, the number of protests was the lowest for many years as a result of further restrictions on public gatherings, demonstrations and rallies. Moreover, class and social fragmentation severely limited the capacity of radical movements to demand economic transformations (Goodwin, 2018).

While state strategies and projects were class-biased, new rules and measures were instituted to ensure a level of social stability and protection. In 2018, the central bank approved the conversion of US dollar-denominated mortgage loans into tenge at the exchange rate of 188.35 tenge per US dollar (Forbes, 2019). It also announced a scheme to offer low-income borrowers the opportunity to rent their repossessed homes from banks with the possibility of buying the property later (Sputnik, 2020). By capping interest rates and penalty fees at 60% and 10% per annum respectively, the state claimed to have instituted a more 'humane' banking practices.

Despite the state rhetoric of tackling indebtedness, many mortgage-holders continued to struggle to make repayments. In 2019, the rate of non-performing loans was one of the highest in the world at 14.1%. In 2020, mortgage debt reached 1.97 trillion tenge (Panchenko, 2020). President Nazarbayev suggested that if people were struggling with debt, then they should give up luxuries, such as lemons.

The Mothers' Movement in Nur-Sultan

On 4 February 2019 five sisters, aged between 3 month and 13 years old, died in a fire, which engulfed their summer wooden house (*vremyanka*) on a harsh winter night in Koktal-1 micro-district of Nur-Sultan. The parents were working the night shift to pay off three overdue bank loans over 100,000 tenge (236 USD). The horrific death of five innocent girls prompted a spontaneous local mobilisation of angry mothers, who were similarly in debt and were forced to rent shabby houses on the outskirts of the city. The state officials did not attend the funeral, and blamed the parents for negligence. Their victim-blaming enraged the mothers.

The Minister of Labour and Social Protection, Madina Abylkasymova, who graduated from Columbia and Harvard Universities and had appeared on the cover of Forbes the day after the tragedy, took sick leave and avoided meeting angry and aggrieved mothers. The tragedy exposed not only a wide class divide, but the shocking depth of class contempt and lack of sympathy for vulnerable and poor groups.

A new wave of protesting mothers demanded housing, debt cancellation and an increase in social assistance for large families. Their calls to cancel debts came at an opportune moment for the mothers' movement, because President Nazarbayev had resigned, and his uncharismatic, unpopular, hand-picked successor, Kassym-Jomart Tokayev had to win the presidential election on 9 June 2019. On 26 June 2019, in a move to secure his political legitimacy, President Tokayev signed a decree on consumer loan debt relief that allowed the government to settle debts of 'socially vulnerable category of citizens' (i.e. families with four or more children, and with disabled or orphaned children).

But the debt relief programme had strict criteria. The total amount of family debt could not exceed 3,000,000 tenge (7900 USD), and each borrower was only eligible for an annulment of 300,000 tenge (790 USD). The government claimed that the programme benefitted nearly 500,000 individuals at a cost of about 276.3 million USD (Eurasianet,

2019a). Moreover, the decree instructed banks and MFIs to write off all fines and penalties accrued on consumer loans for the vulnerable category of borrowers.

In an effort to restrict predatory practices, President Tokayev's decree also ordered the central bank to ban banks accruing penalties, commissions and other charges on unsecured consumer loans that were overdue by more than 90 days. Banks and MFIs were also banned to lend to people, who had income less than the minimum monthly living wage (78 USD), or had overdue loans. Moreover, the central bank was instructed to register and regulate the activity of online lenders and pawnshops. To some extent, the mothers' movement managed to force the government to introduce some measures to regulate predatory lending practices (BakerMckenzie, 2019).

The government's actions were motivated by neoliberal values of individualism, self-responsibility and economic independence. The government framed its measures as a one-time gift to financially irresponsible social groups. Soon after the debt relief decree, it launched a media campaign accusing the mothers of being dependent on the state. The Department for Social Development Affairs commissioned a 26-minute documentary film on 'social dependency', and posted it on the official website of Nur-Sultan's city administration. The film demonised the mothers' movement, and accused the members of being unwilling to work hard or improve themselves.

In September 2019, President Tokayev cut welfare support to large impoverished families, justifying the measure as a mechanism to stimulate the ethic of hard work. There were also amendments to the social security legislation. The changes meant that recipients had to regularly confirm their right to receive social assistance, register at the labour exchange, and engage in retraining programmes. The government articulated a neoliberal moral discourse that attacked working class families for being idle and ignorant (Lawler, 2004). It distinguished between 'deserving' and 'underserving' poor. It individualised poverty and indebtedness, forcing low-income groups to be self-responsible.

In addition, the retired head of the state, Nazarbayev, made a special public appearance to lecture 'greedy mothers' on the need to be self-sufficient, and recommended them to 'buy a pair of cows' and look after themselves (Eurasianet, 2019b). Nazarbayev delegitimised and discredited the mother's movement. His intervention reflected class and gendered moral assumptions that women ought not to interfere in politics, but look after the household. Shortly after Nazarbayev's attack on low-income mothers for lacking family planning and entrepreneurship, news broke that his daughter, Dinara Kulibayeva, who with her husband Timur Kulibayev owned the country's largest bank, Halyk, had purchased a C17th castle outside Geneva that was worth 63 million USD (Azattyq, 2019). Ironically, the castle was partly paid by extracting interest from struggling borrowers. The Kulibayevs were able to live a life of luxury through others' hard work and surplus value, evading social condemnation of their economic dependency.

The Women-Led Anti-Debt Movement in Kyrgyzstan

The Emergence and Development of the Movement

On 26 May 2016, about 700 people, mostly rural women, protested in front of the US Embassy demanding debt amnesty from banks and MFIs that had been created and supported by the US Agency for International Development (USAID) and the World Bank's International Finance Corporation. Holding placards that read 'Occupy FINCA', 'Debt kills', 'Save our homes from banks' and 'Humans above profit', the protesters did something very significant that day. Most of them had travelled over 500 km to attribute blame for their indebtedness to US-led financial institutions. The latter had enforced debt-led strategies of capital accumulation, or the growth-cum-debt development model, for the past thirty years (Soederberg, 2012, 2014). The protesters drew public attention to the role of international finance in generating debt bondage, challenging the myth of women's empowerment through microcredit enterprise. Getting to this point had been a tumultuous long journey.

The history of women's indebtedness started in 1995 when the USAID and the World Bank supported the establishment and development of major MFIs under the banner of poverty reduction and women's empowerment.[7] The top four MFIs (FINCA, Kompanion, Bai Tushum

[7] The country division of FINCA launched its microcredit operations in 1995 with a seven-year grant from the USAID (Yale School of Management, 2011b). In 1996, Mercy Corps, a US NGO, received a USAID grant to launch a microfinance programme to support entrepreneurial women in rural areas. It started four regional micro-lending organisations, which were later reorganised to become Kompanion (Yale School of Management, 2011c). In 2000, Bai Tushum, a small local NGO, was partnered with a US NGO, which received a USAID grant to expand micro-lending in rural areas.

and Mol Bulak) received significant funding from international donors, including International Finance Corporation. By 2010, they served 77% of the microcredit borrowers, and controlled 52% of the microcredit portfolio (Microfinance Centre, 2011).

MFIs later leveraged further commercial capital to scale up and expand their financial operations. International donors and investors mandated MFIs to become fully commercialised, which meant charging high interest rates (up to 44%) to borrowers (Bateman, 2010; Ruziev & Dow, 2013). The process of commercialisation led Bai Tushum, FINCA and Kompanion to become fully fledged banks, though they still handle a significant micro-loan portfolio (Fitzgeorge-Parker, 2018). This shift of microcredit's social mission to profit-making has been referred to as a 'mission drift' (Bateman, 2010).

After almost three decades, there is no conclusive evidence to show that microfinance has significantly improved women's lives in transition and developing countries (Bateman, 2018; Fedirici, 2014; Mader, 2015). Micro-lending is exploitative, unproductive and unjust, and micro-loans are unlikely to be used for innovative enterprise (Soederberg, 2014). In our interview with the director of Microfinance Association in Kyrgyzstan, Maxim admitted that there were no international or domestic indicators to show that household borrowers had improved their lives. Moreover, he observed that 70% of the borrowers were 'very disciplined at paying back the loans . . . . at the cost of sacrificing their food security, education and health,' which 'obviously cause[d] them immense misery.'

In our study, many female borrowers initially internalised the blame for their hardship, because popular moral discourses on finance individualised problems, and demonised them as financially illiterate and unscrupulous, as discussed in Chapter 3. To keep up with interest payments, many borrowers also dragged family members and relatives intodebt bondage, as Roza, a regional leader of the anti-debt movement, observed, 'We've all became slaves to credit. We worked ourselves to death, but the debt kept growing, swallowing us!' The borrowers' hardship and suffering made it impossible for them to carry on as before. They were angry about their situation and wanted change.

Most borrowers began to understand and interpret their situation at the local level. During 2008–2010, they responded in spontaneous, visceral and localised ways to looming evictions and repossessions. For instance, in Atbashy, Naryn some female borrowers acted together to burn down an MFI branch, and destroy its files and documents on borrowers. In Jalal-Abad, a group of women attacked bailiffs to prevent evictions. In Osh, many women mobilised to sue banks and MFIs for refusing to recognise the June 2010 conflict as a *force majeure*, which affected women's trade and ability to make payments. In Bishkek, some borrowers collectively demanded delays to repayments, because of the closure of the Kyrgyz-Kazakh border in 2010.

At this early stage of localised mobilisation, the activists were inexperienced, and prioritised short-term concerns. Most female borrowers were overwhelmed by the prospect of being evicted, and were limited in their ability to evaluate economic practices and attribute blame, as Ainash, one of the anti-debt movement leaders in Osh, explained:

> We didn't even realise that the banks didn't belong to the state. First, we began negotiating [with the banks] for concessions and extending the period of debt payments. Then we began helping women to defend their rights in courts. The banks could repossess homes in 60 days without getting court papers. Our main goal was to prevent the confiscation of property and the eviction of families onto the streets.

Ainash and other women lacked knowledge about banking practices and their rights. They soon learnt that the courts and financial institutions upheld the sanctity of the contract regardless of their circumstances (see Sanghera, 2020). The female activists often resorted to disruptive sit-ins at local branches to gain concessions from banks and MFIs. In our focus group, several female movement leaders explained that their 'attacks' on lenders were so frequent that the police stopped arresting them. They negotiated on behalf of marginalised borrowers to prolong repayment schedules (see also Satybaldieva, 2018). The branch managers had little option but to listen to their demands, and usually responded by prolonging the repayment schedule up to 6 months. They did not waiver penalty fees, lower interest rates or cancel debts.

But short-term solutions did not help the borrowers to reduce or pay off their debt. Their debts increased after penalties and interest were applied to their existing debt. Moreover, the number of borrowers grew significantly, and the activists' strategy of representing each borrower and mediating on an individual basis with lenders became impractical.

By 2012, the women leaders and activists realised that legislative change was required to protect the borrowers' rights, and they pursued rights-based politics. The leaders and activists from Osh and Jalal-Abad travelled to Bishkek, and held a series of protests in front of the presidential building, and in Bishkek's Gorkii park. The news about their protests spread quickly, and attracted the attention of Bishkek-based activists, who joined the protests and built alliances, as Gulnaz described:

> So in 2012, many indebted women gathered in Gorkii park to protest. But no-one was paying attention or helping us. We then threaten to burn ourselves. We brought gasoline canisters. After the threat, three Parliamentarians came out and said, 'Let's set up a committee and try to negotiate with the banks.' In December 2012, we set up this movement, mobilising women across the regions, setting up branches and coordinators in remote areas.

The movement activists used the threat of self-harm to gain access to political institutions, which previously ignored them. For the first time in the country, a parliamentary committee was formed to investigate banking practices. The activists were asked to collect evidence of financial malpractice and fraud throughout the country. This facilitated the establishment of a nationwide movement, which was named the Committee for Protection of the Borrowers' Rights in Kyrgyzstan.

The activists' investigation into financial malpractices helped them to understand that their indebtedness was largely not their fault. The fact that there were thousands of people struggling with debt pointed to how banks and MFIs had behaved in predatory ways as a result of lax regulation. It was at this moment that the movement activists critically reflected on the financial industry and its practices. Their 'situation definition' shifted from individualising debt problems to attributing blame to the industry and the state. The movement's critical assessments of the responsibility and blame for the situation evolved, leading to different goals and strategies (Crossley, 2002b; Porta & Diani, 2006).

The movement's new strategy reflected a shift from individual mediation at a local branch level to legal and structural reforms at the national level. The movement leaders identified the state as a key site of regulation of rent relations, and sought to change banking and microfinance laws to alleviate problems arising from predatory lending and lack of safeguards for borrowers. After gaining access to the Parliamentary Committee on Economic and Fiscal Policy in 2013, the movement leaders submitted large files on financial malpractices and fraud, and demanded amendments to the financial legislation. Their demands were:

1. To ban lenders from repossessing property that would make families homeless.
2. To pass individual bankruptcy law, which would include a debt relief order.
3. To establish a state fund that would offer affordable and long-term loans.
4. To prohibit passing debt obligations to other family members.
5. To prohibit debt repayments from borrowers' pensions and welfare payments.
6. To prohibit the proliferation of pawnshops, and crack down on informal lenders.
7. To restore borrowers' homes, which had been fraudulently repossessed.

These demands evoked the state as a market regulator. At this point, the movement activists did not demand the nationalisation of banks because they were unaware of the role international capital played in their indebtedness. The committee's investigation resulted in several parliamentary resolutions, which recommended amendments to banking and microfinance laws, especially on collateral, borrower's rights and the establishment of a state fund to refinance debt. But these proposals were vehemently opposed by the National Bank of Kyrgyz Republic, the financial industry and business lobbies, including the International Business Council and the Investment Council. The central bank rejected the proposal to set up a state fund, arguing that it would distort market discipline, and would be costly to the state.

After heated negotiations, President Atambaev signed into law a single amendment to restrict usurious practices in 2013. The new amendment capped interest rates on loans at 35%, and penalties and fees at 20% of the loan. It also required a court order for repossessions, and banned borrowers from having multiple loans. As a result of the anti-usury law, the central bank closed 99 MFIs, and increased the requirements of starting capital and reserve funds (Sabi, 2015). But the amendment has been contested. Maxim explained that the microfinance sector has been lobbying to reverse the legislation on capping interest rates.

The anti-debt movement activists felt that the new law did not curtail the lenders' power to charge high interest rates and enact foreclosures. Furthermore, the movement activists were dissatisfied that the state refused to create a public credit fund that could issue cheap long-term loans. Although interest per se had become an established economic rent practice, and most borrowers in our study did not question its validity, the lack of alternative forms of credit allocation was raised. For instance, Ainash remarked, 'Why do all the funds go to private and commercial entities? There are no affordable loans for us, ordinary workers and farmers.' The movement activists observed that there was no real choice in the credit market, because the lenders were for-profit institutions that did not cater for the needs of low-income groups.

Unsatisfied with their engagement and progress with the parliamentarians, the movement leaders brought charges against the financial industry to the State Centre for Judicial Expertise, the Ombudsman's Office and the Supreme Court. But the judicial system overwhelmingly sided with the lenders. For instance, after examining about 8000 cases of financial malpractices in 2014 and about 900 cases in 2015, the Anti-Corruption Business Council concluded that the juridical system protected the creditors' interests (Kudryavtseva, 2016). In cases of default, the courts viewed credit as the lenders' property and assets, and justified its return on the basis of the rule of law and the sanctity of the contract. Borrowers, who failed to pay off the loan, were seen as violating the lenders' property rights over money, and having broken their promise to repay.

In an investigation on repossessions and property seizures, the Committee on Economic and Fiscal Policy found that judges did not believe that banking and microfinance laws violated Article 12 of the Constitution of the Kyrgyz Republic, which stipulates that private property is an inalienable right and people cannot be involuntarily deprived of their property. The judiciary protected the lenders' and other property owners' rights to own, speculate and dispose assets at a profit over the borrowers' and other disadvantaged groups' basic human needs, and it often prioritised the property rights of the rich and powerful over those of the poor (Sanghera, 2020). The judiciary and the central bank sanctioned reckless lending, expanded the 'colonising structures' of debt, and facilitated and normalised secondary forms of exploitation by guaranteeing appropriate laws and governance (Soederberg, 2012).

The class alliance of the political, financial and legal elites created setbacks for the movement leaders. In response to this situation, the activists travelled across the country to mobilise more struggling borrowers, and called on them to join the movement to defend their rights. They organised public forums to inform the people about debt, as Gulnaz explained:

> During our mobilisation efforts we've learnt that a great deal of people were in debt. This was the biggest achievement of the movement. We showed the real scale of the problem to the public. . . . Few years ago people would not admit they were in trouble. They felt so ashamed. For some the sense of shame was so great that they committed suicide. But now people are beginning to wake up! We told people that we had rights and that they shouldn't be trampled over. This awakening is fragile but it's taking place. . . . We didn't anticipate that so many people would join us. There are thousands in our movement. Without this work, so many families would have been completely lost.

In our interviews, many borrowers credited the anti-debt movement for relieving their crushing sense of shame. They also came to understand that their dire predicament was manufactured by the financial industry, and was not a result of their personal or moral failure. Although the movement has struggled to curtail the power of the financial industry, it succeeded at spreading the movement's ideas and demands. According to the leaders, the movement grew from a few hundred to about 40,000 members between 2008 and 2016, challenging the state and financial elites' narrative that only a fraction of borrowers were struggling to make repayments. As Crossley (2002b) observes, social movements progress and grow when leaders and members arrive at new situational definitions that shift the blame from personal to structural factors.

Lack of Support for the Movement

Between 2013 and 2015, the anti-debt movement activists tried to build alliances with social forces to challenge the financial system. But they struggled to gain support from intellectuals, middle class youth activists, international NGOs and established civil society groups. Whereas in Kazakhstan mortgage-holders and apartment shareholders gained the support of left-wing oppositional leaders, in Kyrgyzstan the movement activists struggled alone, having little in common with other social forces. For instance, middle class activism in Bishkek usually involved organising forums, exhibitions and workshops, but according to Mamedov, the director of a left-wing intellectual initiative SHTAB, such activism was often uncritical, unreflexive and 'quite xenophobic towards the urban poor and internal migrants' (Nasritdinov & Schroder, 2017: 122). His stance of promoting the interests and needs of less fortunate groups had alienated middle class activists, who had prevented the expansion of his work. The lack of left-wing politics and class solidarity profoundly undermined the reach and success of the anti-debt movement. Without the support of educated elites and other social groups, the social movement stalled in its evolution, and was unable to launch an effective political challenge.

The lack of support by civil society organisations left the anti-debt movement vulnerable to co-optation by populists and predatory elites. During the 2015 parliamentary elections, a former parliamentarian Kanat Isaev approached the movement leaders with a deal. If the leaders successfully mobilised the population to vote for his new party Kyrgyzstan, Isaev promised to advance the movement's demands. Desperate to find political allies, the leaders and activists campaigned across the country to mobilise voters for Isaev's party. Although Isaev was successful and got re-elected, he refused to honour his promise. His failure to honour the commitment demoralised the movement members and undermined the leaders' legitimacy.

In our focus group, the female leaders described how a self-serving and cynical 'Ostap Bender- type' politician had fooled them. They observed that negotiations with political elites were a frustrating and messy process, and that opportunities to pressurise them only emerged in unique circumstances. In general, pre-electoral agreements between elites and marginalised groups often resulted in broken promises and bitter disappointments. Existing theoretical frameworks often depict the poor as weapons of the wealthy (see Radnitz, 2010). But it would be more accurate to describe them as victims of the wealthy. The political elites tended to exploit social movements' vulnerabilities for their own interests. The anti-debt movement was an unpopular cause, partly because the political elites were in alliance with the financial elites, and several senior politicians had partial ownerships of banks and MFIs, as discussed in Chapter 1.

The Movement's New Manifesto

In 2016, the financial crisis in Russia and the appreciation of the US dollar against the Kyrgyzstani national currency resulted in more people (including some middle class groups) struggling to repay their loans. The US dollar-denominated loans inflated people's debts by more than 30%. A national television channel broadcasted a programme where leading economists discussed the crisis. Arsen, one of the economists, strongly criticised the central bank's monetary policy. The following day, the leaders of the anti-debt movement contacted Arsen to request a meeting with him. He agreed, explaining how impressed he was by the female leaders' determination to tackle indebtedness:

> I've no idea how they found my cell number. What impressed me is that these women were doing all this work on their own without much funding. Everything was based on their energy and enthusiasm. . . . My goal was to shape the national discourse. I agreed to write down my vision for the solution to the debt problem. I see the currency board as a mechanism that can fix the exchange rate and generate extra funds for the state to use to bail out the borrowers.

Arsen had opposed the central bank's monetary policy for several years, and was eager to attract public attention to his ideas, and shape the public discourse. Arsen and the movement leaders needed each other. He wrote his manifesto in Kyrgyz, printed 25,000 copies using his own funds, and then distributed them to rural borrowers across the country. The movement activists finally found an expert as their ally, who was already dealing with the 'problem', and offered a solution to it (Crossley, 2002b).

But the new situational definition did not immediately gain widespread acceptance, though the movement leaders and activists mapped it onto their existing understanding of the problem (Crossley, 2002b). Arsen's novel interpretation of the problem exposed the dependency of the central bank on the International Monetary Fund's directives. He largely attributed blame to international financial institutions for sustaining a financial system that strengthened the US dollar against the national currency, and thereby exacerbating the debt crisis. The movement members did not fully understand the economic theory of currency boards. But they accepted the new attribution of blame that was also emerging in their encounters with bank officials, as Jibek, a national leader, explained:

> We blame these international banks for our problems. They're the main culprits. When we spoke to the officials at the central bank, they said, '*Eje*, do you think we make decisions here? We're absolutely powerless here! The trouble is made by the people on the other side of the ocean.' We came to understand that all these foreign banks, like the World Bank, were to blame. We thought of burning their offices to the ground. But then Arsen said that wouldn't help. So we're trying to make changes through his manifesto.

Arsen's attribution of blame confirmed the leaders' suspicions that the central bank did not have much autonomy, and that international financial institutions shaped lending practices. The movement members began to understand that the funds that were coming from international lenders to local banks came with certain conditions. Although lacking a complete understanding of the situation, the female leaders had a vague sense that the real power lay with international institutions. The opaqueness of power was embedded in the class dependency between local women and international elites. The class dependency was more insidious because 'the exploiters [were] more hidden, more removed', and the mechanisms of exploitation were neither apparent nor transparent (Fedirici, 2014: 235).

In 2016, the new 'situation definition' moved the movement leaders to develop a new strategy to target national and supra-national institutions. They campaigned across the country to promote Arsen's manifesto. Moreover, they appealed to major international agencies to recognise fraudulent financial practices as human rights abuses, and channel their donor funds and capital into state banks rather than commercial lenders. But the movement's appeal to international human rights and democracy organisations were met with silence. The movement activists realised that their cause did not fit the donors' pro-market liberal agenda. Their disillusionment with Western democracy-promoting agencies was shared by most activists in Kazakhstan. They were highly cynical about Western organisations, viewing their presence in the region solely because of its natural resources (Niyazbekov, 2018).

The popularity of the manifesto prompted the movement leaders to organise several large assemblies in Bishkek. The assembles were also attended by the chairpersons of the central bank and the Union of Banks of Kyrgyzstan, some senior parliamentarians and several representatives of state ministries. It was the first time that the chairperson of the central bank had met and responded to questions from a large audience of borrowers. The assemblies consisted of 3000–4000 people from different regions of the country. They held placards in Kyrgyz and Russian languages that denounced commercial banks and demanded reforms. Arsen remarked, 'The sheer number of people that had travelled here affected [the chairperson of the national bank and others]. We let the people speak and they didn't hold back.'

After the assemblies, the Interdepartmental Committee on Borrowers' Appeals was established to investigate cases of fraudulent practices in banking and microfinance sectors, and assist families facing debt-related difficulties. The movement leaders were granted observer status on the committee. Shortly afterwards, the anti-debt movement organised a protest in front of the US Embassy to attribute blame to the USAID and the World Bank for creating and supporting predatory lending in the country. They specifically singled out Bai Tushum, FINCA, Kompanion and Mol Bulak as major culprits of financial malpractices, and as agents of global capital that had indebted and entrapped rural families.

The State's Suppression of the Movement

The Kyrgyzstanistate was a site of contestation between different class interests. Capital-export countries, international financial institutions and foreign investors wielded strong influence over the state through conditionalities on international credit, foreign direct investment flows and threat of economic sanctions, as discussed in Chapter 5. As in Kazakhstan, the state's relationship with the anti-debt movement was not neutral. Its establishment of a debtfare state accommodated the interests of international capital (Soederberg, 2014).

The state and financial elites undertook a range of measures to quell and undermine the anti-debt movement. The central bank intimidated the movement leaders by pressing criminal cases against them, which were later dropped. Moreover, the state created divisions and tensions within the movement. The Committee on Borrowers' Appeals drew on the central bank's guidelines on 'deserving borrowers' to decide who should receive debt assistance. The committee offered to restructure the debt of a small group of borrowers. Some of these borrowers then held a press conference to appeal to other borrowers not to join or remain in the movement, but instead resolve their disputes through the committee.

After reviewing over 3000 applications for debt assistance in 2016, the committee issued a technical report, explaining which groups of borrowers did not qualify for help based on its stringent criteria. Over half of the cases were rejected because the applicants did not have a loan, had repaid theirdebt, or had no difficulties with repayments. Applicants were deemed to have resolved their loans, if they were involved in legal proceedings, or their homes were repossessed. A third of the cases were rejected because the applicants refused to make repayments, and wished to apply for individual bankruptcy. The committee's technical approach sought to discredit the anti-debt movement's claim of a national debt crisis, and delegitimise its leaders. The report was widely disseminated in the national media. The anti-debt movement was framed as unscrupulous, untrustworthy and undeserving of public sympathy and support.

The financial and state elites also aimed to disempower the movement leaders by co-opting them into the Committee on Borrowers' Appeals. By granting the leaders observer status on the committee, it was hoped that the movement would be demobilised. Moreover, by co-opting the leaders into state structures, they would be asked to make compromises and accommodate state demands, and, in the process, risk their legitimacy with grassroots activists and members. Public committees and independent commissions can be symbolic elite gestures to disaffected constituencies, and can be a means of delaying unpopular decisions and actions until quieter times prevail, or weakening oppositional forces through co-optation (Porta & Diani, 2006).

At the same time, the elites sought to appease and pacify the movement. Their encounters with large audiences of angry borrowers prompted them to consider individual bankruptcy (insolvency) law for people struggling with debt. For the past three years, the central bank, under the supervision of the World Bank, met international experts on personal bankruptcy to assess possible proposals and changes to the law. It remains uncertain whether individual bankruptcy law will be adopted.

In response to the state's attempt to discredit the movement, the leaders pursued litigation to tackle the financial sector. They filed lawsuits against lenders for drawing up contracts in violation of banking and microfinance laws. The Supreme Court ruled that their lawsuits could be heard in regional courts. This represented a victory for the movement, because the borrowers could file charges against lenders without incurring expensive and arduous trips to Bishkek. The leaders prepared a legal template to help borrowers file their cases.

During the 2017 presidential elections, several movement activists appeared at the Akipress media centre to denounce the candidacy of Omurbek Babanov, who owns one of the largest commercial banks in the country. In response, Babanov promised to issue bank loans at 7%. The movement questioned his pledge, exposed his bank's malpractices, and explained that the bank had refused to lower interest rates to its existing struggling borrowers. By speaking up against him, the movement leaders contributed to Babanov's low polling and eventual loss, having been a favourite to win at the beginning of the campaign.

In 2020, the Covid-19 pandemic increased unemployment which prompted the movement activists to demand credit holidays. In March

2020, the central bank issued a temporary decree, recommending commercial banks and MFIs to defer loan payments for three months, and stop charges on fines, commissions and penalties. But most lenders did not offer payment deferrals, and obligated borrowers to pay the interest.

After the third political uprising in October 2020, the issue of charging interest rates during the pandemic was raised when Sadyr Japarov was campaigning for presidential office. Eager to mobilise support, Japarov announced that the state would compensate interest on loans up to 100,000 soms (1190 USD) for three months, or pay off part of the principal debt. The Ministry of Finance announced that the measure would help almost 600,000 borrowers at the cost of 1.2 billion soms (14.2 million USD) (Azattyk, 2020).

Conclusion

This chapter examined the struggles of the anti-debt movements in Kazakhstan and Kyrgyzstan. International financial institutions and development agencies created and developed the banking and microfinance sectors in Central Asia. Money was commodified into a property that enabled lenders to extract income through high interest rates (Jessop, 2015). The debt-led economic development was a form of capital accumulation through unequal market inclusion and economic dispossession that enriched the financial elites at the cost of inflicting misery and insecurity on most of the population.

The strain affects (such as anger, shame and moral shock) and fraudulent malpractices were important in galvanising mobilisation (Crossley, 2002b). It was in this context that the struggles of anti-debt activists emerged, as they tried to resist the neoliberal commodification of money. The study showed the importance of paying attention to underlying structural conflicts to gain the intelligibility and normativity of social struggles, as Bourdieu (1998) remarks, human action does not emerge out of 'nothingness'.

The anti-debt movements' struggles against the financial and state elites were hampered by internal social divisions and state tactics of suppression and co-optation. In Kazakhstan, middle and working class borrowers initially united in their demands for social protection. But as the anti-debt movement evolved, different interpretations of the problem and attributions of blame emerged along class lines. The pro-business and middle class factions of the movement chose to depoliticise economic grievances, and demand limited interventions. The working class sought to radicalise the movement, and transform economic arrangements. Whereas the state tolerated and co-optated the pro-market groups, it weakened the radical faction.

In Kyrgyzstan, the largely impoverished rural women led the mobilisation in their social struggle. The urban-based middle class NGOs and established civil society organisations showed little class solidarity with the rural and working class activists. Lacking financial resources and broad social support, the movement failed to undermine the power of finance in society. The state tried to discredit and delegitimise the movement using the mass media to cast aspersions on the leaders' honesty and integrity.

Nevertheless the anti-debt movements in both countries managed to win some state concessions, usually at times of crisis or during election cycles. In Kazakhstan, the grassroots movements united to force the state to allocate funds to complete housing projects, restructure loans, and provide targeted debt relief. In Kyrgyzstan, the state passed a law to restrict usurious interest and extrajudicial seizure of property. Crucially, the movements raised awareness about debt and financial fraud, countering the moral narrative of the financial industry as a benign and empowering force. As Soederberg (2012) argues, it is vital to interrupt the representation of debt as a neutral contract into which the working poor enter voluntarily and on equal terms, and from which they are said to benefit.

The countermovement-state relationship was complex (Goodwin, 2018). The Central Asian political regimes' concessions to the movements were limited in nature and scope. They employed neoliberal moral discourses to demonise and stigmatise recipients of debt relief as the 'undeserving poor'. The movements and activists were discredited and disempowered. Moreover, state measures, including physical and legal assaults, were used to suppress oppositional and movement leaders.

By instituting neoliberal financial policies, the Central Asianstates rewrote the social contract, and created a new class dependency between financial elites and borrowers. Debtfare states were established that facilitated, justified and normalised unequal class relationships to ensure debt-led capital accumulation (Soederberg, 2014). They minimised the oversight of the financial sector, and eliminated strong protections against predatory lending. The political elites legitimised the neoliberal framing of debt as empowering. People were discouraged from relying on state resources and collective capabilities (such as the welfare state and trade unions) that were historically important for reducing poverty in the Global North. The Central Asian debtfare states offered limited redistribution of income, and forced poor groups to escape poverty through self-responsibility and entrepreneurship.

The activities and achievements of the anti-debt movements have to be put in the context of a huge power imbalance between the class alliance of the state, financiers and the judiciary and mostly poor and working class borrowers. The movements confronted the states' discursive, legal and coercive powers. Financial institutions around the world have successfully resisted attempts to strongly regulate and control lending practices. Neoliberalism promoted and expanded the financialisation of economies, and depoliticised and legitimised the growth-cum-debt development model. The passivity over financial regulation reflects the degree to which governments and parts of societies have accepted and naturalised the neoliberal moral order (Hudson, 2015). To overcome such powerful forces, supranational institutions and global anti-corporate movements are required to regulate financial capital (Crossley, 2002b).

References

Aimbetova, M. (2008). *Ostavim Narodu Zhil'e: Chernyj den' uzhe nastupil*. https://www.kn.kz/article/2016/.

Akchabar. (2016). *Obzor rynka kreditovania v Kyrgyzstane za 2015 god*. https://www.akchabar.kg/article/loans/loan-market-review-2015/.

Aliev, T. (2015). Bednost' v Kazakhstane. *Mirovaya Ekonomika i Mezhdunarodnye Otnosheniya, 59*(12), 105–115.

Andreucci, D., García-Lamarca, M., Wedekind, J., & Swyngedouw, E. (2017). 'Value grabbing': A political ecology of rent. *Capitalism Nature Socialism, 28*(3), 28–47.

Asian Development Bank. (2011). *Sector assessment (Summary): private sector and finance*. Bishkek: Asian Development Bank Report. https://www.adb.org/sites/default/files/linked-documents/41544-082-kgz-ssa.pdf. Accessed July 2020.

Azattyk. (2014, February 14). *Ipoteka: sem' raz otmer, potom beri*. https://rus.azattyk.org/a/kazakhstan-mortgage-after-devaluation/25263767.html.

Azattyq. (2019, August 24). *'Korovy' Nazarbayeva i 'shveitsarskij zamok' ego docheri*. https://rus.azattyq.org/a/press-review-kazakhstan-nazarbayev-castles-and-cows/30126599.html.

Azattyk. (2020, December 2). *Pomosh ot gosudarstva? Politicheskii aspect podderzhki zaemshikov*. https://rus.azattyk.org/a/30979450.html.

Baitelova, Z. (2009). Zhilishnyj vopros stal politicheskim. *Kn.kz*. https://www.kn.kz/article/3253/.

BakerMckenzie. (2019). *Kazakhstan president announces consumer debt loan relief*. https://www.bakermckenzie.com/en/insight/publications/2019/07/kazakhstan-president-announces-consumer.

Barisitz, S., & Lahnsteiner, M. (2010). *From stormy expansion to riding out the storm: Banking development in Kazakhstan* (Financial Stability Report 19). Oesterreichische National Bank (Austrian Central Bank), pp. 61–71. https://ideas.repec.org/a/onb/oenbfs/y2010i19b1.html.

Bateman, M. (2010). *Why doesn't microfinance work? The destructive rise of local neoliberalism*. Zed Books.

Bateman, M. (2018). Small loans, big problems: The rise and fall of microcredit as development policy. In H. Fagan & R. Munck (Eds.), *Handbook on development and social change* (pp. 131–150). Edward Elgar Publishing.

Black, W. (2011, May 25). The two documents everyone should read to better understand the crisis. *HuffPost*. https://www.huffpost.com/entry/the-two-documents-everyon_b_169813. Accessed July 2020.

Bocharova, M. (2014). 'Von iz doma!': hronika prinuditelnyh vyselenij. *Vlast.kz*. https://vlast.kz/obsshestvo/_von_iz_doma_hronika_prinuditelnyh_vyselenij-6903.html.

Bourdieu, P. (1998). *Practical reason: On the theory of action*. Polity Press.

Crossley, N. (2002a). *Making sense of social movements*. Open University Press.

Crossley, N. (2002b). Global anti-corporate struggle: A preliminary analysis. *British Journal of Sociology, 35*(4), 667–691.

Djarlygapova, D. (2017). Zaemshiki za bortom: Komu pomogla programma refinasirovaniya zaimov? *Vlast.kz*. https://vlast.kz/amp/jekonomika/21893-zaemsiki-za-bortom-komu-pomogla-programma-refinansirovania-ipotecnyh-zajmov.html.

Engel, S. (2019). Microfinance as poverty-shame debt. *Emotions and Society, 1*(2), 181–196.

Eurasianet. (2016, February 4). *Kazakhstan: Economic woes prompting pot-bangers to target banks*. https://www.refworld.org/docid/56b45ac04.html.

Eurasianet. (2019a, August 24). *Dolgovaya amnistiya v Kazakhstane reshit ili otlozhit problemu?* https://russian.eurasianet.org/долговая-амнистия-в-казахстане-решит-или-отложит-проблему.

Eurasianet. (2019b, August 23). *Kazakhstan: Castles, cows and a grumpy old man*. https://eurasianet.org/kazakhstan-castles-cows-and-a-grumpy-old-man.

Fedirici, S. (2014). From commoning to debt: Financialization, microcredit, and the changing architecture of capital accumulation. *The South Atlantic Quarterly, 113*(2), 231–244.

Fitzgeorge-Parker, L. (2018). Impact banking: Microfinance comes of age in Kyrgyzstan. *Euromoney*. https://www.euromoney.com/article/b1b0967crmxs3m/impact-banking-microfinance-comes-of-age-in-kyrgyzstan.

Forbes. (2019, March 6). Vremya refinansirovatsa. Shans est': srok istekaet 15 iyulya. https://forbes.kz/finances/finance/vremya_refinansirovatsya_shansyi_est_srok_istekaet_15_iyulya/.

Glushkova, S. (2011). Tasmaganbetov otvetil "golodovshikam" razoblacheniyami. *Azzattyq*. https://rus.azattyq.org/a/housing_crisis_astana/2312480.html.

Goodwin, G. (2018). Rethinking the double movement: Expanding the frontiers of Polanyian analysis in the Global South. *Development and Change, 49*(5), 1268–1290.

Graeber, D. (2011). *Debt: The first 5,000 years*. Melville House Publishing.

Hudson, M. (2015). *Killing the host: How financial parasites and debt bondage destroy the global economy*. CounterPunch Books.

International Finance Corporation. (2016). *Islamic banking and finance: Opportunities across micro, small and medium enterprises in Kyrgyz Republic*. International Finance Corporation.

International Monetary Fund. (2010). *Republic of Kazakhstan: 2010 Article IV Consultation* (IMF Country Report No. 10/241). International Monetary Fund.

Janda, K., & Turba, B. (2013). Determinants of the financial performance of microfinance institutions in Central Asia. *Post-Communist Economies, 25*(4), 558–569.

Jessop, B. (2002). *The future of the capitalist state*. Polity.

Jessop, B. (2015). Hard cash, easy credit, fictitious capital: Critical reflections on money as a fetishised social relation. *Finance and Society, 1*(1), 20–37.

Kalashnikova, A. (2015). Chego dobivaetsa Esenbek Ukteshbaev? *Ratel*. https://ratel.kz/raw/21_aprelya.

Karim, L. (2011). *Microfinance and its discontents*. University of Minnesota Press.

Keating, C., Rasmussen, C., & Rishi, P. (2010). The rationality of empowerment: Microcredit, accumulation by dispossession, and the gendered economy. *Signs, 36*(1), 153–176.

Korneeva, O. (2009). Dolshiki i ipotechniki Kazakhtana sozdajut narodnoe dvizenie. *DW*. https://www.dw.com/ru/дольщики-и-ипотечники-в-казахстане-создают-народное-движение/a-4269221.

Kudryavtseva, T. (2016). *Bolee polumillionov Kyrgyzstantsev zashchityat ot proizvola kreditorov. 24.kg*. https://24.kg/finansy/40325_bolee_polumillionа_kyirgyizstantsevzaschityat_ot_proizvola_kreditorov/.

Kushnareva, P. (2008). Obmanutye dol'shiki Astany donesli svoi pretenzii Sergeju Horoshunu lichno. *Azzattyq*. https://rus.azattyq.org/a/1328230.html.

Lawler, S. (2004). Rules of engagement: Habitus, power and resistance. *The Sociological Review, 52*(2), 110–128.

Mader, P. (2015). *The financialisation of poverty*. Palgrave Macmillan.

Microfinance Centre. (2011). *Research on the Level of Indebtedness and Repayment Performance of Individual Borrowers in Kyrgyzstan*. https://mfc.org.pl/kyrgyzstan-research-on-indebtedness-and-repayment-performance/. Accessed July 2020.

Mihailova, E. (2017). Ona torgovala svoim telom, chtoby vyplatit kredit banku, - yurist iz KR. *Sputnik*. https://ru.sputnik.kg/society/20170122/1031388624/yurist-sulajman-usenov-o-dolgah-kyrgyzstancev.html.

Moskovka, I. (2010). *Esenbek Ukteshbaev, lider dvijeniya 'Ostavim narodu jil'e': My ne halyavshiki!* Time. https://time.kz/news/archive/2010/10/16/18354.

Mun, N. (2016). V Almaty ipotechniki postavili grob u vhoda v bank i shvyrali v sotrudnikov nizhnim bel'em. *Nur.kz*. https://www.nur.kz/1010816-v-almaty-ipotechniki-postavili-grob-u-v.html.

Nasritdinov, E., & Schroder, P. (2017). Re/claiming Bishkek: Contestation and activism in the city of two revolutions. *Central Asian Affairs, 4*(2), 97–128.

Niyazbekov, N. (2018). Is Kazakhstan immune to color revolutions? The social movements perspective. *Demokratizatsiya, 26*(3), 401–426.

Ostrowski, W. (2009). The legacy of the 'colored revolutions': The case of Kazakhstan. *Journal of Communist Studies and Transition Politics, 25*(2–3), 347–368.

Panchenko, T. (2020). Voronka kreditnoj aktivnosti. Bolee 80% ekonomicheski aktivnyh kazakhstantsev imejut kredity. *Forbes.kz*. https://forbes.kz//stats/bolee_80_ekonomicheski_aktivnyih_kazahstantsev_imeyut_kredityi/?.

Paprocki, K. (2016). 'Selling our own skin': Social dispossession through microcredit in rural Bangladesh. *Geoforum, 74*, 29–38.

Parenti, C. (2015). The environment making state: Territory, nature and value. *Antipode, 47*(4), 829–848.

Pchelyanskaya, I. (2016). *How much did housing cost 25 years ago?* Krishna. https://krisha.kz/content/articles/2016/skol-ko-stoilo-zhil-yo-25-let-nazad.

Polanyi, K. (1944). *The great transformation: Economic and political origins of our time*. Rinehart.

Porta, D., & Diani, M. (2006). *Social movements: An introduction*. Blackwell Publishing.

Prokopenko, V. (2015). K resheniyu problemy suicyda v armii privlekut banki'. *Tengri News*. https://tengrinews.kz/kazakhstan_news/resheniyu-problemyi-suitsida-armii-iz-za-kreditov-privlekut-269637/.

Radnitz, S. (2010). *Weapons of the wealthy: Predatory regimes and elite-led protests in Central Asia*. Cornell University Press.

Regnum (2010, September 15). *V Kazakhstane destabilizatsiya idet sverhu: interview*. https://regnum.ru/news/polit/1325747.html.

Rojas, Y., & Stenberg, S. (2016). Evictions and suicide: A follow up study of almost 22,000 Swedish households in the wake of the global financial crisis. *Journal of Epidemiology Community Health, 70*(4), 409–413. https://doi.org/10.1136/jech-2015-206419

Rolnik, R. (2011). *Report of the Special Rapporteur on adequate housing as a component of the right to an adequate standard of living, and on the right to non-discrimination in this context*. UN Human Rights Council. https://www.ohchr.org/EN/HRBodies/HRC/RegularSessions/Session25/Documents/A_HRC_25_54_Add.2_ENG.DOC. Accessed July 2020.

Ruziev, K., & Dow, S. (2013). *A review of banking sector reforms in transition economies* (Working Paper 03/13). Centre for Global Finance, University of the West of England.

Sabi, M. (2015). Supply of Islamic microfinance in Central Asia: The case study of Tajikistan and Kyrgyzstan. *International Journal of Islamic Finance, 7*(2), 9–27.

Sanghera, B. (2020). Justice, power and informal settlements: Understanding the juridical view of property rights in Central Asia. *International Sociology, 35*(1), 22–44.

Satybaldieva, E. (2018). A mob for hire? Unpacking older women's political activism in Kyrgyzstan. *Central Asian Survey, 37*(2), 247–264.

Sayer, A. (2015). Time for moral economy? *Geoforum, 65*, 291–293.

Seitz, W. (2020). Urbanization in Kazakhstan: Desirable cities, unaffordable housing, and the missing rental market. *International Journal of Urban Sciences*. https://doi.org/10.1080/12265934.2019.1709534.

Socialism.kz. (2009). *Aktsiya ipotechnikov priostanovlena*. http://socialismkz.info/?p=1040.

Socialism.kz. (2016). *Ipotechniki kak orudie informatsionnoj vojny akordy*. http://socialismkz.info/?p=16191.

Soederberg, S. (2012). The Mexican debtfare state: Dispossession, micro-lending, and the surplus population. *Globalizations, 9*(4), 561–575.

Soederberg, S. (2014). *Debtfare states and the poverty industry*. Routledge.

Sputnik. (2020, January 15). *Вернуть жилье, отобранное банками за долги по ипотеке, может будет по программе рефинансирования ипотечных жилищных займов*. https://ru.sputniknews.kz/economy/20200115/12549755/gosudarstvo-banki-kvartiry.html.

Sultakeev, K., Karymshakov, K., & Sulaimanova, B. (2018). The impact of microfinance on entrepreneurship in Kyrgyzstan. *Acta Oeconomica Pragensia, 26*(2), 24–40.

The Global Economy. (2020). *Real interest rate—Country ranking*. https://www.theglobaleconomy.com/rankings/Real_interest_rate/.

Tombs, S. (2012). State-corporate symbiosis in the production of crime and harm. *State Crime Journal, 1*(2), 170–195.

Vesti. (2012, March 12). *V Kyrgyzstane rastet chislo samoubijstv sredi dolzhnikov po kreditam*. https://vesti.kg/proisshestviya/item/10996-v-kyirgyizstane-rastet-chislo-samoubiystv-sredi-dolzhnikov-po-kreditam.html.

Whyte, D., & Wiegratz, J. (2016). *Neoliberalism and the moral economy of fraud*. Routledge.

Wiegratz, J. (2016). *Neoliberal moral economy: Capitalism, socio-cultural change and fraud in Uganda*. Rowman and Littlefield.

Yale School of Management. (2011a). *Kyrgyz MFI Comparison in 2010*. https://vol11.cases.som.yale.edu/sites/default/files/cases/kompanion_financial_group/Picture%2043.png.

Yale School of Management. (2011b). *Microfinance in Kyrgyzstan: Growth and competition*. https://vol11.cases.som.yale.edu/kompanion-financial-group/kyrgyzstan/microfinance-kyrgyzstan-growth-and-competition.

Yale School of Management. (2011c). *Mercy Corps and Kompanion*. https://vol11.cases.som.yale.edu/kompanion-financial-group/introduction/mercy-corps-and-kompanion.

Yessenova, S. (2010). Borrowed places: Eviction wars and property rights formalization in Kazakhstan. In *Economic action in theory and practice: Anthropological investigations, research in economic anthropology* (30, pp. 11–45).

Yuricyn, V. (2011). Represii protiv "ONZ", "SDK" i Zhanartu. https://zonakz.net/2011/09/06/репрессии-против-онж-сдк-и-жа/.

CHAPTER 9

Fighting the Commodification of the Extractive Industries: The Labour and Environmental Movements

This chapter examines how grassroots labour and environmental movements struggled for justice in Kazakhstan and Kyrgyzstan. Neoliberalism legitimised and promoted a regime of rent extraction in the natural resource sector that also involved extracting surplus value from workers and creating negative externalities for local communities. In response to labour inequality, work insecurity, economic dispossession and environmental destruction, local resistance arose to demand social protection and transformation of economic relations (Burawoy, 2015). The movement leaders and activists were able to develop alliances with other social forces that threatened the political regime's legitimacy in Kazakhstan, and helped to overthrow regimes in Kyrgyzstan.

The politicisation of workers' and local residents' resistance was met with a mix of tactics from co-optation and violent suppression. The host states privileged the interests of transnational capital over those of their citizens, and cooperated with foreign corporations to limit democratic voices and weaken resistance (Gill, 2008; Goodwin, 2018). The class alliance of state elites and transnational corporations had significant legal, economic and political advantages over the local activists. Nevertheless the movement leaders and their supporters continued their struggles. They evaluated the effects of neoliberal marketisation on their lives as harmful and damaging, and wanted to pursue a fair and just society.

B. Sanghera and E. Satybaldieva, *Rentier Capitalism and Its Discontents*,
https://doi.org/10.1007/978-3-030-76303-9_9

The chapter is divided into three sections. Section 'Oil Workers' Resistance in Kazakhstan' explores the exploitative and harmful nature of the oil production regime, and the frequency of strikes in the country. The second section draws on our fourth case study on natural resources to examine how local communities in Kyrgyzstan struggled against mining companies, and demanded better regulations and more benefits. Finally, the conclusion summarises the chapter's key findings and ideas.

Oil Workers' Resistance in Kazakhstan

Labour Unrest

On 29 June 2019, a conflict broke out at the Tengiz shift camp in Zhyloi, Atyrau. Local workers clashed with foreign employees of the Consolidated Contracting Engineering and Procurement (CCEP), one of many subcontractors for the transnational corporation TengizChevroil (TCO) (Toiken, 2019). This latest clash left more than forty foreign employees needing medical help. The violence did not surprise anyone, including the state officials. This and other conflicts were a manifestation of violence and inequality that underpinned the oil industry. The clash was triggered by a photograph of a foreign worker holding a walkie-talkie and its antenna directed towards the mouth of a young ethnic Kazakh woman. The photograph exposed the racialised and gendered labour hierarchies in the industry.

The state officials and the subcontractor quickly downplayed the conflict as a cultural misunderstanding. The Prosecutor's Office conducted labour inspections at 33 out of 17,000 subcontracting companies in the country. It reported that subcontractors committed 300 violations, and issued fines worth 9 million tenge (21,200 USD) (Hairulina, 2019a).

Labour unrest at oil-producing sites was often repressed and concealed. But when clashes got out of control and became public knowledge, they followed a scripted response from the state and transnational companies to ensure security and stability in the industry. Oil corporations would immediately distance themselves from the clashes, claiming no responsibility for the subcontractors' treatment of their workers. Though in reality, transnational corporations controlled the general production process, including contractual obligations and offshore and onshore practices. The state, which had a nominal regulatory capacity, also shifted the blame to foreign subcontractors, while framing itself as the defender of worker's rights. Subcontractors typically accepted the blame and deported the offending foreign workers. The conflict between labour and oil capital would appear to be resolved until the next clash erupted.

Despite the frequent clashes at oil fields, there is strikingly little analysis of the relationship between labour and oil capital that engenders so much violence. Although Zhanaozen case garnered some attention (Evans & Sil, 2020; Human Rights Watch, 2012; Kolesova & Beisembayeva, 2017; Salmon, 2011; Satpayev & Umbetaliyeva, 2015), the role of transnational oil corporations has often been overlooked in shaping labour politics and state responses. The cause of the workers' grievances is often blamed on the autocratic state without understanding how the state is intertwined with transnational corporations. Most scholars (such as Gulbrandsen & Moe, 2005; Kendall-Taylor, 2012; Ostrowski, 2010; Satpayev & Umbetaliyeva, 2015) tend to pathologise the state, and portray oil corporations either as innocent bystanders or benevolent actors.

Yessenova (2012, 2015) offers a critical account of the role of transnational corporations in shaping Kazakhstan's economic and political conditions. Watts (2012) observes that the agency of oil corporations (and adjacent oil service industries and financial institutions) is conspicuously missing in the dominant thinking on oil. Appel (2019: 38) argues that when oil corporations do appear, they are favourably contrasted with the state, and are seen as the proffers of liberalism, in that they promote 'market rationality in the face of corruption, standardisation in the face of irregularity, and universal environmental standards in the face of ignorance.'

It is no coincidence that transnational oil corporations disappear from the dominant accounts of social and political conflicts they engender. The oil industry structures liability and responsibility in such a way that it removes itself from the local social and political context (Appel 2019; Sawyer, 2012). Understanding the oil workers' resistance in Kazakhstan requires interrogating how the global oil capitalism operates, or what Appel (2019) calls 'the modularity' of oil projects that encompass mobile technologies, infrastructures, workforces and risk-avoidance regimes. The oil industry is responsible not only for labour grievances, but a range of social harms, including poor local development, environmental degradation and political violence (Appel, 2019; Ferguson, 2006; Sawyer, 2012; Watts, 2009; Yessenova, 2012).

Enclaves and Subcontracting

Mitchell (2011) urges scholars to analyse how fossil fuels are extracted, produced and distributed in order to understand the structural impotence of labour within the oil industry. During the period from the 1950s to the 1990s, workers and trade unions played a role in the consolidation of oil nationalism (Bini & Petrini, 2019) that transformed the relations between oil-producing and oil-consuming countries. But in the neoliberal era of global oil production, the labour force became weak and fragmented. The neoliberal commodification of labour often produced precarity, insecurity, exploitation and abuse for contracted labour, especially towards the bottom of the production chain (Standing, 2016).

The materiality of oil does not undermine workers' rights, rather it is the way oil corporations design and operate risk-minimising and profit-maximising oil production that disrupts the power of oil workers, thereby impeding their control over the production process. Watts (2012: 441) notes that the oil complex is a global production network 'with particular properties, actors, networks, governance structures, institutions, and organizations but what is, in effect, a regime of accumulation and a mode of regulation.' Enclaves, subcontracting of oil production and the day-to-day operations affected labour practices and relations, which became so radicalised that they threatened the very operations of the industry itself (Appel, 2019; Watts, 2012).

At the beginning of the first TCO project, local oil workers had high hopes for the US oil corporation Chevron, which pledged to upskill local labour and modernise production (Jager, 2014; Yessenova, 2012). But soon they became disillusioned with the Western mode of oil production that dominated large oil projects, such as Tengiz, Kashagan and Karachaganak, accounting for the majority of the country's oil production. The early production sharing agreements (PSAs) signed between the state and transnational corporations ensured the freedom of oil companies to structure production without state regulation and interference.

In 1993, Chevron secured 2000 square kilometres of land for Tengiz production facilities and living quarters (Yessenova, 2012). Today, the Tengiz project is a large onshore production enclave, which consists of more than 60 shift camps, the largest of them holds almost 10,000 workers. Other enclaves exist at other major oil-producing sites. The onshore and offshore production enclaves are sovereign infrastructural spaces defined by strong corporate control, and weak state regulation and taxation (see also Appel, 2019; Watts, 2009). Enclaves are often walled off from the surrounding communities with barbed wire, private security forces and strict identification regime, and are 'tightly integrated with the head offices of transnational corporations' (Ferguson, 2006).

In Kazakhstan's enclaves, the oil workers lacked freedom, autonomy and equality. They were segregated from their families and communities and worked in racially hierarchical and highly supervised ways (Yessenova, 2012). They were stripped of their autonomy through an intense, regimented and controlled work regime. The enclosed regime of micromanagement was justified to minimise accidents. In reality, the work regime enabled oil companies to pursue frictionless and invisible production by distancing themselves from community and labour entitlements (Appel, 2019).

Labour disempowerment and production control were facilitated by subcontracting arrangements, which permeated the value chain. The 1995 Subsoil Law was drafted by US oil corporate lawyers, and it gave 'foreign oil companies a free hand in picking the companies they wanted to cooperate with' and avoid working with Kazakh companies (Ostrowski, 2010: 71). Subcontracting was a highly complex arrangement that allowed oil corporations to enjoy tax loopholes, facilitate transfer pricing, attenuate liability, and maximise profit (Appel, 2019; LeBaron, 2014).

Transnational oil corporations relied on an extensive system of contracts to minimise labour costs and ensure organisational flexibility (Yessenova, 2012). For instance, TCO hired PFD as its lead contractor for one of its major projects. PFD created a network of 60 or so independent contractors for equipment supplies, engineering and construction. TCO and PFD also outsourced their non-core activities, such as equipment maintenance, transport and facilities management. Moreover, most independent contractors, such as Senimdi Kurylis, had similar outsourcing arrangements, subcontracting activities that were smaller and less complex. Subcontracting profited TCO and PFD as subcontractors and sub-subcontractors bore the demands for greater flexibility and smaller profit margins. The system of contracted labour shielded transnational oil corporations and lead contractors from direct responsibility for tensions and conflicts at the low-value production chain.

Furthermore, subcontracting was a ‘divide and conquer’ strategy that racialised and subjugated labour to capital. The exploration and production (E&P) segment of the oil industry production created racialised class divisions among subcontractors and labour. Kazakhstani companies were excluded from greenfield production and operated at the low-value production chain.[1] Nurlan Zhumagulov, the general director of the Union of Oilfield Service Companies, explained that despite recent efforts to increase the local content in production through joint ventures, Kazakhstani companies were unable to secure contracts for the E&P segment of the production process (Suleimenova, 2013, 2015; Yessenova, 2012). New laws on local content did not significantly change the situation, because PSAs’ stability clauses protected the transnational corporations from any adverse impact of new legislation.

The overwhelming majority of Kazakhstani oil workers were in non-essential or brownfield services, which were subcontracted to numerous non-Western foreign companies that allowed transnational oil corporations to disperse liability and reduce labour costs (Hairulina, 2019a, 2019b). Currently, subcontracting companies employ about 150,000–180,000 local workers (Hairulina, 2019b). Most of the local workers, who performed low-skilled tasks, were poorly paid and had precarious employment (see Jager, 2014; Yessenova, 2012). Transnational oil corporations maintained a small number of high-skilled and well-paid staff, and shifted the responsibility of managing low-skilled labour to subcontracting companies. Whereas TCO key staff enjoyed luxury accommodation, most contracted workers stayed in shift camps inside enclaves that lacked proper amenities.

Since the start of oil production in the late 1990s, dominant economic practices and relations have eroded oil workers’ rights and sense of worth. In addition to being largely allocated low-skilled and labour-intensive jobs, the local workers were exposed to dangerous and exploitative work schedules with long shifts and little rest breaks. The managers of subcontracting companies often discriminated and mistreated the workers, and demanded greater effort and productivity. Jager (2014: 507) observed

[1] The share of Kazakhstani companies in the market of geological and geophysical services was only 28% (Global Value Chains Center, 2017). The local content of TCO purchases was merely 3%. Although leading Kazakhstani service companies operated in Russia, Turkmenistan, China and India, thereby demonstrating their international competitiveness, at home they were unable to break into the high-value production chain.

'that young adults working for the oil industry do not tend to boast about their jobs.' Their jobs were undesirable, because they did not lead to skilled or permanent employment.

The Oil Workers' Grievances and Strikes

Although the local workers protested about their pay and conditions, they did not initially blame the transnational corporations for instituting the 'new regime of accumulation and a mode of regulation' (Watts, 2012: 441). Their understanding and interpretation of the situation evolved, as did their attribution of responsibility and blame for their hardship and misery (Crossley, 2002).

The first oil workers' strikes began in 1996, and they have been regular ever since. Evans and Sil (2020) suggest that labour unrest in Kazakhstan is more the exception than the rule. But this is misleading because it neglects clashes and strikes inside the onshore and offshore production enclaves. The oil industry does not publish figures on strikes, accidents and workers' death. The oil industry is shrouded in secrecy, 'a world in which even the most basic statistics can be meaningless' (Watts, 2009: 10).

The first wave of strikes emerged in response to mass redundancies, which the transnational corporations euphemistically described as 'restructuring operations'. From 1998 to 2005, Chevron reduced the TCO workforce from 6000 to 2569 (Yessenova, 2012: 103). In Kyzylorda region, the Canadian company Hurricane Hydrocarbons reduced its staff from over 5100 to 1900. In Aktyubinsk, CNPC made 2000 Kazakhstani workers redundant from AMG (Ostrowski, 2010: 85).

At the time of the restructuring, the local oil workers at TCO protested against unfair and unequal wages, exploitative working conditions, and violations of their rights to organise independent trade unions (Yessenova, 2012). The contracted labour demanded social protection from market forces to ensure dignity, safety, security and well-being (Burawoy, 2015). Their actions opposed the neoliberalisation of labour as low-cost, flexible and contracted work.

Table 9.1 shows the nature and extent of oil workers' strikes in Kazakhstan from 1996 to 2019. The reasons for strike action and labour disputes were consistent over two and a half decades. The table only includes strike actions that were reported in the local media outlets, such as Ak Zhaiyk, Azattyq and Kursive. The actual number of strikes is very likely to be much higher than the reported number.

Table 9.1 Oil workers' strikes in Kazakhstan from 1996 to 2019

Year	*Labour unrest*	*Reasons for dispute*
1996–98	Local oil workers organised a series of strikes and protests at TCO	Mass redundancies, unequal pay, ban on unions
2000	About 100 ethnic Kazakh workers went on strike at a Turkish company Zafer Inshaat, which was contracted to build an American-style town for TCO executives at Atyrau	Unequal wages, poor working conditions, discrimination
2001	Protests at a Turkish-owned company Fintrako-Tepe, a construction subcontractor of TCO. The strike was prompted by the dismissal of several ethnic Kazakh workers, who forced a Turkish supervisor to undress outside in freezing cold, after he had prohibited them from using heaters in cold locker rooms	Unequal wages, poor working conditions, mistreatment by company management
2004	Protests at an Indian-owned company Punj Lloyd, which was subcontracted at the second-generation plant at Tengiz	Unequal wages, discrimination
2005	About 500 workers rioted at a Turkish-owned company Gate Inshaat, which was subcontracted to reconstruct Atyrau oil refinery, operated by the national oil company Karazhanbasmunai	The riot sparked after the beating of a 19-year-old ethnic Kazakh worker by a Turkish supervisor
April 2005	About 3000 local workers rioted at a Turkish-owned company Senimdi Kurylys in Tengiz. The strikers included female workers, who were among the lowest paid and had the poorest working conditions	Workers objected to the dismissal of co-workers, who demanded fair wages and equal treatment
October 2006	A mass riot of local workers at Senimdi Kurylys in Tengiz resulted in 339 Turkish workers injured, 136 of whom had severe injuries	A beating of a local worker sparked the riot; unequal wages, dismissals, discrimination, ban on unions

(continued)

Table 9.1 (continued)

Year	*Labour unrest*	*Reasons for dispute*
October 2006	Ethnic Kazakh workers protested at Gate Inshaat, which operated at the onshore processing facility Bolashak, Kashagan field	Violations of labour and human rights
January 2007	About 300 ethnic Kazakh workers protested at Gate Inshaat, which operated at Atyrau oil refinery	Unequal wages and unfair treatment
August 2007	About 350 foreign employees at Senimdi Kurylys staged a protest at the construction site of the TCO at the second-generation plant	'Language barrier' between Kazakhstani and Filipino workers; unequal wages
December 2008	Protests of over 1000 local workers (employed by several European companies (Bonatti, IGS Sichim and SSS) at the onshore processing facility Bolashak, Kashagan field	Demands for an increase in wages and an introduction of rotational work
2009	A two-week strike of 2000 drillers of Burgylau (a former subsidiary of KazMunaiGas)	Demand for the nationalisation of the enterprise
2010	Several hundred local workers protested at a UAE-owned company Consolidated Contractors Company, which operated on offshore rigs in Kashagan field	Unequal wages, discrimination
April–December 2011	Protests of thousands of workers employed by Kazakhstani company Ozenmunaigas, Karazhanbasmunai (co-owned with Chinese company CITIC), and Italian company Ersai Caspian Contractor (co-owned with ENI)	Unequal wages, ban on independent trade unions

(continued)

Table 9.1 (continued)

Year	*Labour unrest*	*Reasons for dispute*
September 2012	A mass brawl in a canteen on the artificial island D in the Caspian Sea between ethnic Kazakh and Indian workers	Discrimination, wage discrepancies
July 2013	Ethnic Kazakh workers of British companies CAPE Industrial Services and Manpower Services went on strike on the artificial island D at Kashagan field	Workers were forced to write letters of resignation that would allow companies to avoid paying compensation
June 2019	Workers' riots at a UAE-owned company Consolidated Contracting Engineering & Procurement, one of the subcontractors of the TCO at the third-generation plant construction site	Unequal wages, poor working conditions, discrimination

Sources Adapted from media reports from Ak Zhaiyk, Azattyq and Kursive

The table shows that many strikes and protests occurred at various shift camps in the TCO enclave. The oil workers' strikes were largely fragmented, spontaneous and reactive. The anger of the local workers was directed at subcontracted companies, rather than the 'sleek alliance' of transnational corporations and the state that sustained the production regime. Many local workers described how racialised and class divisions were embedded in the oil production regime, engendering bitterness and resentment.

> We work on a rotational basis: 28 working days at sea and 28 days of rest. Our [official] salary is about 70-80 thousand tenge, but we get 35-40 thousand tenge [about 240-270 USD] per month. There's a blatant disrespect for local workers by the foreigners. For example, we're now working at sea in plus 52 degree heat. It's impossible to breathe because of high humidity and stuffiness. Our overalls are literally drenched in sweat. But we're not allowed to drink cold water, and the Arabs themselves don't leave their cool air-conditioned rooms. Is this fair? . . . We also sent letters [to the company asking] to stop communications in English because local workers don't understand what is required of them.

Askar, a worker at Consolidated Contractors Company, Kashagan field (Maitanov, 2010).

> Only 20 minutes are allotted for a meal. If you're a second late, you're fired! Then [a Turkish company] introduced a loud siren to start a meal and to end it. Just like in fascist concentration camps! . . . People became really embittered. [The company] treated us like cattle. . . . Turks are laughing at us. . . . Our workers can't stomach such treatment.
>
> Anonymous worker, Senimdi Kurylys (Maitanov & Guzikov, 2006)

The two workers conveyed their sense of anger and shame that they and other workers experienced. The work regime micromanaged them in a degrading way. The oil infrastructure, which controlled all aspects of work, including water and meal breaks, prevented them from exercising adequate control (Mitchell, 2011). The intense and divisive labour regime engendered sporadic violence directed at foreign workers, who communicated in English and monopolised highly prized supervisory roles. In 2005 and 2006, large and violent clashes occurred in the TCO enclave between Turkish and local workers employed by Senimdi Kurylys, the largest subcontractor at Tengiz (Yessenova, 2012). The subcontractor offered the worst pay and working conditions. TCO remained invisible, leaving the state and the subcontractor to resolve the dispute.

Table 9.1 shows that unfair and unequal wages were a constant source of grievance. The local workers resented the racist evaluation of their labour that diminished their contribution and worth. The oil industry sustained racist practices in violation of the country's Labour Code. Nurlan Zhumagulov, the general director of the Union of Oilfield Service Companies, calculated that on average Kazakhstani workers earned eighteen times less than foreign workers (Murza, 2020).[2] The foreign employees represented about 10% of the total number of oil labour force, mostly occupying key managerial and well-paid positions.

Appel (2019) argues that pay depended on a person's passport, and it had deep colonial roots in the oil industry. The racialised division of labour was justified by claims of differences in skills and talents. Americans and European staff were viewed as skilled and so deserving of high remuneration, while Third World nationals were seen as less talented, and so

[2] At TCO, an average salary for an expat was almost 12 million tenge a month, whereas for a local worker it was about 739 thousand tenge.

merited less income. The racist evaluation of labour was standard practice in the transnational oil industry.

The local workers' other grievances included lack of compensation for overtime and hazardous working conditions and delays in salaries. For instance, at TCO, technical failures were frequent, and the daily inhalation of toxic gases exceeded the maximum allowable limit by 12 times at the main Tengiz shift camp and 40 times in the TCO production area. From 1993 to 2000, 64 TCO employees died at Tengiz. After 2000, TCO mortality statistics were carefully concealed (Crude Accountability, 2013).

Although the workers had some leverage to halt production through unrest, the management could dismiss and blacklist them with ease, so undermining their rights and freedom. The workers who resisted the oil production regime were excluded from the industry. More than 1500 local workers were blacklisted at TCO under codes 400 and 500, which prevented their re-employment at Tengiz (Crude Accountability, 2013). The database of barred individuals was available to all contractors and subcontractors so that they could not be employed at other sites.

Moreover, repeated attempts to unify and increase workers' power through independent trade unions were routinely squashed. The first grassroots union at TCO was defeated in 2003, leaving the workers without any effective mechanism to deal with disputes (Yessenova, 2012). TCO refused to recognise the grassroots union, dismissed its members, and denied its leaders access to company premises. As Crude Accountability (2013: 20) observes, TCO 'actively and openly opposes the establishment of independent trade unions at its contract companies, although it says it supports collective bargaining and respects the rights of workers in contracting companies.' It set up a management-friendly union, which was used to sign collective agreements.

TCO's strategy of crushing independent unions became a blueprint for contractors, subcontractors and other major oil companies. Established TCO contractors and subcontractors did not have trade unions. An absence of independent unions was one of the key favourable conditions to becoming a TCO subcontractor. Eset Uteuliev, the chairperson of the Atyrau regional committee of trade unions for construction and industrial materials, lamented that Senimdi Kurylys disbanded an independent union, and dismissed its chairperson after initially consenting to have a union. Senimdi Kurylys explained the reversal of its decision by noting that 'the establishment of a trade union at the enterprise must be agreed upon with the general contractor' (Crude Accountability, 2013: 20).

The oil workers' solidarity was curtailed by the oil production regime, which not only ensured effective rent extraction but shielded itself from criticisms. Appel (2019: 58) remarks how Western oil managers often complained about local corruption and filth, but were unreflexive about the negative effects of the oil industry on labour rights.

The Politicisation of the Workers' Strike in Zhanaozen

In May 2011, the oil workers of three enterprises (Karazhanbasmunai, Ozenmunaigas and Ersai Caspian Contractor) in Zhanaozen, Mangystau went on strike. Initially, they protested independently of each other, but they raised familiar demands, including recognition of independent unions and equal pay. Satpayev and Umbetaliyeva (2015: 125) observe that 'the peculiar feature of Zhanaozen was that the labour conflict began not in a foreign company but in the subsidiaries of the national state-controlled oil and gas company KazMunaiGas (KMG), which gave the state leadership direct responsibility.' In drawing this distinction between KMG and transnational oil corporations, the authors obfuscate the way the oil complex operates.

KMG corporation is a junior partner in the oil complex, and does not operate outside the oil capitalist logic. KMG is listed on the London Stock Exchange, and private shareholders own 39% of the company (Salmon, 2011). The company aims to prioritise shareholder value and profits over labour rights. The other two enterprises, Ozenmunaigas and Ersai Caspian Contractor, operate under equal foreign ownership, and have similar racialised production structures as at TCO, Karachaganak Petroleum Operating (KPO) and North Caspian Operating Company (NCOC). The workers' protests at these enterprises were similar to those at other sites. The management's response to the workers' demands fitted the general pattern of refusing to negotiate with striking workers and then dismissing them.

But the oil workers' resistance in Zhanaozen was distinct, because it became politicised during an intense seven-month stand-off between the workers and the oil companies. The protests, which took place outside shift camps as a result of mass lay-offs, became visible and attracted the attention of local communities and other oil workers in the region. Wives, mothers and extended relatives of the striking oil workers showed their support by blocking roads (International Partnership for Human Rights, 2011). The non-striking oil workers showed solidarity by donating a share of their salaries to the strike fund, which helped the strikers to survive for seven months. The residents of Aktau and railway workers at Shetpe station donated food to the strikers. In summer of 2011, around 12,000–18,000 people became engaged in the strike (Rysaliev, 2011).

By June 2011, the workers' strike attracted the support of diverse oppositional forces, who further politicised the strike. In June and July, the leaders of the Socialist Resistance of Kazakhstan and Zhanartu trade union participated in strike rallies, and facilitated contact between the local workers and international workers' associations, such as the Committee for a Workers' International (CWI). Paul Murphy, an Irish socialist at CWI, and a Tanja Niemeier, a member of the European United Left/Nordic Green Left travelled to Zhanaozen. They helped to raise the profile of the strike and set up an international solidarity campaign and a support fund for the workers' families (Maitanov, 2011).

Liberal oppositional forces, such as Azat and Alga, which had failed to respond to the 2005 Shanyrak tragedy and the 2008 financial crisis, reached out to the workers to join their oppositional movement called Narodnyi Front (The People' Front) (Mukhametrakhimova, 2012). The Central Committee of the Communist Party and Alga launched the movement to participate in the 2012 parliamentary elections (Reuters, 2011; Toguzbaev, 2011). Narodnyi Front urged the oil workers to participate in the elections by voting for the Communist Party, which was the only registered oppositional party.

But the politicisation of the strike was met with state repression. The workers' radicalisation grew as the state and the oil companies refused to negotiate, dismissed thousands of striking workers, and imprisoned leading trade union leaders and activists, such as Akzhanat Aminov, Natalya Azhigalieva, Kuanysh Sisenbaev and Natalia Sokolova. Attempts to release the leaders were clamped down, as the state allied with the oil companies to crush the resistance. In August 2011, the brutal murder of Zhaksylyk Turbaev, an oil worker and an activist, and Zhansaule Karabalayeva, a 17-year-old daughter of the chairperson of the trade union committee at Ozenmunaigas, marked a turning point in the strike (Human Rights Watch, 2012). Their death sent shockwaves among the strikers, protesters and sympathisers, prompting a mass withdrawal from the ruling Nur Otan political party to join Narodnyi Front.

In late summer, a new wave of grassroots leaders emerged, such as Roza Tuletaeva, Talgat Saktaganov, Amangeldy Lukpanov, Mukhtar Umbetov, and Maksat Dosmagambetov (Toiken, 2011). They organised hunger strikes, and voiced the oil workers' concerns at international platforms, such as the Organisation for Security and Co-operation in Europe, the European Parliament and the Workers' Congress in Moscow (Grishin, 2012; Toiken, 2011). In October 2011, the court in Almaty banned the Central Committee of the Communist Party from participating in the 2012 elections. After this decision, Narodnyi Front became disinterested in mobilising the oil workers to vote in the elections. Roza Tuletaeva accused the leaders of Narodnyi Front of failing to honour their pledge to support the striking workers and their families (Kazinform, 2012).

In November 2011, the grassroots leaders remobilised the oil workers' into a new organisation Rabochii Komitet (the Workers' Committee). This was a significant step in the politicisation of the workers. Rabochii Komitet announced that existing oppositional political parties were not to be trusted, and urged oil workers across the country to boycott the 2012 parliamentary elections. It also planned to form its own political party, and call for a national strike in the natural resource sector (Kenesary, 2011; Kurmanov, 2016).

A key part of Rabochii Komitet's political programme was the nationalisation of the oil industry, so as to secure the workers' control of the oil production. Rabochii Komitet planned a rally for 16 December that would call for the resignation of President Nazarbayev and his government, and a sector-wide strike. As the protesters gathered for the rally, the security forces shot unarmed oil workers, activists and residents (Kurmanov, 2016). The oil workers' movement was squashed before it had a chance to grow and gain national salience.

The existing literature (such as Human Rights Watch, 2012; Satpayev & Umbetaliyeva, 2015) on Zhanaozen violence neglected to examine how the oil workers tried to resist global capital, and struggle against the powerful alliance of the state and transnational oil corporations. In privileging the interests of transnational capital over labour, the state crushed the oil workers' movement (Goodwin, 2018). It protected the regime of capital accumulation that it depended on for state revenues (Jessop, 2002).

The dominant narrative downplayed the class nature of the conflict (Human Rights Watch, 2012; Satpayev & Umbetaliyeva, 2015). The national media demonised the oil workers as terrorists and criminals, helping to maintain the regime's rule and authority. The oil workers' accounts still remain unheard. Their struggle was about the ownership and control of natural resources, as an anonymous oil worker, explained after the Zhanaozen massacre, 'This is not terrorism, not provocation, not pogroms. This is a real class struggle! Struggle against the capitalist invaders and grabbers of the national oil wealth. Lenin would've been proud of us!' (Aslamova, 2011).

After the Zhanaozen tragedy, the oil complex undertook various measures to prevent future labour unrest. The government amended the country's criminal and labour laws to inhibit the creation of independent unions, and introduced criminal sanctions for organising or participating in unsanctioned strikes (Human Rights Watch, 2016). For international legitimacy, the government with the support of a number of Western public relations companies (such as US-based BGR Gabara, London-based Portland Communications and Tony Blair Associates, a consultancy group headed by the former UK prime minister) arranged sympathetic media and think-tank reports on Kazakhstan (Lewis, 2016). Domestically, the government unleashed a media campaign to discredit the oil workers. Many of the oil workers' movement leaders and oppositional activists, who were imprisoned in 2012, were later released, and exited politics.

In pursuit of profits at the expense of workers' well-being, the oil complex was responsible for industrial unrest. Given the structural nature of labour grievances, strikes and protests continued at oil fields and enclaves. Local trade union activists report that after the Zhanaozen tragedy, there were 80 strikes in the industry between 2012 and 2015 (Human Rights Watch, 2016). By oppressing peaceful labour mobilisation, the oil complex risks spawning violent insurrection that has occurred in other oil-producing countries, such as Nigeria (Watts, 2012).

Anti-Mining Protests in Kyrgyzstan

Local and National Opposition to Gold Mining

About two months prior to the October 2020 parliamentary elections, a film drama called 'Meken' was released on YouTube after the state film commission banned it. The film portrays a stand-off between a local community and a Chinese mining company, and it may have been inspired by an actual incident the previous year. In the film, hundreds of local residents attacked the company workers, leading to mining being suspended. Although the political elites criticised the film for being poorly made and stoking anti-Chinese sentiments, the film was widely popular. In its first week of release, it had over a million views, receiving largely positive comments. One comment posted in August 2020 foreshadowed what was to happen later in the year (Solo, 2020):

> While watching the movie, I likened the main character to Sadyr Japarov. Kumtor is far more harmful than this, more terrible things can be discovered there. Sadyr Japarov is still imprisoned for telling the truth. My people, awake!!!

On the night of 5 October 2020, Kyrgyzstan experienced its third political uprising triggered by flawed parliamentary election results. Some protesters seized the opportunity to release the jailed ex-parliamentarian Sadyr Japarov. Before his imprisonment, he had campaigned to nationalise the largest gold mine Kumtor, and on that basis possessed considerable political capital. Many protesters also broke into the properties of foreign-owned mining companies, including Centerra's Bishkek office, the Russian-owned Zherui gold mining site, the Kazakhstani-owned Bozumchak copper-gold mine site, and the Chinese-owned Ishtamberdy deposit site in Jalal-Abad region. In Talas, local protesters set alight the Zherui's gold extraction factory, causing an estimated damage of 15–20 million USD.

Following the uprising, the struggle for power ensued among various factions. The rural protesters ferociously backed Japarov's candidacy for the interim premiership. He was hailed as a Kyrgyz patriot, who could defend rural and national interests. Japarov's trajectory from prison to the head of state revealed the strength of popular and nationalist backlash against neoliberal capitalism and its prescribed extractivist economic strategy.

The popular anger against the natural resource sector started in the late 1990s. The controversy over Kumtor gold mine contributed to the overthrow of the country's first two presidents (Pomfret, 2018). The sector has been a site of social and political contestation, involving local, national and international interests (Fumagalli, 2015; Horrocks-Taylor, 2018). The state attempted to promote foreign investment while defending national and local interests. In practice, it sided with transnational capital. Local communities' resistance against predatory and harmful mining has been difficult against the state-capital symbiosis (Byambajav, 2012).

Almost every mining project in the country faced some level of local resistance. Mining operations were repeatedly suspended, because of road blockades, office raids, burning and looting equipment and attacks on company personnel. The majority of the operations were owned and developed by foreign investors. In Batken, not a single mining project was fully operational because of local protests (Nogoibaeva, 2016). In some cases, companies fully ceased their operations due to local pressure. In 2012, the Russian-owned A.Z. International stopped production at the Aprelskoye gold deposit (Dzyubenko, 2012). In 2013, the Australian-listed Z-Explorer ended its operations at the Shambesai gold field (Trilling, 2013).

Despite the difficulties, many foreign investors continued their operations because of the lucrative potential of rent extraction. Many mining companies became accustomed to national and local opposition, and developed strategies to overcome resistance. After the 2020 political uprising, some companies issued statements to assure their shareholders that the country's political instability was not going to affect their operations. In Kyrgyzstan, there are about 49 gold sites, and 39 companies are involved in gold mining (Asanov, 2018).

Local Communities' Environmental Concerns

The miners' resistance was less significant compared to local residents' opposition. Employment in the mining sector has been small. The workers' unrest was usually triggered by differences in income between foreign and local workers and was short-lived.[3] Local people living close to mines were actively engaged in contestation with the state and mining companies.

The media discourse often portrayed local protesters as a barbaric mob for resisting neoliberal extractivism (Nogoibaeva, 2016). Local grievances were dismissed as political interests masquerading as environmental concerns. The academic discourse tended to attribute anti-mining protests to subversive clientelism. But critical research shows that protests were motivated by genuine concerns (Horrocks-Taylor, 2018; Nogoibaeva, 2016; Oxus International, 2013; Wooden, 2013). In eight mining-affected communities in Talas, Jumgal, Naryn, Jeti Oguz, Chatkal, Ala Buka, Chon Alay and Kadamjai, local residents were deeply

[3] For instance, at Kumtor gold mine where foreign staff were paid 14 times more than local workers, local unrest decreased after local workers' monthly earnings increased to about 3000 USD (Manasov, 2019).

concerned about the impact of gold mining on water supplies due to cyanide spillages or dam failure (Oxus International, 2013). Attempts to protect land and water were cultural and moral struggles to ensure human and environmental well-being.

The neoliberal commodification of nature largely externalised the costs of extractive operations to local communities, thereby minimising transnational corporations' operating costs, liabilities and risks, and increasing their profits and share value. Neoliberal extractivism was also destructive for nature as predatory mining was often unregulated. National and international legal frameworks on mining favoured the interests of foreign investors over national and local interests. As a consequence, mining companies operated in a predatory manner, as if 'there were no people or culture' (Landen & Fotaki, 2018). Drafted under the guidance of International Finance Corporation, the legislation on mining lacked environmental oversight for fear of discouraging foreign investment (International Institute of Sustainable Development, 2018).

For instance, the 2017 amendments to the Water Code allowed the Canadian company Centerra to dump waste rocks on top of two mountain glaciers, and contaminate major rivers as a result of the mine's tailings (openDemocracy, 2018). Moreover, Centerra was not obligated to pay compensation for environmental damage. Over the years, regulatory bodies have had their funding cut, hindering their capacity to monitor pollution, and shifting the responsibility to the industry to regulate itself, as discussed in Chapter 5. Incidents of companies altering data and reports to meet environmental safety standards were common.

Although depicted as ignorant and barbaric, local communities in Batken understood the consequences and dangers of mining. They were exposed to radioactive waste from uranium mining (Nogoibaeva, 2016). They were also bitter that remediation processes had not been carried out, and feared that the erosion of tailings through mudflows or natural destruction would contaminate the transboundary rivers, leading to possible conflicts with neighbouring countries.

The current legislation on tailings and waste dumps does not require mining companies to design, operate and maintain waste structures that correspond to internationally recognised standards and practices. While the legislation requires them to establish up a remediation fund, it does not provide well-defined guidelines for administering remediation actions. Makhmudova and Matsui (2019) argue that policies on post-mining remediation are outdated, and do not include technologically advanced clean-up standards. The legal framework fails to establish sustainable mining policies.

Environmental concerns were exacerbated by lack of economic benefits, such as local employment and infrastructure development. The Law on Subsoil does not have local content provisions that oblige companies to buy national goods and services. Moreover, changes to the Tax Code made in 2014 established a mere 10% profit tax for gold mining companies (International Institute of Sustainable Development, 2018). The average effective tax rate for gold companies was estimated to be around 11%, which was lower than other countries in the region. The gold mining company at Kumtor did not pay most taxes until 2002, and benefitted from a number of tax exemptions (Kronenberg, 2014). The International Institute for Sustainable Development (2018) concludes that Kyrgyzstan's mining laws have favoured transnational companies.

While mining companies articulated their corporate social responsibility goals and activities, lack of clear guidelines on the content and the scope of social package agreements allowed them to set low targets and make minimal contributions (Doolotkeldieva, 2020; International Institute of Sustainable Development, 2018). Neoliberal extractivism addressed social demands within a corporate social responsibility framework, but the latter was limited in its reach and was seen as an attempt to purchase consent and manage risks (Doolotkeldieva, 2020; Watts, 2005). The framework did not correspond to social investments during the Soviet period, which saw extensive spending on physical and social infrastructure (Manasov, 2019).

The Unequal Relationship between Residents and Foreign Companies

In general, local resistance against the extractive industry was protracted, unstructured and episodic. Although most protesters articulated environmental concerns, demands for better redistribution of resources and economic development were also important. Local communities often justified their demands on the basis of their social and moral rights over the land.

The unequal relationship between local communities and mining companies limited the effectiveness of local resistance. A situation compounded by weak local and national state capacity. For instance, the residents of Kok Serek village in Jalal-Abad oblast objected to the development of tailings from Bozumchak copper-gold mine close to a river, which was the only drinking water source. Kazakhmys Gold Kyrgyzstan, a member of a Kazakhstani-owned KAZ Minerals, altered the location of its waste structure to satisfy the local demands, but the change was not approved by environmental specialists or construction engineers (Manasov, 2019). The local residents were unsure if the new waste construction met the required technical and engineering safety standards. The residents could not hold the company to account, because they lacked the knowledge on tailings. The absence of state regulation engendered suspicion and hostility towards the company.

Transnational mining companies learnt to respond to local protests through elites' co-optation. But the co-optation of local and national elites often fragmented local communities, leading to increased social tensions. For example, Kazakhmys faced a wave of protests in 2013, triggered by the selection of a Chinese company as a subcontracting firm, which only employed Chinese workers. Kazakhmys explained that it was not legally required to hire local workers, but promised to increase its local content. The local workers only constituted 20% of the Kazakhmys's employees (Manasov, 2019). The company hired local individuals from rich and powerful families, which exerted significant influence on the local government to secure the operation of the mine.

In some cases, attempts to negotiate with foreign companies backfired. For instance, in our case study, a Chinese company, which purchased a coal mine in Karasuu, faced opposition from residents of a small mountainous village in Alay. The residents refused to allow the company to use the main road through the village to transport coal to China. The company started to negotiate with the *aksakals* (the court of male elders). The *aksakals* listed their demands, which included assistance with the provision of drinking water, asphalting the main road, annual contributions to a village fund, free distribution of two tons of coal annually to each family in the village, compensation for any damage caused to houses along the main road, and measures to support the local ecology. The company agreed to meet three of the conditions: piped water, free distribution of coal and compensation for damages. The company rejected the *aksakals*' demands for a village fund and asphalting the road.

When the negotiations broke down, the Chinese company changed its tactics, and informally recruited two local businessmen to secure a deal. The two local businessmen approached the *aksakals* to ask to use the main road. A group of young men in the village raise objections, sensing that the businessmen were acting on behalf of the Chinese company. At the village meeting, a majority of the participants agreed to grant the businessmen their approval under less stringent social conditions. The decision-making process was dominated by the *aksakals*. The co-optation of local elites allowed the Chinese company to use the road without offering its initial compensation package. This type of negotiating tactic generated hostility and distrust towards Chinese companies, which generally did not offer community programmes, preferring instead to negotiate only with state elites.

Across the country, local residents were frustrated by outcomes of negotiations, and they began to pursue violent strategies. In Batken, residents appealed 36 times to the state authorities and mining companies before resorting to burning down mining camps (Nogoibaeva, 2016). As a result of increased violence, a law was changed in 2012 that required a 2% contribution from mineral sales to Regional Development Funds (RDFs), which primarily benefitted mining villages. From 2014 to 2017, 40 RDFs were created throughout the country (International Institute for Sustainable Development, 2018).

But RDFs did not include neighbouring communities, which had to negotiate their own social package with mining companies. Not surprisingly, companies choose to implement the least costly social projects. For example, Kazakhmys repeatedly rejected a village's demands to asphalt the main roads, instead it bought electricity cables for the village (Manasov, 2019).

In recent years, some local communities have tried to make new mining companies commit to investment in the productive sector, and create jobs unrelated to the extractive sector. In 2018, a mining camp in Jalal-Abad region was set alight by villagers, and the company owner departed. The new owner, a Chinese-owned Manson Group Company, won the tender in 2019 and signed up to an ambitious programme of economic development in the village. The new company agreed to build a honey processing plant, a brick factory, a modular dairy plant, a polycarbonate greenhouse complex, a retail pavilion, a gas filling station, a mini-market, a cafe, a three-storey hotel and a tourist complex. It remains to be seen if the company will actually honour the agreement (Sputnik, 2018).

The Politicisation of the Anti-Kumtor Movement

The local mobilisation against Kumtor gold mine was the only movement in the country that gained national and international visibility. Its profile was sustained for nearly two decades. The movement engaged with a range of actors, partially because local activists pursued several strategies to scale-up their concerns at the national and global level (Horrocks-Taylor, 2018). The anti-Kumtor movement began as a campaign for compensation for a cyanide spillage. It grew in size and vision, calling for the mine to be nationalised and, in the process, challenging the dominant neoliberal order. But the struggle between the local residents and Cameco, a Canadian company, was unequal. While the company secured the backing of the state and its success seemed to be assured, it fuelled national populism in Kyrgyzstan.

After the cyanide spillage in 1998, Cameco downplayed its impact on the local population, though more than 2500 people were poisoned, and four people died. Cameco failed to offer adequate compensation to local communities affected by the 'accident', which spilt nearly two tons of cyanide and sodium hypochlorite into the Barskoon River. The incident exposed the transnational corporation's capacity to harm the population and the environment with impunity. Erkingul Imankojoeva, a former textile worker residing in Issyk-Kul, formed NGO Karek. Its aims were to pursue compensation claims for the spillage, enhance local economic development, and improve ecological monitoring and safety measures (Horrocks-Taylor, 2018).

A group of local women activists played a significant role in the NGO and the movement, though their contributions were often neglected. Imankojoeva lamented that the hard work of women activists, such as Asiya Sasykbaeva, Toleikan Ismailova, Natalia Ablova and the ecologist Kalia Moldogazieva, remained invisible to the public. The women activists were at the heart of the anti-Kumtor movement, and were persecuted by the state. Bacheva-McGrath et al. (2009) report that in Issyk-Kul province more than 54 local activists were forced to flee the country because of arrest warrants.

Karek's campaign for environmental justice was effective at publicising and politicising Cameco's practices, which became Centerra in 2004. Karek blocked a major road from Bishkek to the mine on at least five occasions between 1998 and 2006. Protests over many years contributed to the development of the residents' political agency and a critical understanding of the company's practices. Moreover, Karek cooperated with Bishkek-based NGOs, such as the Tree of Life, and global organisations, including the Dutch NGO Milieukontakt, Mining Injustice Solidarity Network and Bankwatch Network.

Karek's alliances with other organisations helped to politicise Centerra's malpractices through press meetings, critical reports, accident victim photo exhibits and public showings of *Zolotaya Avariya* (Golden Accident), a film about the cyanide spillage (Horrocks-Talor, 2018). Karek invited independent international hydrogeologists to assess Centerra's environmental damage, leading to further international pressure on the company. In addition, Karek tried unsuccessfully to sue Centerra for causing health damage, during which time 12 out of 29 plaintiffs died. The legal proceedings spanning over 15 years added to the political controversy around Kumtor.

Horrocks-Taylor (2018) explains that the local residents' road blockade was the most effective strategy. Five days of road blockade in July 2006 caused Centerra's share price to fall by 28%. After eight years of refusing to accept responsibility, Centerra relented and agreed to compensate 4.4 million USD to five local villages for agricultural damage arising from the spillage. But the compensation did not reach the local residents, because it was appropriated by the Ministry of Health, different state funds, the President's Fund and the state security services (Bacheva-McGrath et al., 2009).

The anti-Kumtor movement was further politicised after Centerra renegotiated its contract in 2009. The new agreement transferred the entire mine to Centerra's ownership. After President Bakiev's violent overthrow in 2010, a succession of governments and oppositional parties tried to renegotiate the 2009 agreement. Centerra's 2009 deal with President Bakiev was 'widely perceived as another diminution of Kyrgyz control over their land' (Gullette & Kalybekova, 2014: 14).

Heated debates and discussions enraged over the mine's ownership structure and Centerra's distribution of profits and dividends. There were two parliamentary motions to nationalise the mine: in 2012 by Sadyr Japarov, one of the leaders of the nationalist Ata-Jurt party; and in 2013 by Omurbek Tekebaev, the leader of Ata-Meken party. After the defeat of each motion, a wave of protests occurred throughout the country.

In 2013, the anti-Kumtor protesters cut the power to the mine, and kidnapped the governor of Issyk-Kul as hostage.

Protracted negotiations ended after Centerra threatened to take the state to international arbitration, and close the mine. In 2017, the government retained the 2009 agreement, and Centerra promised to increase its contribution to an environmental protection fund. Though this came at the price of the state surrendering its right to prosecute Centerra for environmental damage in the future.

The defeat of the government over Kumtor generated more anger and resistance to mining operations in the country. Local mining communities became more restive and militant. In April 2018, the residents of Toguz-Torou set alight a gold recovery plant at Makmal mine, which was operated by a Chinese-owned company Ji El Makmal Development (Rahmankulov, 2018). In the same year, protesters in Batken closed down Shambesai gold mine, which was developed by a Chinese-owned company Tiandi (Djumashova, 2020). In August 2019, local residents in Naryn stopped production at Solton-Sary mine, after they attacked the employees of Zhong Ji Mining. In December 2019, protests in Bishkek and Balykchi led to the Russian-operated uranium mine being suspended in Tash-Bulak, Issyk-Kul. In October 2020, violent attacks suspended operations of eight gold mining companies.

The long embattled dispute with Centerra took a new twist after the October 2020 uprising. Initially, the interim Prime Minister Sadyr Japarov toured the country, and told local residents to desist from violence and allow mining companies to resume their operations. In the context of a decimated economy, exacerbated by the Covid pandemic and rising of international debt payments, Japarov backtracked on his earlier statements of wanting to nationalise Kumtor. But after winning the January 2021 presidential election, Japarov expropriated Kumtor mine in order to increase the flow of revenues into the state budget. In response, Centerra filed a lawsuit against the government, and the status of Kumtor mine is currently the subject of international arbitration. In the past, transnational capital has been successful in preventing developing countries from challenging the basic tenets of the neoliberal economic order and the regime of rent extraction (Gill, 2008).

Conclusion

This chapter examined how the regime of resource extraction created social inequalities, state violence, labour unrest and environmental harms in Kazakhstan and Kyrgyzstan. The neoliberal commodification of labour resulted in most Kazakhstani oil workers lacking adequate protection against injury, sickness, exploitation, insecurity and racial discrimination. Transnational oil corporations used subcontracting companies to extract surplus value in ways that belittled and degraded the oil workers. The neoliberal regime of extractivism in Kyrgyzstan commodified nature, and in so doing was destructive of the local environment. Transnational companies shifted the negative externalities of their mining operations to local communities, and co-opted local and national elites to overcome strong opposition.

As in other parts of the world, the transnational corporations in Central Asia inflicted considerable social suffering and harm. The oil workers' dignity and worth were demeaned, and local residents' well-being and democratic voice were curtailed in favour of foreign investors' rights and income extraction. While state regulation in support of labour and local communities was minimal in the extractive sector, state activism was intense in prosecuting, injuring, and sometimes killing activists and protesters, who threatened the existing status quo and the interests of transnational capital.

The power of transnational capital was legitimised by ideological and media discourses that framed local resistance as mob or criminal activities, oppositional shenanigans or terrorism. Such frames prevented critical scrutiny of transnational corporations' practices and their role in violent suppression and dispossession. Moreover, host states, international financial institutions and transnational corporations used legal, economic and political mechanisms to inflict violence on the population in defence of the neoliberal 'free market' ideology (Gill, 2008; Hudson, 2015).

The social movements were a response to the withdrawal of social protections, violations of laws and codes, and lack of concern for people's safety and well-being (Burawoy, 2015). Most of the population sympathised and shared the activists' concerns, and supported their strikes and protests. There was a common understanding that the neoliberal commodification of things had gone too far. The movement activists and their supporters politicised their struggles against transnational extractive capital.

In Kazakhstan, the oil workers fought for better pay, working conditions and control of production. Their demands progressed from equal pay and independent trade unions to the nationalisation of the industry. As their movement became more politicised, the state used repressive tools to crush dissent and ensure compliance. In its interactions with the grassroots labour movement, the state sided with foreign oil companies against its own citizens.

In Kyrgyzstan, local resistance to the mining industry succeeded in politicising resource extraction and obstructing the operations of foreign companies. The popular nationalist backlash against neoliberal extractivism reached its apogee in 2020 with the country's third political uprising. But local and state attempts to change the ownership and rent structure of natural resources largely failed, because the international investment rule regime protected the rights and power of foreign investors (Schneiderman, 2008).

The unequal relationships between the oil workers and the oil complex and between local communities and the state–corporate alliance meant that movement leaders and activists struggled to achieve social protection or transform economic relations. The host states employed a range of tactics from co-optation to violence to weaken and crush oppositional forces to neoliberal extractivism (Goodwin, 2018). Moreover, the power of local agency to achieve change was curtailed because of state and regulatory capture by transnational corporations (Gill, 2008). The existing oil and mining contracts obligated the host states to protect foreign investors' operations, and in doing so raise revenues for state budgets.

References

Appel, H. (2019). *The licit life of capitalism: US oil in Equatorial Guinea*. Duke University Press.

Asanov, B. (2018). Kyrgyzstan: zolotorudnye mestorojdeniya obrastaushie konfliktami. *Azattyk*. https://rus.azattyk.org/a/kyrgyzstan_gold_mines/29576512.html.

Aslamova, D. (2011). Участник митинга в поддержку казахских нефтяников, разгромивших Жанаозен: Ленин бы нами гордился! *Комсомольская правда*. https://www.irk.kp.ru/daily/25806.5/2786926/.

Bacheva-McGrath, F., Popov, D., Zarafian, I., & Imankozhoeva, E. (2009). Between a rock and a hard place. *CEE Bankwatch Network*. https://bankwatch.org/wp-content/uploads/2011/08/btw_a_rock_and_a_hard_place_web.pdf.

Bini, E., & Petrini, F. (2019). Labor politics in the oil industry: New historical perspectives. *Labor History, 60*(1), 1–7. https://doi.org/10.1080/0023656x.2019.1536497.

Burawoy, M. (2015). Facing an unequal world. *Current Sociology, 63*(1), 5–34.

Byambajav, D. (2012). Mobilizing against dispossession: Gold mining and a local resistance movement in Mongolia. *Journal of the Center for Northern Humanities, 5*, 13–32.

Crossley, N. (2002). Global anti-corporate struggle: A preliminary analysis. *British Journal of Sociology, 35*(4), 667–691.

Crude Accountability (2013). *Republic of Chevron: 20 years in Kazakhstan*. https://crudeaccountability.org/wp-content/uploads/2013/06/20130604-Chevron20YrsInKazakhstan-en.pdf.pdf. Accessed Sept 2020.

Djumashova, A. (2020). Sem' akcij potesta, posle kotoryh investory prekratili rabotu v Kyrgyzstane. *24.kg*. https://24.kg/obschestvo/144008_sem_aktsiy_protesta_posle_kotoryih_investoryi_prekratili_rabotu_vkyirgyizstane/.

Doolotkeldieva, A. (2020). Regulating corporate social responsibility (CSR) in the large-scale mining sector of Kyrgyzstan. *OSCE Academy Policy Briefs*.

Dzyubenko, O. (2012). Kyrgyz villagers attack Russian-owned mining camp. *Reuters*. https://uk.reuters.com/article/us-kyrgyzstan-mining/kyrgyz-villagers-attack-russian-owned-mining-camp-idINBRE8AS0YA20121129.

Evans, A., & Sil, R. (2020). The dynamics of labor militancy in the extractive sector: Kazakhstan's oilfields and South Africa's platinum mines in comparative perspective. *Comparative Political Studies, 53*(6), 992–1024.

Ferguson, J. (2006). Seeing like an oil company: Space, security, and global capital in neoliberal Africa. *American Anthropologist, 107*(3), 377–382.

Fumagalli, M. (2015). *The Kumtor gold mine and the rise of resource nationalism in Kyrgyzstan* (Central Asia Economic Papers No. 16). George Washington University.

Gill, S. (2008). *Power and resistance in the new world order* (2nd ed.). Palgrave.

Global Value Chains Center. (2017, October 17). *The oil and gas services value chain in Kazakhstan*. https://gvcc.duke.edu/cggclisting/the-oil-and-gas-services-value-chain-in-kazakhstan/.

Goodwin, G. (2018). Rethinking the double movement: Expanding the frontiers of Polanyian analysis in the Global South. *Development and Change, 49*(5), 1268–1290.

Grishin, A. (2012). После Жанаозена: 37-ой год в отдельно взятом регионе. *Fergana News*. https://www.fergananews.com/articles/7236.

Gulbrandsen, L., & Moe, A. (2005, Winter). Oil company CSR collaboration in 'new' petro-states. *Journal of Corporate Citizenship, 20*, 53–64.

Gullette, D., & Kalybekova, A. (2014). *Agreement under pressure: Gold mining and protests in the Kyrgyz Republic*. Friedrich Ebert Stiftung.

Hairulina, N. (2019a). Эхо Тенгиза: что выяснила инспекция труда? *Ak Zhaiyk*. https://m.azh.kz/ru/news/view/61392.

Hairulina, N. (2019b). Операторы должны взрастить конкурентоспособные казахстанские компании. *Ak Zhaiyk*. https://azh.kz/ru/news/view/61349.

Horrocks-Taylor, J. (2018). Dirty water, muddied politics: hybridisation of local and national opposition to Kumtor mine, Kyrgyzstan. *Land, 7*(2), -18.

Hudson, M. (2015). *Killing the host: How financial parasites and debt bondage destroy the global economy*. CounterPunch Books.

Human Rights Watch. (2012). *Striking oil, striking workers: Violations of labor rights in Kazakhstan's oil sector.* https://www.hrw.org/sites/default/files/reports/kazakhstan0912ForUpload_0.pdf. Accessed July 2020.

Human Rights Watch. (2016). *We are not the enemy: Violations of workers' rights in Kazakhstan*. https://www.hrw.org/report/2016/11/23/we-are-not-enemy/violations-workers-rights-kazakhstan. Accessed July 2020.

International Institute of Sustainable Development. (2018). *IGF mining policy framework assessment. Kyrgyzstan*. https://www.iisd.org/publications/igf-mining-policy-framework-assessment-kyrgyzstan. Accessed July 2020.

International Partnership for Human Rights. (2011, October 3). *Подавление протестов рабочих в Казахстане*. https://iphronline.org/wp-content/uploads/2011/10/rus_labor_protests_briefing_paper_oct_2011.pdf.

Jager, P. (2014). Flows of oil, flows of people: Resource-extraction industry, labour market and migration in western Kazakhstan. *Central Asian Survey, 33*(4), 500–516.

Jessop, B. (2002). *The future of the capitalist state*. Polity.

Kazinform. (2012, September 20). *Из показаний Р.Тулетаевой на суде в г.Актау: «Народный фронт» разжигал у нефтяников ненависть к власти.* https://www.inform.kz/ru/iz-pokazaniy-r-tuletaevoy-na-sude-v-g-aktau-narodnyy-front-razzhigal-u-neftyanikov-nenavist-k-vlasti_a2496122.

Kendall-Taylor, A. (2012). Purchasing power: Oil, elections and regime durability in Azerbaijan and Kazakhstan. *Europe-Asia Studies, 64*(4), 737–760. https://doi.org/10.1080/09668136.2012.671567.

Kenesary, B. (2011). Komu vugodno sohranat' ochag nyaprazheniya v Zhanaozene? *Nomad*. https://nomad.su/?a=3-201107280016.

Kolesova, E., & Beisembayeva, D. (2017). Understanding the Zhanaozen crisis through the intercultural lenses of Eurasianism in Kazakhstan. In A. M. George & K. Kwansah-Aidoo (Eds.), *Culture and crisis communication: Transboundary cases from Nonwestern perspectives* (pp. 163–183). Wiley.

Kronenberg, J. (2014). Viable alternatives for large-scale unsustainable projects in developing countries: The case of the Kumtor gold mine in Kyrgyzstan. *Sustainable Development, 22*(4), 253–264. https://doi.org/10.1002/sd.1529.

Kurmanov, A. (2016). Pyat' let s momenta rasstrela rabochih Zhanaozena. *Socialnoe Deistvie*. http://socdeistvie.info/analitic/1724-pyat-let-s-momenta-rasstrela-rabochih-zhanaozena.html.

Landen, A., & Fotaki, M. (2018). Gender and struggles for equality in mining resistance movements: Performing critique against neoliberal capitalism in Sweden and Greece. *Social Inclusion, 6*(4), 25–35.

LeBaron, G. (2014). Subcontracting is not illegal, but is it unethical? Business ethics, forced labor, and economic success. *Brown Journal of World Affairs, 20*(2), 237–249.

Lewis, D. (2016). Blogging Zhanaozen: Hegemonic discourse and authoritarian resilience in Kazakhstan. *Central Asian Survey, 35*(3), 421–438.

Maitanov, A. (2010). Казахские рабочие на Кашагане требуют прекратить их дискриминацию. *Azattyq*. https://rus.azattyq.org/a/kashagan_workers_strike/2117559.html.

Maitanov, A. (2011). С бастующими нефтяниками встретился депутат Европарламента. Azattyq. https://rus.azattyq.org/a/strike_kazakh_oil_workers_europarliament_member_visit/24269311.html

Maitanov, A., & Guzikov, L. (2006). *S chego nachalas draka na Tengize: Svidetel'stva ochevidtsev i fotokamer*. https://online.zakon.kz/Document/?doc_id=30074592#pos=7;-22.

Makhmudova, G., & Matsui, K. (2019). The remediation policy after mining works in the Kyrgyz Republic. *Resources Policy, 61*(C), 304–310.

Manasov, Z. (2019). *The theory and the practice of neoliberal transformation in Kyrgyzstan: The case study of gold extraction in the* Bozumchak*mining field*. Unpublished PhD Thesis, Graduate School of Social Sciences of Middle East Technical University.

Mitchell, T. (2011). *Carbon democracy: Political power in the age of oil*. Verso.

Mukhametrakhimova, S. (2012). *Казахстан: протестные группы ищут поддержки у профсоюзов*. Institute for War & Peace Reporting. https://iwpr.net/ru/global-voices/казахстан-протестные-группы-ищут-поддержки-у-профсоюзов.

Murza, J. (2020). Исследование: нефтяники-экспаты зарабатывают в 20 раз больше местных специалистов. *Azattyq Ryhy*. https://rus.azattyq-ruhy.kz/analytics/11169-ekspaty-i-kazakhstantsy-inostrantsy-neftianiki-zarabatyvaiut-v-20-raz-bolshe-mestnykh-spetsialistov.

Nogoibaeva, E. (2016). *The Gold of Batken. Socio-cultural aspects of relationships between local communities and investors in Kyrgyz Republic: Based on field-work research in Batken province in the sphere of natural resources extraction*. Bishkek.

openDemocracy. (2018, April 3). *Gold and water*. https://www.opendemocracy.net/ru/kumtor/. Accessed Sept 2020.

Ostrowski, W. (2010). *Politics and oil in Kazakhstan*. Routledge.

Oxus International. (2013). *Extracting sentiments: The effect of mining exploration and extraction on eight communities in the Kyrgyz Republic*. Bishkek.

Pomfret, R. (2018). *Exploiting a natural resource in a poor country: The good, the bad and the ugly sides of the Kyrgyz Republic's gold mine* (IOS Working Papers, No. 372). Leibniz Institute for East and Southeast European Studies.

Rahmankulov, K. (2018). Судьба Джи Эл Макмал Девелопинг остается под вопросом. *Azattyk*. https://rus.azattyk.org/a/kyrgyzstan-djalal-abad-makmal-toguz-toro/29537425.html.

Reuters. (2011, October 5). *Компартия Казахстана увидела в запрете сигнал к досрочным выборам*. https://fr.reuters.com/article/orutp-kazakhstan-party-suspended-idRURXE79411120111005.

Rysaliev, A. (2011). Nedovols'tvo rabochih neftyannogo sektora Kazakhstana. *Institute for War & Peace Reporting*. https://iwpr.net/ru/global-voices/nedovolstvo-rabochikh-neftyanogo-sektora-kazakhstana.

Salmon, P. (2011). Repression intensifies against Kazakh oil workers. *Journal of Contemporary Central and Eastern Europe, 19*(1–2), 507–510. https://doi.org/10.1080/0965156X.2011.632556.

Satpayev, D., & Umbetaliyeva, T. (2015). The protests in Zhanaozen and the Kazakh oil sector: Conflicting interests in a rentier state. *Journal of Eurasian Studies, 6*(2), 122–129.

Sawyer, S. (2012). The corporation, oil, and the financialization of risk. *American Ethnologist, 39*(4), 710–715.

Schneiderman, D. (2008). *Constitutionalising economic globalisation: Investment rules and democracy's promise*. Cambridge University Press.

Solo. (2020). *Meken toluk metrajduu korkom tasmasy*. https://www.youtube.com/watch?v=63_sxMT2ezM&lc=Ugzf7WvHlC3-U3z1-494AaABAg.

Sputnik. (2018, December 19). *Nazvan pobeditel tendera po razrabotke rudnika Makmal*. https://ru.sputnik.kg/economy/20181219/1042510374/makmal-tender-pobeditel-manson-grupp.html.

Standing, G. (2016). *The corruption of capitalism: Why Rentiers thrive and work does not pay*. Biteback Publishing.

Suleimenova, L. (2013). Казсодержание: Казахская народная сказка про белого бычка. *Ak Zhaiyk*. https://azh.kz/ru/news/view/17397.

Suleimenova, L. (2015). Крошки от нефтяного пирога. *Ak Zhaiyk*. https://azh.kz/ru/news/view/27168.

Toguzbaev, K. (2011). Часть оппозиции создает очередной «Народный фронт». *Azattyq*. https://rus.azattyq.org/a/opposition_parliament_election_/24249814.html.

Toiken, S. (2011). Мангистауцы в Брюсселе. *Ak Zhaiyk*. https://azh.kz/ru/news/view/7551.

Toiken, S. (2019). Конфликт на месторождении Тенгиз и его вероятные причины. *Azattyq*. https://rus.azattyq.org/a/kazakhstan-aterau-tengiz-vozmozhnye-prichiny/30036348.html.

Trilling, D. (2013). Kyrgyzstan: Another gold mine attacked as Kumtor protests continue. *Eurasianet*. https://eurasianet.org/kyrgyzstan-another-gold-mine-attacked-as-kumtor-protests-continue.

Watts, M. (2005). Righteous oil? Human rights, the oil complex, and corporate social responsibility. *Annual Review of Environment and Resources, 30*, 373–407.

Watts, M. (2009). *Crude politics: Life and death on the Nigerian oil fields*. Institute of International Studies, University of Berkeley, USA. https://citeseerx.ist.psu.edu/viewdoc/download?doi=10.1.1.518.4318&rep=rep1&type=pdf.

Watts, M. (2012). A tale of two gulfs: Life, death and dispossession along two oil frontiers. *American Quarterly, 64*(3), 437–467.

Wooden, A. (2013). Another way of saying enough: Environmental concern and popular mobilization in Kyrgyzstan. *Post-Soviet Affairs, 29*(4), 314–353.

Yessenova, S. (2012). The Tengiz Oil enclave: Labor, business and the state. *Political and Legal Anthropology Review, 35*(1), 94–114.

Yessenova, S. (2015). The political economy of oil privatisation in post-Soviet Kazakhstan. In H. Appel, A. Mason, & M. Watts (Eds.), *Subterranean estates: Life worlds of oil and gas* (pp. 291–306). Cornell University Press

PART IV

Evaluating Rentier Capitalism

CHAPTER 10

Critical Discussion: Neoliberalism, Social Suffering and Resistance

This chapter consists of six thematic sections, each of which offers a critical discussion on issues arising from the case studies. The first section examines the nature and force of the neoliberal movement in Central Asia. It reveals the key economic and political powers, mechanisms, countervailing forces and outcomes in Kazakhstan and Kyrgyzstan. The growth and diversity of rent-seeking practices are examined in the second section, moving beyond the usual analysis of natural resources and public corruption in the region. In the third section, the nature of the state's strategic selectivity in Central Asia is explored. It emphasises capital's privileged access and control overstate institutions and capacities.

Section 'The Moral and Political Significance of Class' discusses the significance of class in Kazakhstan and Kyrgyzstan. It reveals how middle and working class groups often had different interpretations and responses to social inequalities and suffering. The fifth section discusses how Kazakhstan's and Kyrgyzstan's countermovements were responses to harms generated by the neoliberal commodification of money, land and labour. It also examines anti-plutocratic uprisings in Kyrgyzstan. Section 'Moral Evaluations of Rentierism and Its Outcomes' evaluates the effects of rentierism in terms of justice and flourishing. It shows that movement leaders and activists posed fundamental moral economic questions.

B. Sanghera and E. Satybaldieva, *Rentier Capitalism and Its Discontents*, https://doi.org/10.1007/978-3-030-76303-9_10

The Neoliberal Movement

This book examined how neoliberalism was a political-economic movement that sought to justify market-friendly constitutions, promote individual freedom, legitimise economic inequalities, and defend rentier interests (Jessop, 2012; Sayer, 2015). Competitive markets with minimal state regulation were assumed to coordinate economic actions better than the public sector. International financial institutions claimed that for markets to be optimal, they ought to be protected from state intervention, democratic decision-making and majoritarian politics. The investor, or the holder of large private property rights, was the dominant political subject of the neoliberal constitutionalism (Gill, 2002).

While many goods and services have both use-value and exchange-value, Part II of this book discussed how neoliberalism privileged the latter over the former. The financial sector expanded money in the form of easy credit to create interest-bearing debt. Banks and microfinance institutions were not simply providing financial services and facilitating transactions, but were offering loans at usurious interest rates. The private construction industry tended to focus on satisfying affluent buyers' wants and desires for high-end apartments. Property developers and owners primarily viewed apartments as an investment to obtain rent and capital gains. The extractive industry acquired a vast amount of scarce natural resources to extract economic rent. Transnational energy and mineral corporations sought to maximise shareholder value to the detriment of local ecosystems.

Neoliberalism contributed to the making of the post-Soviet economic class structure. Power and wealth did not merely shift towards the rich but shifted within the rich (Sayer, 2015). The rise of the rentier class reflected its ability to obtain income from the ownership and control of existing assets, rather than from the production of goods and services. The rentiers' income was dependent on others to produce goods and services and generate a surplus, which was partly siphoned off through rent extraction. Neoliberalism transferred wealth from the asset-poor to the asset-rich, exacerbating economic inequalities and social suffering.

The situation in Kazakhstan and Kyrgyzstan was akin to neo-feudalism in that most people paid real estate rent, interest, monopoly rent, financial fees and other charges to powerful rentiers, whose ownership and control of assets contributed nothing to wealth creation but they possessed property rights to income streams. Whereas the Soviet Union condemned and criminalised rent, or unearned income, as unproductive and a deadweight loss to society, neoliberalism justified and promoted it (Marcuse, 1996). In a reversal of the classical ideal of freeing societies from feudal-like rights and rents, neoliberalism envisaged free markets to mean markets free for rentiers to extract income free of government regulation and taxation (Hudson, 2014).

The neoliberal version of a 'free market' did not merely promote rentierism, it weakened state regulatory and enforcement powers. The production of crimes, fraud, violations and harms in the financial, real estate and natural resources sectors was routinised and conventionalised (see also Tombs & Whyte, 2009). The neoliberal legal and judicial mechanisms (e.g. the rule of law, the investment rules regime and the courts) often protected foreign investors, private property rights and contracts, and restrained state activism to tackle social inequalities and harms (Schneiderman, 2008). Regulatory and state capture and the investor's privileged status limited democratic decision-making (Gill, 2002).

The wave of marketisation in Kazakhstan and Kyrgyzstan spawned grassroots countermovements, in what Polanyi (1944) had earlier called the double movement. The commodification of money, land and labour did not only prioritise exchange-value over use-value, it produced indignation and anger over rent appropriation and labour exploitation. Part III of this book examined how social movements arose out of social suffering and needs, and sought to campaign for human dignity, solidarity and justice.

Each fictitious commodity created its own form of exclusion and unequal inclusion, and provided the basis of particular social movements (Burawoy, 2015). The relations of inequality and indebtedness around the commodification of money mobilised the anti-debt movements. The relations of exclusion and dispossession around the commodification of land and nature created informal settlements, and spurred land, housing and environmental movements. The relations of inequality and insecurity around the commodification of labour power provoked industrial action.

The countermovements in Kazakhstan and Kyrgyzstan struggled against powerful rentiers and foreign investors, who were able to use ideological, material and structural power to advance and entrench free market ideas. Domestic and transnational capital interests had privileged access and control over state capacities so that the states facilitated and protected rentier activities. The countermovement–state relationship was a complex and multidirectional process (Goodwin, 2018). At times, the governments embraced particular movements to gain political legitimacy. Through a repertoire of contention, the countermovements won some significant concessions. But in general, the plutocratic regimes weakened and crushed the movements to preserve the status quo.

The Diversity of Rent-Seeking Practices

This book explained the post-Soviet economic transformation in Central Asia through the lens of rentierism. Rentierism was a relational, diverse, complex and variegated process. The rentier class extracted income through the ownership and control of existing assets that others wanted or needed but lacked (Sayer, 2015). The powerful propertied class was dependent on others to create things of use-value, produce wealth, and generate a surplus value, which was partly siphoned off through interest, rent, dividends, capital gains and other payments. Mere ownership produced nothing, but was a source of unearned income. Whereas the capitalists contributed to wealth creation, the rentiers extracted income by virtue of having property rights to existing assets.

Income extraction was diverse and complex (see also Christophers, 2019; 2020). The big rentiers included commercial banks, property developers, energy corporations, telecommunication companies and large retail owners. The petty rentiers consisted of ordinary people obtaining interest on bank savings, and families renting spare apartments. The former were less passive than the latter because they actively found new sources of unearned income; e.g. the creation of microcredit and mortgage markets, the construction of luxurious apartments, and the development of oil fields. Some professional groups were part of the rentier ecology as intermediaries, such as corporate lawyers, accountants and engineering surveyors. They facilitated rentier activities.

The nature of post-Soviet rentierism varied depending on the countries' natural resources, economic development, foreign direct investment and integration into the world market. Rent extraction was stronger through credit money, real estate and nature than knowledge, digital platforms and trading shares. Natural resource rent was greater in Kazakhstan than in Kyrgyzstan. The housing boom was stronger in Nur-Sultan and Almaty than in Bishkek and Osh. Microcredit loans were relatively more important in rural Kyrgyzstan than elsewhere. Moreover, the state–countermovement relationship shaped what and how economic rent was appropriated and distributed (Andreucci et al., 2017; Goodwin, 2018).

The state alliance with the rentier class meant that attempts to regulate economic and social rights in favour of dispossessed and marginalised groups were weak and short-lived.

Part II of this book was based on an expansive idea of rent-seeking that moved away from the usual preoccupations with natural resource rent and illicit public takings (Engvall, 2014; Pomfret, 2019). Most forms of income extraction were routine and widespread based on 'legalised corruption' (Sayer, 2015). While the public rightly condemned state officials' rent-seeking practices as an abuse of power, private forms of extraction were widely accepted and celebrated as part of the 'free market' system. Both mainstream economics and popular discourse deceptively have referred to rentiers as 'investors' and unearned income as 'profit', so eliding a vital distinction between wealth creation and income extraction.

Neoliberal scholars, especially public choice theorists such as Buchanan (2008), argue that rent-seeking exclusively takes place in the state domain. Rent-seeking is depicted as any collective action that prompts government action to extract money from economic producers through taxes (Maclean, 2017). As rent-seeking monopolies, state institutions can stifle economic enterprise, freedom and growth in pursuit of their own private interests. Moreover, rent-seeking in the private sector escapes criticisms, because rent is seen as an imperfection that can be eliminated in competitive markets (Mazzucato, 2018).

But the public choice treatment of rent-seeking is flawed (Sayer, 2020). First, there is an important moral distinction between state transfers, which can be based on recognition of need and human well-being, and unearned income, which is based on owners' control over existing assets. Whereas the latter arises from economic power and domination, the former can be democratically informed. Second, actually existing markets do not operate according to an idealised model of perfect competition. As Part II showed, quasi-monopoly power and unearned income were prevalent in major economic sectors.

The State's Strategic Selectivity

This book discussed how the post-Soviet political regimes in Kazakhstan and Kyrgyzstan were marked by biases and privileges that made state institutions, capacities and resources more accessible to some political and economic interests, forces, strategies and spatiotemporal horizons than others (Jessop, 2002). The regimes' powers, strategic biases and projects were a product of a balance of social forces located within and beyond the state juridico-political apparatus. Basic class contradictions and social struggles meant that the regimes never achieved a stable and coherent political system, which was inherently fragile, vulnerable and dependent on social forces. While the regimes made concessions and used violence to ensure social cohesion and political legitimacy, they were also prone to failure.

After the collapse of the Soviet Union, the transition to a market economy expanded the role of rent in post-socialist countries (Mihalyi & Szelenyi, 2017). At the behest of international financial institutions and donors, Kazakhstan and Kyrgyzstan privileged capital and rentier interests, or 'value grabbing' (Andreucci et al., 2017). Constitutions and legislations protected private property rights and rent extraction free of state control (Marcuse, 1996). The commodification of money, land and labour meant that lenders, landowners and employers gained more rights to appropriate and exploit others' surplus value. Though the grass-roots movements challenged the state bias, producing a mixture of state concessions and suppression.

International financial institutions and development agencies helped to create a legal infrastructure for a 'free market' system in Central Asia. The rule of law and economic freedom were promoted over other ideals such as democracy and human rights (Waldron, 2012). The judiciary in Kazakhstan and Kyrgyzstan became an important site to defend private property rights. Its rhetoric of impartiality, reason and objectivity masked its ideological bias towards neoliberalism and moral individualism (Bourdieu, 1987). In so doing, the judiciary construed the existing unequal pattern of property ownership as rational and just, and its associated rights and outcomes (including unearned income and harms) as legitimate and fair (Sanghera, 2020).

State capture by business elites and market capture by state elites were significant features of post-Soviet politics (Mihalyi & Szelenyi, 2017). Economic capital was converted into political capital and vice versa. By entering politics, the rich sought to shape policies in their interests. Operating in the shadow of plutocracy, Kazakhstan and Kyrgyzstan instituted lax regulatory regimes, so that not only considerable wealth was amassed but corporate crimes and harms were regularised and normalised (Tombs, 2012). In Central Asia, many plutocrats wholly or partly owned companies that directly or indirectly extracted rent. These political agents engaged in licit but harmful rent-seeking practices within and beyond state boundaries, as well as illicit siphoning of public funds to overseas accounts and tax havens (Cooley & Heathershaw, 2017).

Capital-export countries used legal and juridical mechanisms to discipline the Central Asian states to 'free market' forces and values. International investment treaties, the courts of arbitration and production sharing agreements were not neutral vis-à-vis the balance of class forces in society (Schneiderman, 2008). By endorsing the rule of law and the investment rules regime, the states privileged foreign investors' rights and representation while constraining their citizens' democratic rights and actions (Gill, 2008). Moreover, as joint shareholders of natural resource projects, the states' and transnational corporations' interests were allied to prioritise rentierism over sustainable development. The neoliberal constitutionalism did not merely lock in transnational capital, it sanctioned dangerous extractive practices and consequences.

Domestic and transnational capital interests had privileged access and control over the Kazakhstani and Kyrgyzstani political regimes' institutions and capacities. The countermovements sought to make the regimes more accessible to their interests and needs, but it was difficult to alter the strategic selectivity inscribed into the host states (see also Fischer & Langthaler, 2019). The regimes had little room for political manoeuvre, because they were dependent on the business class to generate revenues and taxes for state budgets and contribute to economic growth. The regimes often diluted popular demands for regulation and nationalisation of predatory rent-extractive sectors. Politics as 'the art of the possible' was limited, because the needs of capital accumulation were invariably prioritised over human flourishing and dignity for all.

The Moral and Political Significance of Class

This book investigated the significance of post-Soviet class structure, which was inherently relational, antagonistic and emotive. Neoliberalism did not produce self-sufficient and autonomous individuals, but rather created new forms of economic dependency (Sayer, 2015). In seeking to liberate the population from the Soviet form of welfare dependency, the neoliberal architects produced new parasitic and exploitative forms of market dependency, in which the powerful propertied class appropriated and exploited surplus value that others generated. The asset-rich and transnational corporations became richer by taking from the asset-poor and the working class through interest, rent, capital gains and low wages.

The massive transfer of wealth left most of the population in a state of indebtedness, poverty, misery and distress.

In the post-Soviet space, differences in people's economic capital (including means of production, assets, occupations and income) were a significant source of economic power, security and inequalities. The upper, middle and working classes possessed different amounts of economic capital, so that they had differential access to economic opportunities and goods, had varied subjective experiences of class inequalities, and pursued different economic strategies for income and survival (Satybaldieva, 2015, 2018b).

Status, gender and ethnic differences contributed to economic inequalities through multiple ways of acquiring wealth, distributing scarce assets, designing jobs, and allocating income. This book explored how the elites privatised and acquired valuable assets through nepotism; the lenders deliberately targeted female borrowers in rural communities for microcredit loans; and the transnational energysubcontractors lowered labour costs through gendered and racialised divisions of labour.

Part III of this book showed how differences in people's lived experiences and understandings were a major obstacle in building social solidarity and cross-party alliances against the rentier class. The social movements struggled to overcome class and other differences to achieve successful mobilisation and collective action. Moreover, neoliberal capitalism encouraged individualistic and self-interested responses to economic hardship; e.g. petty trading, quiet encroachment on land and labour migration.

Transition societies can attempt to protect themselves from the destructive effects of unfettered market forces (Polanyi, 1944). But the process is not inevitable. Some societies can react ferociously against neoliberal restructuring, while others can remain docile even in the face of high levels of social suffering (Kim, 2010). Part III examined how grassroots initiatives and social movements emerged in Kazakhstan and Kyrgyzstan in response to the neoliberal wave of marketisation, differing in their defensive and offensive aspirations and strategies. The defensive countermovements sought to reshape rather than reverse the neoliberal regime of commodification (Goodwin, 2018). The anti-debt movement in Kazakhstan consisted of a significant middle class component, which aimed to reform not transform financial practices. The anti-debt movement in Kyrgyzstan was largely offensive in its nature, and raised demands well beyond capping interest rates.

To account for the dynamics in social resistance, it is important to understand people's lived experiences of class for emotive and normative responses. Without acknowledging the everyday experiences of insecurity and injustice created by neoliberalism-in-practice (Whyte & Wiegratz, 2016), accounts of human agency and politics in post-Soviet societies can become reductionist and distorted. Mainstream accounts of patronage and subversive clientelism provide a spectator's view of action, where working class actors' political practices are explained in instrumental and passive terms, reducing them to mere 'weapons of the wealthy' (Radnitz, 2010). These accounts are based on rational choice and cultural norms that prioritise elites as key actors, and marginalise first-person accounts and ordinary people's evaluations. In so doing, mainstream accounts do not merely ignore people's feelings, concerns, struggles and aspirations, they conceal the harms caused by the neoliberal movement.

The post-Soviet countermovements were largely organised and sustained by the dispossessed working classes, who had experienced indebtedness, evictions, dismissals and ecocide, and had sympathy for others in similar situations. Their responses were informed by social suffering and a mismatch between their class habitus and their neoliberal habitat. They felt angry, ashamed and shocked by the negative consequences of the commodification of money, land and labour. Their class moral sentiments shaped their thoughts and actions, sometimes leading to resistance and collective action. They initially aimed to stop market-related harms, such as debt-related suicides, land and housing evictions, and the stigmatisation of the poor. Their moral actions were not merely shaped by traditional norms and cultural discourses, they were also based on their subjective and emotional experiences of class inequalities, such as pride, shame, fear, envy, compassion and resentment. These emotive and moral responses were embodied evaluative judgements of the social world, moving and motivating working class and marginalised groups to take political action (Sayer, 2005).

The post-Soviet grassroots mobilisations emerged independently of political elites, and so were contingently, not necessarily, related. In Kyrgyzstan, the short-term alliances of some countermovements with oppositional elites led to turnovers of political elites, rather than a change in the nature of the political regime. The intra-elite cleavage was not a sufficient condition for democratic politics (see Junisbai & Junisbai, 2005), because elite self-interests did not translate into emancipatory politics. Oppositional elites were not driven by social problems, but a desire to access scarce resources without open confrontation with the ruling elite and state authorities. In Kazakhstan, oppositional elites, such as Alga and Azat, repeatedly failed to act on working class grievances.

Part III examined how older women emerged to lead resistance against indebtedness, the financialisation of housing, land evictions and corporate environmental damage. They mobilised resistance and collective action from marginalised social positions, structured by patriarchy, capitalism and ageism, and they did so without the support of the international donor class. Their resistance against rentier capitalism was partly gendered, because women were disproportionately affected by its practices of exclusion and unequal inclusion. Moreover, the older women were more motivated by redistributive justice than other social groups, and viewed the state as an important actor for correcting market fundamentalism (Satybaldieva, 2018a).

In Kyrgyzstan, the older women were effective at building alliances with aggrieved young people, who embodied strong ethno-nationalist sentiments and saw Western liberalism as a threat to their national sovereignty and local morality. The stigmatised working class rejected neoliberal subjectivity, and drew on traditional moral and Islamic discourses to define themselves through non-market values (Satybaldieva, 2018b). Most working class actors defined themselves in relation to familial ties and communal roles, and embraced orthodox Islam because of its egalitarian discourse. They often reacted with anger over the colonisation of life by economic values, usually invoking non-market norms and Soviet-era nostalgia for labour, solidarity and equality.

Junisbai (2010: 1697) observes that in Kyrgyzstan 'young and middle-aged people are just as likely to support egalitarian economic justice principles as those who worked most of their life under the Soviet Union and have already retired.' In his study, more than 70% of the population strongly supported values of egalitarianism and redistribution. The working class were often in conflict with middle class individuals, who led comfortable lifestyles in the city and embraced less egalitarian values. In Kazakhstan, there was less support for wealth redistribution, with only 48% of the population in favour of the principle. Junisbai (2010) explains the lack of support as 'an American Dream effect', in that most people held neoliberal moral beliefs and values. The neoliberal moral justifications and discourses were particularly prevalent among the rich and powerful, as discussed in Part II.

Kazakhstan's youth often accepted material inequality and nepotism, and were less engaged in political, social and civic initiatives. This was particularly true of the Western-educated youth, the so-called Bolashak generation (see Marinin, 2020). The Western-educated cadre sought opportunities within the established political order, unwilling to confront the powerful elites. A study found that only 1% of the youth participated in sanctioned rallies, and none took part in unsanctioned protests (Kilybayeva et al., 2017). Although they were active online, about 62% of them believed that their actions could not influence political power, depicting themselves as mere observers.

Junisbai and Junisbai (2019) argue that less than 35% of the population (the so-called 'ardent democrats') in Kazakhstan and Kyrgyzstan exhibited a strong support for liberal democracy. But our study on the countries' countermovements suggests that these 'ardent democrats' were not interested in challenging the political regimes. Rather it was the movement leaders and activists who opposed the regimes' neoliberal market values, advocating instead redistributive justice, egalitarianism, a strong welfare state and traditional values.

The differences in class-based values undermined social solidarity and collective action, contributing to the movements' lack of success. For instance, Kazakhstan's oil workers in Zhanaozen shifted from a defensive countermovement, which demanded equal pay and independent unions, to an offensive one, calling for the nationalisation of the oil industry. But they lacked wider support in the country, so enabling the political regime to violently suppress them.

The Unequal Countermovement–State Relationship

This book explored how Kazakhstan's and Kyrgyzstan's countermovements were responses to exclusions, unequal inclusions and harms generated by the neoliberal commodification of money, land and labour and the associated rentier practices. The movement members' relation to the world was one of concern, and they monitored and evaluated how the things they cared about were faring. Their emotions did not merely provide first-person evaluations of social suffering and injustice, they informed and motivated them towards wanting to remedy the situation (Sayer, 2011). The movement leaders' and activists' understanding of the situation and their assessment of responsibility improved over time, as they shifted the blame from personal to structural factors (Crossley, 2002).

The countermovements did not automatically result in protective measures (Goodwin, 2018). The Central Asian political regimes often weakened, co-opted and neutralised them. Departing from the usual depiction of the state as weak or fragile, Parts II and III showed how state institutions and capacities were biased towards transnational and domestic capital, and were restrictive towards social movements. In Kazakhstan, the state accommodated some of the demands of the anti-debt movement that primarily benefitted the middle class borrowers. In most of its encounters with social movements, the state used intimidation, suppression and violence; e.g. threat of and actual land evictions, attacks on oil workers and opposition leaders, and the criminalisation of strikes and protests. Similarly, the Kyrgyzstani state employed coercive measures against the leaders and activists of anti-debt and environmental movements.

By privileging investor rights, the Central Asian political regimes limited democratic forces and grassroots resistance against transnational and domestic capital (Gill, 2008). The regimes' strategic selectivity arose from their strong dependency on exports of natural resources and foreign capital. Their fiscal and material basis shaped their political manoeuvring. In Kyrgyzstan, constitutional reforms to foster greater democratisation did not alter the power of transnational capital over the state. Although after the political uprising in October 2020, Sadyr Japarov expropriated Kumtor mine, he did not envisage nationalising the mining sector. When violent protests destroyed some mining operations that threatened revenue flows into the state budget, he toured the country, urging his followers to allow transnational companies to operate unimpeded.

The countermovements' outcomes in Central Asia were similar to those in Latin America, where progressive governments failed to diversify their economies from resource extractivism, and prioritised capital accumulation over social expenditure (Fischer & Langthaler, 2019). The dominance of capital explained some key political similarities in Kazakhstan and Kyrgyzstan. Despite their contrasting positions on the democracy-authoritarianism spectrum, both states were dominated by the rentier class and transnational capital.

To describe Central Asian politics in patronage-based terms (Junisbai & Junisbai, 2019) ignores the dominance of capital and plutocracy in Kazakhstan and Kyrgyzstan. The rentier class was dependent on legal and judicial mechanisms rather than informal ties to shape political structures. Moreover, as Isaacs (2014) argues, the concept of patronage is misused and overstretched. It assumes a false dichotomy between formal and informal, and the prevalence of informal practices associated with corruption. The intrinsic normativity of neopatrimonialism/authoritarianism/illiberalism essentialises Central Asia as the deviant 'other', and assumes a trajectory towards a reified liberal democracy.

The crimes of the powerful, including economic fraud and political corruption, were endemic features of neoliberal policies that deregulated industries and facilitated predatory income and resource extraction, labour abuses and ecocide in pursuit of profits. Whyte and Wiegratz (2016) argue that mainstream Western scholarship fails to examine the relationship between neoliberalism and fraud. The assumption that corruption and fraud is predominantly a problem of the Global South and that the Global North sets international standards for economic and political transparency is part of the neoliberal political project imposed by international financial institutions to legitimise intervention on behalf of capital. Such liberal-illiberal imaginary serves to locate 'delinquent' areas for neoliberal interventions (Koch, 2019).

By focusing on Central Asian states' strategic selectivities and plutocratic tendencies, this book offered an alternative perspective to that of the often-quoted binaries to describe political regimes in the Global South and the Global North. Central Asian states share significant commonalities with Western countries: the rentierisation of the economy, increasing indebtedness, obscene levels of economic inequalities, reduced social protection and state and regulatory capture by the rich. Moreover, as in the West, the Central Asian plutocratic structure entrenched the privileges and rights of capital, and blamed the poor for having a dependency culture.

The class dynamics of grassroots resistance cannot be understood through patronage-based frames, which are blind to first-person evaluations of harms and injustice, social struggles against commodification and class-based political activism. In Kyrgyzstan, the three political uprisings were anti-oligarchic in nature, because the majority of the population periodically resisted the dominance of rich elites, or plutocrats. The March 2005 uprising, the so-called Tulip Revolution, was triggered by public anger at President Akayev's family attempt to hold onto power. The popular discontent was fuelled by the presidential family's wealth, which had been amassed since the country's independence.

The second uprising in April 2010 occurred over price hikes by utility and telecommunication companies, which were partly owned by President Bakiev's son, Maxim. His insatiable desire to acquire income and wealth intensified public anger and resentment towards the Bakiev regime. In October 2020, the third uprising was labelled as Oktyabrskaya Narodnaya (the People's October). Many people objected to the wealth and power of the three 'oligarchic' political parties, which consisted of prominent rentiers. The resistance against them resulted in more than 600 people being injured and the death of a young man.

In Kyrgyzstan, the 2020 elections were partly shaped by anti-establishment and anti-oligarchic discourses. Some populist parties, such as Chon Kazat (The War for Just Cause) emerged months prior to the elections to gain social media traction with rural and urban poor groups. Syimyk Zhapykeev, the leader of Chon Kazat, claimed that thirty oligarchs could pay off the national debt, and urged his supporters to go to their homes and force them to renounce their property in favour of the people. The *raskulachivanie* (stripping the rich) was supposed to start with Kubanychbek Zhumaliev, who allegedly owned wealth worth 2.5 billion USD. When the oligarchic parties of Birimdik, Mekenim Kyrgyzstan and Kyrgyzstan emerged as winners through voter fraud, the majority of the population refused to accept the blatant domination of the rich. After the uprising, there were calls to drain the political swamp in Bishkek, and have clean and honest patriotic forces in power.

Kyrgyzstan's figures on protest activity indicate that action against economic injustices occurred on a regular basis over a prolonged period of time. Table 10.1 shows the number of protests from 2010 to 2018. The protests involved political issues, such as political and media freedoms, gender and sexual rights, and socioeconomic issues, including land and housing rights, labour disputes, debt repayments and ecological damage. The available data shows that the average share of socioeconomic protests

Table 10.1 Number of protests in Kyrgyzstan between 2010 and 2018

	2010	*2011*	*2012*	*2013*	*2014*	*2015*	*2016*	*2017*	*2018*
Number of protests	685	1193	1286	849	544	434	596	823	552

Source Adapted from Nasritdinov and Schroder (2017) and Kloop (2017)

Table 10.2 Number of protests in Kazakhstan between 2010 and 2018

	2010	*2011–2012*	*2012–2013*	*2014*	*2015*	*2015*	*2016*	*2018*
Number of protests	64	162	119	114	71	52	36	32

Source Grishin and Duvanov (2018)

was 41%. The average number of protesters per year was 67,000 people. On average, half of all protests took place in Bishkek.

Kazakhstan had a lower level of protest activity, though more focused on socioeconomic issues. Table 10.2 shows the number of protests from 2010 to 2018. The data shows that the average share of socioeconomic protests was about 86%. The average number of protesters per year was about 3890 people. The number of protests declined significantly because of the criminalisation of unsanctioned peaceful gatherings (Grishin & Duvanov, 2018). In 2018, 69% of all peaceful protesters were arrested. The neutralisation of key oppositional figures and countermovement leaders demobilised the population. Many people felt threatened by the state's violent crackdown on protests, and abstained from public demonstrations due to the risks of detention and fines.

The plutocratic regimes were successful in constraining grassroots resistance and democratic forces in Kazakhstan and Kyrgyzstan. The levels of economic inequalities were incompatible with democracy, because the rich capturedstate institutions and capacities, which in turn privileged access to the rentier class. In the face of unequal class and state power, the countermovements struggled to achieve their aims. Democracy was doomed to be flawed with huge economic disparities. Economic equality is a necessary condition for a meaningful democracy, and this means holding the neoliberal movement and its advocates responsible for promoting rentierism to the detriment of democracy.

Moral Evaluations of Rentierism and Its Outcomes

This book analysed and assessed the justifications and fairness of post-Soviet economic relations and practices, which were predominantly related to rent extraction. It did not merely describe and explain the moral, legal and political factors that shaped rentier economies, it evaluated the consequences of rentierism on the environment and people's well-being. If descriptions of economies do not understand what things make people flourish or suffer, they are then deficient descriptions of human existence (Sayer, 2017). Evaluative judgements of good or bad were necessary to adequately understand the effects of rentierism on human flourishing, and people's responses to them.

In modern economies, people depend on market and non-market relations for the provision of goods and services, and most provisioning involves social relations between people. Some forms of dependence are defensible in terms of human dignity and flourishing (Sayer, 2015). Other forms are indefensible if abuse, violence, exploitation, suffering and injustice arise. Part II examined how rentierism consisted of unequal social relationships between those who owned and controlled existing assets and those who wanted and needed but lacked them. In relationships between lenders and borrowers, landowners and tenants, speculative sellers and buyers, monopolies and customers, shareholders and workers, and licensors and licensees, one side was justified and empowered to obtain unearned income.

In Kazakhstan and Kyrgyzstan, rent extraction was celebrated and defended on the basis of individual liberty, economic freedom, private property rights, market choice, the rule of law, the 'free market' ideology and economic prosperity. State regulation or violations of the neoliberal regime of property rights were seen to be unfair and unjust to the propertied class and investors, and corrupt and immoral behaviour on the part of the political and propertyless classes. Moreover, market relations were justified and promoted as a better alternative to state capitalism and welfare dependency, which stifled hard work, entrepreneurship, creativity innovation and growth.

But as Part II argued, actually existing markets did not operate according to neoliberal assumptions and ideals. Post-Soviet rent extraction was far from the idealised picture of an entrepreneurial investor class or a society of equal property owners. Moreover, the neoliberal account failed to consider other concerns that trumped the case for rentierism.

The motives, norms, discourses, mechanisms and outcomes of rentier activities were evaluated in terms of justice, equality, democracy, law, the environment and flourishing. The rentier form of dependence was judged to be indefensible for several reasons.

First, rentierism involved contributive injustice. Although as able-bodied adults, the rentiers were able to work and produce useful goods and services, they chose to contribute little to nothing to wealth creation. They received unearned income on the basis of power and property rights, rather than contribution or function (Tawney, 1921). They were unwarranted to free ride and be parasitic on others' labour to partly siphon off surplus value. Whereas state transfers were usually warranted, unearned income was not.

Second, rent extraction produced distributive injustice. The rentiers benefitted from undeserved distribution of income unconnected to needs, recognition, talents or efforts. Unwarranted economic inequalities emerged through the transfer of unearned income from the asset-poor to the asset-rich, and the accumulation of assets as improperty, which was used not as a means of production or work but as an instrument of income extraction and power (Hobson, 1937). While the rentier class had considerable wealth and power in Kazakhstan and Kyrgyzstan, the majority of the population struggled to make loan repayments, have adequate housing, secure dignified employment, and inhabit a clean and safe environment.

Third, rent-seeking was closely related to plutocratic governance. The post-Soviet rentier class captured state and regulatory bodies (Mihalyi & Szelenyi, 2017). The rentiers often occupied powerful political positions at multi-scalar levels in Kazakhstan and Kyrgyzstan. The political regimes' dependency on natural resource exports also created privileged access and control over state institutions for transnational capital. Moreover, the neoliberal constitutionalism ensured foreign investors' privileged status to the detriment of local needs and interests (Gill, 2002). The pro-market governance structures protected the interests of the rich, deepened social inequalities, limited democratic forces, and contained countermovements.

Fourth, rentier activities encouraged criminogenic environments in key economic sectors. The desire for short-term gains, large returns on investment and maximum shareholder value facilitated and routinised malpractice, corruption and fraud in Kazakhstan and Kyrgyzstan; e.g. extrajudicial debt collection, predatory lending, bribery of state officials, illegal acquisition of land, data falsification, and violations of health and safety code of practice. Moreover, neoliberalism undermined state regulatory and enforcement capabilities, framing regulation as 'bureaucratic' and state intervention as 'rent-seeking'. Deregulation, de-supervision and de facto decriminalisation enabled the production of corporate crimes and harms (Black, 2011; Tombs & Whyte, 2009).

Fifth, rentierism contributed to ecocide (Sayer, 2015). The political regimes selected a specific spatiotemporal horizon that promoted short-term income extraction over long-term economic development. Transnational corporations plundered Central Asia's natural resources at an ever-greater speed to accumulate revenues and profits. Their excessive extraction damaged the region's biodiversity and fragile ecosystem. Issues of economic sustainability and people's health usually received little attention, and compensation for environmental damage and remediation funds were small. The environmental problems in sparsely populated areas of Tengiz, Kashagan and Kumtor were far removed from the cosmopolitan and extravagant lifestyles of the political elites and transnational investors.

Sixth, rent extraction generated social suffering. The majority of the population was trapped in unequal relationships with the rentier class, with little to no alternative means to secure the necessary goods and services for well-being and survival. The rentier class exploited and profited from people's inherent economic dependency. The neoliberal movement created unfettered markets for money, land and labour, so that people were vulnerable to usury, rent, speculation and exploitation (Marcuse, 1996). Whereas the Soviet Union made important moral distinctions between earned and unearned income, property and impropriety, and productive and unproductive capital, neoliberalism elided them to the detriment of society.

The development of rentierism was met with calls for alternative economic arrangements and institutions. People's relation to the world was not merely of adjustment to dominant relations and practices, but of evaluative judgements on their concerns and situations (Sayer, 2017). People's well-being depended on how their concerns, attachments and commitments fared in the world. They monitored and evaluated their situation to determine what they should do. The movement leaders and activists were evaluative beings, who interpreted the world in relation to things that mattered to them. They moved between states of lack and despair and of hope and yearning, between things as they were and as they might be, and between what was and what ought to be.

Moreover, the second part of the double movement posed fundamental and critical questions of what was economic activity for, and what was the nature of economic responsibilities and rights? (Sayer, 2000). The leaders and activists of social movements raised important moral economic questions: what things should and should not be commodified? what were the appropriate sets of rights and responsibilities of lenders and landowners? what were transnational corporations' responsibilities to their workers and local communities? what responsibilities did the state have to its citizens? and to what extent was unearned income acceptable?

References

Andreucci, D., García-Lamarca, M., Wedekind, J., & Swyngedouw, E. (2017). 'Value grabbing': A political ecology of rent. *Capitalism Nature Socialism, 28*(3), 28–47.

Black, W. (2011, May 25). The two documents everyone should read to better understand the crisis. *HuffPost*. https://www.huffpost.com/entry/the-two-documents-everyon_b_169813. Accessed July 2020.

Bourdieu, P. (1987). The force of law: Toward a sociology of the *juridical field. Hastings Law Journal, 38*(5), 805–853.

Buchanan, J. (2008). Same players, different game: How better rules make better politics. *Constitutional Political Economy, 19*(3), 171–179.

Burawoy, M. (2015). Facing an unequal world. *Current Sociology, 63*(1), 5–34.

Christophers, B. (2019). The rentierization of the United Kingdom economy. *Environment and Planning A: Economy and Space*. https://doi.org/10.1177/0308518X19873007.

Christophers, B. (2020). *Rentier capitalism: Who owns the economy, and who pays for it?* Verso.

Cooley, A., & Heathershaw, J. (2017). *Dictators without borders: Power and money in Central Asia*. Yale University Press.

Crossley, N. (2002). Global anti-corporate struggle: A preliminary analysis. *British Journal of Sociology, 35*(4), 667–691.

Engvall, J. (2014). Why are public offices sold in Kyrgyzstan? *Post-Soviet Affairs, 30*(1), 67–85.

Fischer, K., & Langthaler, E. (2019). Soy expansion and countermovements in the Global South: A Polanyian perspective. In A. Roland, B. Aulenbacher, U. Brand, F. Decieux, K. Fischer, & S. Birgit (Eds.), *Capitalism in transformation: Movements and countermovements in the 21st century* (pp. 212–227). Edward Elgar Publishing.

Gill, S. (2002). Constitutionalising inequality and the clash of globalisations. *International Studies Review, 4*(2), 47–65.

Gill, S. (2008). *Power and resistance in the new world order* (2nd ed.). Palgrave.

Goodwin, G. (2018). Rethinking the double movement: Expanding the frontiers of Polanyian analysis in the Global South. *Development and Change, 49*(5), 1268–1290.

Grishin, A., & Duvanov, S. (2018). *Otchet o rezultatah monitoringa realizatsii prava kazakhstantsev na mirnye sobraniya v 2018 godu. Kazakhtanskoe mezhdunarodnoe byuro po pravam cheloveka i soblideniya zakonnosti*. https://bureau.kz/files/bureau/Docs/Reports/2018/Report%20MS%202018%20RUS.pdf.

Hobson, J. (1937). *Property and improperty*. Victor Gollancz Ltd.

Hudson, M. (2014). *The bubble and beyond* (New). ISLET.

Isaacs, R. (2014). Neopatrimonialism and beyond: Reassessing the formal and informal in the study of Central Asian politics. *Contemporary Politics, 20*(2), 229–245.

Jessop, B. (2002). *The future of the capitalist state*. Polity.

Jessop, B. (2012). Neoliberalism. In G. Ritzer (Ed.), *The Wiley-Blackwell encyclopaedia of globalization* (Vol. 3, pp. 1513–1521). Wiley-Blackwell.

Junisbai, A. (2010). Understanding economic justice attitudes in two countries: Kazakhstan and Kyrgyzstan. *Social Forces, 88*(4), 1677–1702.

Junisbai, B., & Junisbai, A. (2005). The democratic choice of Kazakhstan: A case study in economic liberalization, intra-elite cleavage and political opposition. *Demokratizatsiya, 13*(2), 373–392.

Junisbai, B., & Junisbai, A. (2019). Regime type versus patronal politics: A comparison of 'ardent democrats' in Kazakhstan and Kyrgyzstan. *Post-Soviet Affairs, 35*(3), 240–257.

Kilybayeva, S., Nassimova, G., & Masslimova, A. (2017). The Kazakhstani youth's engagement in politics. *Studies of Transition States and Societies, 9*(1), 53–71.

Kim, W. (2010). Polanyi's double movement and neoliberalization in Korea and Japan. *Social Movement Studies, 9*(4), 373–392. https://doi.org/10.1080/14742837.2010.522306.

Kloop. (2017). Кыргызстан: Анатомия митингов. https://kloop.kg/blog/2017/04/19/kyrgyzstan-anatomiya-mitingov; https://kloop.kg/blog/2017/04/19/kyrgyzstan-anatomiya-mitingov/.

Koch, N. (2019). Post-triumphalist geopolitics: Liberal selves, authoritarian others. *ACME: An International Journal for Critical Geographies, 18*(4), 909–924.

Maclean, N. (2017). *Democracy in chains: The deep history of the Radical Right's Stealth Plan for America*. Viking Press.

Marcuse, P. (1996). Privatization and its discontents: Property rights in land and housing in the transition in Eastern Europe. In G. Andrusz, M. Harloe, & I. Szelenyi (Eds.), *Cities after socialism: Urban and regional change and conflict in post-socialist societies* (pp. 119–191). Blackwell.

Marinin, S. (2020). Agents of change? Civic engagement of Western-educated youth in Kazakhstan. In M. Laruelle (Ed.), *New voices from Central Asia: Societal transformations* (pp. 20–30). The George Washington University.

Mazzucato, M. (2018). *The value of everything: Making and taking in the global economy*. Penguin.

Mihalyi, P., & Szelenyi, I. (2017). The role of rents in the transition from socialist redistributive economies to market capitalism. *Comparative Sociology, 16*(1), 13–38.

Nasritdinov, E., & Schroder, P. (2017). Re/claiming Bishkek: Contestation and activism in the city of two revolutions. *Central Asian Affairs, 4*(2), 97–128.

Polanyi, K. (1944). *The great transformation: Economic and political origins of our time*. Rinehart.

Pomfret, R. (2019). *The Central Asia economies in the twenty-first century: Paving a New Silk Road*. Cambridge University Press.

Radnitz, S. (2010). *Weapons of the wealthy: Predatory regimes and elite-led protests in Central Asia*. Cornell University Press.

Sanghera, B. (2020). Justice, power and informal settlements: Understanding the juridical view of property rights in Central Asia. *International Sociology, 35*(1), 22–44. https://doi.org/10.1177/0268580919877596.

Satybaldieva, E. (2015). Why class matters in Kyrgyzstan: Everyday experiences, moral sentiments, and the politics of the poor. In M. Laruelle & J. Engvall (Eds.), *Kyrgyzstan beyond 'Democracy Island' and 'Failing State': Social and political changes in a post-Soviet society* (pp. 99–123). Lexington Books.

Satybaldieva, E. (2018a). A mob for hire? Unpacking older women's political activism in Kyrgyzstan. *Central Asian Survey, 37*(2), 247–264.

Satybaldieva, E. (2018b). Working class subjectivities and neoliberalisation in Kyrgyzstan: Developing alternative moral selves. *International Journal of Politics, Culture, and Society, 31*(1), 31–47. https://doi.org/10.1007/s10767-016-9251-5.

Sayer, A. (2000). Moral economy and political economy. *Studies in Political Economy, 61*(1), 79–103.

Sayer, A. (2005). *The moral significance of class*. Cambridge University Press.

Sayer, A. (2011). *Why things matter to people: Social science, values and ethical life*. Cambridge University Press.

Sayer, A. (2015). *Why we can't afford the rich*. Policy Press.

Sayer, A. (2017). Values within reason. *Canadian Review of Sociology, 54*(4), 468–475.

Sayer, A. (2020). Rentiership, 'improperty' and moral economy. *Environment and Planning A: Economy and Space*. https://doi.org/10.1177/2F0308518X20908287.

Schneiderman, D. (2008). *Constitutionalising economic globalisation: Investment rules and democracy's promise*. Cambridge University Press.

Tawney, R. H. (1921). *The acquisitive society*. G. Bell and Sons.

Tombs, S. (2012). State-corporate symbiosis in the production of crime and harm. *State Crime Journal, 1*(2), 170–195.

Tombs, S., & Whyte, D. (2009). State and corporate crimes. In R. Coleman, J. Sim, S. Tombs, & D. Whyte (Eds.), *State, power, crime* (pp. 103–115). Sage.
Waldron, J. (2012). *The rule of law and the measure of property*. Cambridge University Press.
Whyte, D., & Wiegratz, J. (2016). *Neoliberalism and the moral economy of fraud*. Routledge.

CHAPTER 11

Conclusions

This chapter explores some broader issues arising from the book. Section 'An Economy Fit for the People' poses a fundamental question 'What is the economy for?' It argues that an economy must ensure sustainable development and human flourishing for all, and that rentier capitalism is not fit for purpose. The second section examines what policy measures and social alliances must occur to transform the existing economic system to better serve the people and preserve the planet. In the third section, the Covid-19 pandemic crisis is briefly discussed. It explores how rentier interests and activities were entrenched by countries' responses to the pandemic. Lessons can be drawn from the crisis on how to tackle the threat of rentierism to humanity.

An Economy Fit for the People

The question 'What good is served by the economy?' is essential to understanding economic institutions, relations and activities (Booth, 1994). According to Aristotle, wealth and property are instruments or tools for the purpose of life, and their worth is judged according to ends or purposes external to them. Wealth does not constitute good for human beings if it lacks such ends. Endless desire for wealth merely causes personal harm and social suffering. Property which is used by owners, not as means of production or 'means of work but as an instrument for

B. Sanghera and E. Satybaldieva, *Rentier Capitalism and Its Discontents*, https://doi.org/10.1007/978-3-030-76303-9_11

the acquisition of gain or the exercise of power' fails to perform positive or constructive function (Tawney, 1921: 65–66).

An economic study is unavoidably an ethical inquiry that provides an answer to the question 'To what end?' (Booth, 1994). This question problematises the discussion on economic phenomena that abstracts human beings from their social relations and contexts, or does not appreciate what things are good for human development given that people are economically, socially and psychologically dependent on others for survival and development (Sayer, 2018). Modern economies are constituted by complex webs of social relations (seller–buyer, employer–employee, lender–borrower, landowner–tenant, teacher–student, doctor–patient, state–citizen, parent–child, and so on). While some forms of dependency can be mutually beneficial and life-enhancing, others are likely to be parasitic, exploitative and oppressive.

Moreover, people are needy and vulnerable beings, who require a variety of things and activities to lead a good life. Nussbaum (2006) and Sen (1999) offer their capabilities approach as a way of thinking about human and economic development. In addition to having wealth and property as useful instruments for a worthy and dignified life, individuals need to have adequate food, shelter, health care and education; be able to participate in economic and political decisions that affect their lives; have the freedom to express ideas; be able to interact with others without intimidation and stigma; be treated with respect and equality free from domination and exploitation; be able to care for others and be cared by them; and have safe and sustainable environments without facing risks to health, communities and fragile ecosystems.

The purpose of economic activity is provisioning to enable human flourishing for all in a fair, just and sustainable way (Sayer, 2015). Beneficial forms of dependency based on equality, freedom and respect enhance people's capabilities and well-being. Harmful forms of dependency arising from domination, inequalities and misrecognition are unwarranted. Although their defence is weak and it is possible to eliminate or minimise them, they tend to persist and viewed as how things are and what people deserve, as in the 'belief in a just world' (Lerner, 1980). People can normalise oppressive social relations, especially in the context of little to no alternatives. They can also find a virtue in necessity.

But people are not merely shaped by social positions, they flourish and suffer depending on the nature of their activities, things and relations. People are evaluative beings, and they are partly aware and discriminate between things that have beneficial or damaging effects on them (Sayer, 2011). Their relation to the world is one of concern, and they become habituated to care about some things of value and not about others. Their evaluative judgements do not only passively describe how the world is, but how it ought to be. Their assessment of social suffering can lead to social critique and motivation and pressure for social change, as social arrangements become denaturalised and politicised.

Neoliberalism fails to adequately answer the question 'What is the purpose of an economy?' Wealth, profits and money-making are celebrated as ends in themselves. Self-interest, greed, entrepreneurship and competition are viewed as desirable qualities in an acquisitive society. Moreover, property is acquired for its capacity to extract income, rather than as an instrument of work or a means of production (Tawney, 1921). Exchange-value predominates over use-value, and unproductive investment over productive investment. Neoliberalism promotes endless wealth, unearned income and improperty.

In addition, neoliberalism supports unjust and harmful forms of economic dependency that enable the rich to take advantage of the relative poor. Neoliberalism shifts the balance of power in social relations towards the propertied class: lenders, landowners, investors, employers, international donors, and so on. Those who own and control existing scarce assets extract income from others, who lack them (Sayer, 2015). The rentier class is dependent on others to produce goods and services to generate a surplus, part of which is siphoned off through rent, interest, dividends and capital gains. Moreover, capitalists exploit workers, who lack collective bargaining rights and state regulation to secure good pay and working conditions. The wealthy few are empowered and enriched to the detriment of the majority. Neoliberalism is a class assault.

Grassroots movements' efforts to counter the neoliberal marketisation have proven to be uneven, fragmented and partial (Burawoy, 2015; Fraser, 2013; Goodwin, 2018). Transnational capital, the state, international financial institutions and capital-exporting countries present a formidable alliance against local and poorly resourced fractured social movements. Though having considerable power does not guarantee success. Countermovements can modify, block, override and circumvent market interests and capital power through debt relief, rent and interest caps, recognition of collective bargaining, strike action, lawsuits, land occupations, industrial sabotage and political unrest.

What is to Be Done?

This book has argued that neoliberalism produces indefensible parasitic and exploitative social relations, in particular, those relating to fictitious commodities. The following are some ideas of how to translate the moral economic critique of neoliberalism and rentierism into policies and practices for the provisioning of goods and services that ensures human flourishing for all. Clearly, it is important to tackle the main sources of unearned income.

The first set of measures would not propose a radical change to private property rights. The state could regulate asset prices so as to eliminate or minimise economic rent, and offer essential goods and services at or near cost price. Another proposal could be to cap interest rates, housing rent and utility tariffs so as to curb excessive payments and charges. Prices and caps would be democratically determined, and would vary according to regional and seasonal demand so as to allocate goods and services more efficiently (Sayer, 2015).

The second suggestion would involve taxing unearned income through high land value tax, capital gains tax and dividend tax. Such taxes would reduce incentives for speculation and improperty. Moreover, they would dampen financial, housing and stock market bubbles, thereby ensuring greater economic stability. It is crucial to reverse decades of public policy of tax favouritism for real estate, banks, finance, natural resources and industrial and platform monopolies (Hudson, 2021; Christophers, 2020).

The third set of controls would impose strict restrictions on the ownership of scarce assets. There could be specific limits on financial, property and land holdings per family. These limits would be democratically determined, and would vary according to household size and needs. Such restrictions would minimise wealth concentration and improperty, ensuring greater equal distribution of property. Moreover, credit would be regulated to encourage productive investment and projects, thereby contributing to wealth creation and economic development, rather than income extraction and debt deflation (Hudson, 2014). Lending for consumption and assets would be limited so that it does not fuel asset bubbles.

The fourth set of policy measures would involve more radical changes to the provisioning of goods and services. The state could nationalise key entities, such as banks, housing and natural resource companies so that scarce assets would be under democratic control for the benefit of the whole economy, rather than the interests of private elites. Another proposal could involve an adequate representation of workers, users and other key stakeholders on company boards. This would promote economic democracy by restricting the rights of absentee shareholders. Mutual associations and user/worker-controlled companies (e.g. housing associations and credit unions) could be expanded to devolve control to users and employees and limit appropriation and exploitation.

These measures to curtail unearned income would not only minimise economic inequalities and enlarge the ownership and control of scarce assets, they would also ensure sustainable and equitable development. Though anti-rentierism has to be combined with anti-capitalism and green politics to save the planet (Sayer, 2015). Tackling global warming and resource depletion requires a decrease in the global extraction of fossil fuels, and a reduction in consumption in rich countries. Consumption levels in the Global North are unsustainable, and cannot be replicated in the Global South. An equitable global development would involve a policy of de-growth in developed countries and limited growth elsewhere. Central Asian countries would have a moderate increase in their consumption levels, though less than in poorer parts of Africa.

The challenge is to develop a global and coordinated response to match the scale of the crisis. Countermovements in the world are many and diverse, ranging from anti-debt movements in Central Asia and squatters' movements in Africa to environmental campaigns in Latin American and labour resistance in Europe and North America. They are sometimes treated as disconnected particularisms, or distinctive regional forms of mobilisation (e.g. patron–client politics in Central Asia and clan/tribal politics in Africa). But these countermovements cannot be understood as separate struggles, but rather as part of a global countermovement that seeks to oppose and shackle the harmful and destructive regime of capital accumulation (Burawoy, 2015; Walker, 2017). This does not mean projecting the false universalism of the Western canon, rather it acknowledges the importance of viewing regions in terms of the world market, the world polity and world society (Jessop, 2018).

Building a counter-hegemonic project, which can galvanise opposition to neoliberalism, requires an inclusive alliance of interests beyond those harmed by the commodification process. Social movements more focused on recognition than redistribution demand access, as opposed to protection (Fraser, 2013). Feminism, multiculturalism, LGBT liberation and disability rights activism have criticised the oppressive nature of social protections. Social protections are often premised on unpaid or marginalisation of female labour, the exclusion or unequal inclusion of immigrant and ethnic minority communities, heteronormative understanding of the family and ableist views of mobility and ability.

Social movements critical of social protections are likely to align with neoliberalism to favour marketisation (Fraser, 2013). Market flexibility, diversity and inclusion can trump concerns over economic inequalities, exploitation and domination. As a result, existing solidarities are weakened or fractured. But social movements based on recognition can realign with those based on redistribution to transform the ethical basis of social protections so that countermovements do not simply defend the status quo of the hierarchical, exclusionary and communitarian understandings of social protection. This broad alliance of offensive social movements would not just re-embed the economy, it would radically transform society (Goodwin, 2018).

Rentierism During the Covid-19 Crisis

The Covid-19 pandemic crisis was a missed opportunity to reshape economic relations and institutions, and tackle rentier capitalism. In general, regional and national responses entrenched rent extractive practices, as governments sought to minimise disruption and maintain the status quo. During the global crisis, the sources of earned income and transfers fared much worse than the sources of unearned income. As countries implemented restrictions to curb the spread of coronavirus, the production of goods and services drastically declined. The number of waged and salaried workers and self-employed people dropped, and many people saw their jobs disappear or furloughed. Low-paid, semi-skilled and migrant workers invariably experienced greater hardship than other social groups.

State and voluntary transfers were inadequate to replace the loss of earned income or meet people's basic needs. Social welfare support was meagre, capped or means-tested, designed to help a small minority of poor families. Those above the official poverty line but struggling to make ends meet as well as non-citizens were excluded from state support. Charities offered partial and patchy support to the most vulnerable sections of the population. Moreover in low-income countries, the drop in remittances exacerbated the plight of poor households.

By contrast, unearned income remained relatively unchecked and protected from cuts. It was business as usual for rentiers, who continued to receive interest, rent, dividends and capital gains. Income extraction was neither prohibited nor cancelled. Governments only urged lenders and landowners to postpone repayments for a brief period of time, after which repayments would be recalculated and increased. Many struggling households and businesses were required to pay rent, interest, insurance, mortgage and utility payments, otherwise they faced possible eviction or legal action. People were expected to fulfil their obligations to rentiers on much-reduced income.

Governments and international financial institutions offered loans to struggling families and businesses to mitigate their dire economic circumstances. The loans were at preferential rates and operated through commercial banks and microfinance institutions. This response reflected the neoliberal strategy to individualise, privatise and financialise social and economic problems. Poor and middle-income individuals were encouraged to take on more debt to stimulate the economy, while enriching and empowering wealthy financial elites. Crouch (2009) terms this 'privatised Keynesianism'.

After decades of delegitimising governments as too big, corrupt and dictatorial, most citizens distrusted them, putting their faith in markets and civil society. Markets, philanthropy and charities were asked to do more, justified on the basis of enhancing freedom, choice, compassion and care. The Covid-19 crisis seemed to confirm people's belief that the market contract and charitable sentiments were more important than the social contract and state duties. In many countries, banks and microfinance institutions offered temporary relief by giving or rescheduling loans, and landowners showed some goodwill to postpone rent payments.

But the Covid-19 pandemic also revealed the extraordinary measures that governments took to ensure people's well-being. In general, people expressed broad political support for these measures to keep their societies healthy and safe. It is not inconceivable for political and social forces to align to tackle the dangers that neoliberalism and rentierism pose to people's well-being and the planet's future. Undoubtedly, the challenge is huge. Some readers may be pessimistic, and claim that it is easier to imagine the end of the world than to imagine the end of neoliberalism or rentier capitalism. But this is the 'pessimism of the intellect', and does not reflect people's hopes and aspirations for a better tomorrow.

References

Booth, W. (1994). On the idea of the moral economy. *American Political Science Review, 88*(3), 653–667.

Burawoy, M. (2015). Facing an unequal world. *Current Sociology, 63*(1), 5–34.

Christophers, B. (2020). *Rentier capitalism: Who owns the economy, and who pays for it?* Verso.

Crouch, C. (2009). Privatised Keynesianism: An unacknowledged policy regime. *British Journal of Politics and International Relations, 11*(3), 382–399.

Fraser, N. (2013, May–June). A triple movement? Parsing the politics of crisis after Polanyi. *New Left Review, 81*, 119–132.

Goodwin, G. (2018). Rethinking the double movement: Expanding the frontiers of Polanyian analysis in the Global South. *Development and Change, 49*(5), 1268–1290.

Hudson, M. (2014). *The bubble and beyond* (New). ISLET.

Hudson, M. (2021). Finance capitalism versus industrial capitalism: The*Rentier* resurgence and takeover. *Review of Radical Political Economics.* https://doi.org/10.1177/04866134211011770.

Jessop, B. (2018). The world market, 'North-South' relations and neoliberalism. *Alternate Routes: A Journal of Critical Social Research, 29*, 207–228.

Lerner, M. (1980). *The belief in a just world: A fundamental delusion.* Plenum Press.

Nussbaum, M. (2006). *Frontiers of justice: Disability, nationality and species membership.* Belknap.

Sayer, A. (2011). *Why things matter to people: Social science, values and ethical life.* Cambridge University Press.

Sayer, A. (2015). *Why we can't afford the rich.* Policy Press.

Sayer, A. (2018). Welfare and moral economy. *Ethics and Social Welfare, 12*(1), 20–33.

Sen, A. (1999). *Development as freedom.* Oxford University Press.

Tawney, R. H. (1921). *The acquisitive society.* G. Bell and Sons.

Walker, R. (2017). Value and nature: Rethinking capitalist exploitation and expansion. *Capitalism Nature Socialism, 28*(1), 53–61.

Bibliography

24 Kg. (2019, October 15). *Building by the rules, or attempting to seize property*. https://24.kg/obschestvo/132225_stroitelstvo_ponbsppravilam_ili_popyitka_izyyat_sobstvennost_/.

24 Kg. (2020, February 12). *The building lobby of the Bishkek City Council in the faces. They took the RAP*. https://24.kg/obschestvo/143277_stroitelnoe_lobbi_bishkekskogo_gorkenesha_vlitsah_oni_prinimali_pdp/.

Aalbers, M. (2008). The financialization of home and the mortgage market crisis. *Competition and Change, 12*(2), 148–166.

Abdoubaetova, A. (2020). Secondary schools and inequality: Navigating the fragmented landscape of educational choices in Bishkek. In M. Laruelle (Ed.), *New voices from Central Asia: Societal transformations* (pp. 85–106). The George Washington University.

Adkins, L., Cooper, M., & Konings, M. (2019). Class in the 21st century: Asset inflation and the new logic of inequality. *Environment and Planning A: Economy and Space*. https://doi.org/10.1177/0308518X19873673.

Aidar, S. (2018, October 22). What we know about alleged elite corruption under former Kyrgyz President Almazbek Atambayev. *openDemocracy*.

Aimbetova, M. (2008). *Ostavim Narodu Zhil'e: Chernyj den' uzhe nastupil*. https://www.kn.kz/article/2016/.

Akchabar. (2016). *Obzor rynka kreditovania v Kyrgyzstane za 2015 god*. https://www.akchabar.kg/article/loans/loan-market-review-2015/.

Akipress. (2016). *94 construction incidents including 46 deaths recorded in Kyrgyzstan in 9 months—State Technical Safety Inspection*. https://akipress.com/news:585654/.

B. Sanghera and E. Satybaldieva, *Rentier Capitalism and Its Discontents*, https://doi.org/10.1007/978-3-030-76303-9

Aldashev, A. (2011). *Determinants of internal migration in Kazakhstan* (Working Papers 301). Osteuropa-Institut Regensburg.

Aliev, T. (2015a). Kazakhstan: Resource curse or Dutch disease? *Problems of Economic Transition, 57*(10), 1–28.

Aliev, T. (2015b). Bednost' v Kazakhstane. *Mirovaya Ekonomika i Mezhdunarodnye Otnosheniya, 59*(12), 105–115.

Andreucci, D., García-Lamarca, M., Wedekind, J., & Swyngedouw, E. (2017). 'Value grabbing': A political ecology of rent. *Capitalism Nature Socialism, 28*(3), 28–47.

Andrusz, G. (1990a). A note on the financing of housing in the Soviet Union. *Soviet Studies, 42*(3), 555–570.

Andrusz, G. (1990b). Housing policy in the Soviet Union. In J. A. A. Sillince (Ed.), *Housing policies in Eastern Europe and the Soviet Union* (pp. 288–329). Routledge.

Angioloni, S., Kudabaev, Z., Ames, G., & Wetzstein, M. (2018). Household allocation of microfinance credit in Kyrgyzstan. *Post-Communist Economies, 30*(1), 78–98.

Appadurai, A. (2012). The spirit of calculation. *Cambridge Anthropology, 30*(1), 3–17.

Appel, H. (2019). *The licit life of capitalism: US oil in Equatorial Guinea*. Duke University Press.

Appel, H., & Orenstein, M. (2018). *From triumph to crisis: Neoliberal economic reforms in postcommunist countries*. Cambridge University Press.

Asanov, B. (2018). Kyrgyzstan: zolotorudnye mestorojdeniya obrastaushie konfliktami. *Azattyk*. https://rus.azattyk.org/a/kyrgyzstan_gold_mines/29576512.html.

Asian Development Bank. (2011). *Sector assessment (Summary): private sector and finance*. Bishkek: Asian Development Bank Report. https://www.adb.org/sites/default/files/linked-documents/41544-082-kgz-ssa.pdf. Accessed July 2020.

Asian Development Bank Institute. (2014). *Connecting Central Asia with economic centers*. Asian Development Bank Institute. https://www.adb.org/sites/default/files/publication/159307/adbi-connecting-central-asia-economic-centers-final-report.pdf. Accessed July 2020.

Aslamova, D. (2011). Участник митинга в поддержку казахских нефтяников, разгромивших Жанаозен: Ленин бы нами гордился! *Комсомольская правда*. https://www.irk.kp.ru/daily/25806.5/2786926/.

Auyezkhanuly, A., Manap, A., Akpanov, A., & Karshalova, A. (2019). The study of the residential real estate market in the Republic of Kazakhstan. *Journal of Real Estate Literature, 27*(1), 117–133.

Azattyk. (2014a, August 28). *Bishkek. 13 floors of lawlessness*. https://rus.azattyk.org/a/26554594.html.

Azattyk. (2014b, February 14). *Ipoteka: sem' raz otmer, potom beri*. https://rus.azattyk.org/a/kazakhstan-mortgage-after-devaluation/25263767.html.

Azattyk. (2019a, August 29). *Strategic agreement between Kyrgyzstan and Centerra: What did the parties agree on*. https://rus.azattyk.org/a/kyrgyzstan_kumtor_strategic_agreement/30134766.html.

Azattyq. (2019b, August 24). *'Korovy' Nazarbayeva i 'shveitsarskij zamok' ego docheri*. https://rus.azattyq.org/a/press-review-kazakhstan-nazarbayev-castles-and-cows/30126599.html.

Azattyk. (2020, December 2). *Pomosh ot gosudarstva? Politicheskii aspect podderzhki zaemshikov*. https://rus.azattyk.org/a/30979450.html.

Azattyq Ryhy. (2020a, December 2). *What kind of business do the communists own?* https://rus.azattyq-ruhy.kz/politics/5350-kakim-biznesom-vladeiut-kommunisty.

Azattyq Ryhy. (2020b, February 6). *What kind of business do the defenders of businessmen—MPs from the Ak Zhol party own?* https://rus.azattyq-ruhy.kz/politics/5098-kakim-biznesom-vladeiut-zashchitniki-biznesmenov-deputaty-ot-partii-ak-zhol.

Bacheva-McGrath, F., Popov, D., Zarafian, I., & Imankozhoeva, E. (2009). Between a rock and a hard place. *CEE Bankwatch Network*. https://bankwatch.org/wp-content/uploads/2011/08/btw_a_rock_and_a_hard_place_web.pdf.

Baitelova, Z. (2009). Zhilishnyj vopros stal politicheskim. *Kn.kz*. https://www.kn.kz/article/3253/.

BakerMckenzie. (2019). *Kazakhstan president announces consumer debt loan relief*. https://www.bakermckenzie.com/en/insight/publications/2019/07/kazakhstan-president-announces-consumer.

Bankwatch Network. (2013). *Kyrgyzstan and the conflict over natural resources*. https://bankwatch.org/wp-content/uploads/2014/04/Kutmor-Kygryzstan-Jul2013.pdf. Accessed Sept 2020.

Bankwatch Network. (2016, April 20). *Mining company shirks blame for glacier damage in Kyrgyzstan*. https://bankwatch.org/bw_in_media/mining-company-shirks-blame-for-glacier-damage-in-kyrgyzstan. Accessed Sept 2020.

Barisitz, S., & Lahnsteiner, M. (2010). *From stormy expansion to riding out the storm: Banking development in Kazakhstan* (Financial Stability Report 19). Oesterreichische National Bank (Austrian Central Bank), pp. 61–71. https://ideas.repec.org/a/onb/oenbfs/y2010i19b1.html.

Bastiat, F. (1996). *Economic sophisms* (A. Goddard, Trans.). Foundation for Economic Education.

Bateman, M. (2010). *Why doesn't microfinance work? The destructive rise of local neoliberalism*. Zed Books.

Bateman, M. (2018). Small loans, big problems: The rise and fall of micro-credit as development policy. In H. Fagan & R. Munck (Eds.), *Handbook on development and social change* (pp. 131–150). Edward Elgar Publishing.

Bayat, A. (2000). From 'dangerous classes' to 'quiet rebels': Politics of the urban subaltern in the global south. *International Sociology, 15*(3), 533–557.

Bini, E., & Petrini, F. (2019). Labor politics in the oil industry: New historical perspectives. *Labor History, 60*(1), 1–7. https://doi.org/10.1080/0023656x.2019.1536497.

Bizhanova, M. (2018). Can the Silk Road revive agriculture? Kazakhstan's challenges in attaining economic diversification. In M. Laruelle (Ed.), *China's Belt and Road initiative and its impact in Central Asia* (pp. 54–67). The George Washington University.

Black, W. (2010, May). Neo-classical economic theories, methodology and praxis optimize criminogenic environments and produce recurrent, intensifying crises. *Creighton Law Review, 44*, 597–645.

Black, W. (2011, May 25). The two documents everyone should read to better understand the crisis. *HuffPost*. https://www.huffpost.com/entry/the-two-documents-everyon_b_169813. Accessed July 2020.

Block, F. (2008). Polanyi's double movement and the reconstruction of critical theory. *Revue Interventions économiques*, 38. https://doi.org/10.4000/interventionseconomiques.274.

Bocharova, M. (2014). 'Von iz doma!': hronika prinuditelnyh vyselenij. *Vlast.kz*. https://vlast.kz/obsshestvo/_von_iz_doma_hronika_prinuditelnyh_vyselenij-6903.html.

Booth, W. (1994). On the idea of the moral economy. *American Political Science Review, 88*(3), 653–667.

Botoeva, A. (2018). Islam and the spirits of capitalism: Competing articulations of the Islamic economy. *Politics and Society, 46*(2), 235–264.

Bourdieu, P. (1987). The force of law: Toward a sociology of the *juridical field*. *Hastings Law Journal, 38*(5), 805–853.

Bourdieu, P. (1998). *Practical reason: On the theory of action*. Polity Press.

Bourdieu, P. (2000). *Pascalian mediations*. Polity.

Braguinsky, S. (2009). Postcommunist oligarchs in Russia: Quantitative analysis. *Journal of Law and Economics, 52*(2), 307–350.

Bryman, A. (2012). *Social research methods* (4th ed.). Oxford University Press.

Buchanan, J. (1990). The domain of constitutional economics. *Constitutional Political Economy, 1*(1), 1–18.

Buchanan, J. (2008). Same players, different game: How better rules make better politics. *Constitutional Political Economy, 19*(3), 171–179.

Burawoy, M. (2015). Facing an unequal world. *Current Sociology, 63*(1), 5–34.

Byambajav, D. (2012). Mobilizing against dispossession: Gold mining and a local resistance movement in Mongolia. *Journal of the Center for Northern Humanities, 5*, 13–32.

Cabar. (2020, May 14). *Some residential construction projects may fail due to COVID-19 in Kyrgyzstan*. https://cabar.asia/en/some-residential-construction-projects-may-fail-due-to-covid-19-in-kyrgyzstan/.

Central Asia and Caspian Intelligence. (2008, February 25). *The Salymbekov Clan and the Dordoy Bazaar*. No. 28. https://wikileaks.org/gifiles/attach/177/177775_CACIA27.pdf. Accessed July 2020.

Central Asian News Service. (2016, February 12). *Commercial banks to quit from mortgage, consumer lending markets over National Bank's restrictions—Expert*. https://akipress.com/news:572629:Commercial_banks_to_quit_from_mortgage,_consumer_lending_markets_over_National_Bank_s_restrictions_-_expert/.

Central Asian News Service. (2017, March 2). *Nearly 25,000 teachers in Kyrgyzstan need housing—State mortgage company*. https://24.kg/english/46362_25000_teachers_in_Kyrgyzstan_badly_need_housing/.

Charman, K. (2007). Kazakhstan: A state-led liberalized market economy? In D. Lane & M. Myant (Eds.), *Varieties of capitalism in post-Communist countries* (pp. 165–182). Palgrave Macmillan.

Christophers, B. (2019). The rentierization of the United Kingdom economy. *Environment and Planning A: Economy and Space*. https://doi.org/10.1177/0308518X19873007.

Christophers, B. (2020). *Rentier capitalism: Who owns the economy, and who pays for it?* Verso.

CIS Arbitration Forum. (2013, December 16). *Metal-Tech v Uzbekistan: No jurisdiction because of corruption*. http://www.cisarbitration.com/2013/12/16/metal-tech-v-uzbekistan-no-jurisdiction-because-of-corruption.

Clark, T. D. (2014). Reclaiming Karl Polanyi, socialist intellectual. *Studies in Political Economy, 94*(1), 61–84.

Cooley, A., & Heathershaw, J. (2017). *Dictators without borders: Power and money in Central Asia*. Yale University Press.

Cooley, A., & Sharman, J. C. (2015). Blurring the line between licit and illicit: Transnational corruption networks in Central Asia and beyond. *Central Asian Survey, 34*(1), 11–28.

Crossley, N. (2002a). *Making sense of social movements*. Open University Press.

Crossley, N. (2002b). Global anti-corporate struggle: A preliminary analysis. *British Journal of Sociology, 35*(4), 667–691.

Crouch, C. (2009). Privatised Keynesianism: An unacknowledged policy regime. *British Journal of Politics and International Relations, 11*(3), 382–399.

Crude Accountability (2013). *Republic of Chevron: 20 years in Kazakhstan*. https://crudeaccountability.org/wp-content/uploads/2013/06/20130604-Chevron20YrsInKazakhstan-en.pdf.pdf. Accessed Sept 2020.

Danilovich, N. (2010). Growing inequalities and reproductive health in transitional countries: Kazakhstan and Belarus. *Journal of Public Health Policy, 31*(1), 30–50.

Davis, M. (2004, March–April). Planet of slums. *New Left Review, 26*, 5–34.

Djarlygapova, D. (2017). Zaemshiki za bortom: Komu pomogla programma refinasirovaniya zaimov? *Vlast.kz*. https://vlast.kz/amp/jekonomika/21893-zaemsiki-za-bortom-komu-pomogla-programma-refinansirovania-ipotecnyh-zajmov.html.

Djumashova, A. (2020). Sem' akcij potesta, posle kotoryh investory prekratili rabotu v Kyrgyzstane. *24.kg*.https://24.kg/obschestvo/144008_sem_aktsiy_protesta_posle_kotoryih_investoryi_prekratili_rabotu_vkyirgyizstane/.

Doolot, A., & Heathershaw, J. (2015). State as resource, mediator and performer: Understanding the local and global politics of gold mining in Kyrgyzstan. *Central Asian Survey, 34*(1), 93–109.

Doolotkeldieva, A. (2020). Regulating corporate social responsibility (CSR) in the large-scale mining sector of Kyrgyzstan. *OSCE Academy Policy Briefs*.

Dzyubenko, O. (2012). Kyrgyz villagers attack Russian-owned mining camp. *Reuters*. https://uk.reuters.com/article/us-kyrgyzstan-mining/kyrgyz-villagers-attack-russian-owned-mining-camp-idINBRE8AS0YA20121129.

El-Hodiri, M., Kudasheva, T., & Kunitsa, S. (2015). Methods of measurement of socio-geographical inequality in Kazakhstan, a consequence to the distribution of oil development? *Journal of Economic Sociology, 3*(1), 7–23.

Engel, S. (2019). Microfinance as poverty-shame debt. *Emotions and Society, 1*(2), 181–196.

Engvall, J. (2014). Why are public offices sold in Kyrgyzstan? *Post-Soviet Affairs, 30*(1), 67–85.

Equal Times. (2017, October 12). *Kyrgyz trade unions vow to protect labour rights ahead of Sunday's elections*.https://www.equaltimes.org/kyrgyz-trade-unions-vow-to-protect?lang=en#.X0AUri2ZPBI.

Erturk, I., Froud, J., Johal, S., Leaver, A., & Williams, K. (2007). The democratization of finance? Promises, outcomes and conditions. *Review of International Political Economy, 14*(4), 553–575.

Eurasianet. (2011, May 14). *Kyrgyzstan to pay Osh victims' families: Can it be done fairly*?https://eurasianet.org/kyrgyzstan-to-pay-osh-victims-families-can-it-be-done-fairly.

Eurasianet. (2014, July 22). *Kyrgyzstan: After the revolution came the cranes*. https://eurasianet.org/kyrgyzstan-after-the-revolution-came-the-cranes.

Eurasianet. (2016, February 4). *Kazakhstan: Economic woes prompting pot-bangers to target banks*. https://www.refworld.org/docid/56b45ac04.html.

Eurasianet. (2019a, August 24). *Dolgovaya amnistiya v Kazakhstane reshit ili otlozhit problemu?* https://russian.eurasianet.org/долговая-амнистия-в-казахстане-решит-или-отложит-проблему.

Eurasianet. (2019b, August 23). *Kazakhstan: Castles, cows and a grumpy old man.* https://eurasianet.org/kazakhstan-castles-cows-and-a-grumpy-old-man.

Evans, A., & Sil, R. (2020). The dynamics of labor militancy in the extractive sector: Kazakhstan's oilfields and South Africa's platinum mines in comparative perspective. *Comparative Political Studies, 53*(6), 992–1024.

Fairclough, I., & Fairclough, N. (2012). *Political discourse analysis: A method for advanced students*. Routledge.

Fatyanova, U. (2017). *Eksperty poschitali skol'ko Kazakhstan potratil na EKSPO-2017*. https://the-steppe.com/novosti/eksperty-podschitali-skolko-kazahstan-potratil-na-ekspo-2017.

Fedirici, S. (2014). From commoning to debt: Financialization, microcredit, and the changing architecture of capital accumulation. *The South Atlantic Quarterly, 113*(2), 231–244.

Ferguson, J. (2006). Seeing like an oil company: Space, security, and global capital in neoliberal Africa. *American Anthropologist, 107*(3), 377–382.

Ferguson, J. (2009). The uses of neoliberalism. *Antipode, 41*(S1), 166–184.

Fischer, K., & Langthaler, E. (2019). Soy expansion and countermovements in the Global South: A Polanyian perspective. In A. Roland, B. Aulenbacher, U. Brand, F. Decieux, K. Fischer, & S. Birgit (Eds.), *Capitalism in transformation: Movements and countermovements in the 21st century* (pp. 212–227). Edward Elgar Publishing.

Fitzgeorge-Parker, L. (2018). Impact banking: Microfinance comes of age in Kyrgyzstan. *Euromoney*. https://www.euromoney.com/article/b1b0967crmxs3m/impact-banking-microfinance-comes-of-age-in-kyrgyzstan.

Fletcher, A. (2017). Applying critical realism in qualitative research: Methodology meets method. *International Journal of Social Research Methodology, 20*(2), 181–194.

Forbes. (2019, March 6). Vremya refinansirovatsa. Shans est': srok istekaet 15 iyulya. https://forbes.kz/finances/finance/vremya_refinansirovatsya_shansyi_est_srok_istekaet_15_iyulya/.

Franke, A., Gawrich, A., & Alakbarov, G. (2009). Kazakhstan and Azerbaijan as post-Soviet rentier states: Resource incomes and autocracy as a double 'curse' in post-Soviet regimes. *Europe-Asia Studies, 61*(1), 109–140.

Fraser, N. (2013, May–June). A triple movement? Parsing the politics of crisis after Polanyi. *New Left Review, 81*, 119–132.

Friends of the Earth Europe. (2007). *Kashagan oil field development*. https://www.foeeurope.org/sites/default/files/publications/foee_kashagan_oil_field_development_1207.pdf. Accessed Sept 2020.

Frohlich, C. (2020). Urban citizenship under post-Soviet conditions: Grassroots struggles of residents in contemporary Moscow. *Journal of Urban Affairs, 42*(2), 188–202.

Fryer, P., Nasritdinov, E., & Satybaldieva, E. (2014). Moving toward the brink? Migration in the Kyrgyz Republic. *Central Asian Affairs, 1*(2), 171–198.

Fumagalli, M. (2015). *The Kumtor gold mine and the rise of resource nationalism in Kyrgyzstan* (Central Asia Economic Papers No. 16). George Washington University.

Gawecki, M. (2013). New urbanization of the steppe. Astana: A capital called the capital. *Studia Historiae Oeconomicae, 31*(1), 35–56.

Gentile, M., & Sjoberg, O. (2013). Housing allocation under socialism: The Soviet case revisited. *Post-Soviet Affairs, 29*(2), 173–195.

Gentile, M., & Tammaru, T. (2006). Housing and ethnicity in the post-Soviet city: Ust'-Kamenogorsk, Kazakhstan. *Urban Studies, 43*(10), 1757–1778.

Gill, S. (2002). Constitutionalising inequality and the clash of globalisations. *International Studies Review, 4*(2), 47–65.

Gill, S. (2008). *Power and resistance in the new world order* (2nd ed.). Palgrave.

Global Value Chains Center. (2017, October 17). *The oil and gas services value chain in Kazakhstan*. https://gvcc.duke.edu/cggclisting/the-oil-and-gas-services-value-chain-in-kazakhstan/.

Glushkova, S. (2011). Tasmaganbetov otvetil "golodovshikam" razoblacheniyami. *Azzattyq*. https://rus.azattyq.org/a/housing_crisis_astana/2312480.html.

Glushkova, S. (2013). Protest na krane prodoljaetsya vtorye sutki. *Azattyq*. https://rus.azattyq.org/a/protest-na-krane-vyselenie-nazarbayev-universitet/25165763.html.

Go, J. (2016). *Postcolonial thought and social theory*. Oxford University Press.

Goodwin, G. (2018). Rethinking the double movement: Expanding the frontiers of Polanyian analysis in the Global South. *Development and Change, 49*(5), 1268–1290.

Graeber, D. (2011). *Debt: The first 5,000 years*. Melville House Publishing.

Grassmann, F. (2011). *Protecting vulnerable families in Central Asia: Poverty, vulnerability and the impact of the economic crisis* (Innocenti Working Papers No. 2011-05). https://www.unicef-irc.org/publications/639-protecting-vulnerable-families-in-central-asia-poverty-vulnerability-and-the-impact.html.

Graziani, A. (1989). *The theory of the monetary circuit*. Thames Papers in Political Economy, Thames Polytechnic.

Green, J. E. (2016). Liberalism and the problem of plutocracy. *Constellations, 23*(1), 84–95.

Grishin, A. (2012). После Жанаозена: 37-ой год в отдельно взятом регионе. *Fergana News*.https://www.fergananews.com/articles/7236.

Grishin, A., & Duvanov, S. (2018). *Otchet o rezultatah monitoringa realizatsii prava kazakhstantsev na mirnye sobraniya v 2018 godu. Kazakhtanskoe mezhdunarodnoe byuro po pravam cheloveka i soblideniya zakonnosti*. https://bureau.kz/files/bureau/Docs/Reports/2018/Report%20MS%202018%20RUS.pdf.

Gulbrandsen, L., & Moe, A. (2005, Winter). Oil company CSR collaboration in 'new' petro-states. *Journal of Corporate Citizenship, 20*, 53–64.

Gullette, D., & Kalybekova, A. (2014). *Agreement under pressure: Gold mining and protests in the Kyrgyz Republic*. Friedrich Ebert Stiftung.

Guseva, A. (2005). Building new markets: A comparison of the Russian and American credit card markets. *Socio-Economic Review, 3*(3), 437–466.

Habibov, N. (2014, May). Does reform in Kazakhstan improve access to childcare? Evidence from nationally-representative surveys. *Children and Youth Services Review, 40*, 13–19.

Hairulina, N. (2019a). Эхо Тенгиза: что выяснила инспекция труда? *Ak Zhaiyk*. https://m.azh.kz/ru/news/view/61392.

Hairulina, N. (2019b). Операторы должны взрастить конкурентоспособные казахстанские компании. *Ak Zhaiyk*. https://azh.kz/ru/news/view/61349.

Hann, C. (2016). Cucumbers and courgettes: Rural workfare and the new double movement in Hungary. *Intersections. East Europe Journal Society and Politics, 2*(2), 38–56.

Harvey, D. (2005). *A brief history of neoliberalism*. Oxford University Press.

Harvey, D. (2013). *Rebel cities. From the right to the city to the urban revolution*. Verso.

Hasanova, S. (2018a). Income inequality in Kyrgyzstan: The redistributive effect of social benefits. In M. Laruelle (Ed.), *New voices from Central Asia: Political, economic, and societal challenges and opportunities* (pp. 105–117). The George Washington University.

Hasanova, S. (2018b). *Financial inclusion, financial regulation, financial literacy, and financial education in the Kyrgyz Republic* (ADBI Working Paper Series No. 850). Asian Development Bank Institute.

Hatcher, C. (2015a). Illegal geographies of the state: The legalisation of a 'squatter' settlement in Bishkek, Kyrgyzstan. *International Journal of Law in Built Environment, 7*(1), 39–54.

Hatcher, C. (2015b). Globalising homeownership: Housing privatisation schemes and the private rental sector in post-socialist Bishkek Kyrgyzstan. *International Development Planning Review, 37*(4), 467–486.

Hatcher, C. (2017). Making property in Kyrgyzstan: Bishkek's urban periphery as redistributive space. *Central Asian Affairs, 4*(2), 173–196.

Hayek, F. (1944). *The road to serfdom*. Routledge.

Hirschman, A. (1982). Rival interpretations of market society: Civilising, destructive or feeble? *Journal of Economic Literature, 20*(4), 1463–1484.

Ho, K. (2012). Finance. In D. Fassin (Ed.), *A companion to moral anthropology* (pp. 413–431). Wiley.

Hobson, J. (1937). *Property and improperty*. Victor Gollancz Ltd.

Hoggarth, D. (2016). The rise of Islamic finance: Post-colonial market-building in central Asia and Russia. *International Affairs, 92*(1), 115–136.

Horrocks-Taylor, J. (2018). Dirty water, muddied politics: hybridisation of local and national opposition to Kumtor mine, Kyrgyzstan. *Land, 7*(2), -18.

Hudson, M. (2014). *The bubble and beyond* (New). ISLET.

Hudson, M. (2015). *Killing the host: How financial parasites and debt bondage destroy the global economy*. CounterPunch Books.

Hudson, M. (2017). *J is for junk economics: A guide to reality in an age of deception*. ISLET.

Hudson, M. (2018). . . . *and forgive them their debts: Lending, Foreclosures and redemption from bronze age finance to the jubilee year*. ISLET.

Hudson, M. (2021). Finance capitalism versus industrial capitalism: The*Rentier* resurgence and takeover. *Review of Radical Political Economics*. https://doi.org/10.1177/04866134211011770.

Human Rights Watch. (2012). *Striking oil, striking workers: violations of labor rights in Kazakhstan's oil sector*.https://www.hrw.org/sites/default/files/reports/kazakhstan0912ForUpload_0.pdf. Accessed July 2020.

Human Rights Watch. (2016). *We are not the enemy: Violations of workers' rights in Kazakhstan*. https://www.hrw.org/report/2016/11/23/we-are-not-enemy/violations-workers-rights-kazakhstan. Accessed July 2020.

Ibraimov, B. (2011). *Kyrgyz plan grants land in South*. http://centralasiaonline.com/en_GB/articles/caii/features/main/2011/04/27/feature-01?mobile=true.

Inform Buro. (2017, January 22). *One seat in two chairs: When parliamentary business is not an obstacle to lawmaking*. https://old.informburo.kz/stati/odnim-mestom-na-dvuh-kreslah-kogda-deputatskiy-biznes-zakonotvorchestvu-ne-pomeha.html.

International Institute of Sustainable Development. (2018). *IGF mining policy framework assessment. Kyrgyzstan*. https://www.iisd.org/publications/igf-mining-policy-framework-assessment-kyrgyzstan. Accessed July 2020.

International Crisis Group. (2005). *Kyrgyzstan: A faltering state* (Asia Report No. 109). https://www.crisisgroup.org/europe-central-asia/central-asia/kyrgyzstan/kyrgyzstan-faltering-state.

International Finance Corporation. (2013). *In the Kyrgyz Republic: Cutting red tape*. https://www.ifc.org/wps/wcm/connect/news_ext_content/ifc_external_corporate_site/news+and+events/news/kyrgyz+icpackage.

International Finance Corporation. (2016). *Islamic banking and finance: Opportunities across micro, small and medium enterprises in Kyrgyz Republic*. International Finance Corporation.

International Institute for Environment and Development. (2012). *How to scrutinise a production sharing agreement: A guide for the oil and gas sector based on experience from the Caspian region*. https://pubs.iied.org/pdfs/16031IIED.pdf. Accessed Sept 2020.

International Monetary Fund. (2010). *Republic of Kazakhstan: 2010 Article IV Consultation* (IMF Country Report No. 10/241). International Monetary Fund.

International Partnership for Human Rights. (2011, October 3). *Подавление протестов рабочих в Казахстане*. https://iphronline.org/wp-content/uploads/2011/10/rus_labor_protests_briefing_paper_oct_2011.pdf.

Isaacs, R. (2014). Neopatrimonialism and beyond: Reassessing the formal and informal in the study of Central Asian politics. *Contemporary Politics, 20*(2), 229–245.

Jager, P. (2014). Flows of oil, flows of people: Resource-extraction industry, labour market and migration in western Kazakhstan. *Central Asian Survey, 33*(4), 500–516.

Janda, K., & Turba, B. (2013). Determinants of the financial performance of microfinance institutions in Central Asia. *Post-Communist Economies, 25*(4), 558–569.

Jessop, B. (2002). *The future of the capitalist state*. Polity.

Jessop, B. (2012). Neoliberalism. In G. Ritzer (Ed.), *The Wiley-Blackwell encyclopaedia of globalization* (Vol. 3, pp. 1513–1521). Wiley-Blackwell.

Jessop, B. (2015). Hard cash, easy credit, fictitious capital: Critical reflections on money as a fetishised social relation. *Finance and Society, 1*(1), 20–37.

Jessop, B. (2018). The world market, 'North-South' relations and neoliberalism. *Alternate Routes: A Journal of Critical Social Research, 29*, 207–228.

Jumagulov, M., & Li, A. (2019). Osobnyaki vmesto derev'ev. Kak vlasti Bishkeka unichtojili bol'she treti parka Ata Turk. *Kloop*. https://kloop.kg/t/park-ata turk/osobnyaki-vmesto-derevyev/.

Junisbai, A. (2010). Understanding economic justice attitudes in two countries: Kazakhstan and Kyrgyzstan. *Social Forces, 88*(4), 1677–1702.

Junisbai, B., & Junisbai, A. (2005). The democratic choice of Kazakhstan: A case study in economic liberalization, intra-elite cleavage and political opposition. *Demokratizatsiya, 13*(2), 373–392.

Junisbai, B., & Junisbai, A. (2019). Regime type versus patronal politics: A comparison of 'ardent democrats' in Kazakhstan and Kyrgyzstan. *Post-Soviet Affairs, 35*(3), 240–257.

Kalashnikova, A. (2015). Chego dobivaetsa Esenbek Ukteshbaev? *Ratel*. https://ratel.kz/raw/21_aprelya.

Karim, L. (2011). *Microfinance and its discontents*. University of Minnesota Press.

Karrar, H. (2020). The bazaar in ruins: Rent and fire in Barakholka Almaty. *Central Asian Survey, 39*(1), 80–94.

Kazakhstan Today. (2008, November 24). *Proceeds from illegal monopoly activities of 'Almatyzher' should be collected into the city budget—Human rights activist*. https://www.kt.kz/rus/economy/dohodi_ot_nezakonnoj_monopoljnoj_dejateljnosti_almatizher_sleduet_vziskatj_v_bjudzhet_goroda_pravozashtitnik_1153469649.html.

Kazinform. (2012, September 20). *Из показаний Р.Тулетаевой на суде в г.Актау: «Народный фронт» разжигал у нефтяников ненависть к власти*. https://www.inform.kz/ru/iz-pokazaniy-r-tuletaevoy-na-sude-v-g-aktau-narodnyy-front-razzhigal-u-neftyanikov-nenavist-k-vlasti_a2496122.

Kaztag. (2020). *Nereal'nymi nazval deputat protsenty po kreditam v Kazakhstane*. https://kaztag.kz/ru/news/nerealnymi-nazval-deputat-protsenty-po-kreditam-v-kazakhstane.

Keat, R. (2000). *Cultural goods and the limits of the market*. Macmillan.

Keating, C., Rasmussen, C., & Rishi, P. (2010). The rationality of empowerment: Microcredit, accumulation by dispossession, and the gendered economy. *Signs, 36*(1), 153–176.

Keen, S. (2011). Debunking macroeconomics. *Economic Analysis and Policy, 41*(3), 147–167.

Kendall-Taylor, A. (2012). Purchasing power: Oil, elections and regime durability in Azerbaijan and Kazakhstan. *Europe-Asia Studies, 64*(4), 737–760. https://doi.org/10.1080/09668136.2012.671567.

Kenesary, B. (2011). Komu vugodno sohranat' ochag nyaprazheniya v Zhanaozene? *Nomad*. https://nomad.su/?a=3-201107280016.

Kennedy, M. (1995). *Interest and inflation free money*. Seva International.

Kerimray, A., De Miglio, R., Rojas-Solórzano, L., & Ó Gallachóir, B. (2017). Household energy consumption and energy poverty in Kazakhstan. *IAEE Energy Forum, 26*, 31–34.

Kilybayeva, S., Nassimova, G., & Masslimova, A. (2017). The Kazakhstani youth's engagement in politics. *Studies of Transition States and Societies, 9*(1), 53–71.

Kim, W. (2010). Polanyi's double movement and neoliberalization in Korea and Japan. *Social Movement Studies, 9*(4), 373–392. https://doi.org/10.1080/14742837.2010.522306.

Kloop. (2017). Кыргызстан: Анатомия митингов. https://kloop.kg/blog/2017/04/19/kyrgyzstan-anatomiya-mitingov; https://kloop.kg/blog/2017/04/19/kyrgyzstan-anatomiya-mitingov/.

Kloop (2019a, October 23). *The park that was lost*. https://www.occrp.org/en/public-land-private-hands/the-park-that-was-lost. Accessed July 2020.

Kloop. (2019b, October 23). *The officials who gave it away*. https://www.occrp.org/en/public-land-private-hands/the-officials-who-gave-It-away. Accessed July 2020.

Kloop. (2019c). *How mayors of Bishkek and officials distributed land in Ataturk Park.* https://kloop.kg/t/park-ataturk/kak-chinovniki-razdavali-zemelnyye-uchastki-v-parke-atatyurk/ Accessed July 2020.

Kn.kz (2008, April 8). *Interview of lawyer Sergei Utkin to the agency Kazakhstan Today.* https://www.kn.kz/article/1201/.

Koch, N. (2012). Urban 'utopias': The Disney stigma and discourses of 'false modernity.' *Environment and Planning a: Economy and Space, 44*(10), 2445–2462. https://doi.org/10.1068/a44647.

Koch, N. (2014). Bordering on the modern: Power, practice and exclusion in Astana. *Transactions of the Institute of British Geographers, 39*(3), 432–443. https://doi.org/10.1111/tran.12031.

Koch, N. (2019). Post-triumphalist geopolitics: Liberal selves, authoritarian others. *ACME: An International Journal for Critical Geographies, 18*(4), 909–924.

Kohl, S. (2018). More mortgages, more homes? The effect of housing financialization on homeownership in historical perspective. *Politics and Society, 46*(2), 177–203. https://doi.org/10.1177/0032329218755750.

Kolesova, E., & Beisembayeva, D. (2017). Understanding the Zhanaozen crisis through the intercultural lenses of Eurasianism in Kazakhstan. In A. M. George & K. Kwansah-Aidoo (Eds.), *Culture and crisis communication: Transboundary cases from Nonwestern perspectives* (pp. 163–183). Wiley.

Kopeyeva, A. (2020). Factors behind regional inequality in education in Kazakhstan. In M. Laruelle (Ed.), *New voices from Central Asia: Societal transformations* (pp. 53–85). The George Washington University.

Korneeva, O. (2009). Dolshiki i ipotechniki Kazakhtana sozdajut narodnoe dvizenie. *DW*. https://www.dw.com/ru/дольщики-и-ипотечники-в-казахстане-создают-народное-движение/a-4269221.

KPMG. (2019). *Private equity market in Kazakhstan.* https://assets.kpmg/content/dam/kpmg/kz/pdf/2019/09/KPMG-Private-Equity-Market-in-Kazakhstan-ENG-2019.pdf. Accessed Sept 2020.

Kronenberg, J. (2014). Viable alternatives for large-scale unsustainable projects in developing countries: The case of the Kumtor gold mine in Kyrgyzstan. *Sustainable Development, 22*(4), 253–264. https://doi.org/10.1002/sd.1529.

Kudryavtseva, T. (2016). *Bolee polumillionov Kyrgyzstantsev zashchityat ot proizvola kreditorov. 24.kg.* https://24.kg/finansy/40325_bolee_polumillionа_kyirgyizstantsevzaschityat_ot_proizvola_kreditorov/.

Kuehnast, K., & Dudwick, N. (2002). Better a hundred friends than a hundred rubles? Social networks in transition—The Kyrgyz Republic. *World Bank Economists' Forum, 2*, 51–88.

Kurmanov, A. (2016). Pyat' let s momenta rasstrela rabochih Zhanaozena. *Socialnoe Deistvie*. http://socdeistvie.info/analitic/1724-pyat-let-s-momenta-rasstrela-rabochih-zhanaozena.html.

Kushnareva, P. (2008). Obmanutye dol'shiki Astany donesli svoi pretenzii Sergeju Horoshunu lichno. *Azzattyq*. https://rus.azattyq.org/a/1328230.html.

Kussainov, D. (2018). Inequality in secondary education and Kazakhstan's risk of becoming a fragmented society. In M. Laruelle (Ed.), *New voices from Central Asia: Political, economic, and societal challenges and opportunities* (pp. 117–124). The George Washington University.

Landen, A., & Fotaki, M. (2018). Gender and struggles for equality in mining resistance movements: Performing critique against neoliberal capitalism in Sweden and Greece. *Social Inclusion, 6*(1), 25–35.

Laszczkowski, M. (2011). Building the future: Construction, temporality, and politics in Astana. *Focaal—Journal of Global and Historical Anthropology, 60*(June), 77–92. https://doi.org/10.3167/fcl.2011.600107.

Lawler, S. (2004). Rules of engagement: Habitus, power and resistance. *The Sociological Review, 52*(2), 110–128.

LeBaron, G. (2014). Subcontracting is not illegal, but is it unethical? Business ethics, forced labor, and economic success. *Brown Journal of World Affairs, 20*(2), 237–249.

Lefebvre, H. (1996). *Writing on cities*. Blackwell.

Lerner, M. (1980). *The belief in a just world: A fundamental delusion*. Plenum Press.

Lewis, M. (2007). Comparing Islamic and Christian attitudes to usury. In M. Hassan & M. Lewis (Eds.), *Handbook of Islamic banking* (pp. 64–81). Edward Elgar.

Lewis, D. (2016). Blogging Zhanaozen: Hegemonic discourse and authoritarian resilience in Kazakhstan. *Central Asian Survey, 35*(3), 421–438.

Lexology. (2014, January 27). *Tribunal dismisses the ICSID case KT Asia v Kazakhstan for absence of an investment*. https://www.lexology.com/library/detail.aspx?g=cb52457a-df49-4708-94fc-5c8cd4b1c8c7.

Lister, R. (2015). 'To count for nothing': Poverty beyond the statistics. *Journal of the British Academy, 3*, 139–165.

Liu, M., & Pistorious, T. (2012). Coping with the energy crisis: Impact assessment and potentials of non-traditional renewable energy in rural Kyrgyzstan. *Energy Policy, 44*(C), 130–139. https://doi.org/10.1016/j.enpol.2012.01.025.

Lottholtz, P., Heathershaw, J., Ismailbekova, A., Moldalieva, J., McGlinchey, E., & Owen, C. (2020). Governance and order-making in Central Asia: From illiberalism to post-liberalism? *Central Asian Survey, 39*(3), 420–437. https://doi.org/10.1080/02634937.2020.1803794.

Lukes, S. (2005). *Power: A radical view* (2nd ed.). Palgrave Macmillan.

Maclean, N. (2017). *Democracy in chains: The deep history of the Radical Right's Stealth Plan for America*. Viking Press.

Mader, P. (2015). *The financialisation of poverty*. Palgrave Macmillan.

Maggs, P. (1961). The security of individually-owned property under Soviet law. *Duke Law Journal, 1961*(4), 525–537.

Mahon, R. (1979). Regulatory agencies: Captive agents or hegemonic apparatuses! *Studies in Political Economy, 1*(1), 162–200.

Maitanov, A. (2010). Казахские рабочие на Кашагане требуют прекратить их дискриминацию. *Azattyq*. https://rus.azattyq.org/a/kashagan_workers_strike/2117559.html.

Maitanov, A. (2011). С бастующими нефтяниками встретился депутат Европарламента. Azattyq. https://rus.azattyq.org/a/strike_kazakh_oil_workers_europarliament_member_visit/24269311.html

Maitanov, A., & Guzikov, L. (2006). *S chego nachalas draka na Tengize: Svidetel'stva ochevidtsev i fotokamer*. https://online.zakon.kz/Document/?doc_id=30074592#pos=7;-22.

Makhmudova, G., & Matsui, K. (2019). The remediation policy after mining works in the Kyrgyz Republic. *Resources Policy, 61*(C), 304–310.

Manasov, Z. (2019). *The theory and the practice of neoliberal transformation in Kyrgyzstan: The case study of gold extraction in the* Bozumchak*mining field*. Unpublished PhD Thesis, Graduate School of Social Sciences of Middle East Technical University.

Marcuse, P. (1996). Privatization and its discontents: Property rights in land and housing in the transition in Eastern Europe. In G. Andrusz, M. Harloe, & I. Szelenyi (Eds.), *Cities after socialism: Urban and regional change and conflict in post-socialist societies* (pp. 119–191). Blackwell.

Marinin, S. (2020). Agents of change? Civic engagement of Western-educated youth in Kazakhstan. In M. Laruelle (Ed.), *New voices from Central Asia: Societal transformations* (pp. 20–30). The George Washington University.

Mazzucato, M. (2018). *The value of everything: Making and taking in the global economy*. Penguin.

McGlinchey, E. (2011). *Chaos, violence, dynasty: politics and Islam in Central Asia*. University of Pittsburgh Press.

Microfinance Centre. (2011). *Research on the Level of Indebtedness and Repayment Performance of Individual Borrowers in Kyrgyzstan*. https://mfc.org.pl/kyrgyzstan-research-on-indebtedness-and-repayment-performance/. Accessed July 2020.

Mihailova, E. (2017). Ona torgovala svoim telom, chtoby vyplatit kredit banku, - yurist iz KR. *Sputnik*. https://ru.sputnik.kg/society/20170122/1031388624/yurist-sulajman-usenov-o-dolgah-kyrgyzstancev.html.

Mikhalev,V., & Heinrich, G. (1999). *Kyrgyzstan: A case study of social stratification* (World Institute for Development Economic Research Working Paper

164). http://www.wider.unu.edu/publications/working-papers/previous/en_GB/wp164/_files/82530858910950029/default/wp164.pdf. Accessed Sept 2020.

Mihalyi, P., & Szelenyi, I. (2017). The role of rents in the transition from socialist redistributive economies to market capitalism. *Comparative Sociology, 16*(1), 13–38.

Mihalyi, P., & Szelenyi, I. (2019). *Rent-seekers, profits, wages and inequality: The top 20%.* Palgrave Macmillan.

Millar, J. (2016). Inside Astana, Kazakhstan: The 40 billion dollar city. *GQ*. https://www.gq.com.au/lifestyle/travel/inside-astana-kazakhstan-the-40-billion-dollar-city/news-story/1a3b7b9ac1c751efb23f827e456385d8.

Minsky, H. (1978). *The financial instability hypothesis: A re-statement*. Thames Papers in Political Economy: Thames Polytechnic.

Mitchell, D. (2003). *The right to the city. Social justice and the fight for public space*. The Guildford Press.

Mitchell, T. (2011). *Carbon democracy: Political power in the age of oil*. Verso.

Mogilevskii, R., Abdrazakova, N., Bolotbekova, A., Chalbasova, S., Dzhumaeva, S., & Tilekeyev, K. (2017). *The outcomes of 25 years of agricultural reforms in Kyrgyzstan* (Discussion Paper, No. 162). Leibniz Institute of Agricultural Development in Transition Economies, Halle. http://nbn-resolving.de/urn:nbn:de:gbv:3:2-69129.

Morton, H. (1980). Who gets what, when and how? Housing in the Soviet Union. *Soviet Studies, 32*(2), 235–259.

Moskovka, I. (2010). *Esenbek Ukteshbaev, lider dvijeniya 'Ostavim narodu jil'e': My ne halyavshiki!* Time. https://time.kz/news/archive/2010/10/16/18354.

Mukhametrakhimova, S. (2012). *Казахстан: протестные группы ищут поддержки у профсоюзов*. Institute for War & Peace Reporting. https://iwpr.net/ru/global-voices/казахстан-протестные-группы-ищут-поддержки-у-профсоюзов.

Muminov, F. (2019). Protection of foreign investment in Central Asia. *Russian Law Journal, 7*(4), 125–150.

Mun, N. (2016). V Almaty ipotechniki postavili grob u vhoda v bank i shvyrali v sotrudnikov nizhnim bel'em. *Nur.kz*. https://www.nur.kz/1010816-v-almaty-ipotechniki-postavili-grob-u-v.html.

Murza, J. (2020). Исследование: нефтяники-экспаты зарабатывают в 20 раз больше местных специалистов. *Azattyq Ryhy*. https://rus.azattyq-ruhy.kz/analytics/11169-ekspaty-i-kazakhstantsy-inostrantsy-neftianiki-zarabatyvaiut-v-20-raz-bolshe-mestnykh-spetsialistov.

Myant, M., & Drahokoupil, J. (2011). *Transition economies: Political economy in Russia, Eastern Europe, and Central Asia*. Wiley.

Nasritdinov, E., & Schroder, P. (2017). Re/claiming Bishkek: Contestation and activism in the city of two revolutions. *Central Asian Affairs, 4*(2), 97–128.

National Bank of the Kyrgyz Republic. (2014). *The financial sector stability report of the Kyrgyz Republic*. The National Bank of the Kyrgyz Republic.

National Bank of the Kyrgyz Republic. (2016). *The financial sector stability report of the Kyrgyz Republic*. The National Bank of the Kyrgyz Republic.

Niyazbekov, N. (2018). Is Kazakhstan immune to color revolutions? The social movements perspective. *Demokratizatsiya, 26*(3), 401–426.

Nogoibaeva, E. (2016). *The Gold of Batken. Socio-cultural aspects of relationships between local communities and investors in Kyrgyz Republic: Based on field-work research in Batken province in the sphere of natural resources extraction*. Bishkek.

Nunnally, S. (2017). *Eight facts about water quality in Kyrgyzstan*. The Borgen Project. https://borgenproject.org/eight-facts-about-water-quality-in-kyrgyzstan/.

Nussbaum, M. (2006). *Frontiers of justice: Disability, nationality and species membership*. Belknap.

Ombudsmen Report. (2017). *Novostroiki g. Bishkek: pravo na dostatochnoe jil'e, i inye socialnye, ekonomicheskie i kulturnye prava*. https://ombudsman.kg/index.php?option=com_content&view=article&id=101&catid=52&Itemid=364&lang=ru. Accessed July 2020.

O'Neill, J. (1998). *The market: Ethics, knowledge and politics*. Routledge.

openDemocracy. (2018, April 3). *Gold and water*. https://www.opendemocracy.net/ru/kumtor/. Accessed Sept 2020.

Orazalin, N. (2019). Corporate governance and corporate social responsibility (CSR) disclosure in an emerging economy: Evidence from commercial banks of Kazakhstan. *Corporate Governance, 19*(3), 490–507.

Orazgaliyev, S. (2018). State intervention in Kazakhstan's energy sector: Nationalisation or participation? *Journal of Eurasian Studies, 9*(2), 143–151.

Osenov, S. (2011). Real estate and construction: Market analysis in Bishkek and Kyrgyzstan. *Aki Press*. http://parfenon39.ru/novosti/novosti-20/novost-71.

Osmonova, K. (2016). Experiencing liminality: Housing, renting and informal tenants in Astana. *Central Asian Survey, 35*(2), 237–256. https://doi.org/10.1080/02634937.2016.1146010.

Ost, D. (2015). Class after communism: Introduction to the special issue. *East European Politics and Societies and Cultures, 9*(3), 543–556.

Ostrowski, W. (2009). The legacy of the 'colored revolutions': The case of Kazakhstan. *Journal of Communist Studies and Transition Politics, 25*(2–3), 347–368.

Ostrowski, W. (2010). *Politics and oil in Kazakhstan*. Routledge.

Oxus International. (2013). *Extracting sentiments: The effect of mining exploration and extraction on eight communities in the Kyrgyz Republic*. Bishkek.

Palazuelos, E., & Fernandez, R. (2012). Kazakhstan: Oil endowment and oil empowerment'. *Communist and Post-Communist Studies, 45*(1–2), 27–37.

Panchenko, T. (2020). Voronka kreditnoj aktivnosti. Bolee 80% ekonomicheski aktivnyh kazakhstantsev imejut kredity. *Forbes.kz*. https://forbes.kz//stats/bolee_80_ekonomicheski_aktivnyih_kazahstantsev_imeyut_kredityi/?.

Paprocki, K. (2016). 'Selling our own skin': Social dispossession through microcredit in rural Bangladesh. *Geoforum, 74*, 29–38.

Parenti, C. (2015). The environment making state: Territory, nature and value. *Antipode, 47*(4), 829–848.

Pchelyanskaya, I. (2016). *How much did housing cost 25 years ago?* Krishna. https://krisha.kz/content/articles/2016/skol-ko-stoilo-zhil-yo-25-let-nazad.

Pelkmans, M., & Umetbaeva, D. (2018). Moneylending and moral reasoning on the capitalist frontier in Kyrgyzstan. *Anthropological Quarterly, 91*(3), 1049–1074.

Pettifor, A. (2017). *The production of money: How to break the power of bankers*. Verso.

Peyrouse, S. (2012). The Kazakh neopatrimonial regime: Balancing uncertainties among the 'family', oligarchs and technocrats. *Demokratizatsiya, 20*(4), 345–370.

Polanyi, K. (1944). *The great transformation: Economic and political origins of our time*. Rinehart.

Pomfret, R. (2011). Exploiting energy and mineral resources in Central Asia, Azerbaijan and Mongolia. *Comparative Economic Studies, 53*(1), 5–33.

Pomfret, R. (2018). *Exploiting a natural resource in a poor country: The good, the bad and the ugly sides of the Kyrgyz Republic's gold mine* (IOS Working Papers, No. 372). Leibniz Institute for East and Southeast European Studies.

Pomfret, R. (2019). *The Central Asia economies in the twenty-first century: Paving a New Silk Road*. Cambridge University Press.

Porta, D., & Diani, M. (2006). *Social movements: An introduction*. Blackwell Publishing.

Proactive Investors. (2009, December 9). *Cameco sells 48.5% stake in Centerra Gold for C$872 million*. https://www.proactiveinvestors.co.uk/companies/news/71660/cameco-sells-485-stake-in-centerra-gold-for-c872-million-3205.html.

Prokopenko, V. (2015). K resheniyu problemy suicyda v armii privlekut banki'. *Tengri News*. https://tengrinews.kz/kazakhstan_news/resheniyu-problemyi-suitsida-armii-iz-za-kreditov-privlekut-269637/.

Rahmankulov, K. (2018). Судьба Джи Эл Макмал Девелопинг остается под вопросом. *Azattyk*. https://rus.azattyk.org/a/kyrgyzstan-djalal-abad-makmal-toguz-toro/29537425.html.

Radio Free Europe/Radio Liberty. (1998, May 9). *Kyrgyzstan: Kumtor spill signals further disasters*. https://www.rferl.org/a/1088758.html. Accessed Sept 2020.

Radnitz, S. (2010). *Weapons of the wealthy: Predatory regimes and elite-led protests in Central Asia*. Cornell University Press.

Reeves, M. (2010). The latest revolution. *London Review of Books, 32*, 9.

Regnum (2010, September 15). *V Kazakhstane destabilizatsiya idet sverhu: interview*. https://regnum.ru/news/polit/1325747.html.

Reuters. (2011, October 5). *Компартия Казахстана увидела в запрете сигнал к досрочным выборам*. https://fr.reuters.com/article/orutp-kazakhstan-party-suspended-idRURXE79411120111005.

Roelen, K., & Gassmann, F. (2014). Beyond averages: Child well-being in Kazakhstan. *Journal of Children and Poverty, 20*(2), 91–110. https://doi.org/10.1080/10796126.2014.979139.

Rojas, Y., & Stenberg, S. (2016). Evictions and suicide: A follow up study of almost 22,000 Swedish households in the wake of the global financial crisis. *Journal of Epidemiology Community Health, 70*(4), 409–413. https://doi.org/10.1136/jech-2015-206419.

Rolnik, R. (2011). *Report of the Special Rapporteur on adequate housing as a component of the right to an adequate standard of living, and on the right to non-discrimination in this context*. UN Human Rights Council. https://www.ohchr.org/EN/HRBodies/HRC/RegularSessions/Session25/Documents/A_HRC_25_54_Add.2_ENG.DOC. Accessed July 2020.

Rothe, D., & Kauzlarich, D. (2016). *Crimes of the powerful: An introduction*. Routledge.

Russian-Kyrgyz Development Fund (2015). *Annual report*. Russian-Kyrgyz Development Fund.

Ruziev, K., & Dow, S. (2013). *A review of banking sector reforms in transition economies* (Working Paper 03/13). Centre for Global Finance, University of the West of England.

Ruziev, K., & Majidov, T. (2013). Differing effects of the global financial crisis on the Central Asian countries: Kazakhstan, the Kyrgyz Republic and Uzbekistan. *Europe-Asia Studies, 65*(4), 682–716.

Ruziev, K., & Midmore, P. (2014). Informal credit institutions in transition countries: A study of urban money lenders in post-communist Uzbekistan. *Post-Communist Economies, 26*(3), 415–435.

Rysaliev, A. (2011). Nedovols'tvo rabochih neftyannogo sektora Kazakhstana. *Institute for War & Peace Reporting*. https://iwpr.net/ru/global-voices/nedovolstvo-rabochikh-neftyanogo-sektora-kazakhstana.

Sabi, M. (2015). Supply of Islamic microfinance in Central Asia: The case study of Tajikistan and Kyrgyzstan. *International Journal of Islamic Finance, 7*(2), 9–27.

Sakal, H. B. (2015). Natural resource policies and standard of living in Kazakhstan. *Central Asian Survey, 34*(2), 237–254. https://doi.org/10.1080/02634937.2014.987970.

Salmon, P. (2011). Repression intensifies against Kazakh oil workers. *Journal of Contemporary Central and Eastern Europe, 19*(1–2), 507–510. https://doi.org/10.1080/0965156X.2011.632556.

Samruk Kazyna. (2018). *Overview of investment attractiveness of Central Asian countries*. https://www.sk.kz/upload/iblock/05c/05cd94b6368a1aadd76795e999b7745d.pdf. Accessed Sept 2020.

Sandbrook, R. (2011). Polanyi and post-neoliberalism in the Global South: Dilemmas of re-embedding the economy. *New Political Economy, 16*(4), 415–443. https://doi.org/10.1080/13563467.2010.504300.

Sandbrook, R. (2014). *Reinventing the left in the global south: The politics of the possible*. Cambridge University Press.

Sandel, M. (1984). The procedural republic and the unencumbered self. *Political Theory, 12*(1), 81–96.

Sanghera, B. (2020). Justice, power and informal settlements: Understanding the juridical view of property rights in Central Asia. *International Sociology, 35*(1), 22–44.

Sanghera, B., & Satybaldieva, E. (2012). Ethics of property, illegal settlements and the right to subsistence. *International Journal of Sociology and Social Policy, 32*(1/2), 96–114.

Sanghera, B., Satybaldieva, E., Rodionov, A., Serikzhanova, S., Choibekov, N., & Sultanmuratova, K. (2012). *Illegal settlements and city registration in Kyrgyzstan and Kazakhstan: Implications for legal empowerment*. Open Society Foundations.

Satgar, V., & Williams, M. (2019). Polanyi, nature and the international: The missing dimension of imperial ecocide. In A. Roland, B. Aulenbacher, U. Brand, F. Decieux, K. Fischer, & S. Birgit (Eds.), *Capitalism in transformation: Movements and countermovements in the 21st century* (pp. 198–2011). Edward Elgar Publishing.

Satpayev, D., & Umbetaliyeva, T. (2015). The protests in Zhanaozen and the Kazakh oil sector: Conflicting interests in a rentier state. *Journal of Eurasian Studies, 6*(2), 122–129.

Satybaldieva, E. (2011). *The nature of local politics in rural Kyrgyzstan: A study of social inequalities, everyday politics and neoliberalism*. Unpublished PhD Thesis, School of Politics and International Relations, University of Kent.

Satybaldieva, E. (2015). Why class matters in Kyrgyzstan: Everyday experiences, moral sentiments, and the politics of the poor. In M. Laruelle & J. Engvall

(Eds.), *Kyrgyzstan beyond 'Democracy Island' and 'Failing State': Social and political changes in a post-Soviet society* (pp. 99–123). Lexington Books.

Satybaldieva, E. (2018a). A mob for hire? Unpacking older women's political activism in Kyrgyzstan. *Central Asian Survey, 37*(2), 247–264.

Satybaldieva, E. (2018b). Working class subjectivities and neoliberalisation in Kyrgyzstan: Developing alternative moral selves. *International Journal of Politics, Culture, and Society, 31*(1), 31–47. https://doi.org/10.1007/s10767-016-9251-5.

Sawyer, S. (2012). The corporation, oil, and the financialization of risk. *American Ethnologist, 39*(4), 710–715.

Sayer, A. (1992). *Method in social science: A realist approach* (2nd ed.). Routledge.

Sayer, A. (2000). *Realism and social science*. Sage.

Sayer, A. (2000). Moral economy and political economy. *Studies in Political Economy, 61*(1), 79–103.

Sayer, A. (2005). *The moral significance of class*. Cambridge University Press.

Sayer, A. (2007). Moral economy as critique. *New Political Economy, 12*(2), 261–270.

Sayer, A. (2011). *Why things matter to people: Social science, values and ethical life*. Cambridge University Press.

Sayer, A. (2015a). *Why we can't afford the rich*. Policy Press.

Sayer, A. (2015b). Time for moral economy? *Geoforum, 65*, 291–293.

Sayer, A. (2016). Moral economy, unearned income and legalized corruption. In D. Whyte & J. Wiegratz (Eds.), *Neoliberalism and the moral economy of fraud* (pp. 44–56). Routledge.

Sayer, A. (2017). Values within reason. *Canadian Review of Sociology, 54*(4), 468–475.

Sayer, A. (2018). Welfare and moral economy. *Ethics and Social Welfare, 12*(1), 20–33.

Sayer, A. (2020). Rentiership, 'improperty' and moral economy. *Environment and Planning A: Economy and Space*. https://doi.org/10.1177/2F0308518X20908287.

Schneiderman, D. (2000). Investment rules and the new constitutionalism. *Law and Social Inquiry, 25*(3), 757–787.

Schneiderman, D. (2001). Constitutional approaches to privatisation: An inquiry into the magnitude of neo-liberal constitutionalism. *Law and Contemporary Problems, 63*(4), 83–109.

Schneiderman, D. (2008). *Constitutionalising economic globalisation: Investment rules and democracy's promise*. Cambridge University Press.

Schneiderman, D. (2014). The global regime of investor rights: Return to the standards of civilised justice? *Transnational Legal Theory, 5*(1), 60–80.

Schneiderman, D. (2015). Constitutional property rights and elision of the transnational: Foucauldian misgivings. *Social and Legal Studies, 24*(1), 65–87.

Schroder, P. (2010). 'Urbanizing' Bishkek: Interrelations of boundaries, migration, group size and opportunity structure. *Central Asian Survey, 29*(4), 453–467.

Seitz, W. (2020). Urbanization in Kazakhstan: Desirable cities, unaffordable housing, and the missing rental market. *International Journal of Urban Sciences*. https://doi.org/10.1080/12265934.2019.1709534.

Sen, A. (1999). *Development as freedom*. Oxford University Press.

Sharipova, D. (2015). Who gets what, when and how? Housing and informal institutions in the Soviet Union and post-Soviet Kazakhstan. *Central Asian Affairs, 2*(2), 140–167.

Shaxson, N., & Christensen, J. (2013). *The finance curse: How oversized financial sectors attack democracy and corrupt economies*. Tax Justice Network. http://www.taxjustice.net/cms/upload/pdf/Finance_Curse_Final.pdf. Accessed July 2020.

Shedenova, N., & Beimisheva, A. (2013). Social and economic status of urban and rural households in Kazakhstan. *Procedia—Social and Behavioral Sciences, 82*, 585–591. https://doi.org/10.1016/j.sbspro.2013.06.314.

Shmatenko, L. (2013). An overview of Kazakhstan's investment laws and its investor-state arbitral awards. *The International Law Quarterly, 30*(4), 25–33.

Silva, E. (2012). Exchange rising? Karl Polanyi and contentious politics in contemporary Latin America. *Latin American Politics and Society, 54*(3), 1–32. https://doi.org/10.1111/j.1548-2456.2012.00163.x.

Silverman, D. (2011). *Interpreting qualitative data: A guide to the principles of qualitative research*. Sage.

Smart, A. (2001). Unruly places: Urban governance and the persistence of illegality in Hong Kong's urban squatter areas. *American Anthropologist, 103*(1), 30–44.

Smith, A. (1776). *An inquiry into the nature and causes of the wealth of nations*. https://www.econlib.org/library/Smith/smWN.html. Accessed Nov 2019.

Smith, A. (1976 [1759]). *The theory of moral sentiments*. Liberty Fund.

Snider, L. (2009). Accommodating power: The 'common sense' of regulators. *Social & Legal Studies, 18*(2), 179–197.

Socialism.kz (2009). *Aktsiya ipotechnikov priostanovlena*. http://socialismkz.info/?p=1040.

Socialism.kz. (2016). *Ipotechniki kak orudie informatsionnoj vojny akordy*. http://socialismkz.info/?p=16191.

Soederberg, S. (2012). The Mexican debtfare state: Dispossession, micro-lending, and the surplus population. *Globalizations, 9*(4), 561–575.

Soederberg, S. (2014). *Debtfare states and the poverty industry*. Routledge.

Solidarity Center. (2019, March 8). *Kyrgyz unions find unreported worker death and injuries*. https://www.solidaritycenter.org/kyrgyz-unions-find-unreported-worker-deaths-and-injuries/.

Solo. (2020). *Meken toluk metrajduu korkom tasmasy*. https://www.youtube.com/watch?v=63_sxMT2ezM&lc=Ugzf7WvHlC3-U3z1-494AaABAg.

Spector, R. (2006). *Who governs the marketplace? The politics of bazaars in Kyrgyzstan*. Institute of Public Policy.

Spector, R. (2008). Bazaar politics: The fate of marketplaces in Kazakhstan. *Problems of Post-Communism, 55*(6), 42–53.

Spector, R. (2017). *Order at the bazaar: Power and trade in Central Asia*. Cornell University Press.

Spector, R., & Botoeva, A. (2017). New shop owners in old buildings: Spatial buildings of the apparel industry in Kyrgyzstan. *Post-Soviet Affairs, 33*(3), 235–253.

Sputnik. (2018a, August 8). *How not to turn from a mayor into a prisoner—Learning from the mistakes of ex-mayors*. https://ru.sputnik.kg/politics/20180808/1040543325/bishkek-mehr-ugolovnoe-delo.html.

Sputnik. (2018b, December 19). *Nazvan pobeditel tendera po razrabotke rudnika Makmal*. https://ru.sputnik.kg/economy/20181219/1042510374/makmal-tender-pobeditel-manson-grupp.html.

Sputnik. (2019, November 21). *Surakmatov has 11 apartments, one of 318 square meters*. https://ru.sputnik.kg/politics/20191121/1046305365/kyrgyzstan-surakmatov-11-kvartir.html.

Sputnik. (2020, January 15). *Вернуть жилье, отобранное банками за долги по ипотеке, может будет по программе рефинансирования ипотечных жилищных займов*. https://ru.sputniknews.kz/economy/20200115/12549755/gosudarstvo-banki-kvartiry.html.

Standing, G. (2016). *The corruption of capitalism: Why Rentiers thrive and work does not pay*. Biteback Publishing.

Steimann, B. (2011). *Making a living in uncertainty: Agro-pastoral livelihoods and institutional transformations in post-socialist rural Kyrgyzstan*. University of Zurich.

Stenning, P., Shearing, C., Addario, S., & Condon, M. (1990). Controlling interests: Two conceptions of order in regulating a financial market. In M. Friedland (Ed.), *Securing compliance* (pp. 88–119). University of Toronto Press.

Stiglitz, J. (1994). *The role of the state in financial markets*. The World Bank. http://documents.worldbank.org/curated/en/239281468741290885/pdf/multi-page.pdf.

Stone, L. (2012). Central Asian studies. *Journal of Third World Studies, 29*(1), 175–202.

Suleimenova, L. (2013). Казсодержание: Казахская народная сказка про белого бычка. *Ak Zhaiyk*. https://azh.kz/ru/news/view/17397.

Suleimenova, L. (2015). Крошки от нефтяного пирога. *Ak Zhaiyk*. https://azh.kz/ru/news/view/27168.

Sultakeev, K., Karymshakov, K., & Sulaimanova, B. (2018). The impact of microfinance on entrepreneurship in Kyrgyzstan. *Acta Oeconomica Pragensia, 26*(2), 24–40.

Szelenyi, I. (1987). Housing inequalities and occupational segregation in state socialist cities: Commentary to the special issue of IJURR on east European cities. *International Journal of Urban and Regional Research, 11*(1), 1–8.

Tag El-Din, S., & Hassan, M. (2007). Islam and speculation in the stock exchange. In M. Hassan & M. Lewis (Eds.), *Handbook of Islamic banking* (pp. 240–255). Edward Elgar.

Tawney, R. H. (1921). *The acquisitive society*. G. Bell and Sons.

Tazabek. (2019, June 3). *Blacklist of construction companies: Who are they?* http://www.tazabek.kg/news:1549840.

The Diplomat. (2018, August 9). *Unopposed but protested: Bishkek gets a new mayor*. https://thediplomat.com/2018/08/unopposed-but-protested-bishkek-gets-a-new-mayor/.

The Global Economy. (2020). *Real interest rate—Country ranking*.https://www.theglobaleconomy.com/rankings/Real_interest_rate/.

The Guardian. (2019, October 17). Life in limbo: Inside Bishkek's illegal 'new buildings'. https://www.theguardian.com/cities/2017/oct/17/life-limbo-inside-bishkek-illegal-new-builds-kyrgyzstan.

The Times of Central Asia. (2016, January 16). *State mortgage company starts operating in Kyrgyzstan*. https://www.timesca.com/index.php/news/16215-state-mortgage-company-starts-operating-in-kyrgyzstan.

The Times of Central Asia. (2017, February 27). *'Affordable housing' unaffordable for most public sector employees in Kyrgyzstan*. https://www.timesca.com/index.php/news/17730-affordable-housing-unaffordable-for-most-public-sector-employees-in-kyrgyzstan.

Today. (2009, July 7). *Shareholders ask the president for help*. http://today.kz/news/kazahstan/2009-07-07/15961-sert/.

Toguzbaev, K. (2011). Часть оппозиции создает очередной «Народный фронт». *Azattyq*. https://rus.azattyq.org/a/opposition_parliament_election_/24249814.html.

Toiken, S. (2011). Мангистауцы в Брюсселе. *Ak Zhaiyk*. https://azh.kz/ru/news/view/7551.

Toiken, S. (2019). Конфликт на месторождении Тенгиз и его вероятные причины. *Azattyq*.https://rus.azattyq.org/a/kazakhstan-aterau-tengiz-vozmozhnye-prichiny/30036348.html.

Toktomushev, K. (2015). Regime security, base politics and rent-seeking: The local and global political economies of the American air base in Kyrgyzstan, 2001–2010. *Central Asian Survey, 34*(1), 57–77.

Tombs, S. (2012). State-corporate symbiosis in the production of crime and harm. *State Crime Journal, 1*(2), 170–195.

Tombs, S., & Whyte, D. (2009). State and corporate crimes. In R. Coleman, J. Sim, S. Tombs, & D. Whyte (Eds.), *State, power, crime* (pp. 103–115). Sage.

Tombs, S., & Whyte, D. (2020). The shifting imaginaries of corporate crime. *Journal of White Collar and Corporate Crime, 1*(1), 16–23.

Torebaeva, M., & Ivanov, A. (2006). Imangali Tasmagambetov: Davaite vmeste rassmatrivat' etu problem. *Nomad*. https://nomad.su/?a=10-200607250314.

Transnational Institute. (2017). *Kyrgyz Republic's experience with investment treaties and arbitration cases*. https://www.tni.org/files/publication-downloads/tni_pb_kyrgyz_republic_online_210717.pdf. Accessed Sept 2020.

Transparency International. (2013, January 9). *Overview of corruption and anti-corruption in Kyrgyzstan*. Number 363. https://www.transparency.org/files/content/corruptionqas/363_Overview_of_Corruption_in_Kyrgyzstan.pdf.

Tsenkova, S. (2014). The housing policy nexus and people's responses to housing challenges in post-communist cities. *Urbani Izziv, 25*(2), 90–106.

Trilling, D. (2013). Kyrgyzstan: Another gold mine attacked as Kumtor protests continue. *Eurasianet*. https://eurasianet.org/kyrgyzstan-another-gold-mine-attacked-as-kumtor-protests-continue.

Turganbayev, Y., & Diener, A. (2018). Kazakhstan's evolving regional economic policy: Assessing strategies of post-socialist development. *Eurasian Geography and Economics, 59*(5–6), 657–684. https://doi.org/10.1080/15387216.2019.1586559.

UNCTAD. (2020a). *International investment agreements navigator: Kazakhstan*.https://investmentpolicy.unctad.org/international-investment-agreements/countries/107/kazakhstan. Accessed Sept 2020.

UNCTAD. (2020b). *Investment dispute settlement navigator: Kazakhstan*.https://investmentpolicy.unctad.org/investment-dispute-settlement/country/107/kazakhstan. Accessed Sept 2020.

UNDP. (2010). *Kyrgyzstan: The second progress report on the millennium development goals*. http://www.undp.org/content/dam/undp/library/MDG/english/MDG%20Country%20Reports/Kyrgyzstan/2010.pdf. Accessed Sept 2020.

Ursulenko, K. (2010). Regional development in Kazakhstan. *Kurzanalysen und Informationen*, No 47, 1–10. https://www.dokumente.ios-regensburg.de/publikationen/info/info-47.pdf.

Vesti. (2012, March 12). *V Kyrgyzstane rastet chislo samoubijstv sredi dolzhnikov po kreditam*. https://vesti.kg/proisshestviya/item/10996-v-kyirgyizstane-rastet-chislo-samoubiystv-sredi-dolzhnikov-po-kreditam.html.

Waldron, J. (2012). *The rule of law and the measure of property*. Cambridge University Press.

Walker, R. (2017). Value and nature: Rethinking capitalist exploitation and expansion. *Capitalism Nature Socialism, 28*(1), 53–61.

Watts, M. (2005). Righteous oil? Human rights, the oil complex, and corporate social responsibility. *Annual Review of Environment and Resources, 30*, 373–407.

Watts, M. (2009). *Crude politics: Life and death on the Nigerian oil fields*. Institute of International Studies, University of Berkeley, USA. https://citeseerx.ist.psu.edu/viewdoc/download?doi=10.1.1.518.4318&rep=rep1&type=pdf.

Watts, M. (2012). A tale of two gulfs: Life, death and dispossession along two oil frontiers. *American Quarterly, 64*(3), 437–467.

Weinrib, E. (2002). Corrective justice in a nutshell. *University of Toronto Law Journal, 52*, 349–356.

Whyte, D., & Wiegratz, J. (2016). *Neoliberalism and the moral economy of fraud*. Routledge.

Wiegratz, J. (2016). *Neoliberal moral economy: Capitalism, socio-cultural change and fraud in Uganda*. Rowman and Littlefield.

Wolters, A. (2016). Islamic finance and the state in Central Asia. *Central Asian Affairs, 3*(4), 360–384.

Wooden, A. (2013). Another way of saying enough: Environmental concern and popular mobilization in Kyrgyzstan. *Post-Soviet Affairs, 29*(4), 314–353.

Wooden, A. (2014). Kyrgyzstan's dark ages: Framing and the 2010 hydroelectric revolution. *Central Asian Survey, 33*(4), 463–481.

World Bank. (2009). *Doing business 2010: Kyrgyz Republic*. The World Bank.

World Bank. (2014). *Doing business 2015: Kyrgyz Republic*. The World Bank.

World Bank. (2020a). *Total natural resources rent (% of GDP)—Kazakhstan and Kyrgyz Republic*. https://data.worldbank.org/indicator/NY.GDP.TOTL.RT.ZS?locations=KZ-KG.

World Bank. (2020b). *Personal remittances, received (% of GDP)—Kyrgyz Republic and Kazakhstan*. https://data.worldbank.org/indicator/BX.TRF.PWKR.DT.GD.ZS?locations=KG-KZ.

Yale School of Management. (2011a). *Kyrgyz MFI Comparison in 2010*. https://vol11.cases.som.yale.edu/sites/default/files/cases/kompanion_financial_group/Picture%2043.png.

Yale School of Management. (2011b). *Microfinance in Kyrgyzstan: Growth and competition*. https://vol11.cases.som.yale.edu/kompanion-financial-group/kyrgyzstan/microfinance-kyrgyzstan-growth-and-competition.

Yale School of Management. (2011c). *Mercy Corps and Kompanion*. https://vol11.cases.som.yale.edu/kompanion-financial-group/introduction/mercy-corps-and-kompanion.

Yessenova, S. (2010). Borrowed places: Eviction wars and property rights formalization in Kazakhstan. In *Economic action in theory and practice: Anthropological investigations, research in economic anthropology* (30, pp. 11–45).

Yessenova, S. (2012). The Tengiz Oil enclave: Labor, business and the state. *Political and Legal Anthropology Review, 35*(1), 94–114.

Yessenova, S. (2015). The political economy of oil privatisation in post-Soviet Kazakhstan. In H. Appel, A. Mason, & M. Watts (Eds.), *Subterranean estates: Life worlds of oil and gas* (pp. 291–306). Cornell University Press.

Yuricyn, V. (2011). Represii protiv "ONZ", "SDK" i Zhanartu. https://zonakz.net/2011/09/06/репрессии-против-онж-сдк-и-жа/.

Zavisca, J. (2008). Property without markets: Housing policy and politics in post-Soviet Russia, 1992–2007. *Comparative European Politics, 6*(3), 365–386.

Index

B. Sanghera and E. Satybaldieva, *Rentier Capitalism and Its Discontents*, https://doi.org/10.1007/978-3-030-76303-9

R

S